LATIN AMERICA IN PERSPECTIVE

LATIN AMERICA IN PERSPECTIVE

Oxford Analytica

Houghton Mifflin Company Boston
Dallas Geneva, Illinois Palo Alto Princeton, New Jersey

ISBN: 0-395-52583-7

Library of Congress Card Number: 90-83066

ABCDEFGHIJ-B-9987654321

CONTENTS

Preface xi

Part One

Society 1

1 **The Population** 1
Basic Population Size 3
Fertility 6
Mortality 7
Age Structure 12
International Migration 14

2 **What Sort of People?** 17
Rural-Urban Migration 17
Farmers 19
City Dwellers 24
Ethnic Minorities 31

3 **Social Structure** 40
Classes 40
The Southern Cone and Elsewhere 42
Rural Society 43
Urban Working Classes 46

Middle Classes 47
Upper Classes 50
Mobility 51
Women 52

4 **Education** 55
Primary and Secondary Education 55
Higher Education 59

5 **A Short Note on Culture** 67
Writers and Novels 67
Cinema and Its Influence 70
Television 72
Other Aspects of Mass Culture 75

Part Two
Politics 79

6 **Democracy and Democratization in Latin America** 81
A Democratic Tradition 81
Voters and Elections 90

7 **Political Parties** 101
The Left 101
The Right 104
The Center 105
Populists 107

8 **Political Actors** 113

Employers' Associations and Professional Organizations 113

Labor Unions 115

Organizations of Peasants and Rural Workers 125

Other Social Movements 127

Churches 129

The Armed Forces 134

9 **Political Violence** 145

Guerrillas 145

Violence from the Right 156

10 **Administrative and Judicial Competence** 160

Public Administration 161

Public Corruption 165

The Judicial System 166

11 **Political Prospects** 168

Part Three

Economics 177

12 **Economic Structure: Resilience and Vulnerability** 179

The International Context 180

Trends in Structure Since 1960 181

Vulnerability, Resilience, and Performance in the 1980s 188

13 The Policy Context 193

Currents in Economic Thinking 194

Some Myths About Policymaking 198

Inflation and Stabilization Policy 200

Debt-Management Policy 206

Commercial Policy 210

14 Issues of Employment, Distribution, Poverty, and Welfare 216

Employment: Demand and Supply 217

Inequality, Poverty, and Basic Needs 222

15 Prospects 228

The Debt Problem 229

New Sources of Capital 331

International Trade and the World Economy 234

Economic Policy and Economic Growth 238

Regional Differences 240

Part Four

International Relations 247

16 Latin America and the United States 249

Trends in the 1980s 249

Policy Prospects 253

Cuba 260

17 Latin America and the Soviet Union 263

Commercial Interests 263

Glasnost and *Perestroika* 264

The Soviet Union and Communist Parties in Latin America **266**
Soviet Interest in the Pacific **268**

18 Latin America and Western Europe 271
Historical Ties **271**
The Growth of Relations **272**
Constraints and Limitations **274**
1992 **277**
Europe After the Cold War **279**

19 Latin America and Japan 283
Historical Ties **283**
Pressures for Greater Involvement **285**
Constraints on Japanese Actions **289**
The Future **291**

20 Latin America and Other Regions 293
China **293**
The Middle East **297**
Africa **300**
The Third World Movement **301**

21 International Financial Institutions and Latin America 304
The IMF and the World Bank **304**
Evolution of the IMF in the 1980s **305**
Issues Under Consideration by the IMF **308**
World Bank Response to Latin America in the 1980s **312**

Issues Under Consideration in the World Bank **314**
The Inter-American Development Bank **317**
Prospects for the 1990s **317**

22 Cooperation and Conflict in the Region 319
Patterns of Regional Cooperation **319**
Patterns of Regional Conflict **322**
Brazil and Argentina **325**
Central America **326**

23 Latin America and International Management of the Environment 329

24 Conclusions and Prospects 335

Bibliography 341

Index 351

Preface

In 1988 a body of distinguished Latin American leaders, the Columbus Group, asked Oxford Analytica to undertake a comprehensive appraisal of Latin America and its prospects for the 1990s and beyond. Initiated by Professor Carlos Hank Gonzalez, then president of the Columbus Group, and by Dr. Diego Arria, its executive director, the idea was to bring together a team of scholars from different disciplines to provide a rigorous and detached appraisal of the region. The Columbus Group saw a serious need for a substantive and reflective analysis of the key elements at work that are helping to shape Latin American society, the region's politics, its economy, and its relations with the rest of the world.

To this end Oxford Analytica assembled a study team, led by Malcolm Deas of St. Antony's College, Oxford, into a small core group that commissioned memoranda from a large number of expert contributors from universities throughout Latin America, North America, and Europe. Those who agreed to participate in the project are listed on the following pages. They did so in the knowledge that their texts provided the basic information and insights for the study, but that they would not be responsible for the book's final content.

In 1989 the preliminary findings of the study were presented to the Columbus Group, and since that time the work of the study team has continued. The result is now published for the first time in this volume.

The aim of this project has been to provide the nonspecialist reader with an authoritative account of developments in the region in the recent past, the current state of affairs, and the direction in which events are likely to go. We also hope that this view of Latin America from a distance will be helpful to policymakers in the region who have the difficult job of steering their countries toward the future. Since the Columbus Group urged us to focus particularly on what we think is likely to happen over the next decade and beyond, we have not disguised our judgments in this respect. We have tried to look afresh at the conventional stereotypes about the regions and to challenge received opinions.

In the organization of this book, we have divided our attention among the four major areas: society, politics, the economy, and international relations. Within these four sections we have sought to deal with issues thematically, though with constant reference to the contexts in specific countries. We have tried to balance our coverage, giving more attention to the larger countries but not forgetting the smaller ones.

Our conclusions, broadly speaking, are optimistic. Although most countries of the region will continue to face difficulties in meeting the needs of their people and reducing social inequalities, their economic performance is likely to be more dynamic in the 1990s than in the 1980s. Similarly, though governments will still face strong political challenges from within and from outside the formally constituted political systems, democratic regimes are likely to prevail. Moreover, we believe that Latin America will be more united than in the past and that it will play a more active and collaborative role in world affairs.

In addition to extending thanks to the study team, the contributors, and those who reviewed the text, Oxford Analytica would like to thank the members of the Columbus Group. As well as sponsoring this project and providing valuable suggestions, they gave the team the most complete freedom to reach its own conclusions.

In making the results of the study available to the public, Oxford Analytica shares the Columbus Group's hope that *Latin America in Perspective* will contribute to a richer understanding of the continent's future for everyone.

DAVID R. YOUNG
Managing Director
Oxford Analytica Ltd.

The Study Team

Malcolm Deas (Study Director)
St. Antony's College, Oxford

John Crabtree (Study Coordinator)
Oxford Analytica

Victor Bulmer-Thomas
Queen Mary College, London

Andrew Hurrell
Nuffield College, Oxford

John King
University of Warwick

Rosemary Thorp
St. Antony's College, Oxford

Laurence Whitehead
Nuffield College, Oxford

The Columbus Group

Dr. Angelo Calmon de Sá (Chairman)

Lic. Víctor García Laredo (Coordinator)

Lic. Carlos Abedrop Dávila
Dr. Carlos Ardila Lulle
Dr. Diego Arria
Ing. Gilberto Borja Navarrete
Dr. Carlos Bulgheroni
Dr. Carlos Calvo Galindo
Sr. Osvaldo Cisneros Fajardo
Sr. Manuel Diez
Sr. Agustín Edwards
Sr. Ignacio Fierro Viña
Sr. Franciso Macri
Emb. Manuel de Prado y Colon de Carvajal
Ing. Felipe Thorndike
Dr. Manuel Ulloa
Sr. Juan Carlos Wasmosy

Contributors and Reviewers

Alan Angell
St. Antony's College, Oxford

Leslie Bethell
Institute of Latin American Studies, London

Roberto Briceño
St. Antony's College, Oxford

José María Caballero
FAO, Rome

Rodolfo Cerdas
CIAPA, San José

Henry Dietz
University of Texas, Austin

Robert Dix
Rice University

Eileen Doherty
Ohio University

Charlotte Elton
CEASPA, Panama City

Roberto Espindola
University of Bradford

Adolfo Figueroa
Universidad Católica, Lima

Alan Gilbert
University of London

Stephanie Griffith-Jones
IDS, University of Sussex

Tony Gross
CEDI, São Paulo

Ravi Gulhati
World Bank, Washington, D.C.

Howard Handelman
University of Wisconsin—Milwaukee

Jonathan Hartlyn
University of North Carolina

Rhys Jenkins
University of East Anglia, Norwich

Stephen Hugh-Jones
Kings College, Cambridge

Jane Jaquette
Occidental College

John King
University of Warwick

Maria D'Alva Kinzo
University of São Paulo

Emilio Klein
PREALC, Santiago

Ignacio Klich
London School of Economics

Abraham Lowenthal
Inter-American Dialog

Brian McBeth
The Oxford Consultancy Group

Terry McCoy
University of Florida

Thomas Merrick
Population Reference Bureau, Washington, D.C.

Andrew Nickson
University of Birmingham

José Antonio Ocampo
Fedesarrollo, Bogotá

Robert Orr
East/West Center, Hawaii

Juan Ossio
Universidad Católica, Lima

Marco Palacios
Universidad de los Andes, Bogotá

Alicia Puyana
CRESET, Bogotá

Michael Redclift
Wye College, University of London

Alvaro Reyes
Econometría, Bogotá

Alan Riding
New York Times

Ian Roxborough
London School of Economics

Varun Sahni
Lincoln College, Oxford

Christopher Scott
London School of Economics

Celia Szusterman
North London Polytechnic

Robert Trudeau
Providence College

Louis Turner
Chatham House, London

Diana Tussie
FLASCO, Buenos Aires

Miguel Urrutia
IADB, Washington, D.C.

Peter Wade
University of Liverpool

Philip Williams
University of Florida

LATIN AMERICA IN PERSPECTIVE

Part 1

SOCIETY

1

The Population

Basic Population Size

Around 1950 Latin America's population overtook that of North America. By the year 2000 there will be two Latin Americans for every one North American.

Latin America's population grew by 239 million between 1950 and 1985 to 405 million and is expected to rise by a further 135 million by the year 2000. The projected increase is roughly equivalent to the entire population of Brazil in 1985. In the first two decades of the next century the population will increase by another 170 million. According to projections made in 1988, there will be 537 million Latin Americans in 2000 (around 10 percent of the total world population), including English- and French-speaking people from the Caribbean but excluding Hispanics in the United States. In the year 2020 the total will be near 711 million (Table 1.1).

Latin America at present accounts for 8.4 percent of the world population, and this proportion will increase only slightly over the next few decades. The rate of population growth in Latin America will probably continue at around the same rate as the world average. The average number of children born to Latin American women (3.7), the total fertility rate (TFR), is also only slightly higher than the world average (3.6). The TFR in Asia is about the same as for Latin America; that in Africa (6.3) is much higher. The TFR in North America and Europe is 1.8, lower than the 2.1 required to replace population.

Moreover, the rate of demographic increase in Latin America is falling and will continue to do so. The average annual growth rate for 1950–1985 was 2.5 percent. For the last fifteen years of the century it will be just under 2 percent. With people having smaller families, there has been a corresponding decrease in official expectations of population size for the year 2000. At the

Table 1.1

Latin America in a world perspective

	Total Population (Millions)[a]			TFR[b] (1988)
	1988	2000	2020	
World	5,128	6,178	8,053	3.6
Latin America	429	537	711	3.7
Africa	623	886	1,497	6.3
Asia	2,995	3,612	4,629	3.6
North America	272	296	327	1.8
Europe	497	506	499	1.8
Soviet Union	286	311	354	2.5
Oceania	26	30	36	2.6

[a]Data for 1988 are estimates. Data for 2000 and 2020 are projections.
[b]TFR = total fertility rate, the average number of births per woman aged 15 to 49.

SOURCE: Population Reference Bureau, Inc., *1988 World Population Data Sheet* (Washington, D.C., 1988).

height of fears about a population "explosion" at the beginning of the 1970s, the United Nations was predicting that there would be 652 million Latin Americans in 2000. This forecast was revised downward to 620 million in 1973, 608 million in 1978, 566 million in 1980, and 537 million in 1988. Other organizations that project population trends in the region have also scaled down their estimates in similar fashion.

The numbers continue to rise while growth rates fall because of the phenomenon of "momentum" or "inertia." During previous periods of high fertility the age structure of Latin American populations has developed a particularly youthful profile, with 40 percent of the population under the age of 15. Although the average woman has fewer births than in the 1960s, the number of women of reproductive age will remain large until the generation born during the period of high fertility passes through the age of reproduction. Until that happens, large increases in numbers will continue.

Nor in terms of numbers per square kilometer is Latin America an overcrowded region. Brazil has a population density (16.3 people per square kilometer) that is rather more than that of the Soviet Union (12.5) but less than that of the United States (25.8) and much less than that of Nigeria (78.0). The problem is sometimes one of concentration of population, particularly in one or two major urban centers in each country. In the year 2000 the world's two

Table 1.2

Total population and population growth by country, 1950–2000

	Population (Thousands, Midyear)			Annual Growth Rate	
	1950	1985	2000	1950–1985	1985–2000
All Latin America	165,363	403,699	540,076	2.55	1.94
Argentina	17,150	30,331	36,238	1.63	1.19
Bolivia	2,766	6,371	9,724	2.38	2.82
Brazil	53,444	135,564	179,487	2.66	1.87
Chile	6,082	12,122	15,272	1.97	1.54
Colombia	11,597	28,714	37,999	2.59	1.87
Costa Rica	862	2,642	3,711	3.20	2.27
Cuba	5,858	10,038	11,718	1.54	1.03
Dominican Republic	2,353	6,416	8,621	2.87	1.97
Ecuador	3,310	9,378	13,939	2.98	2.64
El Salvador	1,940	4,768	6,739	2.57	2.31
Guatemala	2,969	7,963	12,222	2.82	2.86
Haiti	3,097	5,922	7,838	1.85	1.87
Honduras	1,401	4,383	6,846	3.26	2.97
Mexico	28,012	79,376	107,233	2.98	2.01
Nicaragua	1,098	3,272	5,261	3.12	3.17
Panama	839	2,180	2,893	2.73	1.89
Paraguay	1,351	3,693	5,538	2.87	2.70
Peru	7,632	19,698	27,952	2.71	2.33
Uruguay	2,239	3,012	3,364	0.85	0.74
Venezuela	5,009	17,317	24,715	3.54	2.37
Other[a]	6,354	10,539	12,766	1.45	1.28

[a]Includes the rest of the Caribbean.

SOURCE: CELADE, *Boletín Demográfico, (Demographic Bulletin)*, no. 41 (January 1988), pp. 21–24.

largest conurbations will be Mexico City and São Paulo. Latin America is much more urbanized than other developing regions of the world. Its 1988 urbanization level of 68 percent comes much closer to the levels of Western Europe or North America than to those of Africa and Asia, 30 percent and 36 percent respectively.

The pattern of population distribution and increase also varies a great deal within Latin America (Table 1.2). Brazil, Mexico, Argentina, Colombia, and Peru are the five largest countries in terms of population, accounting between them for nearly three-quarters of the total. By the year 2000, however, Colombia is expected to overtake Argentina as the region's third most populous country. Over the period 1950–1985 annual population increase was above 3 percent (enough to double the population in twenty-three years) in Costa Rica, Honduras, and Nicaragua, with Venezuela out in the lead with 3.5 percent. At the other end of the scale, under 2 percent a year, came Argentina, Chile, Cuba, Haiti, and Uruguay—Haiti because of high mortality and emigration rates. From 1985 to the end of the century the ranking will be similar, albeit with lower annual growth rates. So, although the growth rate will be down to 0.74 in Uruguay, 1.03 in Cuba, and 1.19 in Argentina, it still will be over 3 percent in Nicaragua and just under in Honduras and Bolivia.

Fertility

There is little doubt from the statistical information available that not only is fertility close to the world average but it has declined significantly in the past twenty years in most Latin American countries. One of the peculiarities of Latin American demographic patterns, however, is that fertility rates initially remained high even after the region had achieved comparatively high levels of urbanization and educational attainment, both of which are usually associated with fertility declines. As late as the 1960s there was strong concern that high fertility would frustrate efforts to improve living standards.

By the mid-1980s fertility rates were falling rapidly in a number of countries, including the three largest high-fertility countries—Brazil, Colombia, and Mexico. They have also declined notably in Venezuela, the Dominican Republic, Costa Rica, Panama, and Peru. Although women of the 15–49 age group could be expected to have six or more births in the early 1960s, the average had fallen to the 3–5 range by the early 1980s.

The wider use of contraceptives by both men and women offers a partial explanation. Many governments of the region were slow to promote family-planning techniques on a widespread basis. Official resistance was greater than in Africa and in Asia, partly because of hostility to such programs for religious reasons and partly because many countries, especially those in South America with large unpopulated regions, sought to increase population.

The use of contraceptives, however, increased significantly during the 1970s and 1980s in the three largest high-fertility countries—Brazil, Colombia, and Mexico. The means of promoting family-planning differed, though. Colombia had the first organized family-planning effort. Initially it had appeared that the government would take the lead, but instead the initiative came from

Colombia's International Planned Parenthood affiliate. This is still the single most important organization supplying contraceptives. In Mexico, by contrast, the government at first prevaricated, but then policy changed in the early 1970s and the government came to play a major role in the supply of contraceptives. Private doctors and commercial outlets also played a role in Colombia and Mexico, but not on the scale that has occurred in Brazil. For at least twenty years, Brazilians have been debating whether the government should be involved in family planning. Meanwhile use of contraceptives has increased dramatically. The main methods are the pill, bought from pharmacies, and surgical sterilization, often carried out in state hospitals without open government approval.

Institutional factors help explain the increased availability of contraceptives, but important social and economic changes have also increased the demand for them:

- Urbanization and increased levels of education have affected family values. In the urban context, unlike in the peasant economy where the number of children a couple has is linked to the family's productive capacity, there is less incentive to have large families. Family values and the role of women have also been affected by the growing influence of the mass media, especially television.
- The growing participation of women in the labor market means that an ever greater number of fertile women combine child-rearing with active employment. Even though women in Latin America participate less in the labor market than do women in the rest of the world (18 percent in 1980, compared with 28 percent in Africa, 33 percent in Asia, and 39 percent in developed countries), that share has been increasing continually. The rate of women's incorporation will continue to be faster than that of men well into the next century.
- Recession and possibly falling real family incomes have made it ever more difficult for families to make ends meet, thereby causing more women to look for work and so delaying or even stopping childbearing. In some countries, like Peru since 1985, government minimum employment schemes designed to help the urban poor have concentrated mainly on employing women.

Mortality

The average Latin American in 1988 could expect to live until age 66, thirteen years longer than in 1958. Although the increase was relatively small for the average Argentine and Uruguayan, who in the 1950s could expect to live considerably longer than most other Latin Americans, there was a substantial increase in most other countries. The countries at the bottom of the scale in the 1950s were the Central American republics (excluding Costa Rica), Bolivia, and Haiti. By the early 1980s the Central American countries achieved higher-than-average gains in life expectancy, but Bolivia and Haiti lagged far behind. Bolivian life expectancy was just over age 50 in the early 1980s, Haitian under 53 (Table 1.3).

Table 1.3

Life expectancy and infant mortality by country, 1950–1985

	Life Expectancy[a]		Infant Mortality[b]	
	1950–1955	1980–1985	1950–1955	1980–1985
All Latin America	51.8	64.9	125.1	62.1
Argentina	62.7	69.7	65.9	36.0
Bolivia	40.4	50.7	175.7	124.4
Brazil	51.0	63.4	134.7	70.7
Chile	53.8	71.0	126.2	23.7
Colombia	50.7	63.6	123.3	53.3
Costa Rica	57.3	73.5	93.8	23.3
Cuba	58.8	73.5	81.9	22.9
Dominican Republic	46.0	64.1	149.4	74.5
Ecuador	48.4	64.3	139.5	69.6
El Salvador	45.3	57.2	151.1	77.0
Guatemala	42.1	59.0	140.6	70.4
Haiti	37.6	52.7	219.6	108.2
Honduras	42.3	61.9	195.7	78.4
Mexico	50.8	67.4	113.9	49.9
Nicaragua	42.3	59.8	167.4	76.4
Panama	55.3	71.0	93.0	25.7
Paraguay	62.6	66.4	73.4	53.0
Peru	43.9	58.6	158.6	98.6
Uruguay	66.3	70.3	57.4	37.6
Venezuela	55.2	69.0	106.4	38.7

[a]At birth, number of years.
[b]Deaths per 1,000 live births.

SOURCE: CELADE, *Boletín Demográfico, (Demographic Bulletin)* no. 40, July 1987, pp. 18–140.

In worldwide terms, at 66 years, life expectancy for the average Latin American was higher than for the average inhabitant of this planet (63 years). It was not much less than in the Soviet Union (69 years), which has a GNP per capita more than four times that of Latin America, and it was considerably more than the average for Africa (52 years) and Asia (61 years). Life expectancy in Europe and North America was 74 and 75 years respectively.

Infant mortality has been significantly reduced in the last thirty years, this being one of the main causes for the fast increase in the size of Latin America's numerical population. The average in the early 1980s was 59 deaths (in the first year of life) per 1,000 live births, relatively low when compared to the averages for African and Asian countries. But the pattern is extremely unequal within Latin America itself. At one extreme are Cuba (22.9), Costa Rica (23.3), and Chile (23.7); at the other are Peru (98.6), Haiti (108.2), and Bolivia (124.4). These last figures are comparable to a number of African countries now.

The drop in infant mortality is clearly related to the growing urbanization of Latin American society, since generally it is easier to provide both preventive and curative medical facilities in areas of high population concentration than in rural areas where population is dispersed. It is also easier to provide drinking water and proper sanitation in cities than in rural communities. The drop in particular reflects the efforts of most Latin American governments over the last few decades to provide vaccination against the most common child illnesses. Again, in this respect there are big differences between countries and in respect of specific diseases, with Cuba, Chile, Panama, and Costa Rica at the top of the league with the great majority of their children vaccinated, and Bolivia, the Dominican Republic, and Haiti at the bottom.

The effects of the debt crisis on many countries of the region during the mid-1980s have tended to reverse the downward infant-mortality tendency, because of falling real incomes among the poor and retrenchment in public health spending. Malnutrition among children has become more widespread since the beginning of the 1980s.

Urbanization coupled with advances in health care has also brought big changes to the overall pattern of causes of death. There is a clear trend away from the classic causes of death in underdeveloped economies (for example, infectious diseases and parasitical diseases) toward causes associated with developed countries (for example, heart disease, cancer, and traffic accidents). Once again, though, the degree to which this is the case varies considerably. The likelihood of dying from an infectious or parasitical disease is the same in Cuba as in the United States. An Argentine, however, is twice as likely to die from such a cause, a Guatemalan fifteen times. The likelihood of dying from a heart illness is three times greater in Cuba or Argentina than

The maps on these facing pages form an overall picture of the natural geographic features of Latin America: Middle America (below) comprised of Mexico, Central America, and the Caribbean Region; and South America (opposite).

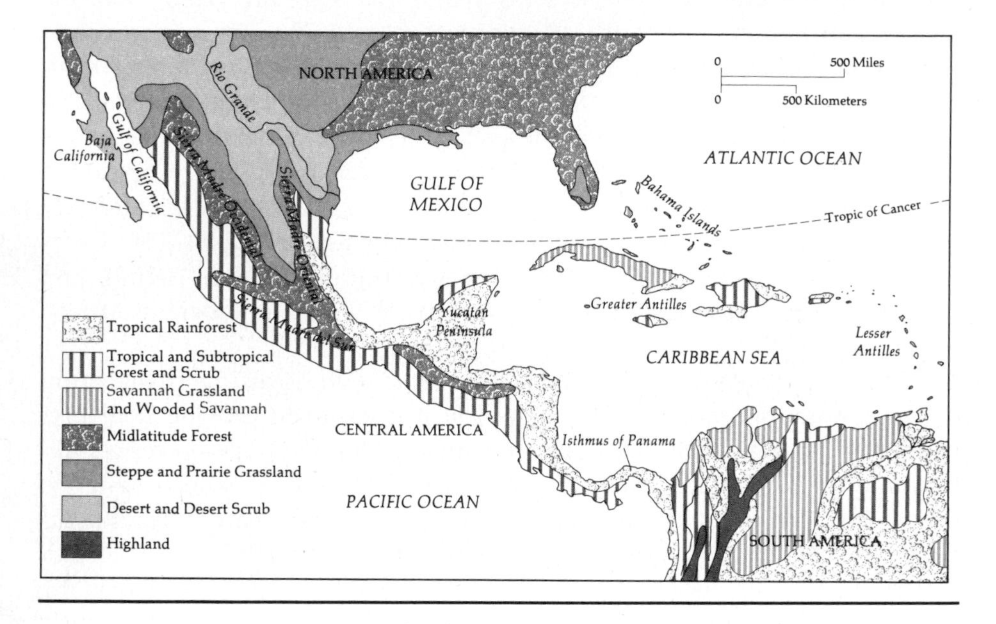

in Guatemala, but the likelihood of dying in a road accident in Argentina is twice what it would be in Guatemala.

AIDS could become a scourge in Latin America unless an appropriate cure is found and made widely available in the last decade of the twentieth century. As elsewhere, its incidence is highest among young adults in cities. The largest numbers of reported cases are in Brazil, Mexico, and Haiti.

In the future, increases in average life expectancy may come more slowly than in the past. Many of the gains that can be derived by eradicating infectious diseases have been realized. There is still room for improvement by reducing infant and child mortality, maternal mortality, and mortality due to violent causes (such as accidents and homicide) and for improvement in life expectancy at older ages. Improvements in maternal and child survival depend on broadening access to primary, preventive health care for the poor and on family planning.

There is also the possibility that the degree of control obtained over certain tropical diseases may diminish. In the case of malaria, the number of cases reported has increased in recent years. Between 1976 and 1985 the figure for Latin America rose from 379,000 cases to 929,000. In 1988, Brazil alone reported more than 500,000 cases; in Venezuela the numbers increased from 3,000 in 1985 to 25,000 in 1989.

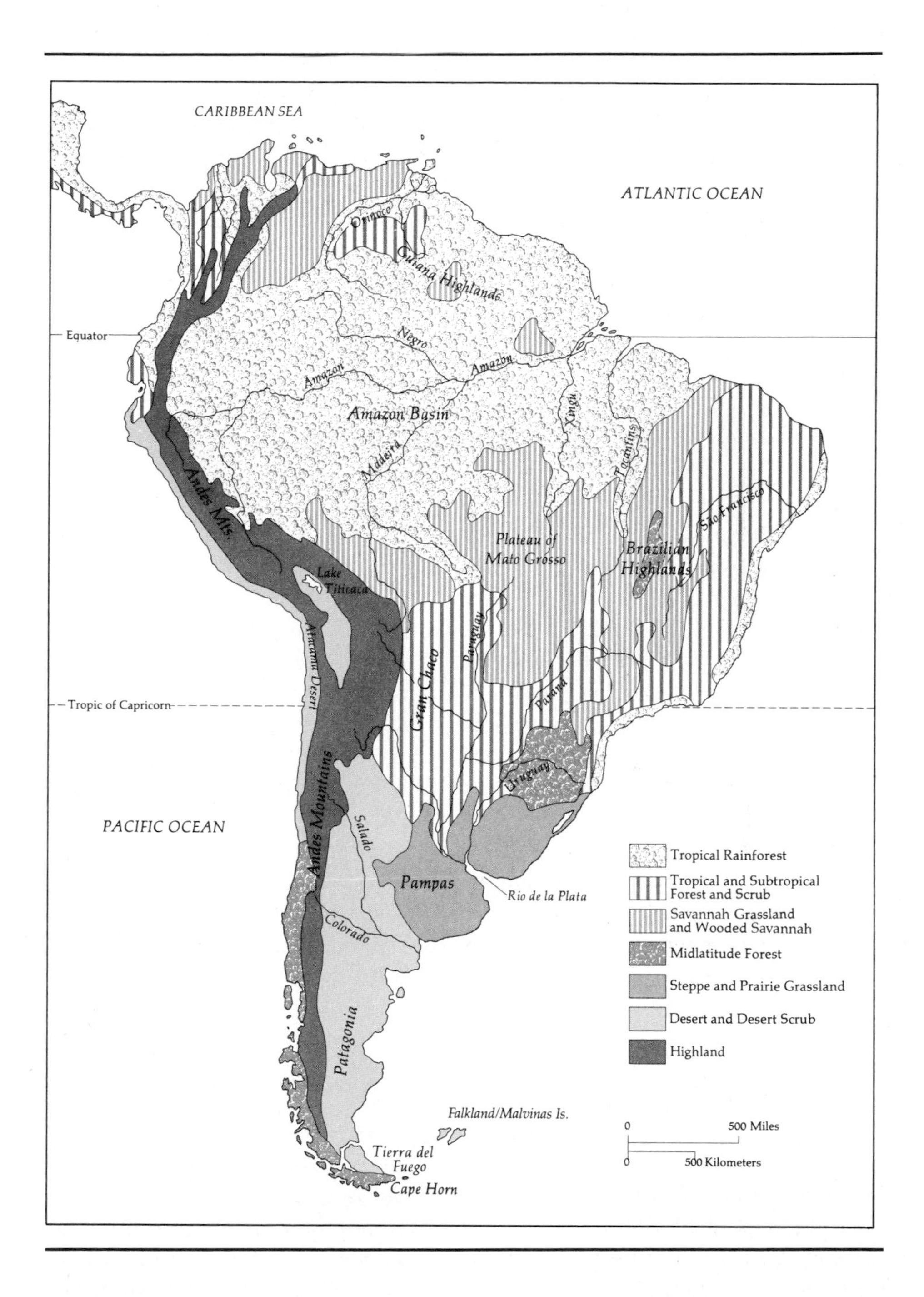
CARIBBEAN SEA
ATLANTIC OCEAN
Orinoco
Guiana Highlands
Equator
Negro
Amazon
Amazon
Amazon Basin
Xingu
Tocantins
Madeira
Andes Mts.
São Francisco
Plateau of
Mato Grosso
Brazilian
Highlands
Lake
Titicaca
Atacama Desert
Paraguay
Gran Chaco
Tropic of Capricorn
Paraná
Uruguay
Andes Mountains
Salado
PACIFIC OCEAN
Pampas
Rio de la Plata
Colorado
Patagonia
Falkland/Malvinas Is.
Tierra del
Fuego
Cape Horn
Tropical Rainforest
Tropical and Subtropical
Forest and Scrub
Savannah Grassland
and Wooded Savannah
Midlatitude Forest
Steppe and Prairie Grassland
Desert and Desert Scrub
Highland
0
500 Miles
0
500 Kilometers

These increases are related to immunity to pesticides among some mosquito populations, frontier migration such as the Brazilian gold rushes, political insecurity in the countryside . . . (for example, that caused by Colombian guerrillas and Nicaraguan *contras*), . . . and the reluctance of less deferential populations to put up with continued immunization. Some experts fear renewed epidemics such as have occurred in India, Sri Lanka, and the western Pacific. They consider that Latin America's spectacular successes in the "attack phase" in combating malaria are threatened by failure in the "concentration phase."

Much also remains to be done in the face of other tropical diseases, such as dengue and chagas. Only three republics—Venezuela, Brazil, and Argentina—have programs for the control of chagas disease.

The use (or nonuse) of tobacco, alcohol, and drugs, as well as diet and exercise, influence mortality levels among adults. The consumption of cigarettes and alcohol varies in the region. Smoking is directly proportional to per capita income: the richer countries smoke more. Beer drinking increased threefold in Central America and the Caribbean between 1960 and 1980 and doubled in tropical South America. By comparison with the United States and Canada however, it is still low—between one-quarter and one-third per adult. Alcohol consumption in the majority of countries—Mexico, Guatemala, Cuba, Dominican Republican, Colombia, Ecuador, Peru, Bolivia, Paraguay, Brazil—is less than 5 liters per year for adults over 15. In Haiti, Venezuela, Uruguay, and Nicaragua, consumption at 5 to 10 liters matches that of Great Britain or Scandinavia; at 10 to 15 liters Chile matches the United States; at 15-plus liters the Argentines equal the French.

Changes in lifestyle have contributed to reductions in mortality from heart disease and cancer, increasing life expectancy among people over 50 in North America and Europe. There is growing public awareness of this in Latin America, but the pace of future increases in life expectancy will depend on how rapidly awareness is translated into changed behavior.

Age Structure

With the exception of countries that have had lower fertility for some time (Argentina, Cuba, and Uruguay, for example), Latin American populations are still comparatively young. The median age is only 21 for the region as a whole, ranging from less than 17 in a number of Central American countries to 30 in Uruguay. The median age is 32 in North America and 34 in Europe.

Table 1.4

Population age composition by country, 1980–2000 (percentage of population)

	1980			2000		
	<15	15–64	>64	<15	15–64	>64
All Latin America	39.3	56.4	4.3	33.3	61.5	5.2
Argentina	30.0	61.8	8.2	28.5	61.9	9.6
Bolivia	43.5	53.3	3.3	43.5	53.2	3.2
Brazil	37.7	58.2	4.0	31.8	62.8	5.4
Chile	32.3	62.3	5.4	27.2	65.9	6.9
Colombia	39.4	57.1	3.5	32.7	62.8	4.5
Costa Rica	38.5	58.0	3.6	32.5	62.5	4.9
Cuba	31.3	61.4	7.3	24.1	66.9	8.9
Dominican Republic	43.9	53.2	2.9	33.6	62.3	4.1
Ecuador	43.3	53.0	3.6	38.3	57.8	4.0
El Salvador	45.2	51.4	3.4	40.7	55.5	3.8
Guatemala	45.9	51.3	2.9	42.9	53.3	3.7
Haiti	43.6	52.9	3.6	43.4	53.5	3.1
Honduras	47.8	49.4	2.7	42.3	54.4	3.3
Mexico	44.7	51.8	3.6	34.1	61.7	4.2
Nicaragua	47.4	50.1	2.4	42.7	54.2	3.1
Panama	40.5	55.4	4.1	31.5	63.1	5.4
Paraguay	42.7	53.9	3.4	37.7	58.5	3.7
Peru	41.8	54.6	3.6	35.6	60.1	4.3
Uruguay	27.1	62.5	10.4	25.0	62.9	12.2
Venezuela	41.1	55.7	3.2	34.5	61.2	4.3

SOURCE: United Nations, *1984 Assessment* (New York, 1986). Used by permission.

This age structure, of course, reflects the tendencies observable for fertility and mortality and relates as well to patterns of international migration. The youthful population profile has led to particular pressure on government services like education and child health.

As birthrates decline, some of this pressure will be lifted and it may be possible to improve the quality of services for the same amount of expense. But as the "bulge" becomes older, it puts a greater degree of stress on other forms of social provision, such as job creation, housing, transport, and other urban services. Priorities in spending, therefore, have to take account of how the age structure in Latin America's population is shifting.

In 1980, just under 40 percent of the total population was under 15 years old; in 2000 the percentage will probably be down to around 33. There will be a slight increase in those aged 64 or more, from 4.3 percent in 1980 to 5.2 percent in 2000. The bulk of the increase in terms of percentage points will be in the middle—the economically active population, which will grow from 56.4 percent of the whole to 61.5 percent. The same sort of regional differentiation will apply, with more than 40 percent under 15 in Bolivia, El Salvador, Guatemala, Haiti, Honduras, and Nicaragua, while at the other end of the scale nearly 10 percent of Argentina's population will be over 64 and more than 12 percent of Uruguay's (Table 1.4).

So, as fertility continues its decline and life expectancy increases, Latin America will have to deal with the aging of its population. The proportion of the population aged 65 or more is likely to rise for Latin America as a whole from 4.5 percent in 1985 to 8.3 percent in 2025. This percentage is, however, a lot lower than those for many developed countries. In Europe, levels of 15 percent or more are fairly common, and both North America and Japan are undergoing rapid aging.

International Migration

Migration to Latin America

Until World War II, many more people migrated to Latin America than from it. The great majority came from southern Europe (Spain and Italy, notably) and settled for the most part in the countries of the so-called Southern Cone—Argentina, Uruguay, and Chile—and in Brazil. There was substantial German migration to southern Brazil and to Chile. In the past century, also, there were flows of indentured workers from China, India, and Japan to Peru and Cuba, Guyana, and Brazil respectively. In addition, there were also specific waves, like the Jewish inflow in the 1930s. About one-third of the more than 50 million who are thought to have migrated from Europe to the Americas between 1821 and 1932 settled in Latin America and the countries of the Caribbean.

Immigration has been much slower since World War II. Transatlantic movements have continued but at much diminished levels. Venezuela became a significant destination for Italian, Spanish, and Portuguese migration, its government adopting a pro-immigrant policy in the late 1940s.

Migration within Latin America

In addition to huge migration flows within individual countries, there have been significant flows between Latin American countries, especially where poor countries with few economic opportunities adjoin richer ones that welcome workers prepared to accept menial jobs and work for low wages. Such is the case of the some 400,000 Colombians who have settled in relatively oil-rich Venezuela, which has also attracted Dominicans, Ecuadoreans, and Peruvians. Similarly, large numbers of Bolivians and Paraguayans have made Buenos Aires and other Argentine provincial centers their home. In both Caracas and Buenos Aires there are large Latin immigrant groups.

The other, statistically less important, category of interregional migrant is the refugee. Political upheavals in Central America have created significant numbers of refugees both in other Central American republics and in Mexico and the United States. So, too, to a lesser degree, political repression in Argentina and Chile caused resettlement of people from these countries elsewhere in the region, notably in Mexico and Venezuela.

Migration from Latin America

Latin American migration to the United States is nothing new: some 167,000 migrants from the region settled in the United States between 1820 and 1900. But it has increased greatly in recent decades. Between 1971 and 1981, 1.8 million Hispanics settled legally in the United States. The numbers of illegal settlers, most of whom clandestinely cross the 2,000-mile U.S.-Mexican land frontier, total several million.

The 1980 census in the United States counted 14.6 million Hispanics, 6.4 percent of the population. Though less than the black community (26.5 million or 11.7 percent of the total), the Hispanic population has grown much faster than the black, partly because of immigration, legal and illegal, and partly because Hispanic fertility is about 50 percent higher than non-Hispanic. The Hispanic population of the United States at the end of the 1980s was close to 20 million, roughly the same as the total population of Venezuela in 1988.

Central America, Mexico, and the Caribbean have been sending the great majority of migrants to the United States. (Canada is also an important destination.)

- Most Caribbean emigration to the United States has been to the metropolises of the Northeast, especially the New York area.
- Florida is the main destination of Cubans and Haitians, many of whom moved as economic and political refugees.

- Mexican and Central American migration has for geographical reasons been concentrated in Texas and California. Metropolitan Los Angeles rivals Monterrey and Guadalajara as being the second largest "Mexican" city after Mexico City. A large number of Mexicans have also settled in the Great Lakes region, especially in Chicago, as have Central Americans (predominantly refugees from El Salvador).

In many ways, patterns of international migration within the Western Hemisphere more closely resemble recent internal migrations within Latin America than they resemble earlier transatlantic movements. The combination of proximity, a very porous land frontier, and the presence of so many Latin Americans, especially Mexicans, in the South and the West makes the United States a major competitor with Mexico City for migrants from Mexico's northern states. The debt crisis in Mexico, the economic adjustment that followed, and the fall in the price of oil have made it even harder for the million Mexicans entering the job market each year to find opportunities. Despite new legal restrictions introduced in the United States to deter immigration from Mexico, the attraction of jobs and higher pay in California and Texas is likely to stimulate continued movement to the end of the century and beyond. The same goes for Central Americans, particularly Salvadoreans and Guatemalans, for whom Mexico is a stepping-stone away from the political convulsions in their own countries.

Migration flows from Latin America to Western Europe have so far been small in comparison to those from the United States. Western Europe is harder to get to, and harder to settle in legally, though many major cities have sizable Latin American colonies, more often of South Americans than of Central Americans and Mexicans. In some cases, migration arose from political events, such as the coups in Chile (1973) and Argentina (1976), though refugees tend to be temporary settlers rather than permanent ones. In other cases the reasons are economic: the lack of job opportunities in Latin America. The existence of a well-established community from any one country is an incentive to more people from that country to arrive and settle. The Colombian community in London is a case in point.

Outward international migration has its positive side for the source countries. It offers relief to the local job market; it also provides a source of repatriated dollars sent by migrants abroad to friends and families. But those who migrate include relatively educated Latin Americans, members of the middle class who find it increasingly difficult to maintain a middle-class way of life in their own countries. They represent a "brain drain" of doctors, dentists, economists, agronomists, engineers, and other beneficiaries of higher education in Latin America, which produces more professionals than it can absorb. Many will never come back even if living conditions in the region improve.

2

What Sort of People?

Rural-Urban Migration

Over the past fifty years the most significant change in Latin American society has been the shift from a predominantly rural, agricultural society to a predominantly urban one. Rapid urban growth has been typical of some parts of Latin America since the beginning of the twentieth century. This was particularly the case in Argentina, Uruguay, and southern Brazil, where large numbers of foreign immigrants settled. In most countries, though, the takeoff in urban growth was a post-1940 phenomenon. Indeed, in Central America and Bolivia it only got started in the 1950s. The process therefore has not been even: Argentina was more urban in 1914 than Bolivia is today. As the twentieth century comes to a close, the urban population will account for an even greater share of the whole. In 1985 some 68 out of every 100 Latin Americans were city dwellers; in the year 2000, 75 out of 100 will be, a far higher ratio than in most other parts of the developing world.

The corollary of urban growth, of course, is the shrinking of rural society in relation to the total population. This does not necessarily mean, however, that numbers are falling in absolute terms. Nor does it mean that ever larger numbers are migrating to the cities, since migration is no longer the most important component of urban growth. The bulk of the new urban population today comes through natural increase. The new city dwellers are the children, even the grandchildren or great-grandchildren, of those who migrated over the past thirty or forty years. This is particularly true of mature urban countries like Argentina, Chile, and Uruguay, but it is also true of urban latecomers like the Central American countries. Even though rural migration may continue, the problem of how to dissuade migrants from moving from rural areas to the cities is no longer the main one facing Latin American governments.

The rate of urban growth in Latin America is no longer accelerating. Both the population itself and the ratio of urban to total population will continue to grow, but the peak in the rate of growth has now past. This has long been the case in the Southern Cone countries—Argentina, Uruguay, and Chile—where rural population is now very small in proportional terms. But the rate is slowing in the late urbanizing countries too (Table 2.1). The average annual rate of change in the percentage of Latin America that is urban was 1.37 percent in the 1970–1975 period. In the 1985–1990 period it was 0.86 percent, and in the 1995–2000 period it will be 0.57 percent. In just Central America, the rates are 1.51 percent (1970–1975), 1.08 percent (1985–1990), and 0.83 percent (1995–2000). This decrease means that the fall in the rural percentage should also slow down.

Table 2.1

Percentage of population residing in urban areas, 1970–2000

	1970	1985	2000
All Latin America	57.7	68.0	74.8
Argentina	78.4	84.7	88.0
Bolivia	38.2	48.2	56.6
Brazil	55.9	70.8	79.0
Chile	75.1	82.2	86.5
Colombia	59.3	69.5	77.4
Costa Rica	38.8	48.2	58.1
Cuba	59.6	70.4	78.9
Dominican Republic	39.2	57.0	70.5
Ecuador	39.5	51.4	61.1
El Salvador	39.5	46.7	54.4
Guatemala	34.4	37.8	43.1
Haiti	19.8	25.0	31.9
Honduras	28.0	39.7	51.5
Mexico	59.0	68.4	76.0
Nicaragua	47.0	57.2	66.0
Panama	47.6	50.1	52.7
Paraguay	37.0	40.0	44.5
Peru	58.1	67.1	74.6
Uruguay	82.0	84.6	86.6
Venezuela	71.8	77.7	82.3

SOURCE: CELADE, *Boletín Demográfico, (Demographic Bulletin)*, no. 34, July 1984, pp. 8–128.

Farmers

A common impression that needs to be dispelled is that, while the growth of cities and the development of the urban economy have proceeded apace over the last thirty years, the rural sphere has remained backward and largely unchanged.

Many of those who wrote about Latin American agriculture and rural life in the 1960s stressed what they described as "dualism." On the one hand they saw there was a "modern" export-oriented agriculture, often organized on plantation lines, which was relatively highly mechanized and enjoyed high rates of productivity. On the other there was a "backward" domestic agriculture, with huge inequalities in landholding (*latifundios* and *minifundios*, estates too large and plots too small) with generally low productivity and extremely inefficient use of existing resources. The need therefore was for domestic agriculture to be modernized and mechanized.

The U.N. Economic Commission for Latin America (ECLA), in particular, highlighted the need to develop rural areas as a means of expanding the size of the domestic market for producers of industrial goods. Agrarian reform was an integral part of ECLA's strategy to promote industrialization in Latin America. Industrial growth would never flourish unless there was a larger market at home for what was produced. Redistribution of rural incomes was seen as vital to the creation of new domestic demand.

The picture in the 1980s has been significantly different from that of the 1960s, and the changes that have taken place are not necessarily those that the experts of the 1960s thought most likely.

Cash-Crop Agriculture

Modernization has been rapid, but not as a result of any radical change in the inequalities of landholding or rural income. Agriculture has become far more capital intensive, and not only in the export sector. Modern agricultural technologies like those of the Green Revolution (and more recently biotechnology) have been applied. Large sums of government farm credit have been channeled into agriculture, with the lion's share going to large and already prosperous producers. Governments have also spent substantial amounts on investment in irrigation and rural infrastructure. Latin American farmers are now large consumers of chemical fertilizers, which has prompted the development of local fertilizer industries.

Plantations continue to exist in some countries, but their importance in agriculture is strictly limited. Most traditional large estates have also disintegrated, either as a consequence of land reform programs or in response to market pressures for them to turn into smaller and more efficient farms. Even peasant farms in long-settled areas with relatively good and plentiful land have been able to modernize.

A sector of modern, middle-sized farms has therefore come into existence. These are farms that hardly existed in most countries forty years ago. They have been growing fast in nearly all countries in Latin America and are of central importance in the agriculture of the economically most important countries. The farmers in this sector have been in the forefront in raising some of the most successful lines in cash-crop agriculture: soybeans and other oil seeds, feed grains, rice and dairy products, poultry and pork, vegetables and fruit, cotton, and coffee.

Thus the distinction between export production and production for the domestic market, previously at opposite poles, has blurred. These new forms of farming supply an expanded domestic urban market with both food staples and raw materials for agro-industrial processing. They also help provide an increasingly important share of export production. These developments, however, do not mean that rural poverty is a thing of the past.

Peasant Agriculture

Latin America continues to suffer from "dualism," though of a rather different type from that which economists and sociologists wrote about in the 1960s. Peasants still continue to be the most numerous kind of farmer in many countries in Latin America, and poverty is still the norm rather than the exception in peasant households. In 1985, ECLA estimated the total number of rural poor at 65 million, just over 60 percent of the total rural population and just under 60 percent of the total "poor," both rural and urban. Despite the fact that, as a result of migration over the last thirty years, the numbers of the rural poor have decreased in relation to the total poor, their numbers have still increased in absolute terms.

As in the past, peasant farming (in which the household consumes a significant part of what it produces) tends to be concentrated in parts of Latin America with poor soils, difficult climates, or both. These are lands that are not attractive for commercial agriculture and where productivity tends to be low. Typically, they are mountainous lands, semiarid ones, or areas prone to drought. They can also include many agricultural areas in the ecologically fragile rain forest. Peasant production, often still organized around the peasant community, is still important in the Andean highlands, the highlands of Mesoamerica, northeastern Brazil, and parts of the Central American and Amazonian tropical rain forests.

The main objective of those who advocated agrarian reform in the 1960s

Caribbean Nations

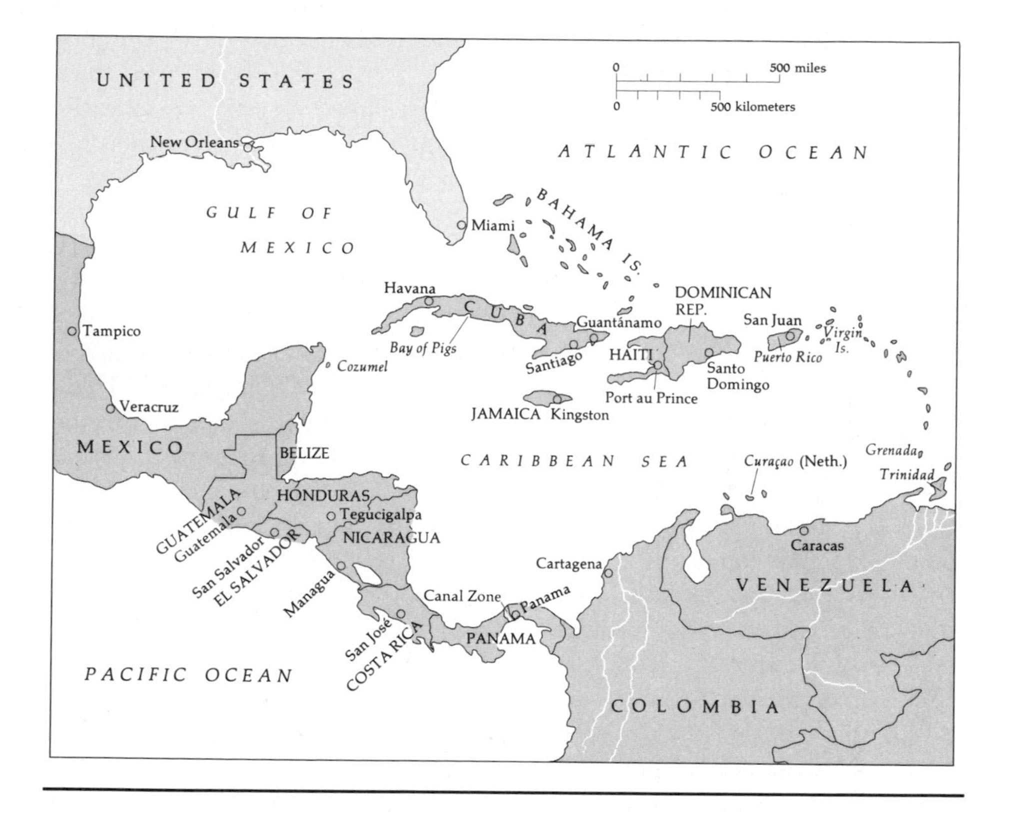

was to raise the living standards of the poor peasantry. The inspiration behind the land reform programs that emerged was the belief that reducing inequalities in rural Latin America would reduce social unrest as well as help the development of a bigger domestic market. In practice, however, in a country that embarked on fairly far-reaching agrarian reform (like Peru) and in one that did not (like Brazil), the outcomes in terms of agricultural development have not been dissimilar.

In both Peru and Brazil the type of agriculture that has been promoted has not been the poorest, the least competitive, or the least capital intensive. The poorest peasants in Peru were not the main beneficiaries; highland communities were often bypassed when land was redistributed. Agrarian reform fulfilled a function similar to the enclosure movement in eighteenth-century England: by breaking the mold of the old system, it helped the development of larger-scale, more commercial agriculture. Even the integrated rural development schemes practiced in Mexico, Colombia, and elsewhere have tended to benefit wealthy peasants with close links to the market by providing them with the credit and technology to improve productivity.

Urban migration clearly has had, and in many places will continue to have, an important effect on the peasant economy. Those people who migrate (like those who leave Latin America for other parts of the world) tend to be the better educated, the better off, and the more skilled. Though poverty, the "push-factor," clearly plays a role in determining migration, the typical rural-urban migrant is not usually the poorest or the least educated. Indeed the poorest regions of most Latin American countries tend to produce proportionately fewer migrants than those regions that are relatively more prosperous. There are exceptions to this general rule: those displaced by war, violence, disease, or natural disasters; or even those who move to the city following friends and relatives who have already established a foothold there.

Nor is all outward migration from rural areas entirely to the city. There have been important flows of people from areas of land shortage to areas of land abundance, partly as a result of official colonization programs but more often than not as a result of spontaneous migration. Examples include movements of population from the Andes (notably Peru, Bolivia, and Colombia) to the Amazon lowlands, especially the jungle and plains fringe along the eastern foothills of the Andes. Similarly, there have been important movements of people from the northeast of Brazil as well as other areas of chronic rural poverty to the Brazilian Amazon. In some cases, as in Brazil recently, there is even a city-to-country migration, the reverse of the normal flow.

Colonization schemes, often viewed by governments as the easier option to land redistribution when dealing with land shortage, have not been unqualified successes. Their success has depended critically on the quality of the land involved, the availability of credit, and access to the market. In many instances, colonists have been unwilling to migrate permanently, either returning to their places of origin or seeking seasonal employment at harvest time on larger-scale agricultural or agro-industrial concerns. Given the inadequacy of the Amazonian soils for agriculture, colonization schemes have damaged not only the habitat of the tribal peoples whose land has been taken but also the ecological balance.

So the question of whether the Latin American peasantry is disappearing—or at what speed—is by no means a simple one. In certain areas, notably in colonization on the agricultural frontier, peasant forms of production are being reproduced, though integrated more than in the past to the market. In other areas, in particular where cash-crop agriculture is advancing fastest, peasant-type production tends to be disappearing in favor of wage labor. There are still important parts of Latin America where peasant agriculture will continue to be the dominant type well into the next century.

However, it seems likely that subsistence agriculture and even semisubsistence agriculture will be further eroded during the next twenty years as peasant producers become more integrated into the market economy. They tend to sell an ever-greater amount of what they grow and to buy an ever-increasing amount of what they consume. This tendency varies greatly from place to place, but even in Peru, where subsistence agriculture is more resilient than in most countries, there are unmistakable signs of peasants forming part of food chains as both producers *and* consumers. Indeed, in highland Bolivia, peasant communities are organizing themselves in such a way as to improve their position in such chains by undertaking transport and marketing themselves.

The speed at which the wage labor in agriculture grows at the cost of the independent producer will depend a great deal on the buoyancy of demand for agricultural produce both in local markets and abroad. What is foreseeable, though, is that increasingly the system of permanent full-time employment, typical of the old *latifundio* estates, will give way to a much more casual labor market in which seasonal workers are hired for the duration of the harvest. Women are likely to play an increasingly important role in this respect. Rural producers will probably spend some of their time in urban employment, while at the same time in the agricultural areas closest to the city farmers will look for seasonal workers in the urban labor market. One example of this is the so-called *boías frías* (cold lunches) in southern Brazil. Under this system, urban workers are collected daily by trucks and taken out to the fields. They carry their cold lunch with them, hence the name.

Rural conflict over landownership seems likely to become less active, especially in those countries where land reforms have at least got rid of the worst excesses of land monopolization and have expanded the use of land titles to demarcate land more clearly. The evidence from these countries is that the demands of peasants and small-scale producers are turning away from the issue of landownership toward issues like the more equitable distribution of agricultural credit and better prices or guaranteed minimum prices for the crops they produce. Rural pressures will therefore represent less of a challenge to the structure of ownership, though pressure for land reform will continue where the pace of growth in commercial farming is producing a growing problem of landless laborers without alternative employment.

At the same time, as the proportion of rural inhabitants continues to decline in relation to the rest of society, their political muscle will thereby weaken and as a consequence so will their ability to exact land reform. Thus, agrarian reform is perceived by governments as being an issue for an ever-smaller proportion of the population. Experience has also shown that modernization of agriculture and enhancement of its capacity to feed quickly expanding urban populations can be achieved without agrarian reform. Finally, the new commercial farmers of Latin America, especially the large ones, are often more economically powerful than their *hacendado* predecessors, the large landowners of the past. There may be growing demand for land reform—in Brazil, for example—but a growing body of entrenched landlord interests is prepared to go to great lengths to make sure that this does not happen.

City Dwellers

Concern among policymakers about the social and political effects of rapidly increasing population in Latin America have been compounded by the concentration of large numbers of poor people in cities. With urban living standards tending to fall during the 1980s as a consequence of the debt crisis, it is at first surprising that urban protest has not been much more violent.

Geographical Concentration

One of the specific features of Latin American urbanization has been its concentration in just one or two urban centers, normally the capital city. There are very few countries where the urban population is spread out into more than four or five large centers. Brazil and Colombia are exceptional. The gap between a country's largest city and second largest is often notable. Mexico City is six times the size of Guadalajara; Buenos Aires is ten times the size of Rosario; Lima is eleven times bigger than Arequipa; Santiago is seven times the size of Valparaiso.

Reasons for population concentration include the traditional centralization of government and the pattern of industrial development, often in and around the country's major port. Migration toward the main center of employment has tended also to feed on itself as relatives of original migrants follow in their footsteps.

Attempts by governments to decentralize have not been successful. New cities have been built, but more often than not they have been closely linked to the exploitation of large reserves of formerly untapped natural resources. This was the case in the building of Las Truchas in Mexico and Ciudad Guyana in Venezuela. Currently, growing urban settlements in parts of the Amazon jungle in Brazil are attracting people from densely populated areas on the coast, both rural and urban.

The most conspicuous example of the "new city" was the building of Brasília, but efforts by governments to decentralize their own bureaucracies by building new capital cities have not been a great success. Other countries have toyed with the idea, but vague promises have not been put into practice. Peru's President Fernando Belaúnde Terry in the early 1980s promised to build a new capital in the jungle. Later, Argentina's Raúl Alfonsín said he would make Viedma, a small town in northern Patagonia, his country's new administrative capital.

Two main obstacles face such schemes: one is resistance from the bureaucrats faced with the possibility of living in provincial obscurity; and the other is the expense involved. Though President Miguel de la Madrid talked of the need to decentralize Mexico's bureaucracy in the wake of the Mexico City earthquake in 1985, such a scheme was clearly going to cost a great deal more than Mexico could then afford.

Despite the obstacles to decentralization, there are welcome signs that excessive concentration is leading to a change:

- In many countries, provincial cities have been growing faster than capital cities, though they have a long way to go before they catch up.
- Within urban centers a tendency toward decentralization has occurred: the major city centers have been losing people to towns and cities within the same metropolitan region. During the 1970s, the city of São Paulo itself grew at a slower rate than other major cities in the state of São Paulo within a 150-kilometer radius of the capital. The same trends are visible also around Buenos Aires, Caracas, and Mexico City.

In the foreseeable future, substantial decentralization of urban population is unlikely, especially if it involves the expense of building new cities and if the recession persists. Decentralization will happen when there is a clear economic motive for it. If the largest cities become so congested that they stimulate firms to relocate, the trend toward bigger provincial centers or dispersion within the metropolitan area is likely to continue; and if it does so, then some of the worst consequences of urban overconcentration may be mitigated.

Employment

The growth of the Latin American city, coupled with the way in which industrial growth has taken place, has led—as in other rapidly developing parts of the world—to a highly differentiated pattern of job creation. Those individuals who receive a decent wage for what they do often represent a relatively small proportion of the economically active population. They include executives, factory workers, professionals, and white-collar government workers. Much more numerous are the workers who earn low wages.

The problem is not so much—as some argue—that urbanization preceded industrialization in Latin America. The pattern varies. Rapid urban growth has taken place in some cities along with industrialization and in some intermediate cities without it. One aspect of the problem is that the kind of industrialization has been capital intensive rather than labor intensive, especially when compared with the industrialization that took place in the nineteenth century in the United States and in Great Britain. The increase in the number of high-productivity jobs brought about by industrialization has not been sufficient to absorb surplus agricultural labor. The result has been the parallel growth of an "informal sector," which employs a large number of people in relation to capital used, where productivity is generally low, where hourly pay rates are minimal, and that provides little or no job security.

Until the 1980s, open unemployment was an overstated problem in most parts of Latin America. The officially unemployed were mainly those who could afford to be unemployed, and generally they formed only a small fraction of the total work force. Most of these "unemployed" were to be found among those who had a family to support them. They were also to be found in jobs where employment was cyclical or fluctuating, such as in construction and among port workers. During the 1980s, as a consequence of recession, rates of open unemployment increased substantially, though not without important variations between countries and within them. The difference between countries is partly explained by the ways in which statistics are compiled, but it also results from differences in government policy. Mexico's figures are lower than Venezuela's partly because Mexico, unlike Venezuela, made sustained attempts to maintain activity in the construction industry. Within Mexico, too, Monterrey, with its heavy industry, suffered much worse than did Guadalajara, with its small-scale manufacturing base.

The real dimensions of unemployment are hidden. The term "underemployment" is a misnomer. Many very poorly paid people in the informal sector work ten to fourteen hours a day. The large numbers of street vendors in any Latin American city work long hours, but their productivity is low. Many of those who work in the informal sector, though by no means all, work in services.

In the Latin American city, compared with the industrializing cities of the United States or Europe in the last century, service industries have proliferated. This proliferation is in part due to the improved technology used in factories and the difficulty of absorbing excess labor within industry. However, there are also many low-productivity "informal" manufacturing industries, which are often tightly integrated into the production systems in the "formal sector": the clothing industry in many countries depends on a large number of contracted outworkers, like seamstresses working at home. Low-productivity, arguably "informal" jobs exist in mining and agriculture too.

There is a widespread belief that service industries are essentially unproductive, but this is not necessarily the case. Productivity depends on the physical product or service involved. Although some of the best-paid services may be the least necessary from an economic point of view, the worst-paid services may be extremely important. The cigarette vendors on street corners comprise an invaluable and very cheap sales force for the companies manufacturing cigarettes.

Disappearance of the informal sector by the first decade of the next century is unlikely. Latin American cities will continue to be relatively poor, exhibiting big differences in wealth and income. Rates of natural increase will continue to fall, but the labor force will continue to grow very quickly, given the young age structure of most urban populations. With this in mind, a substantial reduction of the numbers of the lowly paid is unlikely in what is left of this century, even assuming substantially higher rates of economic growth than in the 1980s. In countries like Peru and Bolivia, informal-sector activity seems likely to increase.

Housing

The rapid growth of Latin American cities and the failure of governments to find housing policies that can cope with the rise in demand have led to a huge expansion in self-help housing—dwellings built by those who inhabit them. Most city centers are surrounded by large areas of self-help housing. Acute housing problems are found in these settlements: overcrowding, lack of basic amenities, poor physical conditions. Such settlements are also generally unplanned, are often far from the main centers of employment, and at times are constructed on land least fit for housing development, such as on steep slopes subject to subsidence, as in Rio de Janeiro. However, it is not necessarily the case that the expansion of self-help housing means that housing conditions are getting inexorably worse.

For a number of reasons the quality of new self-help housing is a doubtful guide to the general quality of housing conditions:

- The self-help shack fairly quickly can become a solid, even well-constructed house. In most cities the age of self-help housing can be gauged from the material with which it is built. Plenty of neighborhoods in Latin American cities have three-story brick-built family houses that provide relatively good housing but that began life as cardboard, reed-matting, or corrugated-iron shacks.
- The provision of basic services like electricity and water has by and large kept pace with that of urbanization. Self-help builders have

proved adept at applying political pressure to get such services installed.

- For some, self-help housing is a welcome relief from rented accommodation. Not all new settlers in self-help housing are rural immigrants. Many come from the city itself, often from tenements in its oldest parts, escaping conditions of overcrowding and lack of basic amenities.
- A growing number of architects and planners have come round to the view that self-help housing is an architecture that works and that as such it is to be encouraged, not discouraged.

A recent survey of Caracas estimated that 61 percent of the population lived in the *ranchos* (settlements of self-help housing). It qualified 53 percent of this housing as "good," and 23 percent as "fair"; 67 percent of the houses had sanitation, 72 percent water, and 80 percent electricity.

Another misconception about self-help housing is that it is all built on private land that has been occupied illegally. In many cases, it is true that land has been invaded against the wishes of the owner, but for the most part, people build on public land. Politicians and officials have tended to cooperate with land squatting, especially when it occurs near election time. Indeed in Venezuela it has been shown that a close link is apparent between elections and the timing of invasions, with the process of land settlement becoming part of the cut and thrust of winning votes. Even some military leaders, notably Peru's General Manuel Odría in the late 1940s, encouraged land invasion. In many instances, though, self-help housing takes place on land that has been purchased. This procedure became the norm rather than the exception in Brazil, Colombia, and Mexico many years ago.

There is scant hope that governments in Latin America will resolve housing problems over the next twenty years. The best that can be expected is a continuation of the post hoc response to illegal subdivision, land reorganization, and servicing. If the provision of basic services—water, electricity, sewers—can be maintained at their current levels, this should at least come somewhere near providing potential increases in urban settlement. The problems occur when governments find themselves obliged to cut back on the public investment projects (like dam construction, which provides water and electricity) required to meet the projected increase in demand.

Government housing policies have tended to consist too often of just building more low-cost houses. The beneficiaries of such programs are generally middle-class or more affluent working-class families. Outside government circles, it is generally agreed that such programs are costly and that they miss the majority of the poor. To avoid this, governments should redirect resources toward providing basic infrastructure and away from building houses and apartment blocks; or governments should lend money to people to build their own or to extend their existing homes. The problem is that many politicians continue to believe that finished or half-finished houses are more exploitable politically than the provision of sewerage or drinking water systems.

Another sector of the urban population that is growing rapidly is made up of those living in private rented accommodations. This sector is no longer confined to tenement areas; but the practice is a fast-growing problem in areas of self-help housing where families subdivide their homes and rent out parts of them to boost their incomes. In several Latin American cities, including Mexico City, Santiago, and Bogotá, between one-third and one-half of all households are renting or sharing accommodations.

Finally, it is important to emphasize that the housing situation can improve only if there is a sustained increase in per capita income. If national income is rising and the poor obtain a decent share of that increase, then they have the resources to improve their own housing and governments can dedicate themselves to providing basic infrastructure, from dams to piped water supplies, to underpin continued urban growth.

Services, Infrastructure, and Transport

Given the size of the increase in urban population, most Latin American governments appear to have coped surprisingly well with the extra strain on the system of basic services. Between 1970 and 1980 the number of people living in Mexico City increased by 5 million, yet services did not deteriorate as rapidly and significantly as this growth would suggest. Few developed countries could have coped with such an increase much better than Mexico did.

However, signs of stress are clear in, for example, basic social services that mainly benefit the poor. The general quality of publicly provided health services and education in cities is poor, and it has probably deteriorated over the last fifteen years. The more prosperous prefer to use private medical facilities and private schools, and those persons with the power and influence to change things have little direct interest in improving social services.

In contrast, public services required by industrial and commercial groups (electricity, water, sewerage, telephones, roads) have tended to respond better to the increased demand. Popular pressure has also become more intense to ensure that newly settled urban areas are provided with at least some of these services. The performance of public utilities, however, appears to suffer from the way in which they are administered. In many Latin American cities they run at a substantial loss and thus do not generate funds for further expansion and investment. The use of blanket subsidies is common, undermining the economic viability of the public companies concerned and subsidizing those who can afford to pay as well as those who cannot. There are some exceptions. In Bogotá the water company has long operated a system of cross-subsidy, charging more for water in wealthy districts and charging less in poor ones.

Public utilities, like all publicly owned, heavily indebted concerns, have been hard hit by the debt crisis: high interest rates on past borrowing and lack of any new lending. They have been forced to increase the rates charged to customers, thus effectively limiting use by poorer customers. In many cases locally contracted debts have been absorbed by national governments because the utilities or the municipal governments administering them just could not pay.

The real impact of the debt crisis may surface only in the future. The lack of investment in the expansion of water and electricity systems during the 1980s may slow economic growth in some cases and cause a crisis of public provision over the next fifteen years. Since public service provision is such a critical issue socially and politically, any major shortfall or any massive increase in the price to consumers is likely to be a potent source of public protest. One way to avoid this is to improve the highly regressive tax system, which generates the inadequate income with which municipalities provide basic services. But tax reform is especially difficult to implement when recession and inflation have lowered most people's real income.

Another major problem facing Latin American cities is road congestion and poor systems of public transport. As cities become more and more extensive geographically, dependency on motorized transport for people to get to work grows. Car ownership in Latin America's largest cities has soared, and with it traffic congestion and air pollution. Air pollution has become a critical problem in certain months of the year in many major cities. Mexico City is a prime example, as are São Paulo and Santiago.

Measures to deal with air pollution have not had much effect. Car ownership in Brazil and Mexico more than tripled between 1970 and 1980, concentrated in the largest cities. Public transit systems, like the Caracas metro, have helped cut journey times for many workers, but expansion of such systems demands huge investment. A Parkinson's law of traffic seems to operate: improve the capacity and new traffic appears to fill the space created. Still, more and better public transport is urgently required in almost all Latin American cities, though not necessarily underground railways, which are immensely expensive. The political will to limit car ownership or restrict the use of the private car may be lacking. If so, more people will spend longer and longer getting to work and the problem of air pollution will get worse.

Ethnic Minorities

Latin America's nonwhite, nonmestizo ethnic groups may be minorities, but two of them are large minorities. Amerindians and blacks form a significant part of the total population in Brazil, in Mesoamerica, in the Andean countries, and in the Caribbean. Smaller ethnic minorities are the descendants of Chinese indentured laborers in Peru and Cuba, and of Indian indentured labor in Guyana. Brazilians of Japanese descent now number over a million and form the largest Japanese colony outside the mother country. The use of the term "ethnic minority" for these groups but not for northern European migrants, for example, is obviously arbitrary. However, it reflects the fact that the latter have suffered little or no discrimination.

Discussion of ethnicity in the Latin American context is complicated by the fact that ethnic boundaries are difficult to identify geographically. Ethnicity exists in both an urban and a rural context. Nor is there always a sharp divide between an ethnic minority and the rest of society. Intermarriage has long blurred the edges of ethnic purity, and a degree of upward mobility has facilitated some racial integration. Latin America does not present the relatively clear-cut situation of South Africa or of (until fairly recently) many parts of the United States. That said, however, Latin American Indians and blacks still represent clearly identifiable groups in a society where racial consciousness is never far from the surface.

Since the last century, the "modernizing" instinct has led Latin American governments to try to integrate their ethnic minorities economically, socially, and even politically. In schools, members of ethnic groups have long been encouraged to believe in the virtues of republican democracy. Policies to modernize agriculture and to integrate peasants into a national economy also sought to incorporate ethnic groups into the "national" society. But despite this, social stratification has generally continued to reflect ethnic origins, exposing the myth of racial democracy. Encouragement of ethnic groups, by the state or by intellectuals, to stand up for their own cultural identities and values also has a long history. The Mexican *indigenistas,* those who defended the Indian past and values, came to prominence after the 1910 revolution, and a degree of *indigenismo* (their doctrines) has passed into the credo of the postrevolutionary Mexican state.

However, increasingly there are many signs of ethnic groups themselves beginning to revindicate their "nationhoods" and champion the rights of the so-called Fourth World, often vigorously supported by vocal pressure groups in the First World. Often ethnic groups do so in ways that go further than questions of land and the more limited traditions of *indigenismo.* At the same time, though, that degree of ethnic self-consciousness may prove to be transitory since, with the drift of members of ethnic groups from a rural to an urban society, the symbols of ethnic identity may become more a folkloric memory than live patterns of belief.

Amerindians

From spread of disease, disruption of settlement patterns, physical extermination, and forced labor by the Spaniards and others, the population of native Amerindians fell dramatically from the time of the conquest onward. The areas where indigenous peoples persisted in largest numbers, where their cultures and language endured, or where indigenous societies proved particularly strongly based and resilient, were either remote or difficult to conquer. These areas are still where most ethnic Amerindians, the direct descendants of pre-Columbian cultures, live today.

The calculation of numbers cannot be at all precise. In the literature on ethnicity no two writers use exactly the same criteria to define ethnic identity. The most recent and comprehensive analysis of the demography of indigenous peoples yields the following figures. The total indigenous population in the whole hemisphere—North and South America— was around 28.5 million people in 1978. Of these 27.9 million were in Latin America, approximately 6.5 percent of Latin America's total population. A previous estimate published in 1962 for the whole of the hemisphere put the indigenous population at just over 13 million. Even discounting inaccuracies and discrepancies in methods used to measure population, it is clear that indigenous populations are not falling. Given these estimates, they appear to have more than doubled in a period of sixteen years.

With the exception of Uruguay, all Latin American countries have indigenous groups. In some, like Guatemala and Bolivia, they represent a majority of the population. The total of 28.5 million for 1978 can be broken down into three component groups:

- Traditional peasant producers, concentrated in highland areas and often organized in peasant communities, who totaled over 21 million in 1978. They are most numerous in Mexico, Guatemala, Peru, Bolivia, and Ecuador.

- Tribal peoples, mainly in jungle areas, primarily but not exclusively in Amazonia. They numbered nearly 1.5 million, concentrated mostly in Brazil, Colombia, Ecuador, Peru, and Venezuela.
- Urban migrants, the great majority of whom were previously peasant producers, who numbered over 5 million in 1978. This group is the hardest to define. Marriage patterns (endogamy versus exogamy) and membership of migrant associations offer clues, however.

Over the next twenty years the overall number of members of ethnic minority groups will probably continue to increase, though the distribution will change. There will be proportionately more of them living in cities and proportionately fewer continuing as peasant producers. The tribal jungle population will also continue to rise, after a long period of decline, though this will vary a great deal from place to place. In parts of Brazilian Amazonia, some ethnic groups, especially the most isolated ones, might disappear by the end of the century.

The number of ethnic groups is also difficult to establish with any precision and depends to a great extent on how language and dialect are defined. According to the same source used to calculate numbers, there were 130 linguistic groups, of which Quechua and Aymara (Bolivia, Peru, and Ecuador) and Aztec and Maya (Mexico and Guatemala) are the largest.

The expansion of education and increasing economic participation have eroded and will continue to erode linguistic differences and to reduce the total of separate languages spoken, further increasing the numbers of people for whom Spanish or Portuguese is a first language. These changes will not necessarily lead to rapid and irreversible acculturation, however. So long as ethnic and racial identity is linked with land rights and political status, ethnic groups will survive. New forms of ethnic and cultural identity may well emerge because of the growing number of ethnic organizations.

The highland Indian communities of Latin America have undergone very significant changes as a result of their progressive incorporation into the national economy. The effects of migration to the cities and the tendency for traditional communal forms of production to disappear, especially in areas like highland Peru where they have traditionally been very important, are often taken as signs that ethnic consciousness is being diluted. Migration supposedly signifies a rupture between rural life and urban life. In most cases no such rupture exists, partly because in many cases migration is not permanent, and even when it is, those who migrate maintain links with their former communities, moving back and forth between their urban and rural spheres. This movement helps explain the proliferation of bus companies in many Latin American countries.

Another reason for the absence of a sudden rupture is that consciousness of ethnicity persists in the urban environment, although the cultural forms it takes may change. Peru is the country with the largest concentration of indigenous people in urban areas. About 30 percent of the total indigenous population now live in cities, mainly in Lima, where new cultural expressions of ethnicity are to be found that represent a fusion of Andean-rural with coastal-urban forms. "Chicha" music is but one. In Guatemala and Bolivia 25 percent of all indigenous people live in cities, and in Mexico and Ecuador the proportion is about 10 percent.

In Peru two specific influences have combined to further alter the pattern of rural life in the highlands: the growth in coca cultivation; and the impact of the Sendero Luminoso (Shining Path) guerrilla organization.

The massive expansion of coca cultivation in the 1980s in response to world demand for cocaine has been concentrated in the Alto Huallaga valley (the Huallaga River is one of the tributaries of the Amazon). The same phenomenon has occurred in the Chapare district of Cochabamba in Bolivia. Because of the profitability of coca farming in both Alto Huallaga and the Chapare and because the crop requires a substantial labor force, coca farming has a strong attraction for people from all over the highlands in both countries. Though some may have been able to acquire land, the majority are wage laborers. Both in terms of the corruption and violence cocaine engenders and in terms of dedication of land to coca rather than food, the growth of narco-agriculture and drug trafficking has had a disturbing influence in rural areas where coca is grown.

Sendero Luminoso, Peru's messianic guerrilla movement, has also had a disturbing influence, especially in the southern and central sierra, where it has been most persistently active. Most victims of the conflict between Sendero and the security forces have been innocent peasants whose loyalty each side tries to win. Depopulation has resulted from migration within the sierra area, from rural communities to provincial towns and to big cities.

Ethnicity undoubtedly plays an important part in defining the characteristics of peasant movements and rural tensions. Indeed, strong ethnic identity is one of the conditions that favors guerrilla warfare. Sendero Luminoso, despite its dogmatic Maoist rhetoric, has a keen sense of the customs and beliefs of Quechua-speaking Indians, whereas the orthodox Peruvian left has always had difficulty in subordinating class to ethnic concepts. In Bolivia, by contrast, the strength of *indigenismo* in peasant unions owes much to a successful blend of class and racial consciousness. In countries like Bolivia and Peru, and to a lesser extent in Ecuador, Colombia, and Mexico, ethnicity will continue to be an important element in rural politics.

Lowland indigenous groups face different problems. In Amazonia, and particularly Brazilian Amazonia, they are confronted by the destruction of their habitat by rapid colonization by outsiders, by the flooding of river valleys as part of hydroelectric schemes, by the penetration of slash-and-burn agriculture, and by the rapid development of extractive industries like logging and mining. They are threatened by the voracious and uncontrolled development of this large but hitherto sparsely populated region.

The economic development of Amazonia began in the early 1970s with a massive program of road construction—both arterial roads that cut across undemarcated tribal lands (and sometimes through designated national parks) and feeder roads. Access to the interior led to rapid colonization and to progressive deforestation, sometimes aided by outside funding for massive projects like the Polonoroeste scheme. The Polonoroeste scheme in northwest Brazil is a land colonization scheme established in 1981 that covers some 41 million hectares, and that sought to promote orderly land occupation and development by supporting productive activities and providing economic and social infrastructure. Rondônia, the size of West Germany, was a state of almost totally virgin forest in 1980. At present rates it will be wholly deforested by the end of the century. Other development schemes like Carajás in Brazil's central Amazon region will also lead to rapid deforestation. The Carajás project, a multifaceted program covering a huge area of the Amazon rain forest, involves the development of mining, charcoal smelting, and agribusinesses like ranching and tropical fruit cultivation.

Adverse conditions for business in South Africa have led to ever-greater interest on the part of international mining companies to move in on Brazil. However, the attraction of mining has also led to the proliferation of small-scale miners, known as *garimpeiros,* prospecting for a wide range of minerals. Gold mining lured not only landless rural workers from other parts of Brazil but also colonizers, professionals, and other people from the cities.

Faced with the problem of loss of their land, conflict with colonizers and *garimpeiros,* the flooding of river valleys, and the poisoning of some rivers with the mercury used in gold processing, Indian groups have become more assertive in defending their interests. This is not just the case in Brazil, but in Colombia, Ecuador, and Peru as well. Church missionaries (especially those with left-wing sympathies) have been prominent in tribal defense organizations, as have individual anthropologists, international Indian protection societies, and the workers in state-run agencies set up to protect tribal peoples. Often unwittingly, church missionaries have educated tribal elites who have come to act as political representatives. Their demands vary from place to place but have a common focus on issues like land rights, shares in the benefits of agriculture and mining, respect for different ethnic groups and their respective cultures, and recognition of a degree of autonomy for indigenous groups within the state. The response of national governments has been more favorable in Peru and Colombia than in Brazil, where indigenous demands have met with hostility from the armed forces as well as from government agencies and some sectors of the Catholic Church.

The tactics of indigenous groups have included armed confrontation with settlers, mutual support between ethnic groups in defense of territorial rights, and campaigns for representation in government agencies, like Brazil's National Indian Foundation (Fundação Nacional do Indio—FUNAI), set up to protect indigenous groups. The problems they have faced include factionalism, disagreements over from whom to seek support, and lack of true representation.

Although many members of indigenous jungle tribes will continue to suffer, even to be killed, over the next twenty years, and although even more will be forced to move from their traditional habitat, Indian organizations, supported by outside pressure groups, will receive greater recognition and gain political influence. Despite its size and remoteness, Amazonia is no longer (as it was twenty years ago) the "least-known" continent. Basic ethnographic information exists for most tribal groups and the land they occupy. The combination of ethnological with ecological concern in developed countries, as well as in the Amazonian countries themselves, means that indigenous issues will be taken increasingly seriously and the representatives of indigenous groups will be listened to. Public opinion and well-marshaled public pressure will become one of the indigenous groups' most powerful weapons in defending their land and way of life.

Blacks

The current location of blacks continues to reflect their introduction into Latin America as slaves by the colonial powers. This distribution followed the demands for labor where the local indigenous population did not suffice. Slaves were imported throughout Latin America. Where numbers were relatively small, as in Argentina, blacks had all but disappeared by the early twentieth century.

Areas where the black presence is still most notable are those where slaves formed a crucial part of the labor force:

- Brazil. Brazil has Latin America's largest black population. According to the 1980 census, 6 percent of the total population is black, 38 percent *pardo* (mulatto). In Bahia, in the northeast, the population is 12 percent black and 65 percent *pardo.*
- The Pacific coast of Colombia, Ecuador, and (to a much lesser degree), Peru. Blacks in Colombia are at least 4 percent of the total population and mulattos 25 percent. At least half of Colombia's blacks live on the

Pacific coast, which is 90 percent black. Almost all Ecuadorean blacks live on the coast as opposed to the highlands.

- The Atlantic coast of Colombia and Venezuela.
- The Caribbean coast of Central America, from Panama north to Belize. The black population includes also Black Caribs, the descendants of escaped slaves who mixed with Carib Indians on the islands of Saint Vincent and were transferred to Honduras in the eighteenth century.
- The Caribbean islands. The main black populations of the Spanish-speaking Caribbean islands live in Cuba, where between one-third and one-half of the total 10 million people are black or mulatto, and in the Dominican Republic, which is predominantly mulatto.

In most parts of Latin America where blacks are numerically important, the vast majority of them continue to occupy the lowest rungs of society. Studies in a number of countries show that blacks tend to do worse than poor whites or mestizos (people of mixed white and Indian ancestry) in situations of growing economic opportunity. This situation is partly because of discrimination of the nonsystematic type. It has also resulted from the effects of cumulative discrimination in the past, which has shaped cultural values in ways that make entering certain professions difficult or work against accumulating wealth.

One classic example of poverty and discrimination on a large scale is to be found along the Pacific coast of Colombia and Ecuador. Here blacks tend to be concentrated in remote, extremely poor, and well-demarcated areas, where there is little chance of racial assimilation or integration. Whites and mestizos, who tend to control access to natural resources, typically view the black majority as lazy and incompetent. In Brazil, too, though demarcation is less clear, blacks are overrepresented in the *favelas* (districts of informal settlement) and in the lowest occupational strata.

As for other rural dwellers, migration to the cities has provided a way out of rural poverty. Evidence from Colombia, however, suggests that black immigrants to the cities are generally worse off than nonblacks. Blacks tend to enter the lowest strata as domestic servants, construction workers, and street vendors. The notion that urbanization provides the mechanism for racial integration is therefore not plausible. Nor does migration to other countries necessarily offer a solution. Haitians working in the sugar plantations of the Dominican Republic have always faced extreme discrimination. Blacks fleeing Haiti for the United States found little welcome there. The official response was to ship them back, though the United States proved more accommodating to refugees from Cuba.

However, the foregoing evaluation does not tell the whole story. More and more blacks in both Colombia and Brazil have reached higher levels of education, and greater numbers are becoming members of the lower middle class than was the case twenty years ago. Particularly if migrants move to basically nonblack cities like Medellín or Bogotá in Colombia, like São Paulo or Rio de Janeiro in Brazil, and like Guatemala City in the case of Black Caribs, there is a greater degree of assimilation and there are better prospects for a degree of social mobility.

But assimilation is not quick and easy and the numbers who rise into the middle class are not many. In Latin American cities—São Paulo and Medellín to name but two that have been the subject of extensive research—just as in other cities of the world, large-scale migration tends to lead to a racist, antiblack sentiment among other groups. Finally, though social mobility for blacks may be becoming easier, it tends to be a lot more difficult than for nonblacks. Many blacks complain that it is much harder for them to succeed in the educational system, in the professions, in the urban labor market, and in the property market than it is for nonblacks. Few are the number of blacks, for instance, who have been elected to Congress in any country of the region.

Black consciousness, stimulated by black power movements in the United States, has become more evident in Latin America over the last twenty years. It is most evident, however, among educated blacks who wish to be accepted as blacks, not as honorary whites. In Brazil there have been Black Rio and Black Salvador movements. In Colombia blacks have founded the groups Cimarrón (fugitive), Panteras Negras (Black Panthers), and the Centro de Estudios e Investigaciónes Franz Fanon (Franz Fanon Study and Research Center). Some groups have managed to survive, even without much money.

Black consciousness is given depth by the existence of black cultural traits, common particularly in music and religion. Black culture as it is understood in Latin America is not necessarily defined by proximity to "pure" African forms but rather by the fact that blacks practice it. Nonblacks are increasingly interested in black culture. Often this interest has the effect of making black culture a picturesque and folkloric entertainment, rather than integrating it fully into national culture.

Blackness as a tool of political mobilization in the struggle for resources and power has never been an important force in Latin America proper. If this situation is compared with black politics in Haiti, Guyana, and Surinam, not to mention the United States and South Africa, vast differences are clear. Political solidarity around the notion of race does not come easily, and for most Latin American blacks, Africa is a primitive place with which they feel little close identification.

In the politics of Latin America, black consciousness will probably continue to be of marginal importance, the intellectual preoccupation of small groups of well-educated blacks. Opportunities for blacks to mobilize *as blacks* will remain limited. In the United States, black consciousness was the result of decades of systematic repression, and a clear demarcation and social definition of blackness created the conditions for racial solidarity. Such conditions do not exist in most parts of Latin America even in pockets like the Colombian Chocó, where color and administrative boundaries coincide and where political protest has clear racial overtones. But such places are few and far between.

In Latin America the clear demarcation between black and white is absent, but there remain a number of obstacles to assimilation, let alone social mobility. "Integration" of blacks may therefore simply mean their becoming more nearly equal members of an unequal society—a few wealthy blacks, a small group of middle-class blacks, and a majority of poor blacks. Yet, there is still a long way to go until even this minimal goal is reached.

3

Social Structure

Classes

So far this study has concerned itself with the numbers, location, and ethnic composition of Latin America's population, though it has also explored some of the implications of demographic change and migration. These are relatively simple matters compared with the evolution of social structure. Not only are empirical data more than usually rare and uncertain, but their interpretation is bound to be controversial. Questions of class and status—their relation to political behavior and economic performance—and questions of the degree of rigidity or fluidity in a society are intricate matters anywhere. The societies of Latin America have never been an exception, though simplified pictures of them have been common in the past and are still common in the present.

Analysis of a society's divisions can range from a statistical account of the distribution of income, which does not necessarily tell a great deal about social relations or social mobility, to an attempt to describe how people picture their own societies—after all, to some degree "class" is about how people define themselves vis-à-vis others—and the categories they use. People, however, may not always be much help. As elsewhere, in Latin America a great many define themselves as in some way middle class or insist on the importance of their geographical origins. Even within a single nuclear family, members' economic circumstances and category of employment or self-employment, whether formal or informal, may vary significantly.

Latin America's societies vary not only across the region but within each republic: the social structure of Popayán is not that of Bogotá; that of Salta is not that of Buenos Aires. The comparisons that might illuminate are hard to choose. To say that such and such a "fluid" aspect of Latin American society is more similar to the United States than to Europe begs a number of questions about both the United States and Europe. European observers tend to assume that aspects of Latin American society that appear familiar—nunneries or Jockey Clubs, for example—are more part of the essence of local society than are those that are not European—cattle ranchers who speak English with North American accents, or baseball players. But the nuns and the ranchers both go back to early colonial days, and the Jockey Clubs and the baseball teams may have been founded at much the same time, at the turn of the century.

Outsiders are prone to believe in pyramids, strata, "oligarchies," "traditional landowners," and "dominant classes" without much inquiry or questioning. Is there in the republic in question one pyramid or several? If there are several—one for each major region, for example—which takes precedence, and why, and how do they fit together? If there are "strata," is there an agreed order in which they lie one on top of the other? Moreover, a stratum is not simply a group. How are smallholders, owner-drivers of taxis, semiskilled workers in multinational companies, and customs officers arranged *as strata?*

"Oligarchy" is another slippery term. In El Salvador until the 1980s "oligarchy" designated a small number of economically powerful families. In El Salvador, a country only a little larger than Massachusetts, it was even possible to find agreement about who was an oligarch, although politically not all those on the list were in agreement, nor did they exercise power consistently in the way that a classic oligarchy might be expected to do. In Colombia, in contrast, "oligarch" is normally used to describe a person of a certain family background, habits, and manners. For at least a hundred years "oligarch" has also been a common political insult, and one should not be misled into thinking that it is a precise term of political or sociological analysis.

"Traditional landowners" no doubt exist here and there in Latin America, but if "traditional" means adhering to the customs and methods of bygone eras, then they are overwhelmingly outnumbered by nontraditional landowners. In visions of the Latin American past the power and prestige of traditional landowners are generally exaggerated. The prestige and power of landowners, in both national and local affairs, varies according to locality. Not all land confers power, and not all land confers prestige.

A phrase such as "dominant classes" begs many questions. What do these classes dominate? How do they do it? And how many of these classes are there?

The argument is not that inequalities of wealth and power do not exist or have been exaggerated. Latin America includes some of the most unequal societies in the world in income distribution. Nor is the argument that analysis and differentiation are impossible. Rather, the argument is that the reader should be on guard against oversimplified accounts of Latin America's social structures and their relations to political power.

"Class" is normally a political term, and analyses of class structure are commonly loaded with barely concealed political judgments. It is still widely felt, though not often directly expressed, that a large middle class is a desirable feature of any society because it fosters political stability. In this view, large middle-income districts mute the urban contrast between rich and poor. Large numbers of family farmers and prosperous peasants create a "cushion" between the large landowner, or *latifundista,* and the landless laborer.

In reality, the correlations between the structure of a society and its politics are much harder to draw. No student of twentieth-century Europe would be unaware of the difficulties in such arguments or unaware that what happens to classes matters as much as what classes exist. Yet students of Latin America, and policymakers, seem more prone to simple notions. The literature of the Alliance for Progress was full of them, particularly the part of it devoted to agrarian reform. It is well to stress, therefore, that though some plausible assertions can be made about the nature and evolution of Latin American society, no obvious political conclusions can be drawn.

Large middle classes do not guarantee political stability and an absence of violence. By most indicators Chile and Argentina were the most middle-class republics of Latin America; yet Argentine politics have been both unstable and violent, and Chilean politics passed through violence to a stability backed by force that was not what the believers in middle-class virtues usually have in mind. In Peru, schoolteachers would probably define themselves, and most categorizers would probably define them too, somewhere in the myriad ranks of the middle classes, but their union is Maoist and their rhetoric revolutionary. Colombia has a great many family farms and numerous prosperous peasants, yet they have hardly been much of a "cushion" in reducing violence in rural Colombia.

The reader is therefore doubly cautioned: not only is the description of social structure fraught with problems even when it tries to confine itself to mere description, but no clear political conclusions follow.

The Southern Cone and Elsewhere

A distinction may be drawn between three republics of the Southern Cone—Argentina, Chile, and Uruguay—and the rest of Latin America. Those three have had low rates of population growth. They are highly urbanized and have not experienced any rapid growth in the industrial labor force in recent years. Indeed, in all three it has declined, in contrast with trends elsewhere in

Latin America. In Argentina, Chile, and Uruguay, one can point to a certain middle-class and working-class cohesiveness, which perhaps derives from those countries' slow growth in the post–World War II period. For example, the Chilean industrial labor force grew by only 9 percent between 1952 and 1970 and has declined since. There is therefore reason to regard those societies as less "fluid" in their structure than societies elsewhere in Latin America.

In recent decades societies above the Southern Cone have experienced rapid population growth, rural-to-urban migration, and industrialization. Insofar as "fluidity" is measured by such indicators, as those other societies cease to grow in numbers and to experience large-scale migrations or rapid industrialization, they too will by definition become less "fluid." In that sense social mobility may eventually decline, though such speculation rests on the crudest sort of measures or indicators, such as equating the horizontal mobility of a shift from country to town with a degree of vertical social mobility.

Rural Society

Nearly all analyses of social stratification place rural workers in the lowest class category. As a result, migration to urban areas by the vast majority of rural workers comes to constitute social mobility *by definition.* Whether the move to urban areas *in itself* really constitutes social mobility may be the subject of discussion. A sizable component of measured social mobility in Latin America is due to rural workers moving to urban areas. In the future this component will be a decreasingly important phenomenon as migration as a component of urban growth declines.

Some of the effects of migration and agrarian change were examined in Chapter 2. Latin America as a whole has experienced increased commercialization of agriculture, both in areas of small peasant agriculture and on large estates. There has been a tendency for large estates to break up as a result of both commercial pressure and, in some areas, significant agrarian reforms. There has been a tendency toward increasing proletarianization of rural labor, and improved transportation systems make it easier for employers to use temporary or migrant labor. Peasants tied to large estates under a variety of service tenure systems are disappearing. Independent smallholders, including sharecroppers and renters, are not.

Cycles of marijuana and coca growing have temporarily raised rural

South America

incomes in parts of Bolivia, Peru, and Colombia in recent years. To a lesser extent this has also happened in Mexico, and it is happening increasingly in Brazil. Marijuana and coca are by no means the only new crops that can have a dramatic regional impact: other examples are rice in Colombia, and citrus fruit and soya in Brazil. Old products in new places can have the same effect: an example is the introduction and expansion of banana production in the Gulf of Urabá, which in some twenty years has raised Colombia from negligible importance in the banana trade to the position of the region's leading exporter. But bananas, unlike cocaine, are not newsworthy. In Brazil the opening up of the Amazon agricultural frontier has employed, often in highly conflictive fashion, seasonal and temporary workers and small peasants.

All these factors add to the complexity of the agrarian scene. It was never safe to generalize about rural Latin America from an image of stagnant, isolated *haciendas* (large estates) on which vegetated an unproductive semiservile labor force. The vast nineteenth- and twentieth-century expansion of coffee production, to give only one example, destroys such illusions. Rural society has frequently changed rapidly. The Urabá banana zone is the scene of numerous conflicts, but it has made new fortunes and continues to attract migrants because banana growers pay high wages.

Other, strictly nonagricultural factors—for example, the discovery of petroleum, gold mining, and coal mining—can also alter rural society. Rural society has never been exclusively agricultural, it has always included artisans, potters, brick makers, and mule-drivers. Not visualizing rural society as exclusively agricultural is still important.

Much of rural Latin American existence is also small-town life, not that of the *hacienda* or farm. Small towns have changed in the last decades: their communications and amenities have improved. The cultural gulf between city and small town is less than it was twenty years ago. In some areas close to large cities, small-town life has experienced a revival and diversification.

Migration to town or city rarely signifies a complete break with rural life. Money is often sent back to the countryside and invested there. A sort of relay system is sometimes adopted, with successive family members taking turns at work elsewhere.

It is not possible here to do more than hint at the varieties of rural society in Latin America and the differing ways they are ordered internally. A student of anthropology or folklore has no difficulty with the notion that there are likely to be vast differences in attitudes, circumstances, prospects, and culture between different types of rural worker, of peasant, of landowner, and in social relations in the countryside. The existence and importance of these distinctions are less easily grasped by those individuals who think in terms of seemingly simple categories, such as "peasant" or "landless laborer."

Urban Working Classes

In the last three decades the numbers employed in industry have grown rapidly outside the Southern Cone. Between 1950 and 1976, industrial workers in Brazil increased fourfold, from 2 million to 8 million. In Mexico their numbers grew threefold, from 1.3 million to 4.3 million. In Chile, by contrast, the increase was only 9 percent. Numbers increased elsewhere too—in Colombia, El Salvador, and Peru.

Urban workers everywhere are a diverse group. It is wrong to think of a typical worker as a factory worker. Most workers do not work in factories, but in a variety of other kinds of establishments. Transport and urban services continue to be major employers.

To what extent do workers think of themselves as belonging to a "working class"? To a considerable extent in the Southern Cone countries, but to a lesser degree elsewhere. Where the industrial working class is large, as in the state of São Paulo, or where there is a recent history of trade-union militancy, as in Bolivia and Peru, class identification may be quite high. Before 1973 it was certainly high in Chile; since then it may have diminished. However, it is often asserted that workers in Latin America place themselves more by their origins and aspirations than by their current situation of work and that there is a marked tendency for them to consider their presence in industry as a temporary stage on the road to some sort of self-employment. Some studies have supported this conclusion, but how general it is, is not known.

Other studies have emphasized that industrial workers' politics derive more from the neighborhood in which the workers live than from the workplace. Outside enclaves like mining areas, low-income neighborhoods contain a variety of people. Nor do the formally employed lead lives segregated from those in the "informal sector." Families have members in both sectors. Indeed, individual workers commonly have a stake in both or alternate between them.

The informal sector is usually defined as providing work without formal contract, without job security or social security, and with generally lower pay. However, the lower pay is not always the case. According to Alain Touraine, recent studies show that numerous young inhabitants of Latin American cities have turned away from low-paying "formal" employment, much of which is less secure than the law intends, toward precarious occasional jobs that they change with great frequency but that bring them a higher income.[1] This movement into the informal sector is particularly striking during periods of very high inflation. In Bolivia in the early 1980s, hyperinflation made a nonsense of formal work contracts, and those workers who could moved into occupations where they could fix the price of their remuneration. Some did well—workers in La Paz offices went off to pan gold, to run contraband, to work in the coca business. All highly informal.

To categorize the informal sector as in some sense archaic or primitive and the formal sector as modern is misleading. Such a categorization would lead to the meaningless conclusion that the Southern Cone is more "modern" than the rest of Latin America and that within the Southern Cone the most "modern" society is that of Uruguay. Neo-liberal doctrines have caused economists and sociologists to revise their views of the informal sector, and many of its activities are palpably modern. The itinerant street vendor is no more typical of the informal sector than the assembly-line factory worker is typical of the formal sector. Official definitions give little or no account of the type of enterprise. In Colombia, for example, "informal sector" applies to any enterprise employing fewer than ten persons. Such businesses can range from boutiques to brick kilns. Conditions of work obviously vary.

Rural migrants are not particularly disadvantaged vis-à-vis other low-income people born in large cities. Migrants tend to do as well as, and often better than, natives in urban labor markets; their success may result from selective migration, if especially well-qualified and dynamic individuals are those who choose to migrate from rural areas.

Estimating the size of the informal sector is a difficult task, replete with methodological problems, and the move from the identification of a sector of the economy to the definition of a social class is even more problematic. Alejandro Portes, in a seminal article of 1983, estimated the formal and informal proletariat as a percentage of the domestic economically active population. Unfortunately Portes's figures, given in Table 3.1, do not distinguish between urban and rural employment, but they convey some idea of orders of magnitude.

All the evidence to date supports a rapid growth in the informal sector throughout Latin America, and the rate of growth of the informal sector seems to be directly correlated with the severity of the crisis. In recent years Peru has seen an extraordinarily rapid rise in the size of the informal sector, and it is no coincidence that a Peruvian writer, Hernando de Soto, has done most to draw attention to its problems and potential.[2]

Middle Classes

Attempts to list the components of the middle classes include white-collar workers in the private and public sectors, independent professionals, small entrepreneurs (formal and informal), managers, shopkeepers, technicians,

Table 3.1

The working class as a percentage of national population, 1970 and 1972

	Formal Proletariat, 1972	Informal Proletariat, 1970
Uruguay	88.5	3.8
Chile	60.5	26.0
Argentina	59.0	22.3
Costa Rica	28.5	48.3
Peru	27.6	69.5
Panama	25.4	60.5
Guatemala	22.3	69.7
Brazil	20.5	65.8
Mexico	15.9	64.0
Colombia	12.9	66.2
Venezuela	12.2	61.6
Ecuador	10.0	80.1
Nicaragua	8.7	69.4
Dominican Republic	6.9	73.3
Paraguay	5.9	na
El Salvador	5.2	68.5
Bolivia	3.3	86.2
Honduras	1.1	82.4

SOURCE: A. Portes, "Latin American Class Structures: Their Composition and Change During the Last Decades," Used by permission of *Latin American Research Review* 20, no. 3 (1985), table 2, pp. 22–23. (The countries have been ranked from the most "formal" to the most "informal.")

schoolteachers and academics, and ranking members of the armed forces (perhaps including noncommissioned officers). Those researchers who make such lists are often hesitant when faced with rural society, unsure what medium or small farmers or peasants they should include or exclude. Such decisions are inevitably arbitrary. Individuals' self-perceptions do not always help. Country people and the inhabitants of small towns are at least as aware of distinctions as city dwellers and probably more so—anonymity is less possible—but they are disinclined to view themselves in simple three class terms. Neighborhood, occupation, lineage, and ethnicity are of more likely importance.

White-collar workers in the private sector and in the bureaucracy and schoolteachers consider themselves "middle class." This label in no way precludes political radicalism. Schoolteachers are generally radical throughout Latin America, as are bank clerks and many public-sector workers.

Few observers doubt that the size of the urban middle classes has greatly expanded in the last decades in the most mobile societies outside the Southern Cone and that old images of a deferential class of servile officials and other petit bourgeois elements no longer hold true, if they ever did. Urbanization, economic growth, the extended role of the state, and the massive expansion of secondary and particularly of higher education not only produced larger middle classes but changed their nature (of particular importance to middle-class Latin America, education is the subject of Chapter 4). With further economic growth most of these changes are likely to persist.

Independent professionals in traditional areas—doctors, dentists, architects, engineers—have grown in number but not as rapidly as professionals employed in large enterprises and by the state. New professions, particularly in the service sector, have also rapidly expanded. As enterprises have modernized and expanded, the numbers of managerial and technical staff have increased, along with the number of private-sector white-collar workers—bank clerks, typists, computer operators—though the automation of office work in recent years may have reduced this effect.

To predict what will happen with small entrepreneurs and property owners is difficult. A reasonable guess is that in the countryside and in small towns their numbers will grow slowly, more or less in line with economic and population growth. What happens in larger cities will depend on the style of economic growth adopted over the next couple of decades.

As many Latin American governments are compelled to reduce the size of the state sector—or at least to contain its growth—a relatively slow growth in the sort of "civil-service" middle class that has been such an important component of the Latin American middle class of the past is likely.

The heterogeneous political views of these groups have attracted much less academic attention than those of organized labor, peasants, or recently arrived urban migrants (all of whom are more easily definable). This lack of attention is surprising. As the French political scientist Alain Rouquié has observed, "the middle classes are nowadays the political class par excellence."[3]

Most of the politicians come from the middle class or classes. These classes also produce the majority of army officers and the leaders of the violent left. The middle classes are the most concerned with the state and its functions, many directly as employees and others—especially if one includes among them workers covered by social security, as many analysts are justifiably tempted to do—through the benefits the state can confer. The middle classes contain what some observers consider the potentially "dangerous class" of today—comprised of those persons who have been educated beyond their probable prospects, those with professional qualifications who are unlikely to be able to exercise their professions. Some of these may become political extremists. Others emigrate or take up some other career. Again, these have been more speculated about than studied. It does not seem likely that such individuals would share a common consciousness or that they could be organized. A sense of rivalry seems as likely among them as one of solidarity.

Statistical estimates of the middle classes are varied to the point of uselessness; they are hard to defend even as indicators of an order of magnitude. More reliable figures, such as the percentage of the population in public employment—most of which one might consider "middle class"—do not provide any certain indication of the total size of the middle classes, because from republic to republic there is a considerable variation in public-sector size that does not correspond to any scale of "social development."

An alternative to this statistical dead end can be sought from urban geography. The trend in Brazil and Mexico, for example, is toward the formation of large, exclusively middle-class residential districts that are spatially removed from low-income housing zones. Naturally, this process takes a considerable time to happen and is constrained by the complexities of the land market. But the process is well under way in São Paulo, Brasília, and Mexico City, and increasing residential differentiation is likely to be an important trend. It is a feature of informal urban settlements as well as of formal ones. As time passes, the original shacks are transformed into substantial dwellings, title is obtained, services improve. So too the status of the inhabitants changes. The importance of neighborhood in the politics of the urban poor is commonly recognized, but it is less frequently considered in assessments of the senses of identity of the middle classes.

Upper Classes

No easily definable "hegemonic" group can be discerned in Latin America or in the individual republics. The list of the rich, powerful, and prestigious includes landowners of various types and lineage, native industrialists, executives of multinational companies, politicians, officers in the armed forces, media proprietors, writers and artists (some of whom are politically influential), and high government officials. They do not form uniformly coherent and successful oligarchies. As Alain Touraine has recently emphasized, there is no durable and stable alliance between the state and capitalist groups in Latin America like the alliances in Japan and Korea.[4] The groups have their sectoral and regional differences. Nevertheless, these differences are not usually acute. Discussions of agrarian oligarchies versus industrialists or of a national bourgeoisie versus foreign capital no longer have much meaning.

Joint ventures between local and multinational capital, often with state participation, have muted tensions between local capitalists and foreign investors. Many of those in the upper reaches of modern enterprise and public administration have finished their education abroad, usually in the United States or Europe. Disagreements over economic policy exist between different groups of businesses, but these disagreements do not correspond to traditional/modern, agricultural/industrial, native/foreign divisions. An analysis of any large Latin American conglomerate reveals a diversity of sectoral interests. In most countries at most times, diverse interests have been a common characteristic of the rich.

New wealth in Latin America has always been rapidly assimilated. Older families tend to assert their status against the wealth of parvenus, but the overall pattern of Latin America is far closer to the general pattern of the United States in this respect than it is to Europe.

Mobility

A major characteristic of the class structure in Latin America has been the high levels of social mobility. For individuals, the probability of upward mobility is enhanced by increased education. As Latin American economies become more formalized, educational qualifications will be increasingly important for access to jobs. Completion of secondary education, for example, is now a prerequisite for employment in the automobile industry in Mexico. From the point of view of individuals, this situation is a mixed blessing. As more individuals are better educated, the economic returns to education tend to decline and ever-higher qualifications are required to obtain any given position in society.

As has been noted, because nearly all analyses of social stratification place rural workers in the lowest class category, migration to cities constitutes social mobility by definition. But as the migration to the cities slackens, it will obviously become a factor of decreasing importance in social mobility.

Another factor promoting social mobility, in particular by expanding the opportunities for employment in the white-collar sector, will be continued economic growth. However, two points should be noted here. First, as in the advanced industrial countries, mobility in one generation seems to be within the ranks of manual labor or within the white-collar section. This is also to a lesser degree true of mobility between generations. Second, not a great deal is known about the nature of white-collar employment, particularly in the lower ranks. How much do standards of living differ from those in the skilled working class? How much mobility is there between the lower ranks of white-collar workers and the professional and propertied middle classes? The data are particularly poor. A reasonable guess is that white-collar workers do enjoy a better standard of living than the majority of manual workers, though the borderlines are blurred. As the size of the white-collar sector expands, and as populations become better educated overall, one might expect the real incomes of white-collar workers to decline relative to those of skilled manual workers.

Mobility into the higher reaches of society, though sometimes spectacular, is much less common than movement into the white-collar sector. Those persons who inherit status and wealth will continue to outnumber the self-made.

As in all societies, a certain amount of downward mobility will continue. Its incidence has yet to receive much scholarly attention. Such downward mobility can affect classes of people as well as individuals. Some observers have detected for certain countries—Bolivia, Brazil, Peru—sharper relative declines in public-sector white-collar circumstances than for organized labor, and they speculate about a crisis of the administrative middle classes. Since 1982 downward mobility among the Argentine armed forces is hard to ignore.

Women

What has been said so far in this chapter does not distinguish between men and women and might lead the reader to assume that no such discrimination is necessary, that women share the same class, the same status as their husbands or partners, and that the broad trends and conditions sketched here do not need any significant modification. That would be a controversial assumption. Much remains unclear about women's position and its evolution in Latin American society; much of the pertinent data are not broken down by sex. In the past decade the role of women and its evolution have nonetheless become much more a focus of scholarly interest, and women's organizations have become more visible in Latin America.

The data on female participation in the labor force are still difficult to interpret. Latin America has usually been assigned a low participation rate by world standards, but such figures can cover only the formal urban labor market and are a most uncertain guide. The same reservation is needed in the face of figures that show past declines in women's participation in contrast with the rising trend in the United States and Europe. The conclusion may be based on the last phase of import-substituting industrialization, which in formal employment favored men. Figures published by the U.N. International Labor Organization (ILO) show a slow rise in formal participation rates—a rise that is projected to continue. Recent writers have sought to go beyond the statistics and to identify trends in agricultural work and in the urban informal sector that the figures do not cover.

Women's agricultural work may actually be increasing, both as wage labor and as unpaid family labor. This seems to be the case in intensive fruit farming and for certain fruit export crops. Women may also be taking on a bigger role in subsistence farming as men migrate to urban work or engage as workers in cash-crop production.

Some have argued that the current crisis has fallen with disproportionate severity on poor urban women, who have been forced from the formal to the informal sector. However, the labor-intensive *maquiladora* (assembly) border industry of Mexico employs predominantly female labor, preferring young unmarried women on the often erroneous assumption that they do not have family responsibilities.

In participation in formal employment, Latin America rates high in comparison with other areas of the world. The reason is that Latin American women have much greater access to education at all levels. Their greater access has become particularly apparent in higher education in the last two decades.

Men do not dominate migration either within Latin America or between Latin America and the United States. Female migration sometimes exceeds that of males. Within Latin America the difference has been attributed to the availability of jobs in domestic service, but such jobs are increasingly seen as only the first stage toward more independent employment for women.

Women and women's organizations have become increasingly prominent in politics. They were particularly prominent in the democratization of Argentina and Uruguay. Politicians are now more interested in detecting and courting specific trends in the female vote. Feminist organizations have focused on expanding the political agenda to include issues such as the revision of health services, in which they have particular interest.

In Colombia and Venezuela, women ministers and deputy ministers and governors are no longer unusual. At least one woman governor is now said to be a Mexican political tradition, although there have been only three women ministers in Mexico. In 1990 a woman became economy minister in Brazil.

The widespread availability of domestic service has enabled many better-off and educated women to enter the professions and do relatively well. There seems to be less sexual discrimination in the professional labor market in Brazil, say, or in Colombia than in many industrialized countries. The particular machismo of the Latin, like the sensuality of the Caribbean, may in part be a product of the Anglo-Saxon imagination.

The 1990s are likely to be a decade of rapid change in laws affecting the relations between women and men. Changes in family law will facilitate divorce, encourage a more egalitarian view of marriage responsibilities, and give women more equal rights to children and property. All legislation will be subject to close feminist scrutiny.

Notes

1. A. Touraine, *La Parole et Le Sang: Politique et Société en Amerique Latine (Words and Blood: Politics and Society in Latin America),* (Paris, 1988), p. 65.
2. H. De Soto, *El otro sendero (The Other Path),* (Lima, 1987). Published in English as *The Other Path* (I. B. Taurus & Co. Ltd., London, 1988).
3. A. Rouquié, *Amérique Latine: Introduction à L'Extrême Occident (Latin America: Introductions to the Far West)* (Éditions du Seuil, Paris, 1987), p. 173.
4. Touraine, p. 79.

4

Education

Primary and Secondary Education

In the 1960s and 1970s the growth of city populations and increased prosperity expanded educational budgets and multiplied schools, scholars, and schoolteachers. It was not uncommon for governments to earmark generous shares of their budgets for educational purposes and to underwrite in other ways the expansion of the state educational systems. The charge that Latin American governments spend only a small proportion of their budgets on education is unjustified. Nevertheless, this expenditure has suffered in many republics in the 1980s, and criticism can be leveled at the direction it takes—too much on higher education, which benefits the relatively well-off, and not enough on primary, where the returns would be greater. Table 4.1 shows a sample of government expenditures for education in 1980. Today more Latin Americans go to school than ever before, and they stay there longer. Urbanization produces a more literate, better educated population. As the demand for education increases, both the governments and private schools respond.

Literacy rates have improved throughout the region. The postrevolutionary literacy campaigns of Cuba and Nicaragua made effective propaganda, but there have been effective campaigns elsewhere—for example, in Ecuador. Everywhere, the proportion of illiterates has declined. By the mid-1970s only two countries, Guatemala and Honduras, had urban illiteracy rates (among population aged 15 and over) of more than 20 percent—28.2 and 21.1 percent respectively. The decline in city and country is more marked among women than among men. Table 4.2 illustrates the not atypical progress of Colombia in the last four decades.

Argentina, Chile, and Uruguay achieved high levels of literacy earlier than the rest of Latin America. Elsewhere the figures indicate a broadly

Table 4.1

Expenditure on education by country, circa 1980

Country	Percentage of GDP	Percentage of Central Government Expenditures	GDP per Capita (U.S. dollars)
Argentina	2.7	10.9	2,210
Bolivia	4.1	30.5	550
Brazil	3.8	6.2	1,770
Chile	3.2	13.0	1,898
Colombia	3.3	25.0	1,180
Costa Rica	8.4	31.1	1,810
Ecuador	6.0	36.7	1,110
El Salvador	3.4	23.1	640
Guatemala	1.7	12.6	1,010
Honduras	3.5	14.3	520
Mexico	4.7	17.0	1,880
Nicaragua	3.0	14.0	610
Panama	5.5	21.8	1,550
Paraguay	1.4	14.2	1,140
Peru	3.6	14.3	1,000
Uruguay	2.5	9.4	2,500
Venezuela	5.1	18.9	3,440

SOURCE: World Bank, *Finanzas y administración del sistema educativo* (Washington, D.C., 1986). Used by permission of the World Bank.

Table 4.2

Percentage of illiteracy in Colombia, 1951–1985

Year	National			Urban			Rural		
	Men	Women	Total	Men	Women	Total	Men	Women	Total
1951[a]	42.5	41.0	43.9	24.8	22.0	27.1	54.6	52.0	57.2
1964[b]	35.7	35.2	36.3	23.3	22.1	24.3	49.6	48.0	51.3
1973[b]	24.9	24.9	25.0	16.1	15.6	16.6	39.3	38.3	40.4
1985[b]	17.9	18.3	17.6	12.3	12.2	12.4	30.6	30.4	30.8
1985[c]	6.2	7.1	5.5	3.2	3.4	3.1	14.1	15.2	11.0

[a]Population 7 years and over.
[b]Population 5 years and over.
[c]Population between 18 and 24 years.

SOURCE: DANE, *Censos de Población (Census of Population)*, (Bogotá, 1951, 1964, 1973, 1985).

similar pattern. Colombia, a middle-of-the-range example of the dimension of the problem and the resources marshaled to combat it, has increased expenditures for education and expanded the numbers of teachers and schools in a pattern broadly typical of the region.

Numbers of students enrolled in schools in cities have followed demographic trends, expanding rapidly in the 1950s and 1960s but showing a falling rate of growth in recent years, a result not only of smaller family size and slower population growth but also of the effects of recession. Recession has had a discernible impact on students in secondary schools and universities. In Mexico, for example, the rates of those students completing the secondary cycle—from age 13 to age 19—are said to have fallen from 42 percent in 1982 to 21 percent in 1986.[1] If growth resumes, the rate of enrollment will continue to increase in most countries, though more slowly than in the 1950s and 1960s. The urban work force typically becomes better educated: a higher proportion of workers completes primary and secondary school; fewer and fewer have no education at all. A Colombian study showed that of the urban employed, 33.5 percent had completed secondary education in 1985, compared with 26.8 percent in 1976. Colombia has been less affected by recession than Mexico.

Students in rural areas are more likely to quit school than those in cities, and more of them need to repeat school years than urban students. To provide education to poor and scattered rural populations, to keep poor rural children in school, to motivate their teachers, and to maintain rural schools with anything more than rudimentary equipment is notoriously difficult. To design distinct curricula and to get teachers to follow them is also hard. Specifically rural schooling is not always popular, and the expansion in the number of teachers has possibly been achieved by a deterioration in training, with fewer teachers coming from the "normal schools" that provide specialized teacher training. Some countries have managed to evolve new methods that show signs of success, but the rural-urban gap remains. Disappointingly little has been achieved through the use of television, though this is true of many other parts of the world besides Latin America. Despite its potential, what little educational television has been attempted has been too much influenced by inappropriate models, such as the British "Open University," an institution aimed largely at adults who wish to take part-time degrees.

In numbers taught, state systems are predominant at the primary level. At the secondary level, however, private schools take a greater proportion of pupils and also receive a degree of direct and indirect state support. Not all of it has been elitist. Various religious orders, such as the Christian Brothers, have a long and honorable tradition of teaching not very privileged pupils. Despite the anticlerical traditions of the Mexican Revolution, Catholic education remains important in Mexico and commands widespread middle-class loyalties. In major cities throughout Latin America it is common to find secondary schools on the American, British, French, and German models that receive some support from their parent countries. Historically, the influence of these schools ranges beyond the small numbers that attend them. This influence can be seen in school uniforms—the universal overall, or *guardapolvo,* of Argentina and Uruguay, and elsewhere the tartan skirts for schoolgirls that are so common that they seem a part of local rather than Scottish folklore.

Latin American governments have made impressive efforts to expand primary and secondary education to meet the enormous challenges of population growth and urbanization. In doing so, they have frequently saddled themselves with fiscal and administrative burdens that they have failed to meet: systems expand beyond the abilities of ministries to control them, and teachers are paid badly and paid late. Teachers' unions tend to be radical—the "class-room Maoists" of Peru are a good example. Their radicalism is more often directed against their paymaster, the state, than it is inculcated into their pupils, and teachers are understandably more concerned with pay and promotion than with educational reform or social revolution. They belong to one of the most prominent parts of the white-collar public-sector unionism that is now a leading element in Latin American trade unionism. One response of governments is to decentralize responsibility for education to the state or departmental level and make appropriate fiscal adjustments. It is too early to say what success this solution will have and whether it will increase regional educational disparities, which are pronounced.

Most governments have made efforts to expand technical and vocational education. The apprenticeship schemes of Brazil and Colombia, for example, are financed by a levy on large business enterprises. Varied secondary curricula have been established, offering commercial and technical options. With the exception of Cuba, no country has attempted to direct students toward specific careers through compulsion. Vocational options, where they are available, remain a matter of pupil or parental choice, which tends to remain conservative. Given the high propensity for those who complete secondary education to go on to higher education, where traditional careers still predominate, technical and commercial education has relatively few takers. The private sector has not exercised much initiative in this area. Showing little faith in local science and technology at the university level, and even less at lower levels, the private sector prefers its own (or imported) solutions and training.

In the absence of reliable studies, what can be said about future trends is speculative. Nonetheless, despite the persistent popularity of "traditional" careers, Latin Americans show no lack of ability in calculating the economic return on educational choices and are much less concerned about old patterns of status than they are sometimes believed to be. If a certain course seems likely to lead to a better job, then it will not lack students. In societies that, against all odds, still consider themselves upwardly mobile, there is a marked reluctance to choose educational options which would appear not to offer more than a limited possibility of social ascent. One Latin American response to such reluctance is to dignify large numbers of activities with the trappings of professional status by founding associations and guilds in unlikely areas of work. Why not? Such organizations may have a positive effect on educational choice, both at the secondary level and in higher education.

Higher Education

The expansion of higher education in recent years has meant more than an increase in numbers of students, especially outside the Southern Cone. Expansion has also brought more postgraduate students, more full-time faculty members in both teaching and research, more careers offered at first-degree and postgraduate levels, and additional universities and other higher educational institutions. In the 1970s the growth in student numbers was sustained at more than 5 percent per year. This expansion has been related to the growth of cities, the increase in numbers in secondary education, and the growth of the modern service sector of the economy.

The expansion also derives from policies of automatic admission to higher education for those who complete secondary education. This *pase automático* often has the status of a democratic right (attempts to revise it in Mexico in 1988 were countered by gigantic student mobilization). The result is the "university of the masses." The University of Mexico (Universidad Autónoma de México—UNAM) has 400,000 students; there are 85,000 first-term students at the start of an academic year in the University of Buenos Aires. Attempts to change the *pase automático* will run into difficulties, particularly in an era of democratization. It is unlikely that numbers will decline, though the rate of increase may slow. The percentage of the age group that is receiving higher education in Latin America roughly conforms to the world average for countries of comparative GDP, as is suggested by Tables 4.3 and 4.4. Some countries show a higher ratio, approaching or even exceeding the level of Italy and Spain: Peru, Ecuador, Costa Rica, Uruguay, Panama, Argentina, and Venezuela.

The increase in the numbers of students with university qualifications does not derive from demands made by the local economies, which have grown, but not to this degree. There are signs that the market for certain professions is saturated, while at the same time persons with technical and

Table 4.3

Gross enrollment ratios of age-groups receiving primary education by country, 1975 and 1987[a]

	Total		Male		Female	
	1975	1987	1975	1987	1975	1987
Low income						
Haiti[a]	62	95	—	105	—	89
Middle income and lower middle income						
Bolivia	85	91	94	97	76	85
Honduras[a]	88	106	88	104	87	108
Nicaragua	82	99	80	94	85	104
Dominican Rep.[a]	102	101	—	99	—	103
El Salvador	74	79	76	77	73	81
Paraguay[a]	100	102	103	104	96	99
Peru[b]	113	122	—	125	—	120
Ecuador	101	117	103	118	99	116
Guatemala[a]	63	76	69	82	53	70
Costa Rica	107	98	108	100	107	97
Chile[c]	112	102	113	103	112	101
Colombia[a]	118	114	116	112	120	115
Brazil	88	103	89	—	87	—
Mexico	105	118	108	119	102	116
Panama[a]	114	106	116	109	111	104
Higher middle income						
Uruguay	107	110	107	111	105	109
Argentina	106	110	106	110	106	110
Venezuela	100	107	99	107	100	107
Industrialized countries with market economies						
Spain[a]	111	113	111	113	111	113
Italy[d]	105	95	106	—	105	—

Note: A gross enrollment ratio is the total enrollment of all ages divided by the population of the specific age-groups that correspond to the age-groups with different levels of education. For countries with almost universal education among the school-age population at the primary level, the gross enrollment ratio will exceed 100 if the actual age distribution of pupils is greater than the official school ages.

[a]The most recent figures for these countries are from 1986.
[b]The most recent figures for Peru are from 1985.
[c]The most recent figures for Chile are from 1988.
[d]The most recent figures for Italy are from 1984.

SOURCE: From the *UNESCO Statistical Yearbook 1989*. © UNESCO 1989.

Table 4.4

Gross enrollment ratios of age-groups receiving secondary and higher education by country, 1975 and 1987[a]

	Secondary						Higher	
	Total		Male		Female		Total	
	1975	*1987*	*1975*	*1987*	*1975*	*1987*	*1975*	*1987*
Low income								
Haiti[b]	8	17	9	18	7	16	0.7	1.2
Middle income and lower middle income								
Bolivia	31	37	—	40	—	35	11.2	16.6
Honduras[c]	16	32	16	29	17	32	4.7	8.8
Nicaragua	24	43	23	29	24	58	8.3	8.4
Dominican Rep.[d]	36	51	—	44	—	57	10.0	18.6
El Salvador	19	29	21	27	17	30	7.8	17.7
Paraguay[a]	19	30	19	30	19	30	6.7	—
Peru[e]	46	65	50	68	41	61	14.6	24.6
Ecuador	39	56	41	55	38	57	26.9	29.6
Guatemala	12	21	13	—	11	—	4.3	8.6
Costa Rica	43	41	40	40	45	43	17.7	24.8
Chile[f]	48	74	44	72	51	76	15.6	17.8
Colombia[a]	39	56	39	55	39	56	8	13.9
Brazil	26	38	24	—	28	—	10.7	10.9
Panama[a]	55	59	52	56	57	63	17.3	28.2
Higher middle income								
Uruguay[a]	60	73	—	—	—	—	16.0	41.61
Argentina	54	74	51	69	57	78	27.2	38.7
Venezuela[a]	45	54	42	48	48	59	18.1	26.5
Industrializing countries with market economies								
Spain[a]	73	102	74	97	71	107	20.4	30.0
Italy	71	75	74	—	67	—	25.6	24.3

[a]More recent figures are from 1986.
[b]Haiti: more recent figures are from 1985.
[c]Honduras: more recent figures are from 1984.
[d]Dominican Rep.: more recent figures are from 1985.
[e]Peru: more recent figures are from 1985.
[f]Chile: more recent figures are from 1988.

SOURCE: From the *UNESCO Statistical Yearbook 1989*. © UNESCO 1989.

business skills are needed. The next decade may see some adjustment as those completing secondary education choose "intermediate" or technical careers in response to this saturation and begin to have doubts that a university degree is the only ticket to improved status. Given a degree's prestige, changes will be slow.

The public universities—national and state—bear the brunt of the avalanche of students and have had to expand staff and plant rapidly. A decline in overall quality, politicized appointments, and the formation of influential unions of academic staff have frequently resulted. Universities, both public and private, have multiplied. Regional forces demand local universities. The new provincial universities are often vulnerable to local political pressures, have difficulty in recruiting good staff, and also suffer from inadequate resources. Governments simply do not have the money to establish the more expensive faculties.

Private universities have been another response; some seek to maintain or set standards outside the public system, and others are more motivated by commercial gain. Some private universities are seen as elitist, seeking to inculcate an exclusive "directing class" mentality. Few have the financial capacity to sustain programs in the physical sciences, which in Latin America as elsewhere are notoriously expensive. Night schools and other speculative ventures have also proliferated.

Quality has not kept pace with quantity. Nevertheless, certain qualitative changes are apparent. The mission of producing successive generations of qualified professionals has ceded some space to a new emphasis on research, particularly in the pure and applied sciences. This development can be seen in a strengthened investigative ethos and in the appearance of new careers, in such areas as biotechnology, informatics, and electronics; it is also visible in the multiplication of postgraduate courses. The new mentality regards research as a collective rather than an individual effort, which requires planning rather than inspiration, and an awareness of the international rather than the local or national context.

Latin American universities have increased their international contacts significantly and are influenced more by international agencies. The Inter-American Development Bank has played an important role in financing certain fields, as have U.S. and European foundations. Latin Americans' individual contacts with universities and scholars abroad have also grown at an unprecedented rate in the last two decades and have had an enormous though as yet unquantified and unstudied influence. This influence is likely to have been as important as more easily identifiable programs of academic assistance in Latin America.

In current circumstances, getting to study abroad is difficult. The massive scholarship programs from Mariscal de Ayacucho (named after the soldier and patriot Antonio José de Sucre, 1795–1830) in Venezuela and of the National Council for Science and Technology (Consejo Nacional de Ciencia y Technología—CONACYT) in Mexico have succumbed to the debt crisis, and funds for study abroad are short everywhere. Local postgraduate courses have become more common partly for this reason and partly because of the increased competence of Latin American universities themselves. The diminished flow of students to study abroad shows the following order of preference by country: United States, West Germany or France, Spain, United Kingdom, Soviet Union and Eastern Europe, and Japan. In terms of curricula chosen, the exact sciences are the most popular, followed by economics and the social sciences, then humanities.

Research remains a minority concern. It has received scant government support. Most politicians are unaware of the potential usefulness of local research; many of those in power today have a picture of the university as it was twenty or thirty years ago. Local business is also often skeptical about local science and technology.

The proportion of university budgets spent on research is low and tends to be concentrated in metropolitan public and private universities. The cost of science puts much of it beyond the reach of other universities—a small astronomy department, for example, can be as expensive as an entire large faculty of philosophy and literature. No university can meet such expenditures out of fees charged, especially where low fees are the norm. The "free" public university does have the effect of keeping private university fees down.

The expansion of postgraduate courses has sometimes had the effect of producing two universities in the place of one, a postgraduate university in uneasy coexistence with the old routine "degree factory," with the former having little influence on the latter. Statistically, the latter continues to occupy the predominant position. Within it, law, medicine, and engineering still take the major share of students, and these faculties are often notoriously impervious to change.

Despite a growing consciousness that changes must occur—there is at least an awareness that judicial reform is a matter of urgency among an influential minority of teachers of law—law schools remain the degree factories par excellence. Most of their alumni now seek state employment. The independent professional is more and more a figure of the past. Societies of former alumni form networks that link universities and faculties with different parts of the bureaucracy, and these networks are significant channels of recruitment. The links between the public university and the state are therefore often much closer than one would conclude from displays of academic hostility.

Of all institutions, the universities hold the greatest importance for the middle classes. In all countries they continue to symbolize the "career open to talent" without barriers of class, wealth, or religious belief. The old camaraderie of the Córdoba (Argentina) University reform of 1918, which encapsulated an ideal of a self-governing autonomous university of the middle classes of that era, has been overwhelmed by numbers. Autonomy is no longer the shibboleth it was, but the egalitarian ideal persists.

Private universities are now at pains to distinguish themselves from their rivals—other private universities as well as public ones—by what they teach or how they teach it or by religious affiliation, not by whom they teach. Not all are elitist; they all have scholarship schemes. Some compete with the public university by teaching the "cheap" degrees, that is, by offering degrees from faculties which are comparably inexpensive to set up. Private universities have the advantage of being less subject to disruption by strikes and closures. In some public universities strikes and closures have at times become so frequent that potential students calculate that attending a private university may be cheaper because their programs will be finished more quickly.

However, since the 1960s the political atmosphere in universities has changed. Today the Cuban Revolution, Fidel and Che, Algeria, Mao, Camillo Torres, Fanon, Sartre, Althusser, Trotsky, Vietnam, and Ho Chi Minh mean little to students born in 1970 and much less than they once did to most of their teachers. The intervening years have seen a series of crises in world communism, not yet ended, which have had divisive and usually disillusioning consequences in university circles in Latin America. Latin American experiences of military rule revalued liberal democratic theory. Though Brazilian universities remained relatively unscathed, Uruguayan, Chilean, and Argentine universities did not. The Argentine university system, once the finest in Latin America, suffered severely in the 1960s and 1970s, and has still not recovered.

Though right-wing currents exist and some private universities do have a conservative ethos, the political mood at most universities remains dissident but less overtly political than before. Revolutionary violence has little support, and the universities have lost political weight. There are more alternative movements and the student today is no longer the one obvious source of demonstrations and agitation. Governments have learned how to be more adroit in their handling of the universities. "Postmodern" students are often less radical than the unions of university teachers or university employees; they want to complete their degree work.

How many students graduate? The highest completion rates are in the old-fashioned degrees like law and engineering and in the private universities. Student dropout rates may be as high as 80 percent in the "mega-universities" of Buenos Aires and Mexico and 50 percent in the large state universities of Caracas, Bogotá, and Quito. High dropout rates are caused by poor preparation, particularly in mathematics and the exact sciences, lack of vocation, poor information about the chosen career, and lack of resources. Fewer female than male students drop out, so certain courses with a high female enrollment have lower dropout rates.

University student dropouts are less common than those in primary education or in the first three years of secondary education. A pupil who completes four-fifths of secondary school is more likely to go on to complete university education than is a pupil beginning primary school likely to complete four-fifths of secondary. There is of course much variation from country to country. Dropout figures are inflated at the university level by the failure to account for students changing careers or changing universities. Such changes are certainly frequent. Dropping out is most frequent in "universities of the masses" for courses with a high mathematical and scientific content, among men, and among older students.

The availability of relatively inexpensive university education is a middle-class privilege that it is politically hazardous to challenge. Latin American educational budgets will therefore probably continue to reflect the general distribution of income, and within them the universities will continue to command a substantial share. It is not so clear that pressure from the universities will succeed in increasing this share, and expenditure per student may fall. Unions may be more successful in ensuring that a high and growing proportion of expenditure goes for salaries and that less goes for further development of the universities. A majority of Latin American universities may already be spending 80 to 90 percent of their resources to pay their employees. Like universities elsewhere, they resist rapid change. Once created, a career, a department, or a course is hard to remove from the list.

A strictly industrial or scientific survey would detect few Latin Americans engaged in research and development. Figures from the United Nations Educational, Scientific, and Cultural Organization (UNESCO), which are often hard to interpret and to compare country by country, show small numbers professionally engaged in the exact and applied sciences. Persons termed "full-time equivalent" in these areas numbered 10,486 in Argentina in 1982, 52,863 in Brazil in 1985, 11,225 in Cuba in 1987, and 16,679 in Mexico in 1984. How many of these people are researching and developing in the sense of attacking the frontiers of pure and applied science is anybody's guess. Commentators oscillate between an exaggerated pride in individual achievement—a Mexican transplant operation, a vaccine developed in Colombia, a useful piece of Brazilian military hardware—and a general sense of inadequacy. UNESCO records 787,400 U.S. scientists engaged in research and development in 1986, and nobody needs to be told how much better supported they are than their Argentine colleagues.[2]

Nevertheless, in the social sciences there has been a revolution in Latin America in the last three decades. The designers of the Alliance for Progress—despite its faults, one of the most coherent efforts to transform Latin American society since the Wars of Independence—worked by the seats of their pants. They could find few interlocutors with any professional training, few studies that were more than intuitive. Since the 1960s a bibliographical explosion has taken place. Much of what has been written has yet to be digested, but successive generations who are immensely better informed about their own societies have come to the fore. Information is not a sufficient condition for intelligent action, but it is a necessary one, and much information which was previously lacking now exists, as well as personnel trained to gather it. The revolution in the social sciences is present not only in the universities (though it *is* there, to a degree that few local politicians seem to realize), but also in independent think tanks and research institutes of high quality.

Notes

1. H. Aguilar Camín, *Después del milagro (After the Miracle),* (Mexico City, 1988), pp. 217–218.
2. Figures from UNESCO, *Statistical Yearbook 1989* (Paris, 1989).

5

A Short Note on Culture

In surveys of Latin America, cultural matters are commonly treated as an afterthought, something that has to be put in for the sake of completeness, to demonstrate that neither the author nor the reader is a complete Philistine. Twenty years ago such afterthoughts rarely avoided a note of condescension. In 1967 Gabriel García Márquez published *Cien años de soledad (One Hundred Years of Solitude)*. Hundreds of thousands of copies of the novel were sold throughout Latin America, and the book was also a best seller throughout the world. The note of condescension has had to disappear.

This study is not the place for a detailed account of the cultural achievements of Latin America in recent years, so only a few themes will be reviewed. Little will be said about music, the graphic arts, and folk culture, though this risks the criticism of readers who would have stressed the enduring importance of dance in the region, before and after the tango, or the criticism of anthropologically inclined readers who rightly argue that the following discussion merely analyzes a few characteristics of urban popular culture.[1] Cultural futures cannot be easily predicted—even less so than economic and political futures. But culture—literature, cinema, television, academic life, newspapers and magazines, comics, *telenovelas* (soap operas), intellectuals, fiestas, carnivals—influences how people feel about themselves. It must, therefore, be an important part of any estimate of the quality of life and its likely evolution.

Writers and Novels

Cultural success in the wider world—and the last two-and-a-half decades have seen spectacular Latin American successes—compensates for other failures. The cultural impact of Hispanics in the United States has been far greater than their political or diplomatic influence and is more important for their integration—and ultimately for affecting the attitudes of other U.S. citizens toward Latin America—than is the election of Hispanic mayors and governors or the formation of Hispanic electoral caucuses. Self-esteem generated by cultural achievement can have significant political and diplomatic effects.

One Hundred Years of Solitude, a work rooted in a province of the Colombian Caribbean coast, made some sort of human sense of provincial life everywhere and conferred on it a certain dignity and heroism. The book was gratefully recognized by all Latin Americans for doing so. García Márquez, Carlos Fuentes, Jorge Luis Borges, and the other writers of the so-called "boom"—the sudden unprecedented success of Latin American authors at this time—have gained and consolidated a region-wide readership that did not exist previously. This increased reading public took up not just "boom" writers but also works by older Latin American writers, who became best-sellers. The whole editorial field gained. The "boom" allowed the professionalization of the writer. Before the 1960s, most writers who did not have independent incomes needed another job—in diplomacy, education, or journalism—to support their writing. In the 1960s a small but significant number of writers began to be supported by their writing. Some became media stars. Now, writers are firmly in the cultural marketplace.

The "boom" created among Latin American writers a sense of community that persists despite ideological differences. The "boom" also boosted self-confidence. Latin American writers, in Mario Vargas Llosa's words of 1968, were "creators," not "primitives"; they were, in Octavio Paz's phrase, "contemporaries of the rest of the world." This self-confidence has lasted, for Latin American fiction is as good as anything being written elsewhere in the world. Gabriel García Márquez, Mario Vargas Llosa, Julio Cortázar, Jorge Luis Borges, Manuel Puig, Carlos Fuentes, Alejo Carpentier, Juan Carlos Onetti, Augusto Roa Bastos, Isabel Allende, Elena Poniatowski, and Clarice Lispector will cast a long shadow over the next generation.

Most writers perceive that they have a political role, either in writing about their societies or, in some notable cases, by intervening directly in politics. Carlos Fuentes gave one possible explanation in an interview:

> *Fuentes:* But generally for us the main motive of writing is the weakness of the civil societies. If you don't say certain things they won't be said. It is a very powerful motivation. I think that this is a generalized feeling among writers, independent of political positions.
>
> *Question:* Is this a continuing need?
>
> *Fuentes:* When you consider that the most developed civil societies of Latin America would be Uruguay, Chile, Argentina, and look what they've gone

> through and are going through. You get Pinochet, *desaparecidos* [the disappeared], torture, generals, *juntas*. Think of countries that have no civil society like Nicaragua, El Salvador, Honduras, what do you expect from them? It's still a long road to be travelled. Good for novelists, bad for people.[2]

Some writers are overt political protagonists. Mario Vargas Llosa, who has always stated his political views with admirable clarity, was in 1990 the (losing) candidate of the center-right for president of Peru—serious politics, not a symbolic salute to the flag. Octavio Paz's Mexican monthly *Vuelta (Return)* is an influential critic of the ruling Institutional Revolutionary Party (Partido Revolucionario Institucional—PRI). It stands, in the phrase of its editor Enrique Krauze, "for democracy without adjectives." Gabriel García Márquez's personal politics are less clear, though he has continued to produce political journalism and is one of the few authors who is still on friendly, even intimate, terms with Fidel Castro. In December 1983, Ernesto Sábato, not the most political of writers, agreed to President Raúl Alfonsín's request that he should head the National Commission on the Disappeared (Comision Nacional Sobre las Desaparicíon de Personas, CONADEP) set up by the new civilian government of Argentina to inquire into the thousands of disappearances under military rule.

There is no uniformity in the political views expressed. Writers are less likely to be on the revolutionary left than they were in the 1960s. They speculate less about the "Latin American identity" and have more interest in the problems of each specific country.

The role of writers as popularizers of debate has expanded. Television, radio, newspapers, and magazines provide opportunities—and rewards—that were unknown twenty years ago. Thus a writer's influence may extend beyond the printed page; it may be exercised in another medium.

At present it is hard to discern any "cultural lead" being exercised by any particular Latin American country. There is no equivalent today to the attraction that Cuba held in the early years of the revolution for large numbers of the region's intellectuals. That attraction waned, disenchantment culminating in the Padilla affair of 1968, when nearly every major Latin American author (the exceptions were García Márquez, Cortázar, Mario Benedetti, and Roa Bastos) and large numbers of European and North American writers (Sartre, de Beauvoir, Sontag, Goytisolo) signed two protest letters concerning the official denunciations and censorship of the Cuban poet Heberto Padilla. Castro replied with his usual vehemence, saying that he was not much interested in the bleatings of petit-bourgeois intellectuals. Since then, the attacks on Cuba of Cuban writers in exile (Guillermo Cabrera Infante, Carlos Franqui, Reynaldo Arenas) have been more effective than the apologies for Castro's Cuba, from either Cubans or visitors. The official line in Cuba has been somewhat modified, and two writers of the 1960s who were banned for their homosexuality and elaborate prose, Virgilio Piñera and José Lezama Lima, are now *autores faros* (cultural heroes). Fidel Castro's interest lies more in films and sports than in books.

The Nicaraguan revolution for a time made a novelist the vice president of Nicaragua and a poet a minister. Its cultural attraction, however, never had the pull of Cuba in the honeymoon period of the 1960s.

Cinema and Its Influence

The Cubans, with the assistance of García Márquez and the Latin American Film Foundation, have established a school to train Cuban filmmakers and others from Latin America, Asia, and Africa. But Cuban films in recent years have not had much impact. The political history and significance of Argentine films is more revealing.

In the late 1960s, Argentina produced *La hora de los hornos (The Hour of the Furnaces),* a powerful thesis film with a heady discourse on third-worldism *(tercermundismo),* anticolonialism, nationalism, socialism, and Peronism. Many young people went to their deaths believing in its simplifications, just as many inside and outside Latin America swallowed the image of the heroic guerrilla portrayed in Constantin Costa-Gavras's *State of Siege,* set in the Uruguay of the Tupamaro guerrillas. Both films look uncritical today, and the contrast with the new Argentine movies could hardly be more marked.

The Argentine military governments of 1976–1983 did not favor movie-making, but it survived with sufficient vigor to provide some criticism before the juntas ended and since then has enjoyed great success with both Argentine and international audiences. María Luisa Bemberg's *Señora de Nadie* helped to break the authoritarian moralism of the regime in its treatment of themes of women's independence and of homosexuality. A military censor told Bemberg that he would prefer to have his son die of cancer than become a homosexual. Bemberg's *Camila* employed an episode in the tyranny of Rosas (Juan Manuel de Rosas was the autocratic ruler of Argentina from 1830 to 1852) as a parallel to the "dirty war" from which Argentina was emerging. *Camila* and Luis Puenzo's *La historia official (The Official Version),* the recent Argentine films that are also best known abroad, were both seen by over 2 million Argentines, approaching one-tenth of the population. Such films have therefore provided some of the catharsis that the country needs to experience after what it has been through. Many recent films have attempted to analyze the immediate past and set out alternatives for the future.

Argentine cinema has also been extremely important in changing attitudes to Argentina abroad. Both *La historia official* and *Verónico Cruz* impressed British audiences in the wake of the Falklands war. The Argentine government has seen the importance of cultural diplomacy: the recent Argentine film season at London's South Bank National Film Theatre had the support of the Argentine foreign ministry. Hardhearted, hardheaded governments should realize that support for films is not a waste of money. Today Argentine cinema is suffering acute financial difficulty due to the poor economic climate and the withdrawal of state credits.

What are Latin American films like outside Argentina, and what are their prospects? After some national, nonimitative successes in the 1960s, moviemaking was particularly hard hit by censorship and many film-makers were forced into exile in the countries that came under military government. Mexico has a large commercial industry that produces films of little merit. Nothing else has been encouraged by the government since the term of President Luis Echeverría. Independent directors have had little chance, but some directors such as Paul Ceduc, Arturo Ripstein, and Jaime Hermosillo have made notable films with few resources. In the main, the Mexican cinema has stagnated, but this may change in the atmosphere of general questioning that now pervades Mexico. Colombia, Venezuela, Peru, and Bolivia have all produced interesting films for the home market, and cinema enjoys some rather haphazard and ill-audited state support.

The strongest South American film industry has intermittently been that of Brazil, which has from time to time received generous credits from a state-funded body, Embrafilme. The industry achieved a reasonable home market, healthy exports to Latin America, and an art-house following in the United States and Europe. Even the Brazilian industry, however, has come into crisis in recent years, with declining movie audiences (down 40 percent in the period 1978–1984), the closure of movie houses (from 3,276 in 1975 to 1,553 in 1984), as well as a massive increase in the television industry. Also Embrafilme has been recently closed down: the state, that philanthropic ogre in Octavio Paz's evocative phrase, is withdrawing its philanthropy. The number of television sets rose from 1.2 million in 1962 to over 18 million in 1980, with an estimated potential audience of about 80 million. Television can reach more Brazilians in one evening than a movie can reach in one year. Brazilian films are not shown much on Brazilian television: in 1980 only one film in fifty shown was Brazilian.

Latin American cinema thus remains a precarious industry. It is capital intensive and depends on imported technology. In Argentina, despite the recent successes, only two or three films a year out of around thirty releases cover their costs in the home market. Coproductions help; they attract foreign stars (María Luisa Bemberg made *Miss Mary* with Julie Christie). But audiences are down everywhere. Films have to compete with television, video, cable, and satellite. Audiences still prefer well-made Hollywood movies to most local products. Only an occasional film meets with international success. Nevertheless, there is a record of achievement, which will be added to if films get more protection at home and more exposure abroad. Spanish television is currently investing heavily in Latin American filmmakers; some forty features have been commissioned.

Television

By 1985, 60 to 70 percent of Brazilians, Cubans, and Mexicans, 80 percent of Venezuelans, and 90 percent of Colombians had regular access to television. In most urbanized countries like Argentina and Uruguay, television spread rapidly and early and now reaches over 90 percent of the population. In countries like El Salvador, Bolivia, and Paraguay, television is still limited to the main cities.

In most countries, television broadcasting is primarily commercial. Experiments in state control have been made, but most have been enforced by authoritarian governments so that the notion has been discredited. Television is run by private companies and supported by advertising. In Mexican *telenovelas* (soaps), for example, commercial breaks seem to come about every three minutes. Although a good deal of television programming is imported from the United States, the tendency is increasing either to produce programming locally or to buy it from regional producers in Brazil, Mexico, or Venezuela. The two big companies are Televisa in Mexico, created by Emilio Azcarraga and Miguel Alemán, and TV-Globo in Brazil, under Roberto Marinho. Both are much more than just TV companies—they are conglomerates. Televisa is probably the largest private TV monopoly in the world. Except in Cuba and Nicaragua, Latin American television tends not to be an instrument of the state.

The influence of U.S. television on the Latin American networks is apparent but not overwhelming. Commercial television draws much revenue from foreign or multinational corporations, and they therefore influence the styles of programming. Many Latin American stations and networks are affiliated with U.S. networks in order to buy programming, particularly low-cost programs like variety shows, soaps, and game shows. Such programming leads to accusations of cultural imperialism.

A number of popular television genres have been created in Latin America. Most notable are the *telenovelas,* which make up the bulk of program sales between Latin American countries and which sometimes reach Europe. Britain's Channel 4 bought TV-Globo's *Marilu* and *Isaura the Slavegirl.* Brazil exports *telenovelas* to nineteen countries. Mexico's *El Derecho de Nacer* (The Right to Be Born), one of the most successful *telenovelas* of romance and family intrigue, was seen throughout the region. The Peruvian *telenovela Simplemente Maria* (Simply Maria), which treated the themes of poverty and social mobility, was also seen widely outside Peru. *Telenovelas,* carefully calculated for the widest audience and largely innocuous, represent an enormous business. García Márquez has pointed out that more people in Latin America watch one episode of a *telenova* than have read his entire *oeuvre* in Spanish. He is at present writing a *telenova* to reach this enormous potential audience. The Televisa studios in Mexico produce a large number, all with high budgets and huge followings. The Mexican soap opera *Cuna de Lobos* (Cradle of Wolves) was recently seen by about half the population. The same extraordinary figures were being registered for the Brazilian *Pantanal* (Swamp), an ecological soap opera set in the swamp regions of that country. Variety programs are also important, as are comedies. *Hogar Dulce Hogar* (Home Sweet Home) is one of Televisa's most popular exports.

Imported U.S. programs are criticized from many angles. Critics are concerned about their violence, materialism or consumerism, and individualism. They worry that U.S. programs may erode the distinctive in the national or regional culture. These fears are not confined to Latin America and may well be as exaggerated there as they are in Europe. Cultures are not easily changed. U.S. television may be a minor contributory factor in Colombian violence, for example, but it is obviously not a large one.

More difficult is the analysis of Televisa. Some critics argue that the concentration of programming in a few hands is dangerous because when certain ideologies and commercial interests hold a monopoly, the result is likely to be a censorship as extensive as and more insidious than any exercised by the state. Other critics say that Televisa at least maintains a certain level of quality and that programs would be worse if a larger number of commercial networks fought it out: they would lower standards to capture viewers. It is possible to hold both views.[3]

Latin American television also faces the uncertainties that derive from new technologies. Videocassette players are widespread among the better off. Perhaps their ownership spread faster in Latin America than it did in Europe because of the poorer quality of many local stations. The most important questions, however, concern satellite and cable television. Many critics predict that the programs from these sources will have a disastrous effect, pumping out all kinds of rubbish. Satellite is seen as the perfect modern way of penetrating cultural and commercial areas hitherto controlled or regulated by local national authorities. In the distribution plans of film, television and sport program producers, in the marketing and advertising strategies of multinational companies, satellites and satellites with cable are important new ways of gaining access to larger audiences. Satellite can also penetrate *politically* closed areas.

Raymond Williams presented the possible dystopia of satellites in his 1974 work *Television:*

> A world-wide television service, with genuinely open skies, would be an enormous gain to the peoples of the world, as short-wave radio, by-passing national controls, has already clearly been. Against the rhetoric of open skies, which in fact, given the expense and sophistication of satellite technology, would be monopolized by a few large corporations and authoritarian governments, it will sound strange and reactionary to defend national autonomy. But the probable users of the technology are not internationalists, in the sense of any significant mutuality. The national or local components in *their* services would be matters merely of consent and publicity—tokenism. In most countries, if these systems gained control, independent production would become very difficult or impossible. Most of the inhabitants of the "global village" would be saying nothing in these new terms, while a few powerful corporations and governments, and the people they could hire, would speak in ways never before known to most of the peoples of the world.[4]

The issues raised by Williams are now questions of current debate, and in Latin America the arguments will intensify in the near future. Televisa and TV-Globo are powerful corporations, but both, politically and technologically, have up to now led relatively sheltered lives.

In Cuba, television programming is used for educational purposes and political mobilization: there are a lot of programs on women, race, children's education, history, music, and sports. Fidel Castro makes good use of the medium. Most programs are produced locally. Cuba is linked by satellite to the Soviet and East European broadcasting consortium Intervision. Most Cubans would much rather be linked to something else: when a *telenovela* comes out, the country tends to shut down as everyone watches it.

Politicians are all acutely conscious of television's importance to them. Chile's General Augusto Pinochet and his advisers, who performed ineptly on television in the campaigning leading up to the 1988 plebiscite, were atypical. Ministers of communication are going to be increasingly important figures, faced by increasingly important and urgent problems.

Other Aspects of Mass Culture

Television is essentially a popular medium. Two other areas of mass culture are the popular literature of comic books and *fotonovelas* (a form of photographic story), and sport.

Comic strips and comic books are enormously popular throughout Latin America, especially in the cities. Their readership ranges from respectable adults—few could deny that they had ever read the Chilean *Condorito,* for example—to *gamines* (street children). Mexico has the largest comic-book industry in the world, and a section of the ministry of education is involved in efforts to produce a more worthy product. Contrary to the impression left by at least the title of the best-known work on the subject—*How to Read Donald Duck: Imperialist Ideology in the Disney Comic* (1975), by Ariel Dorfman and Armand Mattelart—this area of publishing shows little sign of coming under foreign dominance. A strong Latin American tradition of comics dates back at least to the 1920s, particularly in Mexico, Brazil, and Argentina. Mexican productions are not copies of those of the United States. They are most carefully designed for the Mexican and Latin American market. Little unprejudiced study of this impressively large readership has been attempted except by the publishers, who obviously know their audience's tastes very well. Comics provide entertainment cheaply and maintain literacy; some of the best are as good as can be found anywhere. The comic is a lively and healthy cultural form.

Fotonovelas, a form of photographic story originally imported from Spain, are also extremely popular. The original Cinderella romance, the *fotonovela rosa* (the "pink" photonovel), has been supplemented by the more realistic and materialist *fotonovela suave* (the "soft" photonovel) and the more violent and pornographic *fotonovela roja* (the "red" photonovel). A feature of all three is the extraordinary care taken to make the figures and backgrounds both familiar and not too familiar: the scenes of wealth in the Cinderella stories are never of unimaginable wealth. These predominantly innocent fantasies sell in the millions weekly. They reveal something about the dreams of their buyers, as do their equivalents elsewhere.

Considering the prominence of soccer in all Latin America, it is surprising that less has been written and thought about its significance than about *tlachtli,* a sacred Mesoamerican ball game of preconquest times, the Aztec equivalent of rollerball. Soccer was carried to all parts of the region by the British—residents, teachers, miners. By the 1990s the "locals" were showing signs of promise. As Sir David Kelly wrote sometime later of Argentina:

> The ease with which the plutocracy has acquired wealth and political influence was paralleled by a patient determination to wait until a foreign community had done the spade work in building up some institution and then quietly absorb it. Thus the British community had introduced tennis, golf, polo and football [soccer], and started and built up all the first clubs: but already in 1919 all these, with the exception of cricket (which, as in most countries, remained a purely British amusement), are being absorbed by the Argentineans.[5]

It was an intimation that the British would soon be suffering at the feet of an Alfredo Di Stefano or at the hand (or head) of Diego Maradona.

Soccer is seen as a major mechanism of social integration at all levels of society. Janet Lever's *Soccer Madness,* a sociologist's account of soccer in Brazil, argues that it gives a meaning to people's lives, it provides a talking point for strangers, it crosses class barriers and gives cohesiveness to local communities and to the nation. National teams instill pride. In the past twenty years Brazil has been recognized as fielding the most skillful and inventive team in the world. And nobody disputed the fact that Argentina was the best team in the 1986 World Cup and that Maradona was the best player. Argentina's performance in the 1990 World Cup, however, showed a team bankrupt of ideas. The economic crisis, the pauperization of the local leagues, and the scattering of the best talent to teams all over the world have all adversely affected the national teams. South American pre-eminence is no longer assured.

Soccer holds out some political temptations. Juan Perón, who called himself (for skiing) *"el primer deportista"* (the first sportsman), refused to let Argentina compete in the World Cup in the late 1940s for fear of being beaten by Uruguay. The government of General Jorge Videla installed color television in Argentina with great rapidity (and at an astronomical cost) in time for the World Cup of 1978. If, as has often been alleged, Argentine victory was then obtained through massive bribes, it shows clearly the manipulation and brutality of the regime's cultural policies.

A heavy government emphasis on sport does not appear to correlate with much concern for freedom. Cuba has become a major sporting power. The island provides the best example in Latin America of sport financed and organized by the state, a good strategy for coping with a youthful and healthy population prone to let its mind dwell on forbidden things. Cuban achievements—of Alberto Juantorena in middle-distance running and of the world high-jump record holder Javier Sotomayor, for example—would be better known if Cuba boycotted fewer competitions.

There are other examples of sports excellence. The first bicycle was taken to Colombia by a British diplomat in the last century. Nevertheless, even Sir

David Kelly would have been surprised by the popularity cycling at present enjoys in Colombia and by the international successes of Colombian cyclists, living as they do in one of the world's most mountainous countries, where road building and road maintenance face extraordinary difficulties. Panama has enjoyed disproportionate success in boxing, a sport favored by the National Guard. Boxing is also popular on the Colombian Caribbean coast: in the politically more quiescent early 1970s, the only "left" in the country was said to be the fist of Kid Pambele.

Latin America's populations are youthful. Much can be done for sport without great resources. Good policies have been made with imagination—an example is the Venezuelan and Colombian *ciclovia,* the turning over of city streets to cyclists and roller skaters on Sundays and holidays, a scheme that costs virtually nothing and has proved enduringly popular. *Narcotraficantes* (drug dealers) also see investment in sport as both lucrative and legitimizing. In Colombia in the past they have bought whole football teams. Governments are too prone to concentrate on spectacular events like the World Cup, to the detriment of other less occasional, more genuinely popular programs that deserve greater support. Mexico is a case in point, having hosted the World Cup twice in twenty years at enormous expense.

The Latin American impact on European and U.S. culture has recently been greater than that of any other part of the world. That is a surprising statement to make about an area that lacks vital strategic importance, that presents a picture of general economic malaise, and whose participation in world trade is declining. But the impact has been greater in cultural terms than anything coming from the newly industrialized nations of the Pacific rim—Korea, Taiwan, the Philippines, Singapore, and Thailand. The cultural influence of Japan and China is also far less than the economic weight of the one and the share in world population of the other. Japanese culture is, without the presence of the Japanese, unexportable, unlike the products of Japanese technology. In culture in the old-fashioned sense, Australian and Canadian writers and artists have not succeeded in rivaling what has come out of Latin America: García Márquez and Mario Vargas Llosa are far better known, even in Britain, than Patrick White or Peter Carey, and they have as yet no consistent rivals from India, Africa, or the Middle East. The contrast of Latin American writing with domestic British culture must be made. An English reviewer quoted, with approval, and with a recognition of the critic's cosmopolitan authority, Carlos Fuentes having referred to the postwar English novel as "a large pot of tea stewing comfortably under a tea-cosy." A judgment that is not, one feels uneasily, far wrong.

In the United States the Hispanic Americans are leading an assault on WASP culture that Latin Americans are following with interest. The television may be a Sony, but it may well be tuned to Edward James Olmos as Lieutenant Castillo in *Miami Vice*. The cassette recorder or boom box may be an Aiwa, but the chances are high that it is playing salsa and Ruben Blades.

Notes

1. For a detailed analysis of rural and urban culture, see William Rowe and Vivian Schelling, *Popular Culture in Latin America* (Verso, London, 1991).
2. John King (ed.), *Modern Latin American Fiction: A Survey* (Faber and Faber Ltd., London, 1987) pp. 150–151.
3. See Joseph Strubhaar's analysis of television in H. Hind and C. Tatumed (eds.), *Handbook of Latin American Popular Culture* (Greenwood Press, Westport and London, 1985). Also see Cornelia Butler Flora's analysis of photonovels in the same volume.
4. R. Williams, *Television: Technology and Cultural Form* (Fontana, London, 1974), p. 144.
5. Sir D. Kelly, *The Ruling Few* (London, 1952), pp. 114–115.

Part

2

POLITICS

6

Democracy and Democratization in Latin America

A Democratic Tradition

The revival of liberal democracy was the most common focus of interest among observers of Latin American politics in the mid-1980s, and it has indeed been a common experience. The process and its limitations can be explored in a long list of republics: Argentina, Brazil, Peru, Uruguay, Bolivia, Ecuador, El Salvador, Guatemala, Honduras, Mexico, and Chile. They are states of different sizes, levels of development, histories, and prospects, but all seem to be experiencing the same cycle of democratization. This theme of the 1980s contrasts with the preoccupations of the 1960s and 1970s.

In those two decades the focus shifted from revolution or reform (respectively embodied by Fidel Castro's Cuba and the Alliance for Progress) to the study of what seemed to be a new type of authoritarian regime that had emerged as the inevitable response to a certain stage of development: the bureaucratic-authoritarian governments of Brazil, Argentina, Uruguay, and Chile.

It is salutary to remember that liberal democracy as something to be valued for itself did not have so many defenders in those years. The emphasis in the 1960s, even where democracies survived, was reformist and technocratic, not so much on the liberties that the system could guarantee but on the goods that it could deliver. Even though containing the influence of revolutionary Cuba was the political end in view, the designers of the Alliance for Progress were not much interested in politics. Their new men were planners, economists, experts—rarely politicians. The role of politicians was pictured as the subservient one of giving the technocrats a clear run. Politics was not seen as offering a "modern" career. At best, the enlightened politician kept archaic or perverse populist forces at bay while others carried through essential reforms. Many governments responded by striving to appear technocratic so as to receive more aid.

In the 1970s the verdict on politics was even more severe. Such were the contradictions and antagonisms of Latin American development that civilian government was judged unlikely to survive: it would have to give way to military rule—and to a new sort of military rule. The new iron surgeons would not be treating a few occasional symptoms but would carry out prolonged and profound restructuring operations for which few suitable anesthetics were available.

The brief résumé of the conventional wisdoms that preceded the present enthusiasm for, and preoccupation about, democracy and democratization serves first of all to warn against fashion. Revolutionaries, reformists, and authoritarians with their respective admirers, and those who theorized about them without admiring them, all came unstuck in the 1960s and 1970s and early 1980s. The superficial similarities of Latin American politics, the common and Western aspirations of the various republics, the need for commentators to generalize, and the natural vanities of those in power all combine to produce a persistent illusion that the current flavor is going to last forever.

Moreover, one should note that those fashions in analysis not only simplified the politics of the countries that appeared to fit, but also ignored those that did not. Exceptions included Colombia, Venezuela, and Costa Rica, which avoided the authoritarian cycle of the 1970s. Another exception was Mexico, where single-party government persisted until the late 1980s, unaffected by what happened elsewhere in the hemisphere. That government remained in many ways authoritarian, but Mexican politics cannot be seen as part of any cycle. Mexico, viewed from South America, looks distinctly self-absorbed, its politics not affected by the activities of Brazilian, Argentine, Peruvian, or Chilean soldiers or by the achievements of Venezuelan democrats.

The rest of the world, particularly the Anglo-Saxon world, tends both to simplify and to denigrate Latin American politics. There is a tendency to agglomerate, to assume that the worst is typical, and to apply standards that are not applied to other parts of the world: to Africa, Asia, to southern Europe, even to parts of the United States. Structures tend to be simplified as nowhere else. Such-and-such a republic is allegedly run by "fourteen," another by "forty" families. Corruption is held to be universal. Contrasts in wealth are considered to make democracy locally meaningless, and all signs of democratic activity are explained in terms of *clientelismo*—the distribution of resources, jobs, and funds, and the shaping of official decisions, in return for political support.

Phenomena such as inequalities of wealth and power, corruption, and the widespread use of political patronage are not exclusively Latin American. Italy, for example, has much in common with Latin America in its political practices—terrorism, patronage, bureaucratic inefficiency, lack of party principle, ministerial instability, Mafia, to mention just a few—but no one concludes that Italian democracy is meaningless. Southern European politics and much of Latin American politics can often be usefully viewed in a continuum. The average European observer, however, knows something of the recent history of Italy and Spain (though probably not much of Greece or Portugal) but very little of the recent history of Venezuela or Argentina. There is nothing like ignorance of a country's past to make its politics look simple.

Latin Americans tend to make external criticism their own, and they remain acutely conscious of their failure to live up to the expectations of the currently (though not historically) more peaceful and more prosperous quarters of the Western world. Such self-criticism was not so marked in historically proud countries fallen on hard times such as Spain and Italy, and is far less characteristic of nonwestern countries. Indonesians, for example, neither expect themselves, nor are they expected, to run their affairs like the Dutch. Argentines, it was long thought, ought to run their affairs rather better than the Italians.

The present moment is one in which the critics' agenda is going to make impossible demands on Latin American governments for the coming decade. To ask the impossible is to invite failure as well as to forget the essence of politics. Latin American governments are currently expected by their distant critics to perform the following difficult, if not impossible tasks: to pay their debts; to reduce inflation; to redistribute income and attack absolute poverty; to provide for basic needs; to halt the destruction and degradation of the environment; to guarantee human rights and to bring an end to extremist subversion; to provide higher levels of employment and better and more universal education; to end drug trafficking; to reduce crime; to reduce military influence in national affairs and spend less on the military; to avoid populism while consolidating liberal democracy through reform; to privatize their state sectors and "open" their economies; not only to go on having elections but to go on winning them with these sorts of planks in the platform.

That is not a realistic set of expectations, yet it is at the back of the minds of many when they look at the prospects of the elected governments presently in power. An assessment of political probabilities and possibilities ought to have a more down-to-earth point of departure.

After all, these are not new countries. The length and intensity of their previous democratic experiences vary, but they are not political neophytes.

Central America

Although Latin America may have extensively redemocratized in the 1980s, politically it is anything but *tabula rasa,* a blank sheet.

Most of the republics have been independent for more than 150 years (the most important exceptions are Cuba, which did not gain independence until 1901, and Panama, which separated from Colombia in 1903). That makes them older *as nation states* than Italy, Germany, or any of the successor states of the Habsburg monarchy—not older as cultures but in some ways older in terms of their autonomous political traditions.

The dominant political parties of Colombia and Uruguay have their roots far back in the nineteenth century. Though they may at first look more modern than the Colombian Liberals and Conservatives or Uruguay's Blancos and Colorados, parties such as the Peruvian American Popular Revolutionary Alliance (Alianza Popular Revolucionaria Americana—APRA), the Argentine Radicals, the Venezuelan Democratic Action, (Acción Democrática) and the Mexican Institutional Revolutionary Party (Partido Revolucionario

Institucional—PRI) are all more than fifty years old, as are most of the Communist parties of the region and the Socialist parties of Argentina, Uruguay, Chile, and Ecuador. The United States is not the only republic in the hemisphere whose politics are dominated by amorphous currents with their origins in the past century, whose distinctions, while real to the native voter, are hard for the foreigner to grasp.

In some countries the persistence of patterns of party allegiance may be obscured by divisions and changes of party name. Such is the case in Ecuador. But Latin America is no exception to the general rule that a well-established political party tends to survive from generation to generation, despite changes in society and most episodes of authoritarian government—even the rare sort that attempts to achieve some fundamental party realignment or suppress party activity altogether. General Juan Vicente Gómez's long rule in Venezuela (1908–1935) did force the demise of all previous party life, hence the relative modernity in names, ideologies, and organization of Venezuelan parties since. But no such clearing away of old party loyalties has been achieved by successive Argentine military regimes—most have inclined to make tactical alliances with parties rather than to attempt anything more drastic—by Uruguayan or Peruvian soldiers, by milder Ecuadoreans, or even by Chile's General Augusto Pinochet. Brazil's party systems, far less well established at the national level at the onset of military government in 1964, have certainly been more influenced by military direction. But even in Brazil old patterns of coalition and alliance reemerged in the late 1980s, some of them in the hands of those displaced in 1964.

The existence of such patterns of persistent loyalties and political traditions is not easily accepted by those who regard Latin America as being at one and the same time deplorably conservative socially and "volatile" politically. The notion of volatility derives from the tendency to lump together all the apparently bewildering surface phenomena of Latin America's politics. In some ways it is similar to the false equation of the rapid succession of Italian governments with some underlying instability.

The persistence of party allegiances, which in Latin America as elsewhere are bound up with lineage, local solidarity, education, class interest, and a host of other factors including memories of injuries given and received in past conflicts, should come as no surprise. Party allegiance is not specifically Latin American, and in no way is it irrational. What is not rational is the presumption that such allegiances should be promptly abandoned for something that seems more "rational" to the outside observer. Such expectations are not entertained about other parts of the world.

The argument is not that one should expect no movement or change in the panorama of Latin American political parties. Indeed there is quite as much movement as exists in established Western democracies. Sometimes there is much more than many expect, as in the Argentine elections of 1983 and the Mexican elections of 1988. The argument is that the same weight given elsewhere has to be given to long-established party loyalties and traditions in Latin America.

Moreover, the explanation of change should not be exclusively or excessively mechanistic: Latin Americans vote for reasons of jobs and pork-barrel politics, at the behest of bosses, as small cogs in machines, as do many of the inhabitants of California, Louisiana, or Delaware. They also vote for the other reasons: civic duty, habit, affirmation of personality, regional sentiment, group and class interest, and party mystique. Though the eras of intense party mobilization nearly everywhere lie in the past and are unlikely to be revived, party mystique is not dead, and a talented leader can often revive it.

Whatever the shortfalls of liberal democracy in reality, the rhetoric of democracy has been longer established in Latin America than in any other part of the world with the exception of the northern United States. After Haiti, the first colonies of the "Third World" (not a particularly popular or useful term in Latin America) to free themselves from the status of colonies, the Spanish American republics had radical beginnings. And neither was the Empire of Brazil immune to radical currents—Emperor, court, and slavery notwithstanding. "What else could the emancipated colonies do except proclaim the democratic republic?" asked one of their defenders in 1861, pointing out that monarchical and aristocratic alternatives were unavailable.[1] Republics were radical at the time. Some, such as Colombia and at times Venezuela, attempted constitutional practices that emulated the most advanced in Europe. In Chile, Argentina, and Mexico, in different ways and with varying degrees of success, there was a more marked search for the model of a conservative republic.

Independent Latin America has rarely abandoned democratic rhetoric. Few authoritarian regimes have ever offered or threatened a permanent departure from democratic practices. Even the dictatorship of General Rafael Trujillo in the Dominican Republic made sure that at regular intervals all citizens participated in the charade of electing him. There are controlled elections in Fidel Castro's Cuba, as there were in General Alfredo Stroessner's Paraguay.

The electoral record of the region as a whole is uneven but long. There has frequently been heavy manipulation through government machinery and patronage, coercion, corruption, violence, and fraud, and through property and literacy restrictions on the franchise. But these artificial stimuli, abuses, and limitations have been present at the beginning of all Western democracies. They are not peculiarly Latin American, and in Latin America as elsewhere methods evolve.

The importance of the flawed but persistent democratic tradition in Latin America should not be ignored: it has proved its ability to survive numerous disappointments, and it will survive more.

The close of the 1980s saw once again some disillusionment with liberal democracy, doubtless deepened by prolonged economic crisis. Yet this generalization must be applied with care. Disillusionment with the lackluster transitional government of President José Sarney in Brazil, for example, should not be equated with despair about democratic political practices. In Brazil, prior to the election of Fernando Collor in 1990, democracy had been exercised to only a limited extent. Mexico has just begun its probable evolution toward more democratic practices, and Chile has just recently returned to them. Democracy in Venezuela may emerge strengthened from the shock of the February 1989 Caracas riots (which are discussed more fully in Chapter 11), its leaders had become more responsible and less overconfident. Civilian rule has survived tenaciously in Colombia in the face of mounting violence, and it has also performed much better than anyone expected in Bolivia and the Dominican Republic.

The two republics in which liberal democracy seemed especially at risk were Argentina and Peru. But the failure of Raúl Alfonsín's Radical party to perform a series of difficult feats—to satisfy the army and its victims, to stabilize and revive the Argentine economy with minimum austerity, to change the speculative habits of a generation, and then to get itself reelected—should be no surprise. Its "failure" should be seen as part of the normal course of democratic politics, not as a failure of the system. Alfonsín did not give way to another military government; in fact, almost all shades of civilian opinion in Argentina remain resolutely opposed to military government. Even in Peru, where economic depression is complicated by unprecedented problems of internal order, a return to military rule, though a possibility, is certainly not a foregone conclusion. Few there desire it.

The alternatives to elected civilian rule must be considered, though at present no models to the left or to the right attract much interest or support.

On the left, the Cuban Revolution is now viewed as distinctly Cuban in the intellectual and university circles where its attraction was once greatest. Fidel Castro may be recognized as a grand historic figure, and he can make himself the center of attraction at a presidential inauguration as he did in 1987 and 1989 in Quito, Mexico City, and Caracas. He can also still exercise some influence over revolutionary groups elsewhere. But the rigidities and austerities of the Cuban model do not attract; nor does its dependence on Moscow, particularly now that the Soviet Union is in crisis. Havana no longer has the same cultural importance for the left as it had twenty years ago. Fidel Castro has had some success in rebuilding bridges with Latin America, but in doing so, he has muted his support for revolution.

The Nicaraguan Revolution did not command the attention or exert the attraction that the Cuban Revolution did in the 1960s. Significantly, the Latin American response to the Nicaraguan Revolution that drew most support was not a movement of solidarity, though there have been plenty of displays of solidarity on the left. It was the mediating diplomacy of the Contadora Group (Mexico, Venezuela, Colombia, and Panama), which, along with its aim of restraining the United States, always sought to modify the revolutionary aims of the Sandinistas not only in their foreign policy but also in internal Nicaraguan affairs. The Sandinistas were also, at least verbally, committed to pluralist elections and a mixed economy and so did not offer the clear revolutionary alternative that Cuba once did.

The uncertainties for the left were increased by the changes of the 1980s in both China and the Soviet Union. These changes pose problems to Marxists, Communists, and Socialists everywhere, and Latin America is again in no way immune. Western in its dominant culture, in its founding independence ideologies, the region has always been an easy importer of doctrine, and the permeability has increased with the ease of communications. The likely consequences of this crisis on the left are explored below.

The decade of the 1970s bequeathed a parallel crisis on the right. The military regimes that came to power then all achieved much less than they promised or threatened. "Bureaucratic authoritarianism"—the term for the governments of Brazil, Uruguay, Argentina, and Chile invented by Guillermo O'Donnell, the author of the best-known attempt to find common structural origins for these military regimes—turned out to be neither so bureaucratic (in the sense of rational and technical) nor so authoritative (in the medium and the long run these governments failed to generate genuine authority). In Brazil the long-drawn-out transition to democracy, under close military tutelage and with extensive, reserved military powers, produced the least commanding and least authoritative government of all—that of President Sarney. Chile's General Pinochet, who began his rule in 1973 by burning the country's electoral rolls, was defeated in 1988 in a plebiscite of his own designing by a "no" campaign put together by many of the same parties that had dominated the political scene before his coup. The Chilean Communist party, though theoretically still unconstitutional, will shortly return to the scene too. Earlier, the Uruguayan armed forces also unseated themselves in a plebiscite, and President Julio Mario Sanguinetti managed to negotiate a return to full civilian rule with some military vetoes still in the air. Finally, the failure of the Argentine armed forces to generate true authority, or to maintain any sort of bureaucratic order, became apparent to the world in 1982.

This is not to say that such governments have altogether failed to alter the politics of their countries. In Argentina the slogan "*Nunca más*" ("Never again") covers not only the excesses of repression after the armed forces took power in 1976 but also the terrorism and urban guerrilla warfare that preceded the coup. Though the Chileans voted—not so overwhelmingly—that General Pinochet should cease to rule them after 1990, there was no sign of nostalgia for the chaos and polarization of former president Salvador Allende's Unidad Popular (Popular Unity) or for its policies. Political learning processes do occur in Latin America, and these two examples may show that at a heavy cost lessons have been learned, that perhaps some of the aims of military intervention have been achieved.

Military ambitions were never so modest. Military regimes were meant to show a superior consistency, better and more technical economic management, less of a tendency to yield to any populist temptations. The record here shows no discernible superiority to the civilian alternative. General Pinochet started out against the background of the mismanagement of the Allende years and went into his plebiscite willingly because he thought voters would be influenced by a recent boom. But even his government—the most unified, powerful, unchallenged, and doctrinaire of all the authoritarian governments of the 1960s and 1970s—had to bend at times to economic resistance and eventually to electoral expediency.

The economic practices of successive Argentine juntas after 1976 never matched their free-market pronouncements and ended with a populist adventure, the invasion of the Falklands/Malvinas. Along with Mexico, Latin America's largest debtors are Brazil and Argentina, and in all three cases the debts were incurred by regimes that lacked democratic control. In Argentina they were incurred to a particularly large degree, around a quarter of the total, for military purposes.

Faced with tough economic decisions, the iron surgeons flinched. It is still possible to imagine circumstances in which the military will resume power here and there in Latin America. The armed forces have reserved extensive influence in Brazil: civilian control over the armed forces ministries and a number of agencies is expressly denied. The retreat to barracks in Guatemala has been equally orderly, and the Guatemalan army retains extensive powers. General Pinochet remains commander-in-chief in Chile. There have always been a variety of types of military intervention, some more justifiable than others. Civilian leaders themselves are not always constitutional. But after the last cycle of military government, few civilian conservative sectors inside or outside Latin America regard the armed forces as more reliable than civilians, and some military establishments look distinctly less reliable.

International influences, including the U.S. government in most of its manifestations, are predominantly on the side of liberal democracy in Latin America, though their effectiveness is limited and in certain sectors declining. The United States placed its influence squarely behind the electoral process in the Dominican Republic and El Salvador. The United States also clearly favored the "no" vote in the Chilean plebiscite and opposed any coup in Peru in advance of the 1990 general election.

Many Latin Americans remain peculiarly sensitive to North American and European influence. The relative isolation that was a consequence of authoritarian rule was painful for intellectuals, and their experience of exile often revived respect for the undramatic advantages of the rule of law, regular elections, and the preservation of civil liberties.

The duration, intensity, repressiveness, competence, and ambition of military rule varied, and it is reasonable to expect that its legacy will vary too. The subsequent position of the armed forces of the region is considered in Chapter 8. Here the sum of the argument is that despite the strains placed on civilian governments by the most severe economic crisis since the 1930s, there is no alternative to elected civilian government readily to hand: memories of military failure are too recent and too profound. They will be effaced only by civilian failure so general or so critical that it cannot find or await any electoral solution.

Voters and Elections

How credible, how legitimate are elected Latin American governments? How do Latin American elections compare with elections elsewhere in participation rates, in honesty, as free expressions of the will of the electorate? Does the ideological spectrum presented for the voters' choice match what is normally available elsewhere in the West, or are some elements clearly missing? What role is played by government machinery, by private coercion, by fraud and corruption? What part do the media play? How do newspapers, radio, and television compare in importance in Latin American elections, and who controls them? What weight should be given to electoral processes subject to a great deal of government interference, such as in Mexico; or to elections carried out in circumstances of conflict, such as in El Salvador or Nicaragua; or to elections carried out under some element of military veto, as, in their different ways, in Uruguay, Chile, or Guatemala? How advanced are electoral techniques, campaigns, opinion polls?

Participation

Latin America has a long electoral history, and Latin Americans from the Rio Grande southward to Cape Horn have recently been voting with a high degree of effectiveness—results have not been easily predictable and results

Table 6.1

Share of adult population voting, by country

	Year	Type of Election[a]	Total Vote[b] (Thousands)	Adult Percentage of Population Voting[b]
Argentina	1983	P, L	15,180	89
Brazil	1982	L	48,440	81
Colombia	1982	P	6,816	68
Costa Rica	1982	P, L	992	87
Ecuador	1984	L	2,204	53
El Salvador	1984	P	1,524	69
Guatemala	1984	CA	1,856	57
Honduras	1981	P, L	1,171	79
Mexico	1982	P, L	22,523	75
Nicaragua	1984	P, CA	1,170	91
Peru	1980	P, L	4,030	49
Venezuela	1983	P, L	6,741	90
United States	1984	P, L	92,000	53

[a]P = Presidential; L = Legislative; CA = Constituent Assembly.
[b]Aged 20 and over. Estimates based on votes cast as a percentage of total population age 20 or over. (N.B.: This is not the same as the official electorate.)

SOURCE: *LASA Forum* (Latin American Studies Association) Reproduced as publ. 1001, p. 167, in James W. Wilkie and Adam Pevkal (eds.), *Statistical Abstract of Latin America*, vol. 24, UCLA, Los Angeles, 1986. Used by permission of Latin American Studies Association.

have mattered. In 1979, two-thirds of Latin America's population lived under military rule; in 1985, nine-tenths lived in countries where meaningful elections were held.

In the past, property, literacy, and gender qualifications restricted the right to vote. These restrictions no longer exist. A number of republics grant the vote at 18 years of age, some even at 16. In a number the vote is obligatory, though penalties for not voting tend to be negligible and unenforceable. No barriers impede the voting of ethnic minorities: Bolivian, Peruvian, Ecuadorean, Mexican, Colombian, and Guatemalan Indians can all vote, and they do. The bounds of all these electorates are therefore set wide.

Participation, however, shows much variation (Table 6.1). Venezuela has one of the world's highest voting participation records in presidential elections (over 90 percent) and one of the highest known indexes for other forms of participation in elections: attending rallies, sticking up posters, manning the polls. The Venezuelan voting level has until recently been as high as the Italian—one of the world's highest, a statistic showing that participation is not easily correlated with any simple notion of stability or governmental efficiency. In neighboring Colombia, however, participation in presidential elections is much lower, between 40 and 60 percent in recent years.

Such variations do not have simple explanations. Voting is obligatory in Venezuela and not in Colombia. But there is no evidence to show that that is why Venezuelans vote, any more than legal obligation explains why Italians vote. Colombians express a high level of disillusion and cynicism about party politics, but so do Italians. Venezuelan parties have far greater resources at their disposal for mobilizing their supporters than do their Colombian counterparts. Venezuelan parties—Democratic Action (Acción Democrática), the Christian Democrat Party (Comité de Organizacíon Politica Electoral Independiente—COPEI), Movement to Socialism (Moviemiento al Socialismo—MAS)—all have their origins in comparatively recent times and in opposition. They show far stronger autonomous organizational capacity than do the Colombian parties, which have evolved over a much longer period and remain obstinately fluid, informal, and undisciplined. Venezuelans appear to enjoy the mystique of voting. In Colombia, though interest in elections is palpably present and political competition is keen, people vote much less; at between 40 and 60 percent of the electorate, turnout in presidential elections in recent years is broadly similar to that which prevails among the citizens of the United States.

There are as yet few comprehensive and comparative studies of the evolution of suffrage in Latin American and of comparative participation, so conclusions have to be tentative. Participation rates vary from country to country, and what determines their variation is complicated. Party organization and resources, electoral laws, and local traditions are all part of the explanation. Conclusions are hard to draw. The health of a country's democracy is not a simple matter of its participation rate, and one cannot conclude that Venezuela's high rate makes that country more democratic than its neighbor, any more than one can conclude that Italians are more democratic than the French or the British, who vote in smaller proportionate numbers. Within a given country, some elections attract more voters than others. Certain elections—those immediately after military rule, for example—have a plebiscitary quality. Some results are also more predictable than others: predictability can either cause a bandwagon to roll, or it can lead indifferent voters to stay at home.

In elections that by general consent would be recognized as open and competitive—Venezuelan, Colombian, and Costa Rican elections, for example, or the 1986 mid-term Argentine elections—there is nothing abnormal to be seen in the rates of participation. In novel or plebiscitary elections, like the Argentine presidential contest of 1983, participation is usually higher. Some have also looked for a different pattern in what they have called "demonstration elections"—elections carried out in what are obviously far from ideal conditions, where a government seeks to legitimize itself but the opposition either abstains or can organize in restricted fashion only. One can look, for example, at the Salvadorean election of 1982 and the Nicaraguan elections of 1984, at Guatemalan elections between 1954 and 1985, and at all Mexican elections of recent years.

Observers of these Salvadorean and the Nicaraguan elections differed in their conclusions—many of them had made up their minds before they observed—but on balance neither process can be regarded as meaningless, and participation rates were unexceptional. Guatemalan abstention rates vary from 2 percent in 1944 to 64 percent in 1978; but in 1985, when the presidency was to return to civilian hands, abstention dropped to 31 percent. Mexican official figures are not much believed, but it is admitted that a growing rate of abstention, especially in the cities, was behind the efforts made by the government to liberalize the system in the 1970s. Abstention is not something that governments welcome: it saps authority. In the past, militant abstentions have frequently been used as an opposition tactic, and even unmilitant abstention has been a cause for concern.

In many Latin American electorates the rural and small-town vote is more easily brought out than the city vote. In the rural municipalities, traditional loyalties are stronger and traditional methods of getting the vote out are more easily applied. The urbanization of the last three decades has made electorates somewhat less predictable. Competition for the urban vote is often intense, and politicians have not been slow to appreciate its importance and to devise new techniques to capture or to influence it. Many politicians dream that they will make some unprecedented breakthrough against urban abstention. It is not confined to the less well-off sectors of the city population, and some studies show that it is more pronounced among the middle and upper classes.

Some safe general conclusions can be drawn from the electoral statistics of the majority of republics, those where one delicate observation of nineteenth-century practice—that "losing an election was not a common reason for a government to leave office"—no longer holds true. The extent of outright fraud in genuinely competitive elections is now marginal and can usually be disregarded. Elections may still include practices that are surprising to North American, Swiss, or English observers—one should remember that all Latin America anticipated the Swiss in the matter of votes for women—but rigging results or stuffing ballot boxes is not normally important. Exceptions occur when results are exceptionally close, when the small percentage of possible fraud makes a difference—in Panama in 1984, in the 1986 municipal elections in Lima, and in Mexico, where the PRI has made extensive use of blatant fraud and where there have been no effective multiparty checks on the results the PRI chooses to announce.

The Mexican elections of 1988 showed that the PRI could no longer maintain its unquestioned superiority. In forty years the opposition has never been permitted to win even a third of the vote. Then in 1988 Corriente Democrática (Democratic Current), a broad, dissident coalition emerging from the PRI, achieved 31 percent; the National Action Party (Partido de Acción Nacional—PAN) maintained its 17 percent; and the PRI registered 50.4 percent, the lowest rate in its history.

Between 1964 and 1988 the PRI lost 30 percent of the country's vote, and the decline was fairly steady:

Year	PRI Vote (% of Total)
1964	86.3
1967	83.3
1970	80.1
1973	69.7
1976	80.1
1979	69.7
1982	69.3
1985	64.8
1988	50.4

An analysis by electoral district shows that the PRI vote holds up best in rural Mexico. One comparison between the votes of 1961 and 1982 showed that in rural districts the decline was some 15 percent, from 100 percent to 85 percent, whereas in the cities the decline was from 82 percent to 55 percent. This decline has been especially pronounced since 1979. The PRI has lost its dominion precisely in the sector of Mexico that has grown fastest.[2]

To judge the degree to which elections give credible and legitimating results, one must look not at old-fashioned fraud but rather at other aspects of Latin American elections.

Vetoes and Exclusions

Is the range of the electors' choice narrowed by any imposed veto or exclusion? Sometimes it has been. For years in Peru the armed forces successfully prevented the APRA party from taking power through an electoral victory, and between 1955 and 1970 the Argentine armed forces proscribed the followers of Juan Perón. The Uruguayan military could not bring itself to relinquish power without vetoing the presidential candidacy of Wilson Ferreira. Though it tolerated any degree of faction and did not deny legal existence to other parties, the Colombian "Frente Nacional" (National Front) power-sharing and alternation agreement of 1958–1974 obliged candidates to declare some sort of membership in one or other of the country's two traditional Liberal and Conservative currents. This did not prevent the near-victory of a protest vote in the 1970 elections, but it generated a sense of exclusion.

From time to time Communist parties have been declared illegal here and there. The party was denied legal existence, for example, by Article 8 of the 1980 Chilean constitution. Such exclusion is exceptional but, in any case, Communist parties do not usually get a big vote. The Chilean party has in the past been unusually successful, but even at its height it commanded no more than 16.2 percent of the national vote. The Costa Rican Communist party was banned between 1948 and 1970. In the 1940s it had won around 15 percent of the vote. Here and there individuals have also been deprived of their political rights. The practice was employed in Chile by the Pinochet government.

Outright proscription of parties or individuals under the law is uncommon. The degree of difficulty in acquiring legal status for a political party varies from republic to republic, and within countries it has varied over time. The Mexican government's harassment or encouragement of minority parties has been frequently manipulative, obeying the convenience of the ruling party, but this capriciousness is not likely to be maintained in the future. The minorities are now too strong to be dealt with in the old ways.

In general, it cannot be said that the countries of the region erect unreasonable legal obstacles against the existence and participation of a wide range of political parties. Many employ electoral systems that go further than countries elsewhere in the West to ensure minority party representation.

Criticism is not as tellingly leveled at legal or even constitutional provisions as at political practice. The credibility of electoral results, the degree to which they generate genuine authority, is frequently seen to be limited by defects less quantifiable than fraud: by extralegal vetoes, violence, and the threat of violence; by the excessive use of governmental patronage and official machinery; by extensive clientelism *(clientelismo)*; by the persistent power of *caciques* (local political bosses); by widespread bribery; by unequal access to influential media under political control; by lack of democracy within the parties themselves; by lack of any control or limits on electoral expenditure. The list could of course be longer.

Violence and Intimidation

In some parts of Latin America—for example, parts of Guatemala, El Salvador, Colombia, and Peru—guerrilla or counterguerrilla violence robs elections of much of their meaning. These areas are much less extensive than the outside world imagines. Within some of them, elections are not totally devoid of meaning. In some guerrilla-dominated areas of Colombia the electoral "form of struggle" is not neglected; in 1988 the local population was encouraged to vote for the candidates of the Unión Patriótica (Patriotic Union), the political arm of the Colombian Revolutionary Armed Forces (Fuerzas Armadas Revolucionarias de Colombia—FARC) guerrillas. In El Salvador the Farabundo Marti National Liberation Front (Frente Farabundo Martí de Liberación Nacional—FMLN) also has a civil front, the Revolutionary Democratic Front (Frente Democratio Revolutionarío—the FDR), which toys with the notion of electoral participation. The Salvadorean guerrillas themselves have been halfhearted in executing their threats to disrupt elections. If people want to vote—and an overwhelming majority of Salvadoreans clearly do want to—obstructing them has a political cost. Few revolutionaries have the frankness to dismiss elections out of hand. Most talk of waiting for the right conditions and of guarantees. Sendero Luminoso (Shining Path) in Peru, however, rejects elections altogether.

Violence and intimidation can be employed outside areas of guerrilla domination. In addition to the republics mentioned above, such violence is exercised on occasions in Mexico, and examples can be found elsewhere. It is often hard to detect because it precedes or follows elections. Election days themselves are usually peaceful. One should not, however, generalize from extreme cases. In the not-so-distant past, elections in the United States as a whole were not rendered meaningless by abuses in, for example, Alabama, though they may have had no democratic meaning for a substantial part of the population of that state. The map of intimidation even in El Salvador or Guatemala, the two republics that show the highest levels of politically motivated homicide, varies significantly from one part of the country to another. It should also be noted that intimidation can come from both extremes of the political spectrum, as well as from governments and ruling parties. It can also be the product of local situations and conflicts that cannot easily be reduced to any such schema.

Violence and intimidation, like fraud, are far from characteristic of most Latin American elections. In Costa Rica, Venezuela, Ecuador, Uruguay, Argentina, and most of Brazil there is no such tradition in recent times. In Peru there are signs that give cause for concern, but in that country's somewhat intermittent electoral history no systematic pattern of electoral violence can be discerned. Elections have been annulled by military interventions rather than "made" by forcible methods, although those are not unknown. The Bolivian electorate since the revolution of 1952 has not been easy to overawe, though there have been notable examples of electoral fraud and army coups in 1971, 1978, 1979, and 1980. General Pinochet and his supporters exercised a measure of intimidation in the 1988 plebiscite in Chile, but without success.

Clientelism

A broader base for questioning the credibility of elections can be found in clientelism, the excessive reliance by political parties on government patronage. Employment in the state sector and bureaucratic careers are often governed by partisan criteria. State services are distributed according to partisan criteria—health, education, and justice among others. Contracts are also frequently awarded according to partisan criteria.

It is important to distinguish the large range of activities and organizations that may be governed by clientelistic methods from the old-time but still persistent domination of territory, large or small, by a political boss—in most of Spanish America, by the "*cacique*"; in Argentina, by the term "*caudillo*" (the word is used of grander national figures elsewhere); in Brazil, by the "*coronel.*"

Neither type of domination seems as archaic, as condemned to disappear with spreading "modernity" as critics would like. Many aspects of *clientelismo,* are modern. The expansion of social services and education provide new opportunities for clientelistic practices, and no part of the political spectrum can afford to abstain from them. Clientelism does not imply a lack of political competition. Government jobs are of great importance to the educated middle classes as well as to many more humble people. It has been estimated that around six out of ten Latin American professionals are employed by the state. The rapid expansion of higher education in the last decades has brought both new demands for patronage and new forms of patronage. State universities and educational institutes are part of that pattern. The vast state universities of Mexico, and the sensitivity of all aspiring Mexicans to any attempt to cut down their size or restrict access to them, are an obvious example. It is no less a form of patronage, no less a field for clientelism, that the patrons and clients in many Latin American state universities are frequently on the left.

However, few simple spoils systems remain. In the typical Latin American bureaucracy, posts in the upper reaches are subject to political appointment and removal, but changes in labor legislation and the growing significance of public-sector unions make the dismissal of civil servants difficult. Political, partisan, and patronage calculation may still influence appointments and promotions, and much political time and effort is everywhere spent on these matters. But once someone is appointed, his or her loyalty and willingness to serve cannot be taken for granted. Civil servants vote—a proportion of their salaries may even go to party funds—but the assertion that in many republics the size of the effective electorate is the sum of the civil servants, their families, and their dependents is an exaggeration. Nevertheless, patronage in jobs remains a most important element in getting votes, and the fact that this is the case breeds cynicism. Again, that phenomenon is not in any way confined to Latin America. Though it can be a stabilizing influence, it is not a legitimizing influence.

Beyond jobs, there is an array of further material inducements to vote, ranging from building materials to scholarships—Colombian politicians set much store by numerous *"becas"* (scholarships), the most thinly disguised bribe—to cash itself. Everywhere elections have gotten more and more expensive and votes less and less captive. Even where votes are bought, they cost more. Bought votes themselves are evidence that the vote is no longer captive, as nobody pays for a captive vote with anything more than transport and a fiesta. It is possible that some corrupt practices will have to be abandoned because of excessive expense. At present the use of indivisible material rewards—rewards that go to the individual and not to the community—continues to be an important element in certain elections, and this too diminishes their credibility.

There is also logic to the argument that the more an election costs the politician, the more likely is the winner to resort to corruption once elected. The force of this argument varies according to the political arena in question. Venezuelan elections, for example, are perhaps the most expensive in the world, but the legitimate resources available in Venezuela for electioneering are abnormally large. It is therefore possible for an expensive Venezuelan election to be less corrupt and corrupting than a much cheaper contest across the border in Colombia. The increase in election costs tends to work to the disadvantage of candidates who represent low-income strata. The consequence of campaigns of unrestricted expense, frequently far more expensive than anything seen in Western Europe, combined with the lack of official funding, is greater corruption.

Elections and the Media

The conduct of electoral campaigns is everywhere increasingly sophisticated, and expertise is now commonly sought and bought from outside the region. Opinion polls are now commonplace, and for politicians television is the most important of the media at election time. (Questions of the overall influence of the media, of their ownership and orientation, are considered in Chapter 5.) Although most republics have some provision for minority access, the common electoral effect of television tends to favor the big battalions, which were not unfavored by radio and the press in earlier times. However, dissidents can sometimes make a surprisingly good showing. In the Chilean plebiscite campaign of 1988, which drew record viewing figures, the advantage went to the opposition against a government that had not bothered to learn how to present itself competently on television.

Television has made electoral fraud harder. The coverage of elections in northern Mexico by U.S. television is one factor that has made it more difficult for the local PRI to engage in fraud. Television has also influenced the way candidates present themselves, and televised debates have a growing importance. The medium does not favor an intransigent adversarial style.

Conclusions

Assessment of the staying power of Latin America's democracy is clearly part of any attempt to predict the political evolution of the region. It is only part, however, for the democratic process itself can have startling and extreme results. Demagogues, unprincipled populists, can win elections: Juan Domingo Perón never lost one. Electoral competition can also become so acute that it produces uncontainable polarizations. This was the case in Chile, where years of increasingly unconstrained bidding for votes culminated in the intense mobilization of the Unidad Popular (Popular Unity) period and the coup of 1973. Figures give the degree of participation but not the quality of participation. They do not convey whether or not in a given country, even in a given electorate, there is a strong consensus that recognizes certain rules of the game. They do not show what is available across the political spectrum. Before a consideration of such questions, some conclusions can be set down:

- Most of Latin America has a long electoral history, and most republics have experienced intense electoral mobilizations at one time or another. In electoral terms little of Latin America is virgin territory.
- Rates of participation vary, but at both extremes, high and low, they are not exceptional when compared with the rates of other Western democracies.
- Fraud is not widespread. It can influence the outcome of close contests, and it has remained a frequent recourse in Mexico and in Panama. Improved communications, electoral technology, and greater international interest all make fraud more difficult than in the past.
- Clienteles and patronage are still important in elections and are likely to remain so, but they do not preclude competition or make it easy to determine an election's outcome. The manner in which clienteles are built and patronage is employed has evolved and adapted to the social changes of recent decades.
- "Demonstration elections"—for example, in El Salvador in 1982, in Nicaragua in 1984—cannot be dismissed as insignificant. Heavily

manipulated systems can also produce surprises—for example, in Mexico in 1988, in Nicaragua in 1990.

- The quality of an election can vary significantly in different parts of the same country or even in different parts of the same city. In general, urban votes are less easily controlled than small-town or rural votes. The potential electorate is now much more urban.
- Party loyalties and traditions show much the same capacity to survive as they do elsewhere in the West. Latin America contains a number of vigorous parties that were founded in the last century. Two of these are even in power, the Liberals in Colombia and the Blancos in Uruguay. Electoral maps tend to be stable and change slowly.
- The Brazilian party system at the *national* level is the most fluid exception to that last generalization. At the *state* level, despite changing party labels, more persistent patterns are to be found.
- It is not correct to view the return to democratic practices and free elections as just a phenomenon of the early 1980s. The process began in the 1970s, and the transition was still incomplete in early 1990. Brazil had only just elected a president. In Chile the return to democracy began only in 1988, the same year as Mexico's first large-scale electoral surprise. Elections in themselves are not generally novel, nor is the current cycle of democratization, insofar as such can be discerned, confined to the early 1980s. So the novelty cannot be simply expected to wear off.

The next chapter considers the range of choice offered by the political parties.

Notes

1. J. M. Samper, *Ensayo sobre las revoluciones y la condicion social de las Repúblicas Colombianas (hispano-americanas) (Essay on the Revolutions and the Social Condition of the Colombian (Hispanic-American) Republics)* (Paris, 1861), p. 172.
2. See H. Aguilar Camín, *Despúes del milagro (After the Miracle)* (Mexico City, 1988), ch. 4.

7

Political Parties

Any attempt at a survey of Latin America's political parties runs the risk of bewildering the reader with acronyms and overwhelming the reader with a large dose of exegesis. In Latin America, as in so many other places, a party's name does not necessarily provide a clue to its nature. Here it is necessary to use a broad brush, but to use it as precisely as possible.

Without forgetting that the spectrum afforded by any national array of political parties is the party spectrum, not the whole range of possible politics (military regimes have been and remain an option), one can examine left, right, and center; one can also examine populists.

The Left

Parties of marked socialist—not social democrat but socialist—ideology and program commonly meet with small success at the polls. They have a poor record in Argentina, Uruguay, Colombia, Venezuela, the Dominican Republic, and Costa Rica. They do not figure significantly in recent Mexican developments. The three most obvious exceptions are Chile, Peru, and Bolivia, where parties that can be defined as "socialist" have proved themselves capable of attracting a substantial proportion of votes.

In Chile Salvador Allende's Unidad Popular (Popular Unity) coalition, whose two chief components were his own Socialist party and the somewhat more staid but historically important Chilean Communist party, gained power in 1970 with 36.2 percent of the vote. The two parties polled 18.7 percent and 16.2 percent respectively in the 1973 congressional elections, compared with 29.1 percent for the Christian Democrats and 21.3 percent for the National party.

In Peru after 1980 the Izquierda Unida (United Left) emerged as the leading left rival to the more social democrat APRA party. The leaders of Izquierda Unida are avowedly Marxist, although where social democracy ends and Marxism begins is in practice hard to define in Peru today.

In Bolivian politics since the 1952 revolution there have been strong left-wing currents. They figure significantly in elections, though now much less so than previously.

A fourth case, but one where circumstances are clearly exceptional, is provided by Nicaragua.

In Brazil, the Workers' Party (Partido dos Trabalhadores—PT), with a national organization and a socialist ideology, has emerged as a significant national force, the most authentic left-wing party in postwar Brazil. The party scored significant successes in the local elections of 1988. It elected a woman mayor of São Paulo. Its leader, Luis Inacio da Silva, better known as "Lula," was only narrowly defeated in the eliminating round of the 1990 presidential elections. The PT, too, has its social democrats.

Nor should one be too dismissive about the left's electoral record elsewhere. In Ecuador the Socialist party and the two Communist parties together in 1988 totaled some 15 percent of the vote, more than the Guayaquil populist Assad Bucaram. The Venezuelan Movement to Socialism (Movimiento al Socialismo—MAS) in the same year increased its share of the vote to 10 percent.

The cases of Chile, Peru, and Bolivia thus appear less exceptional under closer examination. In all three the socialist left is now a great deal less socialist than it at first looks.

Most Chileans have no desire to repeat the experiences of Unidad Popular, and any party that hinted that it might be eager to do so would be unelectable. The years of military government, 1973 to 1988, have altered the bounds of possibility in Chilean politics: experiences in exile and changes in the socialist camp reinforce the memory of failure in 1970–1973. Chilean politicians also have to take into account the degree of support for General Augusto Pinochet that the 1988 plebiscite showed: 43 percent is by no means a contemptible showing, even if several points should be knocked off that percentage to allow for the pressures he and his followers exerted in their bid to win.

The Chilean Communist party has played a prominent role in the opposition to the Pinochet government and has strong support in poor urban districts. It is still influential in the labor movement. Proscription has preserved it from compromise; but in the altered circumstances that now seem likely, it will probably revert to its pre-1973 patterns of activity in Congress and elsewhere. It was the more circumspect element of the Unidad Popular coalition.

It is also doubtful that Izquierda Unida in Peru, if it had come to power in

Peru, would have attempted to repeat anything like the Chilean experiments of Unidad Popular. Izquierda Unida is far more aware than Salvador Allende was of the opposing forces within the democratic arena. In this circumstance Izquierda Unida does not dominate. The APRA, after all, is a party with great historical staying power and will survive the debacle of the post-1985 administration of Alan García. The Peruvian left is also aware of having to deal with forces outside the confines of formal politics, such as an army (not entirely disgraced) that has a long history of intervention and Sendero Luminoso, the most active and fundamentalist guerrilla threat in Latin America. The socialist left in Peru did badly in the 1990 presidential elections.

Likewise in Bolivia, the most left-wing of the main contenders for the succession to President Víctor Paz Estenssoro did not base their appeals on a socialist program. Jaime Paz Zamora, leader of the once left-wing Movement of the Revolutionary Left (Movimiento de la Izquierda Revolucionaria—MIR), has made no pretense of implementing a socialist program since becoming president in August 1989. The Trotskyite left in Bolivia, in common with other leftist political movements based on the mining unions, was in eclipse by the late 1980s.

Elsewhere the performance of parties of Marxist orientation in national elections is unimpressive. Communist parties, independent Marxist parties, Trotskyites, and numerous combinations of the left do participate in national elections in most republics, but typically they make only a small showing. Their importance may be greater than one would conclude from national electoral figures. Many Communist parties are more active in other forms of politics, and even a small minority representation can have significant influence if its representatives are skilled. Party successes may be more significant at various local levels. Participation in elections may form part of a combination of strategies aimed at legitimizing the party concerned. Coalitions may offer useful gains when their minority representation holds a balance, and this can occur in the obscurity of a congressional committee as well as on a more visible stage. Participation likewise brings some share of patronage, and the left builds its clienteles, struggles to protect and increase its slices, just like everyone else. Membership of Communist parties outside Cuba remains small. The largest is that of Argentina, around 70,000. That of Chile is estimated at between 20,000 and 50,000; Brazil, 30,000; Colombia, 18,000.

The activity of the left in trade unions, universities, demonstrations, and in all sorts of other movements, commonly makes it appear more numerous and powerful than it really is. There is a constant cycle of alarm among opponents and disillusion among supporters. Elections bring greater realism to both sides. The general tendency in recent decades has been for more extreme left-wing parties to lose belief in violence as the midwife of change and to come within the pale of the formal electoral system, where the opportunity is available. This was an unnoticed achievement of the second phase of the last Peruvian military government, which set up rules that encouraged, one by one, all the main factions of the Peruvian left (with the exception of Sendero Luminoso) to accept the notion that participation was legitimate.

The Right

Conservative parties—those that can be defined as overtly supporting free-market doctrines, the reduction of state intervention, the paramount importance of anticommunism—are likewise electorally relatively unsuccessful, all in all perhaps even more so than the socialist left.

Confessedly conservative parties, those that go by the name, are now not so common. Even in the nineteenth century, in a Latin America that came to independence under various forms of liberalism, they were a minority. Some of those nineteenth-century parties still exist—in Colombia, for example—and they have elsewhere more or less direct heirs that go by other names. These survivals, however, have survived by evolving.

The Colombian Social Conservative party—it added "Social" to its name in 1988—maintains a regard for tradition and for the Catholic Church when it is conventional or convenient to do so but has long been careful to appeal to all sections of the population. Its economic doctrines are hardly distinguishable from those of the Liberal party, with which it competes for more than nine out of ten Colombian votes. Like the Liberal party, it is a party of the center.

Parties of the old Conservative type persist here and there as provincial survivals, but the 1980s have also seen the emergence of a new conservatism, brought into being by a combination of the pressures of the debt crisis and by developments elsewhere, the free market, and libertarian fashions of the Anglo-Saxon world. The new conservatives are the Latin American proponents of privatization, deregulation, and the drastic reduction of the state sector. One such government was elected in 1982, that of President León Febres Cordero in Ecuador. It emerged from the usual Ecuadorean combination of existing regional and party forces, and its performance was not as extreme as its rhetoric suggested. But it did show that conservative programs do not make a candidate unelectable.

Criticism of the state from this new vantage of the right can find an echo, as the campaign against the nationalization of the banks in Peru and Mario Vargas Llosa's subsequent run for the presidency showed. It can draw on support from private-sector organizations, especially when they overlook the degree to which the private sector depends on the state. It can be backed also by some of the small "informal" sector entrepreneurs, the heroes of Hernando de Soto's *El otro sendero (The Other Path).* De Soto himself is the most widely read popularizer of neo-liberal economic theory in Latin America, and his doctrines have some electoral appeal. Economic liberalism is also the tenet of the Union of the Democratic Center (Unión del Centro Democrático—UCD) in Argentina, where conservative currents can no longer look to the military for support. Despite a poor showing in the 1989 elections, the subsequent UCD alliance with President Carlos Saúl Menem has given UCD substantial influence in economic policy. The revival of conservative ideology can also be seen in Mexico, both in the fortunes of the National Action Party (Partido de Acción Nacional—PAN) and in intellectual circles. In Chile National Renewal (Renovación Nacional), a cross between neo-liberalism and traditional conservatism, is a powerful party with some 20 percent of the vote.

In Central America an avowedly conservative party gained national power through outright electoral victory in March 1989—the National Republican Alliance (Alianza Republicana Nacionalista—ARENA) of El Salvador, where the Christian Democrats failed in the difficult tasks of either coming to terms with or defeating a prolonged guerrilla insurrection. Conservative parties are also strong in Guatemala, where a visceral anticommunism lingers on.

Anticommunism, however, is a misleading note on which to end this short survey of Latin American conservatism. The new conservative elements are more properly ideological. Their arguments are supported by a widespread recognition that interventionist economic models have not guaranteed growth, that social security has not brought welfare to many, and that much of what has been done has been at the expense of the excluded. There are still many obstacles to privatization and deregulation. One is the sensitivity of clientelist politics, which cannot be wished away by political fashion. Another is the vulnerability of much of that vaunted private sector, which depends on the state more than it is often prepared to recognize. Nonetheless, the new conservatism in the air is a force and an influence: in terms of policy, forgetting the rhetoric and labels, the "center" has in recent years shifted to the right.

The Center

Electoral politics is dominated by parties of the center. This is also true of the limited electoral freedoms of Mexico. The PRI is not exactly a party of the right. Its chief contender in the 1988 presidential elections was not the PAN (a party at least capitalist and business oriented in its origins) nor any of the various splinters of the Mexican left. It was Democratic Current (Corriente Democrática), a dissident coalition emerging from the PRI that did not risk defining its own doctrines too narrowly.

In Guatemala conservative parties are indeed important contenders, but the leading party is undoubtedly the Christian Democrats, a party of the center. In the well-established democratic system of Costa Rica the competition is likewise for the middle ground, as it is in the two other long-standing democracies of the region—Colombia and Venezuela. No candidate who fails to maintain a broad appeal to all classes stands a chance of election to the presidency in Colombia and Venezuela. This does not rule out differences of emphasis, various strategies of appeal that emphasize the needs of the poor, and a rhetoric that frequently confuses inexperienced foreign observers. Reading between and behind the lines of the political rhetoric of any unfamiliar country takes a bit of practice. President Rodrigo Borja's Izquierda Democrática (Democratic Left) in Ecuador, for example, may look like a left-wing party. It is certainly less wedded to free-market methods than the preceding administration of León Febres Cordero was, but its only really left-wing attribute is its name. It is moderate social democrat in its policies, and many staid upland bureaucrats, the sort that in earlier eras voted Conservative, figure among its supporters.

Politicians plan their careers. They study the shape of the electorate and what the electorate wants. Radical dissidence from the centrist current plays a part in many a political career, but in the history of elected government in Latin America an emphasis on a narrow sector of the electorate has rarely made a man president. Surveys, admittedly of limited use for probing wider hypotheses about the sort of politics people would like, commonly belie the notion that voters demand revolutionary solutions. Surveys show that voters are interested above all in the hard and immediate facts of life: employment, inflation, the cost of living. Their voting, or their abstaining from voting, normally obeys the most realistic calculation, and it is misleading to view Latin American electorates as peculiarly volatile, the likely victims of unreasoning populist enthusiasms.

The electoral patterns of Latin America show the same persistent patterns as electoral maps elsewhere. There are still areas of uncertainty. The real as opposed to the imposed pattern of Mexican voting has yet to emerge clearly. In Nicaragua and in El Salvador elections have been held only in disturbed circumstances. In parts of Guatemala and Colombia the process is obscured by violence. In Brazil the size of the country and the diversity of its regional politics, combined with the long absence of national elections—no Brazilian under the age of 48 had ever voted for a president before the 1990 elections—makes for a high degree of unpredictability. In Peru increasing violence may distort elections, and in Chile again the new pattern has yet to emerge after sixteen years of General Pinochet. In Paraguay General Stroessner's one-party dominance was until February 1989 the most long established in the hemisphere, five years older than Castro's. Vertically controlled though they were, elections in Paraguay occurred with some regularity under Stroessner's rule, and the most likely evolution of Paraguayan politics after his departure from power will be some parallel to that of the Dominican Republic after the death of Trujillo.

Though to some this successful transition to a system in which governments can lose elections has been surprising, electoral politics only rarely produce big surprises. Voters in general do not vote for the unpredictable. They may not vote for what economists consider the orthodox. The degree to which they will vote against inflation, for example, varies according to the different experiences of the republics. Inflation is never popular, but an inflation rate that an Argentine or Brazilian voter finds not too difficult to live with—a high but steady rate is perfectly compatible with a predictable future—would horrify a Colombian or a Venezuelan. Any government in Colombia or Venezuela that permitted such a rate would suffer inevitable defeat at the next election, if nothing worse. The point is that electorates are not gullible. They do not favor leaps in the dark. Not only are voters connected through many clientelistic and instrumental ties with existing structures of government and administration—there is nothing essentially antidemocratic about many of these ties—but radical structural changes also rarely figure high on their list of priorities.

Populists

What of populism? Voters who do not vote for radical structural change may still be led astray in sufficient numbers by populists: those who put short-term popularity above sober economic calculation, whose programs are not only unsustainable but damaging, who blandish some corruptible sectors of society—unions, or national industrialists, or some region—to the detriment of the whole.

That is a loose description. "Populism" is notoriously difficult to define, and in defining it value judgments are hard to avoid. Most politicians seek in their different ways to be popular, and the technique of Coriolanus, who "did not fawn upon the people," is not a common choice. Most oppositions are less bound by the constraints of reality than most governments. But there have been leaders who surely fit any definition of populism. Juan Perón will always be among the first to come to mind, then a range of prominent Brazilians before 1964, some of whom have lately reappeared—Jânio Quadros, Leonel Brizola. There still are such leaders: Alan García, the former president of Peru (1985–1990), is a good example.

Such figures are not all that common. Nor is their conduct consistent: Perón was not always a populist if the short-term economic calculation is considered an essential part of the definition. In his second term his economic management was rather conventional.

Military rule has not given way to populism in Argentina, Uruguay, or Ecuador, and if Alan García's government in Peru can be categorized as populist, two things must be remembered: first, he succeeded a more orthodox civilian government, that of President Fernando Belaúnde; and then he ended his term facing civilian opposition to the right and to the left that was distinctly less populist. The opposition to General Pinochet in Chile shows no sign of any populist revival.

In the nontransitional case of Colombia, President Belisario Betancur, a Conservative, might be considered more populist than his Liberal successor, Virgilio Barco or Barco's successor, César Gaviria. Betancur had more of the common touch and was for most of his government popular. Nonetheless his economic policies remained wholly orthodox, and when other programs came into conflict with that orthodoxy, they were sacrificed.

The nearest approach to a populist that the Venezuelan electoral system has produced in three decades of uninterrupted competition is Carlos Andrés Pérez. His first presidency coincided with years of extraordinarily high oil revenue in the 1970s, and his return to power in the 1988 elections saw oil prices low and scant prospect of foreign borrowing. The mismanagements of his first period of office were more the result of the euphoria of unprecedented revenues than of populism as such, and it is hard to think that any other Venezuelan president would have resisted that euphoria.

Carlos Andrés Pérez may look for a larger part on the international stage, where Latin America has few experienced and authoritative voices. At home, he is more likely to confound critics who say he will be unorthodox. He is an acute political calculator, knows that he has little room to maneuver, knows the value of surprise, knows that a presidency lasts five years, and now has his eye above all on his place in the history books. His congressional position is also weak.

Fears of returning populism are strongest in the republic that produced Péron, the most striking populist. Many Argentines, faced with the prospect of a third dose of Peronism and with the memory of the 1973–1976 disaster still relatively fresh, reacted with gloom and despair to the prospect of another Peronist government under Carlos Menem. They saw the party's "unreformed" wing as dominant. They feared its dependence on corrupt elements in the labor movement, its lack of experience in national government, its ignorance of the world beyond Argentina, and its propensity to strike dubious political bargains with the military.

To assume, however, that the Peronists have learned nothing from the past would be a mistake. They lost the elections in 1983 because they inspired insufficient trust both as economic managers and as politicians whose relations with the military were equivocal. Menem knows that unless he can do much better than the party did in the mid-1970s, his period of government could lead to the movement's eclipse. Nevertheless, the party is not going to be easily and rapidly transformed by its leaders. It still has memories of historic success: the postwar redistribution of income and civic advance of large numbers of Argentines under Perón's first government. There are good, as well as less good, reasons why the rank and file may prefer old Peronists to the *renovadores* (renovators) who wish to show the movement's more responsible face, a face that is almost indistinguishable from that of certain sorts of Radical.

If elections were so obviously to be won by overtly populist appeals and promises, then such platforms would be universal. They are relatively rare. The renewed appeal of populism in the early 1990s is by no means universal, but where it exists it arises at least in part from the results of eight or more years since the onset of the debt crisis in 1982, in which imports have been suppressed to boost trade surpluses, consumption held down to increase savings, social programs cut, trade unions forced into retreat, state enterprises liquidated, and foreign investors elaborately courted—all to disappointing effect. Furthermore, many nonpopulist governments, including military ones, have contravened economic orthodoxy themselves.

The recent emergence of candidates from the media, or of candidates who make unprecedentedly intense use of the media in their campaigns—Carlos Palenque in Bolivia in 1989, Ricardo Belmont in Lima in 1989, and Fernando Collor in Brazil—might signal a new form of populism. The political views of these figures, however, are mostly conservative.

The danger of populism is not seen exclusively or even principally as one of possible economic mismanagement, however distressing that may be to economists' sensibilities (which should in any case have been blunted by what nonpopulist governments can do and have done). The danger is that some contender in the electoral arena will so far abandon the unstated rules that the game will once again not survive and there will be a return to authoritarian rule.

One essential for the survival of liberal democracy is a degree of consensus about the limits of competition. This consensus can break down in various ways. In Chile in the years prior to the September 1973 coup, the struggle between the Allende coalition and its opponents took on an unsustainable intensity. No country can withstand for long the vast mobilizations of supporters and opponents of the government that became such a frequent feature of political life, and the consequent polarization of the citizenry and lack of any accord on the limits of government action or of opposition response. Had there not been a coup in Chile, there might even have been a civil war. In Colombia after 1946 the attempt by a Conservative government, elected on a minority vote against a divided Liberal party, to sustain and consolidate its power against Liberal attempts to make its exercise of government impossible led to lengthy and widespread violence and eventually to military rule. In Venezuela the first Acción Democrática (Democratic Action) government of 1945–1948 came to an untimely end in part because it gave no sense of security to its civilian political opponents.

The survival of liberal democratic politics cannot be correlated so simply with economic cycles—with "delivering the goods"—as some observers like to think (and some practitioners of politics like to say), and economic factors may well continue to have less importance than a basic consensus on the limits of political competition. Relative prosperity, ascending in gentle curves, doubtless makes the task of governing easier; and persistent breakdowns in basic public services, with their consequent disorders, help destroy consensus. But it is still a mistake to think that the value of democracy in Latin America is that of some short- or medium-term economic plan of a mildly redistributive nature, and that democracy will have somehow failed unless such a plan both emerges and succeeds. A high level of rhetorical criticism of the government in power—no bad thing in any democracy—should not lead one to the conclusion that the critics really believe that all is the government's fault and that a change of system will better their circumstances. For a trade-union movement, recent years of stagnation and recession may have been—frequently have been—a time of frustration and weakening, even in an atmosphere of relative liberty. But even worse times might occur under all conceivable alternative governments—a speculation with which many of the region's union leaders are quite familiar.

The degree of consensus likewise in any particular republic has to be gauged by looking both within and without the formal political system. It does not match simply with the normal indicators of "development." Argentina is the region's notorious example of a society in many ways "advanced" that has lacked political consensus, though it is a particularly Argentine vanity to believe that the country's peculiar breakdowns are "stages" through which all Latin American republics must somehow pass in Argentina's wake. Nor is there a simple progression in time toward greater consensus. Mexicans, for example, were much less divided politically in the 1950s than they are today. The elections of 1988 revealed that the strains of the 1980s had shattered the conventional assumptions of Mexican politics, and it is as yet far from clear how and with what those assumptions are going to be replaced. The Peruvian elections of 1990 did show some sharpening of left-right divisions. The Colombian elections did not.

All the same, within the spectrum of those who practice electoral politics in the region, there may now be more realism and tolerance, less "triumphalism" among the victors and "catastrophism" among the defeated. Venezuela is the clearest example of a system in which such an agreement on political practices derives from a formal agreement between contenders, the Punto Fijo Pact of 1959. This agreement, which was signed prior to Venezuela's first free elections after the dictatorship of Marcos Pérez Jiménez by all presidential candidates, bound all signatories to recognize certain ground rules of politics regardless of the electoral outcome. It has been reinforced by over thirty years of practice, a period which has included two cycles of alternation between the main contending parties. In Colombia the habits of electoral politics persist and even grow, despite high levels of left-wing and right-wing and drug-related violence. In Ecuador liberal democracy has so far survived the recession of the 1980s, the neo-liberal experiment, sporadic military mutinies, and the astonishing level of verbal insult that has always been a part of the comparatively unviolent Ecuadorean political scene. What appears to be emerging in Chile is a civilian politics far removed from the intense rivalries and ideological antagonisms of the late 1960s and early 1970s.

In Argentina, the Peronist defeat of 1983 changed the assumptions of three decades about the electorate; the Peronist victory of 1989 and President Menem's subsequent choice of policies changed some of the assumptions about Peronism. Unfortunately, some observers had entertained an illusion that a middle-of-the-road radicalism was likely to dominate Argentine politics for a much longer period. This was never likely. Argentina's problems are such that they were bound to erode the support of whatever government was elected, and it is unwise to link the survival of the democratic system with the fate of any one party, let alone of any one policy. A chastened Peronism was bound soon to pose a formidable challenge, and much as some Argentines would like somehow to proscribe all but carefully selected Peronists from participation or victory—forgetting that it was in part proscription that for so long preserved Peronism's post-1955 allure—it was wishful thinking to believe that such a historic force would fade rapidly from the scene.

Democratic practices in Latin America must not only give expression to currents that are largely absent from North American politics, such as Marxists, socialists, and other interventionists, but also to others that offend other sensibilities because their ideology is less well defined.

8

Political Actors

Employers' Associations and Professional Organizations

Economic and professional interest groups have been long established in most Latin American countries. Many rural and agricultural societies date back to the last century, as do medical associations. The prime function of most of these associations is to lobby successive governments in their members' interest.

Latin American business, like business in most parts of the world, is closely concerned with government policy. Many professionals are employed by the state and, not surprisingly, business and professional organizations are generous with their pronouncements. John W. Sloan, author of a recent survey of public policy in Latin America, gives this picture of the context of their activity:

> Because of this lack of legitimacy and the political instability that inevitably follows, each sector demands special protection, special administrative representation, special funds, earmarked taxes, constitutional provisions and so forth, to assure that whatever happens politically or economically their particular social sector will maintain its benefits and security. No group has faith in the honesty, impartiality and efficiency of the government. These attitudes then contribute to the inability of the state to rationalize distributive policies in some overall development plan.[1]

Particular economic interest groups are rarely well represented in Latin American political parties, and studies do not show that they commonly exert much direct political pressure. Their role in financing campaigns, for example, is hesitant and indecisive. Few associations are rich, and their members' politics are not necessarily uniform. They do not control or influence votes. Many depend to some degree on government subsidy and support.

Though they often obtain representation on the boards of state entities, they rarely have a predominant say. Most of them regard most governments at best with apprehension.

It is not common for Latin American governments to identify their interests with business. As the Colombian economist Miguel Urrutia has pointed out, there is no Latin American parallel to the dictum "What is good for General Motors is good for the United States."[2] Even an interest group as powerful as the Colombian National Federation of Coffee Growers would only say such a thing in private.

There is no necessary uniformity of opinion on policy among different private-sector organizations. A general defense of private enterprise may unite them, but on specific issues of economic policy—the minimum wage, tariffs, exchange rates—they may well be surprisingly opposed. In Colombia, for example, the National Industrialists' Association (Asociación Nacional de Industriales—ANDI) tends to side with the trade-union federations on proposals to raise the minimum wage. It represents large industries that normally pay well above the minimum wage and whose costs are not affected by such a move, though their markets may be widened.

In their efforts to influence government policy, such associations rely heavily on press coverage of their criticisms. As a free and critical press offers them more scope, they can in that sense be considered a pro-democratic influence. In certain junctures they can play a major political role. In Colombia in 1957 they engineered the overthrow of the military government of General Gustavo Rojas Pinilla. In Chile the *gremio* (association) of independent transport, the truckers, helped to end the government of Unidad Popular in 1973. In the other direction, the Chilean Colegio de Médicos (College of Physicians) became a respected center of opposition to the government of General Pinochet. Under authoritarian governments the direct political role of private-sector organizations sometimes grows, but in opposition rather than in collaboration. Defensive attitudes toward government persist.

Associations are most effective when they can identify their interests with those of a region. Without being ostensibly partisan—most associations avoid party politics, though in Venezuela they tend to mirror them—a regional identification gives an association added political force.

Governments are reluctant to enter into formal agreements on major items of economic policy with private-sector organizations unless trade unions are included in such "*concertación*" (consensus-building). As the beleaguered representative of the general interest of the nation, a government may have an attitude toward a particular association that is as defensive as that association's attitude toward the government. When faced with trade-union pressure, governments commonly seek out employers' associations as a counterweight.

Most Latin American societies do not seem to favor the creation of large monopolies such as those found in Korea, Japan, and Indonesia. The political systems and culture seem hostile to them, though Mexico is something of an exception. There is no clear evidence that the crisis of the 1980s has increased the power of monopolies and large conglomerates.

The power and influence of employers' organizations have been frequently exaggerated. Their interests diverge, and government policies often run counter to them. They vary in the leverage they can exert, and such leverage often depends on the particular conjuncture. The evidence leads one to conclude that employers' organizations can pursue their ends better in open democratic systems, though they will be frequently frustrated and always defensive.

Some associations show signs of enthusiasm for neo-liberal thinking. De Soto's *El otro sendero* is sometimes alluded to by employers who wish to argue for convenient deregulation and to picture the "formal" enterprise as unfairly hampered in its operations in comparison with the "informal." These arguments may be sincere, but they overlook how dependent on state support many Latin American private-sector enterprises are. Most *gremios* tread a delicate path, hoping to obtain measures of state support while avoiding other threats of state interference.

Labor Unions

The current state of Latin America's labor unions and their future prospects must be seen against the background of the evolution of the last two decades.

The Labor Market

From 1960 to 1982 there was rapid economic growth, rapid population growth, and rural-urban migration, as well as the natural increase of urban populations. The economically active population expanded. There were debates about whether employment opportunities could expand sufficiently rapidly, about the significance of the expansion of the service and "informal" sectors of the economy. Without much evidence—the service sector is after all far from homogeneous, and the jobs it offers range from executives to shoeshines—it was assumed that service-sector jobs were low-paying, low-productivity jobs that were nearly a form of unemployment. Broadly, what

Mexico

CALIFORNIA
Tijuana
ARIZONA
NEW MEXICO
Ciudad Juárez
TEXAS
BAJA CALIFORNIA
SONORA
Hermosillo
CHIHUAHUA
Chihuahua
COAHUILA
Monterrey
NUEVO LEÓN
Saltillo
Torreón
TERRITORY OF BAJA CALIFORNIA
DURANGO
Culiacán
SINALOA
Mazatlán
ZACATECAS
Zacatecas
TAMAULIPAS
SAN LUIS POTOSÍ
Tampico
San Luis Potosí
NAYARIT
Aguascalientes
AGUASCALIENTES
GUANAJUATO
QUERÉTARO
Guadalajara
HIDALGO
JALISCO
Morelia
MEXICO
TLAXCALA
Veracruz
Mexico City
FEDERAL DISTRICT
Puebla
PUEBLA
VERACRUZ
COLIMA
MICHOACÁN
MORELOS
Cuernavaca
GUERRERO
Acapulco
Oaxaca
OAXACA
TABASCO
CHIAPAS
GULF OF MEXICO
PACIFIC OCEAN
Mérida
YUCATÁN
Campeche
CAMPECHE
QUINTANA ROO
BELIZE
GUATEMALA
0
400 miles
0
400 kilometers

occurred seems to have been a slow net improvement in the labor market of the countries that industrialized most rapidly—Brazil, Mexico, and Colombia. In Chile, Uruguay, and Argentina—countries with slow population growth rates and a high percentage of employment in the formal sector—there also seems to have been a similarly slow net improvement. Elsewhere high rates of population growth and low rates of industrial growth *probably* meant that there was little significant improvement in the labor market.

A slowing in the growth of the labor force is anticipated for the rest of the century as population growth rates decline, and this slowdown will result in a significant reduction in the pressure on the labor market. It does look, from this point of view, as if at least for the bigger countries the corner has been turned. However, since the debt crisis the labor market has worsened. It cannot be stressed too much that what happens to employment depends on what happens to economic growth generally.

Two other factors affecting the labor market should be mentioned: female participation in the labor force and the changing capital intensity of production.

By international standards female participation in the labor force is low but rising rapidly:

1960: 19.2%
1970: 21.7%
1980: 26.1%
2000: 27.5%

The impact of this trend on the labor market is likely to remain gradual. Women are frequently secondary workers, and their willingness to work depends partly on the income of the male head of the household. Female labor supply is subject to short-term fluctuation. Many women work in areas that are not unionized, especially in domestic service, but there may be scope in white-collar employment for an increase in the numbers of unionized women. Female labor is conspicuously important in the *maquiladora* industries on the Mexican–U.S. border.

There is also a secular trend toward improved labor productivity, which means that the employment effect of new investments will be less. This trend, however, is not likely to make a major impact on the employment situation.

The labor force in agriculture has continued to grow in absolute terms, but it has declined as a percentage of the total—from 54.1 percent in 1950 to 32.4 percent in 1980—while both industry and services have grown rapidly in both absolute and relative terms. From 1950 to 1970 the urban labor force increased from 46 percent to 61 percent of the total, and in 1985 it was estimated at 70 percent. The creation of new jobs will be overwhelmingly in urban areas. Although measures to increase labor absorption in agriculture will continue to be important, the main concern will be with the creation of employment in urban areas.

Most places of work are small and employ fewer than ten workers, but there is in both the public and the private sectors a small number of very large enterprises, which employ a substantial proportion of the labor force. Union strength is concentrated in the large enterprises. The massive number of small enterprises is not likely to decline significantly by the end of the century.

Union Militancy

Everything about unions is highly dependent on the national political context, and things can change very rapidly. Changes in the regulation of industrial relations are frequently associated with changes of regime. Labor law can be altered to make unionization, strikes, and political activity more or less difficult. Unions are frequently involved in politics. Not only do unions bargain with employers to improve wages and conditions, but they also direct their efforts toward the state, in order to improve conditions for labor and in the defense of the general interests of low-income groups. Unions and their confederations often become the spokespersons for popular discontent, and one-day general strikes against government economic policy are not uncommon. Public-sector unions, which make up an increasing share of the unionized total, are of course involved with the state.

From the mid-1970s onward—though with some notable exceptions, particularly Chile—and possibly from an even earlier date, there has been an upsurge in union militancy in Latin America. The extent to which it is associated with the recent trend toward redemocratization is hard to say. In Peru the height of union militancy was reached in opposition to the last phase of military rule, when the unions were in the forefront of much wider agitation for return to civilian rule. Such an explanation, however, does not cover the changes in Colombian unions. Since the onset of the debt crisis the situation has further changed. In some countries the overall level of militancy has remained high (for example, in Brazil) but has become more markedly defensive. In other countries strike activity has declined.

Union Membership and Organization

Growth in union membership is partly a function of growth in the labor force in industry and in government employment and partly a result of changing political conditions. The statistics are more than usually unreliable. Argentina, Brazil, Mexico, and Venezuela tend to have unionization rates between 25 percent and 35 percent, not dissimilar to rates for OECD (Organization for Economic Cooperation and Development) countries. Colombia, Costa Rica, Panama, Ecuador, and Peru have unionization rates of between 10 percent and 17 percent. Unionization rates are highest in mining, plantations, banking, railways, and manufacturing.

Union organization varies from country to country. Enterprise unions predominate. Thus the average size of unions tends to be small, though there is a growing trend to form industrial unions that cover a whole branch of activity. The industrial unions are often large and powerful. The smaller enterprise unions, to promote their interests, usually rely on affiliation with a national confederation and on the political influence the confederation can exert. Regional confederations are often overlooked, though they can be much more consistently effective than national confederations. Unions tend to have exclusive representation at the enterprise level. Most Latin American unions are affiliated with one or another of the international trade-union organizations, most frequently the Regional Inter-American Organization of Labor (Organización Regional Inter-Americana del Trabajo—ORIT), which is affiliated with the social democratic International Confederation of Free Trade Unions (ICFTU). The Christian democratic Latin American Central of Workers (Central Latinoamericana de Trabajadores—CLAT) and the Communist Permanent Congress of Trade Union Unity of Latin American Workers (Congreso Permanente de Unidad Sindical de los Trabajadores de America Latina—CPUSTAL) have much less influence.

Union Corruption

In recent years it has been widely held that many Latin American trade unions were run in an undemocratic and corrupt manner. In lack of union democracy Latin America is not exceptional—outside Scandinavia, unions are not particularly democratic anywhere. *Pelegos* in Brazil and *charros* in Mexico are names for corrupt and accommodating union leaders, though such terms have little precision. Nevertheless, there is a great deal of corruption of one sort or another, and internal democracy in Latin American unions is not widespread. One consequence is faction and division. One reason for corruption is that government subsidies to unions are frequently more important than membership dues, and in many countries union finances are extremely scarce. Yet unions run by bosses can be aggressive when the occasion demands, and union corruption is not incompatible with rising real wages. Indeed, in Argentina union bosses tend to enjoy solid rank-and-file support. As with political parties, tradition counts for a lot. In many Latin American countries the trend may be toward greater internal democracy in unions, though the data are poor. Shifts in union affiliation between one confederation and another sometimes result from frustration with corrupt and ineffectual leadership.

Union Relationships with Government

The degree of independence that union leaders have vis-à-vis government also varies from country to country and over time. In some republics, notably Mexico and Brazil, the general pattern since the 1960s has been for the state to control union activities closely. There is greater freedom now in Brazil, but in Mexico the government is reasserting its control. Union leaders have tended to serve the interests of the state rather than those of their members. But this situation is changing, and it is now fair to say that union leaders in most countries have a great deal of independence from the state.

Neither Alfonsín, Belaúnde, García, nor Sarney, to mention four leaders of the current democratic transition, owed his position to union support. Not one attempted to build a union following while in office. Recent Colombian presidents have been indifferent to the unions as a possible source of party strength, recognizing that the old confederations are dead and that unions do not control votes.

In Mexico 90 percent of unions and union members are affiliated with the umbrella organization Congreso del Trabajo (Congress of Labor), and nearly all of them are affiliated with the ruling party, the PRI. The Congreso is composed of several confederations and a number of individual unions. Major confederations are the Confederation of Mexican Workers (Confederación de Trabajadores de Mexico—CTM) (the largest), the Revolutionary Confederation of Workers and Peasants (Confederación Revolucionaria de Obreros y Campesinos—CROC), the Regional Confederation of Mexican Workers (Confederación Regional Obrera Mexicana—CROM), and the General Confederation of Labor (Confederación General de Trabajo—CGT). The large national industrial unions—mining, metalworkers, railways, oil, electrical workers—and the teachers have weight on their own.

Mexican governments have habitually followed policies of selective favors, sometimes to the detriment of the CTM. Unions linked with the PRI have been rewarded with congressional seats and other political posts all the way down the ladder, and a high level of corruption in the union movement, particularly in the oil workers' union and in the CTM, is generally accepted. In part, policies of selective favors stem from the role of unions in providing applicants for jobs, and from the *planta* (shop-floor) agreements which are widespread in Mexico. Union leaders can sell jobs to individual workers. Unions are believed to receive most of their financing from government sources.

In Mexico the immediate future of unionism is less certain than it is elsewhere in the region. To the long-awaited succession crisis in the CTM that will follow the death of Fidel Velazquez (b. 1900) must be added the poor showing within the PRI of union bosses in the elections of 1988. Their whole relationship with the PRI is now in question. This has been dramatically shown by President Carlos Salinas's decision to jail the notoriously corrupt oil union leadership on charges of gunrunning and conspiracy.

Brazilian unions expanded rapidly during the presidency of João Goulart (1961–1964). After the military coup of 1964, the new military government moved quickly to disable radical unions, removing leftist leaders, totally outlawing some unions, and forcibly suppressing dissent. The present union movement consists of two confederations and a number of independent unions. The General Confederation of Labor (Confederaçao General do Trabalho—CGT) is a politically moderate organization that supports the Brazilian Democratic Movement Party (Partido do Movimento Democrático Brasileiro—PMDB) and the two Communist parties. The Confederation of Workers (Central Unica dos Trabalhadores—CUT) is linked to the Workers' Party (Partido dos Trabalhadores—PT) and has adopted more left-wing and aggressive positions. "Lula", the most well-known leader of the PT, led the metalworkers' strikes in the late 1970s and early 1980s.

During the 1964–1985 military dictatorship, wages dropped initially and then rose for skilled workers while remaining unchanged for unskilled in the "miracle" period 1967–1975. Turnover in the labor force was very high; employers used layoffs and dismissals to keep wage costs down. The most rapid growth in industrial employment occurred in the region of greater São Paulo, where the metalworkers' union became the nucleus of the CUT.

Since 1985 there has been no consistent policy toward the unions. The Sarney government was unsuccessful in appealing for a "social pact," that is an agreement between the government and the unions on restraining wage claims and the broad direction of economic policy. Since the failure of the Cruzado Plan—a drastic attempt to curb the inflation psychology with the creation of a new currency, which dropped three zeros from the old cruzeiro—strike rates have shot up and there were massive strikes, mainly by public-sector employees.

Although most Argentine unions have been Peronist in affiliation, they have normally been riven by factionalism, and the CGT has often existed in the form of two or more separate wings. A central issue that has divided Argentine unions is their relationship with the official Peronist party. Some sections have seen their best strategy in a political struggle for the return of a Peronist government. They rely on state patronage to raise wages. Other sections have sought to deal pragmatically with whichever government has been in office and have adopted the strategy of using their industrial muscle to obtain improvements for their membership. This pragmatism is perfectly compatible with militant tactics.

At the shop-floor level, Argentine unions tend to be strong and well organized, in contrast with unions in nearly every other country. The initial efforts of the Alfonsín government were directed at weakening the hold of Peronism over the unions, but they were unsuccessful. Alfonsín's government also on several occasions proposed some form of social pact or incomes policy. The union response was to enter negotiations but to accept nothing that would result in a fall in real wages. A series of general strikes put pressure on the government. The decline in manufacturing industry somewhat weakened the unions, and the importance within the union movement of the state employees has increased.

Those three brief surveys of Mexico, Brazil, and Argentina help give some impression of a range of different circumstances and union attitudes and practices. Surveys of other countries require different emphases.

Unions in Chile, Peru, and Bolivia

In Chile, before the 1973 coup the union movement had strong links with political parties, the Communists followed by the Socialists, and centered on industry and mining. General Pinochet's government attempted to institute the enterprise union and made lengthy strikes impossible. Restriction, deindustrialization, and high unemployment took their toll of the movement in the sixteen years of his regime.

In recent years Peruvian unions have been among the most militant on the continent. Maoists are particularly strong in the teachers' union, in Peru as elsewhere the largest sector of state employees. Miners and bank workers have been equally militant. The left is at the same time riven with faction, though the last ten years have seen the ascendancy of the Communist-dominated General Confederation of Peruvian Workers (Confederación General de Trabajadores del Perú—CGTP).

In Colombia public-sector employees also showed a marked increase in militancy in the late 1970s. The older confederations, the Confederation of Colombian Workers (Confederación de Trabajadores Colombianos—CTC) and the Union of Colombian Workers (Unión de Trabajadores Colombianos—UTC), which had their origins in alliance with the traditional Liberal and Conservative parties, lost membership to more effective Communist and independent leadership. The movement has remained deeply divided, and industrial membership appears to have fallen in recent years. The problems facing unions in certain sectors, particularly bananas and petroleum, are compounded by physical insecurity and guerrilla infiltration.

In Bolivia the erstwhile mighty Bolivian Workers Central (Central Obrera Boliviana—COB) has suffered a major reverse with the rapid decline of tin mining. This is perhaps the most dramatic example in Latin America of how union fortunes are tied to the industrial structure of a country.

The Political Role of Organized Labor

What general observations can be made about the political role of organized labor in Latin America? The experience of military government has not usually been positive for unions, but qualifications are needed. The Peruvian military radicals for a time encouraged unionization. Then they discovered (as Perón had discovered earlier) that their pet unions were not so docile as they had expected. In Argentina some Peronists have always been willing to work pragmatically with the military. All the same, most military governments attempt to hold down the rate of growth of wages and place severe limits on union organization. For these reasons, unions in countries recently under military rule may prefer democracy. Under democracy they usually have greater organizational autonomy and the scope to maximize their industrial bargaining power.

There are a number of other effects of military government that it is also necessary to note. First it has often, although inadvertently, fostered the emergence of new union leadership. In the past, military governments have attempted to weaken what they considered as politically motivated unionism by a number of means: by shifting power from the central confederations to the enterprise level; by removing those union leaders associated with union activism; by efforts to improve labor productivity and facilitate the dismissal and layoff of workers; and by restricting strikes. Although these policies have been successful in some instances, they have also tended to make it easier for new, younger, and more militant, leaders to emerge from the unions' rank and file. Furthermore, under military government, union actions were most successful when the unions adopted militant and confrontational tactics. One significant consequence of this has been that the unions' leadership is not readily disposed toward cooperation with the civilian successors of the military regimes of the past two decades.

Strikes are relatively infrequent in Latin America. Inflation and the general state of the economy are the principal factors affecting strike activity. When unions strike, they do so overwhelmingly because of wage issues, and strikes are frequently associated with contract renewal. General strikes to protest at government policy are not common, except in Argentina, Colombia, and Peru, but are a factor to be reckoned with in nearly all countries. In general the more common and the more subversive, the less effective they are.

Conflicts between individual unions and employers are about a wide range of issues. Data from several countries indicate that many conflicts arise from complaints of arbitrary dismissal.

Which sectors of the labor force are most likely to resort to strikes? Miners usually have a high strike propensity. Foreign companies are not usually the favorite targets—some observers argue that their unions are the most "domesticated." In the 1970s the metalworkers tended to be the most militant, closely followed by white-collar workers in the public sector and in banking. It now appears that public-sector workers have taken the lead. Bureaucratic productivity is low, and so are wages; teachers' wages in several republics are often in arrears. Governments have attempted to reduce the size of the public sector and to hold the line on wage increases in general by holding down public-sector pay. Legislation that prohibits strikes by public employees often has little effect.

The state sector has been a major employer and a major focus for union organization. What will happen to the state sector? Will it be reduced in size? Will industrial conflicts increase in the state sector? How will governments attempt to control unions in this area now that old party ties and clientelistic methods are no longer so effective? What does the new weight of white-collar public-sector unionism imply for union movements in general? Will the forms of union strength move away from the state sector toward private industry? Little objective study of union affairs is carried out by either employers or universities; and recent changes, the weakening of "traditional" industrial unionism, and the role of public-sector unionism have yet to be generally recognized.

Thinking trade unionists in Latin America might be pessimistic or at least decidedly defensive about the state sector. They would expect layoffs and an increasing number of unwinnable industrial disputes. As a result, while recognizing that the state sector will tend to be a focus for conflict, they would be looking to expand their base elsewhere. They might be too pessimistic. Most government departments have no defense in the form of adequate personnel policies, and most ministers have little experience in industrial relations. Ministers tend to prefer a quiet life within their own ministries and have little to gain politically by intransigence toward their employees' wages, fringe benefits, and perks. An intelligent unionist will want, first, a resumption of economic growth, a *sine qua non* for anything else, but at the same time will be concerned that this growth does not occur at the expense of the workers. All this does not point unequivocally toward any single strategy, but neither does it point to the advantage of *concertación*.

In the immediate future inflationary pressures are likely to be strong, so one option that governments will attempt to explore will be some sort of incomes policy with union support. Are unions willing to cooperate with incomes policies? The arguments are the same as those that have been voiced in the advanced industrial countries. In theory, union support for a well-designed incomes policy will reduce inflation, stabilize the economy, and help provide the basis for sustained economic growth. As a result, real wages and employment ought to grow at an optimal rate.

However, unions typically fear that a number of things may go wrong with this scenario. Governments may not control profits, and there may therefore be a shift in income distribution from wages to profits. For all sorts of reasons, economic growth may not occur, and union restraint will have been in vain. Small groups of workers, perhaps in collusion with employers, may not abide by the incomes policy and may obtain higher wages.

Unions therefore see support for an incomes policy as risky. Where incomes policies have been tried and have failed without substantial political change, workers will be less likely to experiment again. It may be that the democratic process can generate conjunctures that favor a renewal of agreements. The range of their possible content extends from the minimum wage, which is still influential in the level of average wages especially in the least industrialized countries, to social security, health, and housing. The rights of public-sector unions and the more effective judicial enforcement of agreements are also concerns common throughout the region.

Unions cannot be primarily concerned with the establishment or survival of a particular type of regime, and a democracy that fails to enable them to deliver will inevitably be regarded without enthusiasm, despite in some cases memories and in other cases calculations that point to the conclusion that the alternatives are worse. Union membership does not generally determine political attitudes, though in some places correlation is high. Citizens vote, or abstain, and conduct themselves politically according to a variety of determinants—family, locality, education, for example—that may have nothing to do with union membership. Just as the unions played a minor role in the breakdowns of democracy in the 1960s and 1970s in all the countries concerned—in Brazil, Peru, Uruguay, Chile, or Argentina union miscalculations pale into insignificance beside those of the politicians—they are not necessarily a major pillar of democracy restored. In Mexico the union leadership has declared itself against free, open, and competitive elections.

Organizations of Peasants and Rural Workers

Rural-urban migration, the expansion of modern commercial agriculture, some measures of agrarian reform, improved communications, the much diminished importance of old forms of rural dependence, the colonization of new lands, new crops (including marijuana and coca), the increased presence and complexity of the state agencies in rural areas—these have all brought changes to rural politics. They have not all made rural politics less conflictive.

Both *campesinos* (peasants) and landless workers remain hard to organize. Settlement patterns are often dispersed; migrant labor is vulnerable and seasonal; legal and physical protection may be lacking; cultural barriers may inhibit; local situations are bewilderingly varied; and the resistance of landowners and employers can be violent and determined.

The last decades have seen a demise in expectations of radical agrarian reform, despite reforms and expropriations of some significance in Peru, Nicaragua, El Salvador, and Ecuador and piecemeal intervention elsewhere. They have also seen a continuation of "the process in which direct confrontations between those who controlled access to resources and those who desired access to them gives way to one in which the state pays a more prominent and multifaceted role."[3] By the 1960s and 1970s, demands made by the rural poor were no longer directed primarily toward landowners or other elites at the local level but were instead addressed to the state. Governments now have a wide repertoire of responses: limited agrarian reform measures, infrastructural projects, colonization schemes, organizational initiatives, credit programs, social services, and "integrated" development schemes to respond to or to counter specific demands. "Frequently, these responses were sufficient to disaggregate, coopt, diffuse, or relocate potentially threatening peasant protest."[4]

The thrust of popular rural demands is likely to move away from land to the provision of credit, the conditions of marketing, and the provision of services. In Mexico the controversial expropriation of lands in Sonora and Sinaloa by President Luis Echeverría in 1976, rather than marking the revival of an old *agrarista* (pro-agrarian) tradition as he had hoped, seems in retrospect the last gasp of that tradition as well as of his presidency. New currents concentrate more on the reform and democratization of the *ejido* system—the unique form of inalienable village landholding that emerged from the 1910 revolution—to free it from the hands of an overly mighty bureaucracy. In Brazil the supporters of radical agrarian reform were defeated in the 1988 debates in the Constituent Assembly by a more confident, determined, and better organized opposition that was by no means dominated by traditional landowners.

A similar decline in the prominence of demands for the redistribution of land can be detected elsewhere. Conflicts over land are common in Colombia: in regions of colonization and in certain areas where Indian communities have survived and are increasing in population. But agrarian reform is seen as only an ancillary element in any solution to the country's public-order problems, not only by the government but also by the guerrillas, whose rural roots are less apparent now than they once were. The same conclusions can be drawn for Peru.

Bolivia carried out a radical agrarian reform after the revolution of 1952. There is no significant agrarian agitation in Chile, Argentina, Uruguay, or Venezuela.

Elsewhere in this survey it has been pointed out that the absolute numbers of the rural poor have increased. Though their relative political prominence will probably decrease, there is no reason to suppose that the number of conflicts and organizations will decline. The Pastoral Land Commission of the National Council of Brazilian Bishops recorded 916 land conflicts and the murder of 47 rural leaders between 1979 and 1981, involving 260,000 families and more than 37 million hectares (91 million acres). Though such conflicts are often violent, they do not aim at violent confrontation with the state. Where rural movements have become involved with guerrilla movements, they have suffered repression. Attempts to radicalize them for wider political ends have not been successful. Drug cultivation has usually resulted in a decline in rural militancy.

The modernization of agriculture has frequently prejudiced the interests of peasants, whose way of life was often more secure and whose presence on the land more easily tolerated under traditional systems that now occupy less and less of the rural scene. The years of maximum stress resulting from agricultural modernization may be over, as are the years of maximum rural migration.

Other Social Movements

A certain disappointment with the political performance of the organized working classes, or even with the working classes themselves, has focused attention in recent years on a range of movements and organizations that appear to offer a new politics: neighborhood groups, civic movements and strikes, women's movements, ecological and Indian rights organizations, human-rights organizations, single-issue campaigns for specific once-only ends. The 1970s and 1980s have seen a proliferation of such groups. Some are a response to the urbanization of recent decades. The issues that mobilize immigrants and the "informal" sector have little to do with the workplace and the means of production and much more to do with basic living conditions such as housing and transport. Their mobilization is therefore residential rather than workplace. In some countries—Chile and Brazil, for example—the increase in the number of such groups has reflected the restrictions on other forms of political activity under authoritarian governments.

The groups are widely divergent in their size, nature, scope of action, and make-up; and the view that they represent a new politics, popular and autonomous, is exaggerated. They certainly play a widening and deepening role in any democracy, and some offer new opportunities of participation, but their relation with a national-level democratic order is neither clear nor uniform. Some groups are not novel. It has long been recognized that recent migrants in cities are commonly highly organized and politically well integrated. Their neighborhood organizations are neither autonomous, in the sense of separate from the common political system, nor wish to be so. Many of these organizations and movements are directed toward ends that clearly require state intervention, even when such intervention is not explicitly demanded. New movements and tactics—the Colombian *paro cívico* (civic strike) is a good example—are open to infiltration from conventional politics or even from subversive organizations.

Political virginity is always hard to preserve. Movements may start off resolved to have nothing to do with established political parties or the old ways of doing things, but they may soon be faced with the alternative of remaining small and isolated or suffering some degree of co-optation. Many are not as popular as they would like to appear, and they are inevitably composed of citizens who at other times are voters or who may possess or seek government jobs, whose lives are certainly touched elsewhere by politics and the state. These movements still represent hitherto a relatively small percentage of any country's population and frequently lack political sophistication. Nonetheless their ideas may be taken up by major parties. Ecological consciousness has been raised among politicians to a degree unimaginable ten years ago. The Brazilian Workers' Party (PT) has adopted feminist ideas.

Small groups can be effective on single issues. For instance, the Argentine Mothers of the Plaza de Mayo, the most prominent group who focused attention on the disappeared *(los desaparecidos)* during the 1980s, defied government threats and intimidation by holding protest meetings in the Plaza de Mayo. Small groups can be effective at particular times. For example, the Chilean housewives who organized and carried out the "pots and pans" demonstration of December 1971 against the Unidad Popular, in which around 5,000 women marched through the streets of Santiago beating pots and pans in protest against food shortages and Allende's government. Many groups have good international connections and bring international pressures to bear. They make the political atmosphere less parochial and are a channel by which ideas from outside enter the local political process. They are sometimes a useful disguise for hiding the usual electoral ambitions, providing relief from the boredom generated by familiar politicians and familiar parties.

Urban law and order demands attention and has become a political issue in Brazil, Colombia, and Venezuela. It will be improved only in collaboration with neighborhood organizations. The poor suffer more from insecurity than the rich do.

Many movements focus on the problems of life in cities. Urban issues, especially transport and services, are important areas of potential conflict. The activities of neighborhood groups and civic movements may not bring about a "new politics," but it will give these issues greater prominence within the old politics.

Churches

It is an indication of the decline in the Church's role in politics, a decline that has accelerated in the last decades, that more mention has not been made of the Roman Catholic Church in this survey. It is an indication of the relative rise in numbers of Fundamentalist sects that it is now necessary to point out that the Roman Catholic is one among many Latin American churches. The Roman Catholic Church is still by far the largest and politically the most influential. But it is not the fastest-growing church, not the only church with political influence, and in many places not the most successful in its appeal to the urban poor.

The power and influence of the Roman Catholic Church, both as a conservative force and as a potentially radical force in Latin America, is still substantial though commonly exaggerated. An estimated 90 percent of Latin Americans are baptized Catholic, yet only 10 to 15 percent attend mass regularly. The region has a long history of Church-state conflict in republican times. If one had to name a single current, the dominant ideology of Latin America since independence has been liberalism; and liberalism, though the fact is now frequently forgotten, was long anathema to the Church. Political parties in which the Catholic Church exercises some influence, Conservative or Christian Democrat, are outnumbered and commonly outvoted by parties of the secular center, some of which maintain traditions of mistrust or at least wariness toward Church influence.

The role of the Church in education varies from republic to republic but is generally far from dominant. In most countries there are some Church-directed universities and networks of Catholic schools. Nevertheless, even in Mexico, where the Catholic education system is probably the most extensive anywhere in Latin America, slightly less than 10 percent of children attend Catholic schools. Urbanization has reduced the Church's influence further. Urban dwellers are less likely to be practicing Catholics, and clerical influence faces much more competition. Even twenty years ago a prominent Colombian cleric could believe that the Church's hold on the faithful could be preserved by a powerful radio transmitter beaming its message to owners of fixed-band receivers, but the cheap and changeable Japanese transistor made the idea obsolete almost overnight.

The Church's efforts in politics have to be seen against this background: a society still Catholic but less Catholic than the outside world often supposes, and political systems where both lay and anticlerical traditions are strong and where having the Church in opposition (or at least at a distance from power) is not the novelty that outsiders commonly suppose it to be. These limitations are overlooked by those who fear the retrograde influence of "conservative hierarchies" and by those who pin hopes or fears on the progressive forces of "liberation theology." But with this in mind, to what degree can the Catholic Church be seen as supporting democratic systems in Latin America, and where within such systems is its emphasis placed?

The record of the Church in Latin America in the 1970s is not one of consistent opposition to authoritarian rule. In Chile, as the repressive nature of the Pinochet dictatorship became rapidly apparent, the Church did assume an increasingly critical attitude toward the government. The archbishop of Santiago, Cardinal Raúl Silva, was particularly outspoken in his criticism of the regime's abuses of human rights. Together with Protestant and Jewish leaders, the Church helped to establish the Committee of Peace, which provided legal and humanitarian assistance to the victims of repression and their families. By as early as 1975 more than three hundred full-time lawyers, social workers, and medical personnel were working throughout Chile with an annual budget of over $2 million. When this committee was forced to disband, Cardinal Silva replaced it with the Vicariate of Solidarity. The Church's open criticism of the regime was nonetheless cautious, under both Cardinal Silva and his successor Cardinal Fresno. By avoiding confrontation with the government, the Church obtained space to conduct its defense of human rights.

The Church's reaction to the 1964 military coup in Brazil was not nearly as swift as its reaction to similar events in Chile. A significant number of Church leaders viewed the coup as a welcome respite from the social and political turmoil of the Goulart government, and the Brazilian military did not immediately resort to widespread repression as did the Pinochet dictatorship. Not until 1968 was repression intensified, a repression that the Church did not escape. Its publications, radio stations, and rural projects were affected. A number of progressive priests and religious were imprisoned; some were murdered. The hierarchy's opposition to the military grew steadily during the 1970s, and in Brazil the bishops' criticism went beyond simply criticizing violations of human rights to denouncing the injustices of the economic model, the unequal distribution of land, and the treatment of the Indian population. Justice and peace commissions were set up in a number of dioceses, and the Church founded land commissions to promote agrarian reform.

The most striking innovation during the 1970s was the formation of Christian base communities in a number of Brazilian dioceses. Base communities are small groups of Christians from the same barrio or rural community that gather regularly to relate the Bible to sociopolitical reality. They aim to function as the fundamental organizational units of the Church, a goal that necessarily implies a certain decentralization. In the absence of many other channels for political participation, base communities by 1984 were said to number as many as 70,000 throughout Brazil.

The theological and pastoral innovations of the Catholic Church in Brazil make it the most progressive in Latin America. This substantive change occurred in the context of an authoritarian military regime and owed much to the social views of a small but significant number of churchmen. The contrast with Argentina is marked.

The Argentine hierarchy was hostile to Peronism, disliked the violence of the Montoneros (the Peronist guerrilla group), and was concerned about the involvement with them of the small Third World Priests movement. The hierarchy not only greeted the coup of 1976 with a measure of relief—as did many Argentines—but remained mostly silent in the repression that followed. The archbishop of Buenos Aires, Cardinal Aramburu, was quite explicit in his support for the military regime, and in 1982 he embraced General Galtieri in public to express his approval of the Falklands/Malvinas invasion. Despite government persecution of progressive elements within the Argentine Church, it was one of the least effective in defending human rights in Latin America.

The Roman Catholic hierarchies of Chile, Brazil, and Argentina show three quite distinct reactions to the military governments of the 1970s, varying from support to outright rejection. Analyzing the reasons for such variety in great detail is not possible here. The antecedent politics of all three regimes varied, as did the Roman Catholic traditions and cultures of the countries. Argentine Catholicism shares as many characteristics with the Catholicism of Spain and Italy as it does with that of Argentina's Latin American neighbors. Though in Chile, Brazil, and Argentina there was some variety of response from different prelates, far more is at work than the personalities of individual bishops. The fact is that the Church's record as a pillar of democracy is inconsistent. This observation should come as no surprise to anyone with a knowledge of the history of the Church or of the history of Europe.

Nevertheless, the Latin American Church remains the object of naive expectation. Recent changes have not evenly or deeply penetrated the structures of the institutional Church. Although bishops' conferences today speak a more progressive language, and the Church in general tends to show more interest in social issues, the primary objectives remain unchanged. Most bishops continue to see the Church's mission as that of evangelism, the diffusion of an eschatological message of human salvation. Fundamental to this mission is the preservation of the institution of the Church and the Church's influence in society. The centrality of this mission implies stability, unity, and central authority within the Church and all sorts of political alliances. It is not surprising that the Church has responded to social, political, and economic change in a defensive manner.

How strong is the progressive current? The Second Vatican Council and the Second General Conference of Latin American Bishops, which met in Medellín, Colombia, in 1968, stimulated a renewed concern for poverty and injustice. In their wake came the theology of liberation, heavily influenced by Marxism and theories of dependency and by certain currents in European Catholicism. A substantial number of Catholic priests in Latin America are foreign (the region does not produce enough vocations for its own needs). On balance, since the 1960s, the majority of foreign priests have been inclined toward the progressive wing of the Church.

Liberation theologians advocate a complete structural transformation of society. The influence of Marxist analysis, particularly the acceptance of the notion that change is rooted in class conflict, has been a continuing source of controversy. Of no less concern to Church authorities has been the effort to build a grassroots Catholic Church in Latin America, with the base communities as the fundamental units.

In the early 1970s the conservative hierarchies began a counteroffensive. They gained control of the Latin American Bishops' Conference in 1972 with the election of the archbishop of Medellín, Alfonso López Trujillo, as general secretary. In 1979 the Third General Conference of Latin American Bishops at Puebla denounced inequality and injustice in its "consensus document" but was also critical of the use of Marxist analysis and of the political activities of progressive clergy. Base communities were encouraged but were to be subordinated to the Church hierarchy. In Rome, López Trujillo could count on the support of the prefect of the Congregation of Bishops, Cardinal Sebastino Baggio. Baggio controlled the appointments of Latin American bishops and was responsible for formulating the Vatican's Latin American policy.

Baggio's hostility toward liberation theology has been shared by Pope

John Paul II, who made his own views clear at the Puebla conference and on subsequent visits to the region. During his visit to Nicaragua in 1983 the pope expressed particular concern with the matter of doctrinal orthodoxy. He blamed progressive clergy for creating divisions within the Church and ordered them to obey the doctrinal and pastoral directives of their bishops.

The Vatican has good reason to be concerned with the advances made by the progressive sector of the Latin American Church. By the year 2000, Latin Americans will make up almost half of the world's Catholics. Presently, Latin American bishops account for approximately a quarter of the total number of bishops. As long as John Paul remains pope, the Vatican can be expected to continue its efforts to check the influence of liberation theology and progressive elements within the Church. Conservative bishops will be appointed, and more warnings will be issued.

The vision of the Catholic Church swinging its vast influence from the side of the established order to the side of profound social change because of the influence of a new theology is therefore in all respects incomplete and greatly exaggerated. A similar skepticism needs to be directed at the wilder surmises concerning the influence of progressive Catholicism.

Though much attention has been paid to the nuances of papal and episcopal pronouncements, little attention has been paid to their practical political effect. On occasions the Church's power has turned out to be an illusion. Colombia in the 1960s was a republic where the Church was still seen to be both politically influential and, despite exceptions like Camilo Torres, a prominent priest who abandoned his vocation to join the guerrillas, doctrinally conservative. Pope Paul VI issued his denunciation of birth control, the encyclical *Humanae Vitae (Of Human Life)*, just before his visit to Colombia, the first visit of a pope to the New World. Yet the Colombian government and the Colombian people paid little attention.

Further indications of the political implications of religious practices can be found in the growth of fundamentalist sects, usually though not altogether correctly referred to locally as *protestantes*. It is estimated that at the beginning of the century there were only 50,000 Protestants in Latin America. By 1980 there were 10 million, some 3 percent of the total population. They made up then an estimated 22 percent of the population of Guatemala and 18.5 percent of the population of Chile. The rapid increase of Protestantism has been largely the result of the growth of Pentecostal sects among the working classes in urban areas of Chile, Brazil, Mexico, and Central America, especially in Guatemala and El Salvador. Their growth has been exponential since the early 1970s, as high as 15 percent annually in some countries. The sects have had most of their success among the urban poor, particularly newly arrived migrants. The Catholic Church, both through lack of clergy and through its particular nature, may not be able to offer what these people require. The success of Pentecostalism partly derives from its success in the selection and training of leaders, the emphasis on growth, and the mobilization of the entire membership to the winning of converts (traditional Protestants and Fundamentalists rely on the pastor or evangelist).

The rapid increase in Pentecostal sects is likely to continue during the next 10 to 15 years. This growth has political implications. Within Protestantism as a whole in Latin America, one can find a wide spectrum of positions on social and political issues. Pentecostal sects, however, are known for being apolitical and for lacking social commitment. Except for their pronounced anticommunism, most Pentecostals show very little interest in political issues. While the Catholic Church became increasingly involved with social issues during the 1970s, the Pentecostal churches were commonly marked by their withdrawal, though in Chile they were strong supporters of General Pinochet.

It is sometimes argued that since the late 1970s the links between Pentecostals and political conservatives have been growing, particularly in Central America. Many of these sects are financed in part by parent churches in the United States.

The Armed Forces

In the next chapter this survey of the political spectrum—of actors formal and informal, institutional and occasional—examines the forces and potential of the violent left and the violent right. But first attention must be paid to the military—the institution that should monopolize violence, that should stand guard against the adversaries of constitutional government. The object of a degree of study when in power, the armed forces attract little attention when out of power. That is one of the reasons that studies of their political role often appear incomplete.

As the French political scientist Alain Rouquié points out in a recent study, in 1961 the only surviving military dictatorship in South America was that of General Stroessner in Paraguay. He then lists the series of military interventions that followed the March 1962 overthrow of President Arturo Frondizi of Argentina:

July 1962	Peru
March 1963	Guatemala
July 1963	Ecuador

September 1963	Dominican Republic
October 1963	Honduras
April 1964	Brazil
November 1964	Bolivia
June 1966	Argentina
October 1968	Peru
August 1971	Bolivia
February 1972	Ecuador
February–June 1973	Uruguay
September 1973	Chile

Rouquié's observation on the absence of military governments in 1961 and on the foregoing list not only serves as a warning against excessive optimism about civilian government but prompts one to recall the different origins of these successive coups.[5]

Theorists of the mid-1970s, when the entire Southern Cone and Brazil, Bolivia, Peru, and Ecuador were experiencing military rule, were tempted to construct a model of the bureaucratic-authoritarian state and to see it as the logical response to a certain stage in the social and economic development of the region. Though there were similarities in the circumstances that brought about military intervention in, for example, Brazil and Chile (to give only a tactical instance, in both countries left-wing politicians were foolish enough to get involved in naval mutinies), there were greater dissimilarities. The "excesses of populism" can, loosely, be accounted the cause in Brazil, but such a phrase is not accurate for Uruguay, Argentina, or Chile. The recent presence of a not very effective though famous subversive organization, the Tupamaros, contributed to the demise of civilian politics in Uruguay, though it is worth remembering that that occurred some time after the subversion had been defeated. There was large-scale guerrilla, terrorist, and death-squad activity in Argentina, but also hyperinflation and a political conjunction that was spectacularly "exhausted" before the Argentine army took over in 1976. Yet Argentine society, Argentines as a whole, were less polarized than were the Chileans in 1973.

The Peruvian military government took power from a lackluster president without violence, in the absence of any threat to public order, and for its first few years was radical and reformist. There was little repression in Peru and not much in Brazil, even when the Brazilian military became more repressive between 1968 and 1970. The Uruguayan armed forces tortured suspected Tupamaros and jailed a large number, and many Uruguayans went into exile. (Many more Uruguayans died in Argentina and in Chile than in Uruguay.) General Pinochet's repression in the aftermath of the coup in Chile was severe, and violations of human rights continued throughout the sixteen years of his government. But nowhere else outside Guatemala and El Salvador were there as many victims as in Argentina, and nowhere else did repression take such extreme and seemingly irrational forms.

Other dissimilarities are also soon apparent. The Brazilian military evolved a collegiate system of government that on occasion managed the change in the presidency with impressive smoothness. The commanders conducted a gradual and orderly retreat to barracks, reserving their power in many spheres of national life, a retreat that has already occupied more than a decade. After 1976, as before, the Argentine military juntas were riven by faction. Their rule ended in the debacle of the Falklands/Malvinas invasion. The Chilean armed forces showed little sign of disunity in the fifteen years between General Pinochet's seizure of power and his defeat in the plebiscite of 1988, and they seem set to preserve a constitution in which they take a fatherly pride, even after General Pinochet's departure from the center of the political stage.

Circumstances of departure from power are as varied as circumstances of entry into it. Simple explanations do not fit. For example, the desire to avoid responsibility in times of acute economic malaise does not account for General Pinochet's miscalculation in 1988, when he clearly thought that the relative buoyancy of the Chilean economy would favor him.

Nor can one find any high degree of uniformity in the economic policies pursued by these governments. The depth, persistence, and consistency of the free-market models to which in Argentina, Brazil, and Chile (though not in Peru and Ecuador) they at times proclaimed their support varied. Even Chilean severity itself departed from consistency when faced with financial collapse in the early 1980s. That consistency was never matched by the Argentine juntas, which insisted on no interference with military industries—a substantial slice of the public sector—and worried about the level of employment.

It is therefore hard to discern a common bureaucratic-authoritarian theory of economic management. Given that the repercussions of major economic events of the 1970s, such as the first OPEC oil shock, were far from being uniform, the lack of a common theory is not surprising. Nevertheless, some simple conclusions can be drawn. The records of military governments in economic management are variable and not particularly successful. They did not guarantee stabilization, a welcome for foreign capital, or an atmosphere that avoided the extremes of speculation, let alone prudent management of foreign borrowing.

That the legacy of military governments is not impressive is widely recognized within and beyond the region. Achievements and failures naturally vary, but those who sought economic panaceas through military rule were disappointed. The debt crisis, itself related to authoritarian rule, has underlined a disappointment that was already justified before 1982.

The political legacy is naturally harder to measure and in the euphoria of the widespread "transition to democracy" has only recently begun to be analyzed. The experiences of military misgovernment, of repression and exile, certainly revived the appreciation of bourgeois liberties. The theories of the "national security state" were discredited, as were the theories of some guerrillas and terrorists who believed in the late 1960s and the early 1970s that "things had to get worse before they got better" and that provoking repression would forward revolution by "unmasking the oppressors." Though such groups have not entirely disappeared from the countries that experienced severe repression—as the raid at the beginning of 1989 by left-wing guerrillas on the Tablada barracks in Buenos Aires shows—they have no future. Certain revolutionary illusions will never be common again in Brazil, where they were never widespread, or in Uruguay, Argentina, or Chile.

In Chile the rule of General Pinochet shifted the political spectrum to the right. The survival of a substantial Communist party, which is still theoretically proscribed from legal participation by the constitution and which does not disavow the legitimacy of armed struggle in certain circumstances, is not evidence to the contrary. The party's history, one of prudent parliamentary and trade-union action, weighs more heavily than this nuance of doctrine. So does the nature of Chilean society, the relatively peaceful traditions of Chilean politics, and the geography of the country: Chile, in military and policing terms, is a relatively easy country to control.

It is often stated that the experiences of military rule must have brought a learning process to each country concerned. That process has varied, just as the experiences varied. Ecuadorean military governments were particularly bland, and some generals were rather less authoritarian in temperament than were some Ecuadorean civilians. The Peruvian experience remains ambivalent.

In the countries that experienced systematic repression there is a natural tendency to give much prominence to the question of how military violations of human rights should be investigated and sanctioned and to what degree they should be covered by amnesty. There is no indication that either the Brazilian or the Chilean armed forces will tolerate any debate on this matter. Uruguay has been more successful in reaching an acceptable compromise than Argentina, where the issue haunted the entire six-year period of office of President Alfonsín. The judicial problems are as numerous as the political.

Military establishments will naturally remain powerful. Contrary to widespread belief inside and outside Latin America, the armed forces of the region are not disproportionately large nor disproportionately expensive. The clearest exception has in the past been Argentina, where since 1983 numbers and share of budget have been drastically reduced. Nor are these forces by any normal criteria—by the sort of estimates that are used elsewhere in the world—unnecessary. Nor can they be harmlessly deployed in nebulous developmentalist tasks.

Table 8.1

Military establishments as a percentage of population by country, 1984

Country	Population	Active Military Personnel	Force Level as a Percentage of Population
Argentina	28,000,000	187,000	0.67
Bolivia	5,600,000	28,000	0.50
Brazil	125,000,000	264,000	0.21
Chile	11,300,000	93,000	0.82
Colombia	27,520,000	72,500	0.26
Costa Rica	2,200,000	5,000	0.23
Cuba	9,900,000	130,000	1.31
Dominican Republic	5,900,000	22,500	0.38
Ecuador	8,350,000	39,300	0.47
El Salvador	4,800,000	23,130	0.48
Guatemala	7,260,000	18,500	0.26
Haiti	6,000,000	6,575	0.11
Honduras	4,000,000	11,300	0.28
Mexico	71,500,000	123,132	0.17
Nicaragua	2,700,000	16,700	0.62
Panama	1,890,000	10,000	0.53
Paraguay	3,300,000	19,000	0.58
Peru	18,300,000	105,000	0.57
Uruguay	3,000,000	28,500	0.95
Venezuela	17,000,000	40,500	0.24

SOURCE: A. J. English, *Armed Forces of Latin America: Their Histories, Development, Present Strength, and Military Potential* (London: Jane's Publishing Co Ltd, 1984), Appendix 1. Reproduced with the permission of Jane's Information Group.

Table 8.1 shows Latin American military establishments as a percentage of population at the end of 1984. The world average percentage is around 0.65. The highest percentages in Latin America are those of Cuba, Uruguay, Chile, and Argentina. All the rest are below the world average. The percentages of Brazil and Mexico, the two most populous countries of the region, are particularly low. The Latin American average is higher than the African, roughly comparable to that of Asia. In recent years Central American armies have expanded rapidly (Table 8.2).

Military expenditure is likely to fluctuate strongly from year to year because of the occasional purchase of advanced weapons. Recent estimates as

Table 8.2

Expansion of Central American armies between 1977 and 1985

	1977	1980	1985	Percentage of Increase
Guatemala	14,300	14,900	51,600	360
Nicaragua	7,100	[a]	61,800	870
Honduras	14,200	11,300	23,000	160
El Salvador	7,130	7,250	51,150	717
Costa Rica	5,000	5,000	19,800	396

[a]The National Guard had been broken up. No figures are available for Sandinista forces in 1980.

SOURCE: Adapted from R. Benítez, in A. Varas, comp., *Paz, desarme y desarrollo en América Latina [Peace, Disarmament and Development in Latin America]* (Buenos Aires, 1987), p. 89.

Table 8.3

Military expenditure as a percentage of GNP

Country	Percent
Central America and the Caribbean	
Cuba	7.6
Honduras	5.1
Nicaragua	4.2
El Salvador	3.0
Mexico	0.6
South America	
Chile	7.3
Peru	6.4
Bolivia	3.9
Venezuela	2.6

SOURCES: A. Varas, comp., *Paz, desarme y desarrollo en América Latina* (Buenos Aires, 1987), Varas, various; A. J. English, *Armed Forces of Latin America* (London, 1984), Appendix 2.

a percentage of GNP show an average of around 2.7 percent in Central America and the Caribbean and around 3.4 percent in South America (Table 8.3). Argentine figures fluctuate in recent years more than most and have been as high as 8.1 percent of GNP.

Military expenditure in Latin America grew by some 6 percent per year between 1975 and 1985. The rate slowed for South America but increased in

Central America. Total expenditure between 1975 and 1984 was some $150 billion. Seven countries account for 85 percent of the total for that decade:[6]

Argentina	32%
Brazil	12
Chile	12
Cuba	6
Mexico	17
Peru	6
Venezuela	10

Prior to 1982 Argentina and Cuba together accounted for more than one-third of this expenditure. Between 1979 and 1983, four Latin American countries were among the leading twenty arms importers of the Third World: Cuba, Argentina, Peru, and Venezuela. As a proportion of foreign public debt, arms purchases accounted for the following percentages of accumulated debt in 1983:[7]

Peru	50%
Ecuador	33
Chile	31
Argentina	18
Venezuela	17

The highest total of arms debt outstanding was that of Peru, $4.55 billion. Argentina owed $4.45 billion. Latin American total defense expenditures are loosely estimated at around $20 billion a year, or 8 percent of U.S. defense expenditures.

Latin American armed forces buy their arms from increasingly diverse sources and do not depend on U.S. suppliers as they did in the immediate post–World War II era. A study of contracts made between 1969 and 1982 listed[8]

United States	77 contracts
France	47
Great Britain	31
Italy	15
Israel	14
Soviet Union	13
Brazil	10

Brazil and Argentina are the leading arms producers of the region.

U.S. military aid is of little significance apart from the cases of El Salvador and Honduras. Nor is the influence of the United States pervasive in training and doctrine. Israel is particularly active in the region. British naval influence is still visible—for example, in the case of Chile—and the lessons of the Falklands/Malvinas War are a common subject of study. As a result of that conflict, the United States lost some military influence. The Guatemalan army had no difficulty in surviving a U.S. arms embargo (1975–1985) while its campaign of repression was at its height.

It is a characteristic of Latin American political and academic life that civilians show extraordinarily little interest in military or strategic studies, the definition of the military's proper role, and the design of the appropriate establishments for fulfilling that role. Ministers of defense are customarily serving soldiers. There are arguments in favor of this arrangement, which once established is hard to change, but it is symptomatic of a lack of civilian expertise and interest. Proposals for "military reform" are usually conceived solely to restrict military interference in civilian spheres. Their limited scope is understandable enough in the light of recent experience but shortsighted all the same.

Those who would reform the military hope to restrict the armed forces' role to the defense of the nation's territory. This limitation is neither traditional nor realistic. The defense of frontiers and maritime zones is not an illusory preoccupation among Latin American nations, and no country, not even Costa Rica, can delegate it to any benign neighboring power. These considerations, however, are at times overshadowed by concerns of internal order. Peru, Colombia, El Salvador, and Guatemala, for example, are all scenes of guerrilla warfare with no early prospect of peace, situations that are analyzed further below.

The need for an army for the maintenance of internal order is not dependent on the presence or absence of guerrillas or armed subversives. Throughout recent history most countries have maintained substantial armies in peacetime for reasons other than the possibility of wars against their neighbors. The chief exception to that judgment is the United States, at least prior to 1898. Europeans who know something of their own nineteenth- and twentieth-century history should not be surprised that Latin American states maintain armies for the purposes of maintaining internal order. European armies have frequently been larger, and not just because international wars have been more common. In proportion to population, no Latin American republic now maintains an army comparable to that of Spain, with the exception of Cuba. Demonstrations, strikes, "civic strikes," (city- or region-based demonstrations against central government) and peasant marches pose problems of public order, sometimes beyond the containing capacities of the police.

There is no likelihood that these circumstances will rapidly change. Yet there is little evidence of any new thinking in military circles and hardly any evidence at all of civilian thinking in Latin America on the important theme of what each republic's appropriate military establishment should be. Generals as ministers of defense—in 1989 only Argentina had a civilian minister of defense—may learn more about politics, but at the cost of politicians learning less about military matters.

Latin American armies have been slow to adapt to the challenges posed by guerrillas. Nearly all the armies of the region are based on conscription. Only in Argentina has there been some rethinking of conscription, a result of President Alfonsín's drive to professionalize the armed forces, and ironically only in Argentina has conscription approached the universal. Elsewhere it falls overwhelmingly on the rural poor. It is cheap, but it does not produce professional soldiers. The term of enrollment is usually short, and the time of effective service, after training and before demobilization, is even shorter. The educational level of recruits is commonly poor, which limits their effectiveness still further. Though some recruits learn skills and some volunteer for further service in noncommissioned ranks where standards are better, the common systems of recruitment are antidemocratic. Because the sons of the articulate or influential do not serve, wide divisions between civil and military society tend to be perpetuated.

As a result of the Central American crisis and the Falklands/Malvinas War, international preoccupations have taken an expanded role in Latin American military thinking, and there is an increased eclecticism in the military's contacts outside the region and in arms purchases. It cannot be said that the military side of the learning process entailed in military rule has yielded uniform lessons. The different national experiences of Brazilians, Chileans, Peruvians, and others preclude that. Nor can it be said that within a single country the lessons learned are the same for all ranks of the officer corps. The formation of successive generations of officers is a complex process and can produce sharp contrasts within a single army.

The political beliefs of officers are not likely to have been transformed by the recent and current processes of transition. The old belief that professionalization would remove soldiers from the political scene has long been abandoned in its simple version, but there is renewed emphasis on the professional and the technical in the syllabus of army cadets in Argentina. However, it will be some time before some of them become generals. To change the doctrines of officers of higher rank requires authority and tact that few civilians possess, nor do many institutions exist where the transformation can be attempted. Contrary to left-wing beliefs, the United States exercises little influence in these quarters, and even less after the Falklands/Malvinas affair.

Armies will continue to defend their corporate interests. They are normally well placed to do so. The Brazilian military, for example, retains several cabinet positions that it has no intention of relinquishing, and its representatives discuss all policies—including the future of Amazonia, economic policy, and the computer industry—not just those of direct military concern.

Few armies find themselves in so weak a position as the Argentine army after 1982, and military reform in Argentina has proved hard to carry through. The armed forces recovered some ground through the events at La Tablada arsenal in February 1989, which appeared to show that their role would not be confined to defending the frontiers and which clearly demonstrated their need to reequip. Of the forty tanks that were ordered against the arsenal, only seventeen made it halfway and only one arrived at its destination.

Though international tensions in Latin America are not confined to Central America and, beyond Central America, are not at present acute, they do exist, and it is unlikely that they will all be settled by the Columbus anniversary celebrations of 1992. Their consequences in terms of arms expenditure are particularly heavy. The Argentine arms buildup of the late 1970s, the most spectacular in the region in recent times, has to be seen in the context of tensions with Chile. The Peruvian purchase of Mirage jets was justified by reference to potential conflicts with Chile and Ecuador. The Colombian-Venezuelan differences over the Gulf of Maracaibo led Colombia to purchase frigates, Exocet missiles, and submarines. These are expensive items that have little usefulness in dealing with pressing everyday problems of internal order, which are met with inadequate resources.

Some governments are faced with insurgency on a substantial scale. The challenges are not static. Guerrillas in Peru and Colombia are richer and better armed, largely through drug money, than they were ten years ago. The politics of guerrilla warfare is also fluid and does not always favor the guerrillas, but the serious problems posed—widespread insecurity, human-rights violations by both sides, loss of production and investment, sabotage, demoralization, distraction, refugees, counterterror—need to be faced by a far better military and police response than they have received so far. Security and justice at the most basic levels are involved. It is unfortunately the case that policing, too, has also usually been absent from the political agendas of Latin America. Throughout the region private policing, the employment of security guards, has become more and more extensive. It is a resort of the rich and powerful. The acute security problems of the poor are ignored.

Notes

1. J. W. Sloan, *Public Policy in Latin America: A Comparative Survey* (University of Pittsburgh Press, Pittsburgh, PA, 1984), p. 247.

2. M. Urrutia, *Gremios, política económica y democracia (Interest Groups, Economic Policy and Democracy)*, (Bogotá, 1983), p. 76.
3. For a useful summary, see M. S. Grindle, *State and Countryside Development Policy and Agrarian Politics in Latin America* (The Johns Hopkins University Press, Baltimore, Md., 1986), ch. 9, from which these quotations are taken.
4. Ibid. ch. 9
5. Amérique latine: Introduction à l'extrème Occident (Latin America: Introduction to the Far West) by Alain Rouquié, © Editions du Seuil, 1987. Used by permission.
6. A. Varas, comp., *Paz, desarme y desarrollo en América Latina (Peace, Disarmament and Development in Latin America)* (Buenos Aires, 1987), p. 30.
7. Ibid., p. 160.
8. Ibid., p. 60.

9

Political Violence

Guerrillas

There are guerrillas in only four republics. Their numbers are not large. But their resilience stands in marked contrast to the earlier 1960s *foquista* type of guerrilla movement—isolated groups often fighting in remote areas with scant resources, inspired to no small degree by Fidel Castro's victory in Cuba in 1959.

At present four countries have functioning leftist guerrilla armies that have become to a greater or lesser extent part of the political landscape: Guatemala, El Salvador, Colombia, and Peru. In Nicaragua, in contrast, the *contra* guerrillas tried to bring down a left-wing regime, itself the product of a successful guerrilla war. Indeed it was the success of the Sandinistas that led the left in other countries in Latin America and elsewhere to reevaluate the notion of guerrilla struggle, even though the ousting of Anastasio Somoza in 1979 was the result of specific circumstances that do not necessarily repeat themselves elsewhere.

The Threat

The threat posed by the guerrilla movements of the 1980s to the governments they seek to bring down varies significantly.

The strongest and best organized guerrilla movement in Central America is the Farabundo Martí National Liberation Front (Frente Farabundo Martí de Liberación Nacional—FMLN) in El Salvador. It has some 8,000 armed members. Despite the massive economic and military aid channeled by the United States to the Salvadorean government since the beginning of the 1980s, the FMLN continues to maintain control over a broad swath of the highlands along the Honduran border from Chalaltenango in the north to Morazán in the southeast, and in isolated pockets like the Guazapa volcano to the north of San Salvador. Since the FMLN's failed "final offensive" in 1981, El Salvador has become the scene of what is known as a low-intensity war. Neither the government nor the guerrillas are capable of destroying the other. Skirmishes take place more in the rural than in the urban areas. The FMLN is capable of inflicting sharp and spectacular reverses on the government—for instance, attacks on garrison towns and its November 1989 offensive in San Salvador—but is unable to hold such positions for any length of time.

In Colombia, in contrast, despite a long history, the guerrilla movement does not pose the same sort of threat, though it is a major nuisance to the government. There are four separate, though sometimes interlinked, guerrilla organizations: FARC, ELN, EPL, and M-19.

The oldest, best organized, and most numerous force is the Colombian Revolutionary Armed Forces (Fuerzas Armadas Revolucionarias de Colombia—FARC). It has some 6,000 guerrillas in the field, divided between 48 "fronts" that differ considerably in size, effectiveness, and militancy from one area to another. Though its strongest bastion is the so-called *bloque sur* (southern block), the southern departments of Huila and Caquetá, the FARC has fronts also in points as distant as Antioquia, Arauca, and the middle Magdalena valley. In common with other rural guerrilla groups—the National Liberation Army (Ejército de Liberación Nacional—ELN) and the Popular Liberation Army (Ejército Popular de Liberación—EPL), both of them numerically far smaller—the numbers the FARC has in the field grew substantially in the 1980s following a period of stagnation in the 1970s.

The ELN and the EPL are thought to have around 1,000 men each. The ELN concentrates its attacks on the lengthy oil pipeline from the Arauca oil fields to the coast, and the EPL has most of its men in the highly conflictive Urabá banana-growing area and other parts of the northwest.

The M-19, more urban based and given more to guerrilla "theatricals" like the occupation of the Dominican Embassy in 1980 and the Palace of Justice seizure in 1985, has a less stable numerical following than the other groups. In late 1988 armed M-19 militants were thought to number some 500, compared with over 1,000 in the organization's heyday in 1982. The M-19 also had a rural presence, especially around Cali. In the spring of 1990, after prolonged negotiations, the M-19 made its peace with the government of President Virgilio Barco. It sought to change into an unarmed political movement. In this it has been followed by the EPL.

Contrary to the relative complacency with which it was initially greeted in the early 1980s, Peru's Sendero Luminoso grew very rapidly during the 1980s in members and in the geographical area in which it operates. Numbers are impossible to calculate with any precision, particularly as Sendero involves people with different degrees of militancy. The central core is probably quite small (less than 1,000), but those in the outer rims of lesser militancy are undoubtedly a great deal more numerous. Sendero has diversified from the area from which it originated (Peru's poorest and least developed departments of Ayacucho, Huancavelica, and Apurímac in the south) to initiate armed attacks in the central highlands (Junín and Pasco), the northern highlands (Cajamarca and La Libertad), the coca-producing Huallaga valley (Huánuco and San Martín), and, most importantly, to Lima. In Lima, Sendero has seemingly modified its rural-based strategy in favor of building urban support.

In addition to Sendero, and distinct from it, Peru in the mid-1980s saw the appearance of the Revolutionary Tupac Amaru Movement (Movimiento Revolucionario Tupac Amarú—MRTA). (Tupac Amarú was the leader of a major Peruvian revolt against Spanish rule in 1780.) MRTA is more urban based than Sendero, though in 1987 it initiated an unsuccessful *foquista*-type guerrilla action in San Martín. Its numbers do not exceed a few hundred, but its sympathizers may be more numerous, especially in the universities.

The Guatemalan guerrillas, whose roots go back to the late 1950s and who exerted great influence in the mid-1970s, have survived in spite of persistent and often brutal repression by the Guatemalan army. They are concentrated in the departments of Petén and Alta Verapaz, to the northeast of Guatemala City, jungle areas of recent colonization, though they are also present elsewhere. Though numerically small and boxed in by the military, the Guatemalan guerrillas enjoy support among some indigenous groups, which count on the guerrillas to help them defend themselves from outsiders (often from the military) who are increasingly taking control of the land. But in comparison with guerrillas in El Salvador, the Guatemalan guerrillas face a much stronger and determined counterinsurgency apparatus that in the past has played a conspicuous and controversial role in applying techniques novel to Latin America, many of them derived from the U.S. experience in Vietnam. The Guatemalan army has close links with the Israelis and does not rely on air power, the effectiveness of which is commonly overrated in this type of conflict.

The size and extent of the Nicaraguan *contras* is better documented than are those of left-wing guerrillas. At their peak—before the collapse of Edén Pastora's southern front in 1984—the *contras* numbered some 12,000. Until the late 1970s, their main areas of operation were similar to those that initially harbored the Sandinistas, though (more than was the case for the Sandinistas) geared to supply routes from neighboring Honduras and Costa Rica. Major guerrilla zones included the northern coffee-producing area (Jinotega), the southeastern jungle swamps, traditionally rebellious areas in the central highlands, and (unlike the Sandinistas) among the culturally distinct Miskito Indians of the northern Atlantic coast. The pronounced fall in *contra* activity in 1988 with the blocking of U.S. arms supplies by the U.S. Congress and the *contras'* withdrawal back into Honduras indicated one of the major weaknesses of this guerrilla army—its dependence on outside funding.

Ideology of Guerrilla Groups

The leaders of most other guerrilla forces are Marxists of some sort. There is, however, much ideological diversity between different guerrilla groups and even within them.

The Salvadorean FMLN, as was the Nicaraguan Sandinista National Liberation Front (Frente Sandinista de Liberación Nacional—FSLN) before it, is an alliance embracing Social Democrats and even dissident Christian Democrats through to most hard-line Marxists. Their ideological center of gravity has changed with time and according to circumstances, not without violent internal conflicts. The movement's propaganda is strongly nationalist.

In striking contrast stands Peru's Sendero Luminoso, which has its origins in various splinter groups that broke off from the Maoist Communist party in the 1970s. Unlike the rest of Peru's Marxist-oriented parties, which between 1975 and 1981 became involved in electoral politics, Sendero not only spurned the electoral road but rejected any alliance with any of the left-wing parties that joined up to form the Izquierda Unida coalition in 1980. It accused them of being "parliamentary cretins." Strongly sectarian in its ideology and uncompromising in its methods, Sendero sees itself as the successor of Mao and the "gang of four." Though in practice its conduct reveals some degree of pragmatism in adapting its ideology to Peruvian circumstances, it remains a doctrinaire grouping that purveys a spirit of messianic fundamentalism. The MRTA is not out of the same stable, being politically much closer to the more radical wing of the Izquierda Unida. One of its leaders was once a prominent member of APRA.

The Colombian guerrilla scene is more complex. Ideological, tactical, and personal rifts separate the four main guerrilla organizations. The FARC maintains historical but uneasy relation with Moscow-line communism. The ELN has a more strongly defined Castroist ideology reminiscent of 1960s *foquismo.* The EPL comes from a Maoist background—it used to proclaim solidarity with Albania. The politics of the M-19 in its subversive phase were altogether harder to pinpoint, though it was influenced most by the example of the Uruguayan Tupamaros of the late 1960s and early 1970s. The propaganda of both M-19 and the ELN has a strong nationalist streak.

Factors Favoring Guerrilla Movements

It is helpful to identify factors that favor the development of guerrilla groups: social and ethnic conflict, large areas where the institutions of the state are weak, access to funds, and the guerrillas' success in balancing military and political strategies.

Successful guerrilla warfare takes place against a background or tradition of social and ethnic conflict. In rural Latin America a frequent cause of conflict has been disputes over land and access to resources. A common source of conflict is the interaction of modern cash-crop agriculture with traditional forms of landowning. This clash was the driving force of peasant risings such as that of the followers of Emiliano Zapata in revolutionary Mexico. More recently it has given force to guerrillas in Guatemala and parts of El Salvador.

Not all guerrilla leaders seek to mobilize displaced peasants, however. The strength of guerrillas in areas of colonization in Peru and Colombia reflects land disputes of a different sort. And there are land conflicts in areas like Ayacucho in Peru where the old *haciendas* tended to survive the 1970s agrarian reform. The social base for rural guerrilla movements is far from uniform.

Social conflict is also often an expression of ethnic or even regional antagonisms. It is not accidental that many guerrilla movements have a clear ethnic dimension, notably in Guatemala and Peru. In Peru, Sendero Luminoso has been able to take advantage of a long tradition in which whites are seen as oppressors. Despite Sendero's preoccupation with Maoist doctrine, it has successfully adopted the symbols and practices of Indian Peru. In this sense Sendero Luminosa enjoys a strong advantage over a largely non-Indian army. In Nicaragua, the insensitivity of the Sandinistas to the ethnic separateness of the Miskito Indians of the Atlantic coast was instrumental in turning the Miskitos into one of the most strongly motivated of the various *contra* groups.

The leadership of guerrilla groups, however, is seldom drawn from a peasant background. Leaders tend to be better educated, the sons or daughters of middle or even upper-class families. They proclaim frustration with the limitations of conventional politics and argue that they are driven into taking up arms because the political system offers no other methods of opposition or even of survival. In Guatemala, successive military governments drove all opposition underground. In Nicaragua in the 1970s and 1980s and in El Salvador under the military, the regime pushed political dissidents into siding with those engaged in armed subversion. The leadership of Peru's Sendero Luminoso, in contrast, are ultra-radical intellectuals who first ventured into insurrectional politics from a provincial university background.

Nor, too, are the rank and file of guerrilla movements exclusively of rural or peasant extraction. Increasingly members are recruited in cities among the young and underemployed. The Colombian M-19 drew its rank and file mostly from this source. Even Sendero, with its rural bias, is also involved in urban activities, recruiting among teenagers in the poor quarters of Lima and other cities.

The ease with which guerrilla groups mobilize discontent depends a great deal on the existence, or rather the *absence,* of genuinely representative organizations that command popular respect and are able to bargain successfully at the national level. One of the main reasons guerrillas have become active in Andean Peru but not in Andean Bolivia is that in Bolivia peasant unions (as well as other organizations) have had a powerful representative at the national level in the shape of the National Peasant Confederation, a constituent element of the Central Obrera Boliviana (COB). The COB, though driven underground on many occasions, has played the role of mediator. Some see in the decline of its status in recent years a worrisome signal that political tensions may no longer have the same channels through which they can be relieved.

A second key factor that is a requirement for successful guerrilla warfare is the existence of large areas where the institutions of the state are weak, affording guerrilla groups a degree of basic security. Indeed, it was one of the paradoxes of 1960s *foquismo*—the theory that successful guerrilla war could originate from the establishment of *focos,* isolated bases of guerrilla forces—that the *focos* were set up in remote areas, but areas so far from the centers of political power that their direct political impact was negligible. Che Guevara's foray into rural Santa Cruz in Bolivia is but one example. The quest for security is the same today, and either the existence of areas where the state is weak or neighboring countries prepared to turn a blind eye to guerrillas' use of territory are important conditions.

Guerrillas have made the greatest impact in places where remoteness coincides with areas that have economic or strategic significance. The *llanos* (eastern plains) of Colombia are important for the FARC partly because they have become one of the centers for cocaine manufacture. The Huallaga valley in Peru, the country's foremost coca-growing area, has been the scene of struggles for control between Sendero Luminoso and the MRTA. Also, where vital communications pass through remote areas, such infrastructure becomes an attractive target for guerrillas: the various Mantaro-Lima electricity grid transmission lines for Sendero, the Caño Limon–Coveñas oil pipeline for the Colombian ELN.

A third major factor is access to funds. During the 1960s and 1970s political kidnapping and ransoming was the standard means of raising money. Though kidnapping has not disappeared, the drug trade in the 1980s became for many the main source of income. There is a strong correlation between coca and cocaine production and guerrilla activity, especially in Peru and Colombia. This is not to say that the *narcotraficantes* (drug traffickers) and the guerrillas are one and the same. The evidence suggests that they are not, although some working relationships have obviously been established. *Narcos* are the source of money and arms; guerrillas provide military protection, though in some parts of Colombia guerrillas and *narcos* are increasingly hard to distinguish. *Narcos* are even known to recruit their own paramilitary forces from guerrilla ranks. *Narcos* are nonetheless not always well disposed to guerrillas, especially in areas like Urabá and the Middle Magdalena in Colombia, where they have invested in land and have not hesitated to eliminate those who threaten that investment. Nor are *narcos* the only source of money. In Colombia guerrillas have successfully extorted large sums of protection money from oil companies, banana planters, and cattle ranchers.

Financial support from abroad is now more the exception than the rule, especially since Cuba has become less interested in exporting its own revolution. Though Cuba has provided cash and training to the FMLN in El Salvador as well as to other groups, the FMLN has never been wholly reliant on this support. Reliance on foreign assistance would have been a source of vulnerability and weakness. The Nicaraguan *contras* who relied heavily on U.S. financial support are a case in point.

Finally, the development of successful guerrilla warfare tends to hinge crucially on the guerrillas' capacity successfully to combine and balance military and political strategies, either by developing their own political organizations or through establishing ties with other nonguerrilla political organizations. Examples of the synchronization of military and political strategies are to be found in El Salvador, where the FDR and the Convergencia Democrática (Democratic Convergence) have provided the FMLN with political associates capable of building wider public support and acting as intermediaries. The Salvadorean guerrillas have sometimes been able to link their military activities to more widely felt political demands. In Colombia, however, the ties between the FARC and the Communist party have become more of a problem for the party and for the Unión Patriótica (Patriotic Union). Guerrilla activity, uncoordinated with national political strategies, provokes counterviolence from the right and increases public distrust.

Clandestine organizations in seeking to become involved in overt political work face danger. Widening the area of their support without compromising their security is a classic problem faced by all guerrilla organizations. One of Sendero's strengths has been its cellular clandestine structure, which has proved highly effective against infiltration. Sendero compromised this security when it sought to work on a different level through publishing a daily newspaper.

Guerrillas tend to appear in fairly specific circumstances. The "contagion" effect is less automatic than is often supposed: guerrilla conflict on one side of a national border does not necessarily spark conflict on the other side. It is in Central America that possible "domino" effects caused most concern. Though there may be ties between rural or urban insurgents in different countries, circumstances are rarely the same even when countries exhibit many socioeconomic similarities. Conditions differ significantly between Central American countries. Elsewhere, there are fears that the rural violence now so common in Peru and Colombia will spread into Ecuador. Though this could happen, it is significant that Ecuador's tiny Alfaro Vive guerrilla force has not developed in recent years. Southern Peru and Bolivia are similar in many ways, yet the political context is different. Though there is evidence that Sendero-type groups have been at work in Bolivia, they are unlikely to have a major impact there, however unpopular the government in La Paz may be.

Government Response to Guerrilla Activities

Just as the ideologies, tactics, strategies, and composition of different groups differs from country to country, so has the response of the governments they seek to bring down. Responses vary from relentless repression in Guatemala to dialogue and bargaining in Colombia, aimed eventually at disarming the guerrillas and bringing them within the compass of the formal political system.

The response of the military too varies significantly. At its most extreme it has sought physically to eliminate not only the guerrillas but sectors of the population that are potential sympathizers. During the late 1970s and early 1980s the Guatemalan approach involved indiscriminate killing, a scorched-earth policy, and the practice of uprooting whole communities and setting them in new closely supervised "model" villages. This policy was carried out by a combination of regular troops, death squads, and members of the population dragooned into civil defense patrols.

Similar techniques have been adopted by the Peruvian military in their fight with Sendero Luminoso, though the military aims more at meeting terrorist tactics with counterterrorism than at wholesale elimination. Even so, killing (18,000 plus) has been widespread since 1980. The Peruvians have also tried to organize civilian patrols, using local groups to do the fighting as well as troops. But the success rate of the Peruvian military has been less than that of the Guatemalans. They find it difficult to pin down Sendero members or to rally popular support among the peasant communities against Sendero.

The counterinsurgency strategy in El Salvador is different again. The United States is much more directly involved there than in other areas of the region. Anxious to avoid the mistakes of Vietnam, the military has been holding back from trying to wipe the guerrillas out, adopting a less confrontational approach within a low-intensity war. The strategy has centered on responding quickly to guerrilla actions and trying to drive a wedge between the guerrillas and the civilian population. No one loses and no one wins.

As well as creating new economic and political problems for the governments concerned (higher military expenditure, greater power to the military establishment, problems abroad over human-rights violations), the anti-guerrilla approaches have revealed strictly military shortcomings:

- ▼ Weak loyalties and the low degree of professionalism among Latin American armies. Even the Salvadorean army, after a decade of U.S. attention, is still largely a conscript army with only one or two crack units thoroughly versed in counterinsurgency methods. Cases are common of soldiers selling their arms to the guerrillas. The Colombian and Peruvian armies are also largely conscript armies in which morale is usually low and at least half of the period of active service is spent on rudimentary military training.
- ▼ Inadequate logistics in most armies, with the lion's share of military spending going on military equipment that is irrelevant to the conduct of counterinsurgency. More emphasis has to go on communications equipment and basic transport. Helicopters play an important role but suffer the disadvantage of constant mechanical faults that are costly to repair. In 1988 only 15 percent of Colombia's helicopters were said to be operative at any one time.
- ▼ The inadequacy of military intelligence in penetrating guerrilla organizations. Some guerrilla groups, notably Sendero Luminoso, have proved particularly difficult to penetrate. They maintain a tight cell structure and kill people suspected of being informers.

Various governments in the region have examined ways to achieve negotiated peace settlements or at least ceasefires during which talks can take place. Long-term negotiated settlements have proved extremely difficult to achieve.

The Colombian case presents the best example. Colombia's experience has been closely studied by some other governments facing similar problems. President Belisario Betancur's peace policy of the mid-1980s included these key components:

- ▼ Direct and informal contact with guerrilla organizations through peace commissions made up not just of government officials but of a variety of representative persons.

- The offer of full amnesty for those leaving the guerrilla movements and reentering civil life.
- Political reforms aimed at making the system less exclusive and providing political opportunities for former guerrillas.
- The formation of political parties by guerrilla organizations (the Unión Patriótica in the case of the FARC).
- Providing development and rehabilitation programs in areas affected by violence.

The Betancur plan was modified by Betancur's successor Virgilio Barco, but its essential elements remained in place. The plan was an important influence in the thinking that went into the much more ambitious and multilateral peace plan for Central America for which Oscar Arias, president of Costa Rica, won the Nobel Peace Prize in 1987.

There are, however, many stumbling blocks in the way of any peacemaking:

- The difficulty of pursuing a peace process beyond a ceasefire. The Colombian case shows clearly that the guerrillas on most occasions had no intention of handing in their arms. The murder of many Unión Patriótica figures showed the personal risks they were taking in emerging into mainstream politics, and the same has been true of the M-19. The decision by Rubén Zamora and others in El Salvador to run for election in 1989 was a risky strategy.
- Even if a government is prepared to honor a peace process, it may not be able to control those who are not. Colombian *narcos* shot the UP leaders Jaime Pardo Leal and Bernardo Jaramillo, and someone as yet unidentified killed Carlos Pizarro of the M-19 (guerrillas make many enemies). The existence of death squads in Guatemala, El Salvador, Colombia, and Peru gives the guerrillas the justification of self-defense.
- On the other hand, guerrilla leaders prepared to talk peace may not be able to control their own organizations. Dissident factions of the FARC were not prepared to accept the peace process. Assaults on army patrols, kidnappings, and extortions continued to occur.
- Hostility from the military. In Colombia the military was deeply distrustful of the government's ability to handle peacemaking without giving too much away to the guerrillas and affording them all the publicity and prominence they sought.

- The practical difficulties of implementing rural development programs in remote areas when budget restraints are tight and the financial commitment is open-ended. Though Alan García in Peru started off by talking of the need to get rid of poverty, which he linked to violence, his government's achievement in rural development in places like Ayacucho was negligible. The connections between poverty and guerrilla violence, however, are not clear: several Colombian guerrilla zones are particularly rich. Rural development programs can obviously have only a long-term impact.
- The existence of some groups that resolutely refuse to accept any form of discussion or dialogue. Not only military opposition forced Alan García in 1985 to drop his proposal for a peace commission, but also the fact that Sendero Luminoso was totally uninterested in talking to his government or even to representatives of the more left-wing Izquierda Unida. The refusal of Sendero to negotiate about anything is one of the reasons that the Peruvian situation is so difficult.

The Future

As Latin America moves toward the twenty-first century, there is no reason to believe that the present conflicts will be easily resolved, though no likely guerrilla victories are in the offing. In most countries effective state control is likely to expand into remote areas as roads are built and communications are improved. Most countries, too, now have political systems that are more pluralistic and less exclusive than those of the 1960s and 1970s, though that does not necessarily mean (as Peru shows) that all types of guerrillas will respond to peace overtures. With détente proceeding among the superpowers and their surrogates, there appears to be less rather than more foreign collusion in subversion.

A worrisome sign for the future, however, is the growing influence of the drug trade, not just in the producer countries but in transit countries. Few countries in Latin America will be immune as new drug routes are opened up. With the drug trade come plentiful cash and trade in arms, which are likely to stimulate both rural and urban violence, though of a less ideological variety. Guerrillas are corruptible. Drug money may reduce their "legitimate" revolutionary appeal, but Colombian evidence suggests that it increases their numbers, improves their armament, and increases their autonomy. Conflicts will not be solved quickly or easily.

In El Salvador it is hard to envisage how or from where the FMLN will gain the extra military muscle it would require for a successful final offensive.

Nicaragua after the electoral defeat of the Sandinistas in 1990 is not likely to play a belligerent role in El Salvador. It is unlikely that the Bush and future U.S. administrations will stop the flow of aid that has been of crucial importance in improving the Salvadorean army's fighting capacity as well as in underpinning the whole Salvadorean economy. The United States will not desert ARENA as it did Somoza in 1979.

Colombia's own peace plans will also continue to be fraught with difficulties. Though the FARC will continue to be interested in having a quota of at least local political power within formal politics, its members are still reluctant to lay down their arms, since—at the very least—the government cannot provide the guarantees that this action would require. The multifaceted nature of dialogue—not just with four rival groups but with several subgroups within each—makes coordinated negotiation difficult. The political activities of the *narcos* provide a further element that is hard for either side to control.

Finally, Peru is possibly the most intractable situation of all. The military strategy adopted in 1982 has not worked, and Sendero's influence has spread greatly. The route to negotiated pacification is not *transitable* (passable). The virtual certainty that Peru's economy will see further decline means not only that Peru's social problems will get worse but that the capacity of the Peruvian state to respond will deteriorate too. The army, for one, is extremely concerned about its ability to fight a war of counterinsurgency on as many as five or six fronts. In Peru, also, there is the possibility that sections of the hitherto "parliamentary" Marxist left may take up arms against the government.

Violence from the Right

The presence of guerrilla movements, as the Colombian, Salvadorean, and Peruvian cases show, does not necessarily inhibit democratic processes in the wider society. They may even become more significant, as could be argued from the recent electoral history of El Salvador. Guerrillas are nonetheless not only costly in military and economic terms; they exact a high price in distraction and increase the "short-termism" that economic crisis has made such a feature of many Latin American administrations. Threats to public order demand immediate response. But the more threats there are, the harder it is for a government to stick to any coherent plan and muster the executive energy needed to carry it out. Violence frequently obscures the problems of the regions where it occurs, making diagnosis as well as cure difficult.

Violence can intensify friction between constitutional governments and military establishments about how to proceed. Its immediate effect is rarely progressive, and its beneficiaries are not commonly the forces of reform. A common and spectacular consequence is the emergence to new prominence of violence from the right.

Right-wing violence is not always a response to revolutionary violence. Abuses of private power and the private exercise of coercion have a long history and flourish where the power of the state is weak. Latin America still contains areas of frontier far from effective government control. In parts of Brazil and Colombia, for example, these areas can be the scene of violent conflict. Geographical remoteness, however, does not account for much of the death-squad and vigilante activity that takes place in Guatemala, El Salvador, and Colombia, has begun to appear in Peru, and was intense in Argentina in the mid-1970s.

The left has no monopoly of unofficial violence. For a time in Argentina the Montoneros and the People's Revolutionary Army (Ejército Revolucionario del Pueblo—ERP) behaved as if they had, and their leaders may even have believed that they could one-sidedly determine the rhythm of assassination and kidnapping. If so, the response of the "Triple A," the *Alianza Anticomunista Argentina* (Argentine Anticommunist Alliance), must have come as a terrible surprise. It is a simple fact that violence breeds violence. Prior to the 1970s, Argentina was not a particularly violent society. It has no recent legacy of political killing, and neither territory nor society offered what looked like a fertile breeding ground for guerrillas or terrorists. It had once possessed what was regarded as the best and most efficient police force in the hemisphere. All the same, in the chaotic political conditions of the first half of the 1970s, in the absence of any coherent government policy for preventing confrontation, a violent minority on the left was able to provoke an equally violent minority on the right. Argentine governments colluded with death squads before and after the coup of 1976, and Argentine expertise was exported to Central America and to Bolivia.

In Guatemala a self-confident, extremely anticommunist army, for long unchallenged in its exercise of power and indifferent toward international pressures, was prepared to tolerate and to encourage all sorts of methods in exterminating guerrillas and their putative sympathizers. In El Salvador a much less confident and less efficient army and uncertain civilian governments were unable, as well as not always willing, to contain right-wing assassins.

In Colombia, the increase in numbers and prominence of death squads in the 1980s derived from persistent guerrilla and terrorist kidnappings and extortions, the rise of the drug cartels, and the ineffectiveness of the country's judicial system. Explanations must be sought in the pages of Thomas Hobbes rather than in those of Karl Marx. Groups of landowners, sometimes including peasants and often including *narcotraficantes* who had acquired land, responded to guerrilla extortion tactics such as the *boleteo* (sending demand notes backed by unequivocal threats), the *vacuna* ("vaccination" of cattle against rustling and kidnapping by protection payments), and kidnappings (in which Colombia is a statistical world leader) with massacres among populations suspected of collaboration with guerrillas and with assassinations and threats directed against those considered to be sympathizers or apologists.

The Colombian army and the police were often accused of involvement. The judicial system was as incapable of dealing effectively with these accusations as it was of convicting subversives, and a number of vicious circles were in motion. Death squads were the best justification for guerrillas who wished to persist with a strategy that enjoyed no wide popular support and obstructed the exercise of other forms of popular pressure on the government. Guerrillas killed soldiers and policemen, who regarded charges that they were involved with *paramilitares* (as the irregulars of the right are termed) as further evidence of a lack of public sympathy. The police and the military had no confidence in the effectiveness of the civil courts or the military courts in dealing with their opponents. Judicial investigation of charges against military personnel was a thorny, lengthy, and ineffective business.

The examples of Colombia, El Salvador, Guatemala, and even Nicaragua show that guerrilla wars once begun are hard to end. An essential element in the elimination of violence from the right has to be abandonment of the strategy of armed struggle by the left. Such an abandonment, which is not likely to take place as long as violence from the right persists, would be historically and politically complicated. The revolutionary credentials of the Colombian Communist party, for example, are so bound up with the long history of the FARC that any simple disavowal of the FARC's present existence is inconceivable. This explains the Communists' elaborate theorizing about "the combination of various forms of struggle." But without such a disavowal, the electoral front of the Communist party is likely to be the victim of right-wing violence that its perpetrators see as retaliation.

There are other necessary, though not sufficient, conditions for the elimination of violence:

- Greater military competence and sophistication, as well as discipline.
- Better policing. There is a lack of awareness that many of the problems lie more in the realm of policing than in the realm of military action.

- Better civilian intelligence. Civilian governments are often woefully ill served and ill informed.
- Better civil-military relations.

Few of the items on that list can be improvised in the short term. Two further aspects must be stressed. The first is the role of the cocaine trade in the increased violence. It is certainly the single most powerful contributory factor in Colombia in this decade. The second is the fundamental importance of a strengthened and improved judiciary, discussed in the next chapter.

10

Administrative and Judicial Competence

This survey has covered changes of regime, the characteristics of Latin American democracy, political parties, labor unions, the Church, the military, and groups to the left and right outside the spectrum of peaceful and legal politics. It now considers the capacities and competence of government, which do not change so drastically with change of regime.

Military regimes and democratically elected governments alike govern predominantly with civilians, who make up the public administration, the bureaucracy. Relations between citizen and citizen, between citizen and state, are likewise ultimately governed by the judiciary, and it is also ultimately the judiciary that should provide the sanction for the execution of any government's decisions. No survey of political possibilities can be complete that does not explore these dimensions.

Governments' capacities to meet citizens' needs and wants depend on resources, on the performance of economies. The capacities of most, though not all Latin American governments were severely curtailed by the depression of the 1980s. Resources, however, are not the only item to consider when measuring a government's capacity to "deliver the goods." It would be simplistic to argue that the survival of democracy depends on the rapid and favorable resolution of the debt question. That would make of democracy too tender a plant, too inflexible a system, and would imply that the electorate is either irredeemably ignorant or takes an entirely immediate and material approach to politics.

Political performance is also influenced by the quality and degree of honesty of public administration, which is in turn related to the effectiveness of the judicial system. Administrative and judicial competence has received far too little attention not only from political analysts but also from politicians themselves.

Public Administration

Latin American bureaucracies are not especially large. The proportion of the urban labor force in bureaucratic employment is higher than in Western Europe but lower than in Africa. Latin America occupies in this respect an intermediate position (Table 10.1). The expansion of bureaucracies roughly keeps pace with the expansion of GNP. That they are all excessive *in numbers* is therefore open to question.

Bureaucracies have grown with the expansion of state services—education, health, social security—and state enterprise. Public-sector numbers and proportions vary throughout the region.

The complaint that is frequently brought against sheer size is better directed against inefficiency. Most Latin American bureaucrats are poorly paid (notorious exceptions are the so-called "maharajahs" of the Brazilian public sector and the upper reaches of the Mexican and Venezuelan administrations), and bureaucratic productivity is low. Public officials frequently moonlight in other jobs, and corruption is common. One author summarizes criticism of Latin American public-sector bureaucracies as follows:

> Varying proportions of Latin American bureaucracies are characterized by *personalismo* [favoritism], nepotism, job insecurity, high turnover rates, lack of expertise, inadequate use of existing expertise, failure to delegate authority, formalism, stultifying legalism, unsatisfactory information gathering

Table 10.1

Nonfinancial public-service workers as a percentage of nonagricultural employment and of total population

	Percentage of Nonfinancial Public-Service Workers	
	Nonagricultural Employment	Total Population
OECD countries	24.2	9.0
Developing countries	43.9	3.7
Africa	54.4	2.9
Asia	36.0	4.6
Latin America	27.4	4.8

SOURCE: P. Haller and A. Tait, *Government, Employment and Pay: Some International Comparisons*, IMF Occasional Paper No. 24 (Washington, D.C., 1983). Used by permission of the International Monetary Fund.

> and communication, use of bureaucracy to relieve unemployment and lack of coordination among agencies and departments.[1]

Although those complaints are familiar, they do not all have common causes and some are contradictory. Job insecurity is not common in state employment; rather, job security is one of the main attractions of state employment. However poor the conditions, employment is relatively stable. Favoritism and nepotism are insignificant beside the wide range of politically motivated appointments and practices that Latin American bureaucracies share with those of southern Europe, the pervasiveness of which has already been discussed in the context of electoral politics in this study and which are loosely covered by the term *clientelismo* (clientelism).

National Bureaucracies

Clientelismo is not necessarily unpopular and is certainly politically effective. It can be found in many types of regime and flourishes equally in times of prosperity and in times of adversity. It cannot be eradicated by administrative reforms unsupported by strong political forces. Its prevalence is one reason the current economic crisis has not produced greater political instability than it has.

Public-sector unions fight for better conditions for their members, but they do not fight much for greater bureaucratic rationality and increased efficiency. They are too entwined in the patron-client relationships. As a result, poor countries pay too much for inefficient administrations. There are few bureaucratic successes in Latin America. Autonomous agencies, set up in large numbers in the 1960s with the idea that they should avoid the contamination of the old ministries, did not commonly retain their innocence for long.

Responsiveness to the public is in general remote, insensitive, and slow unless members of the public can bring influence or some other form of persuasion to bear. Procedures designed to lay down numerous checks and counterchecks to prevent improper practices—a perpetual ongoing audit that baffles Anglo-Saxon observers—make for delay and actually increase the opportunities for impropriety. Few areas of government administration can attract talent, not only because salaries are low but also because there are no prospects for advancement and no glamour. Ambitious economists may find that spending some time in a well-placed part of a national planning department or in a ministry of finance will help their careers both at home and abroad. Few lawyers, however, will find the same of time spent in a ministry of justice, and even fewer educators will find the same of time spent in a ministry of education.

Talent is attracted to dramatic large-scale projects or to the World Bank's programs, for which governments must raise matching funds and for the furtherance of which they put forward their best people. The consequence is that a government may successfully execute somewhere a major hydroelectric scheme while remaining totally incapable of providing adequate justice or education in the same locality.

For all those reasons, reform of the state apparatus is no simple task and cannot be carried out by ignoring reality. Bureaucrats may be unpopular with the nonbureaucratic public, but they constitute a substantial force and, given their low pay and low status, many are part of the *pueblo* (the common people). Scope and support for privatization in Latin America exist, but the short-term political costs of any attempt rapidly to reduce numbers in the state sector are high. Possible alternatives include avoiding further ill-judged expansion and making administrations work better.

Local Bureaucracies

Local government is relatively underdeveloped in Latin America and typically accounts for no more than 5 percent of total public-sector current expenditure, a low share by comparison with Africa and Asia. The centralist tradition derived from the colonial past has often extended from revenue and expenditure to the direct appointment of local officials by central government.

Local bureaucracies have been characterized by an absence of professionalism. Available funds have been absorbed by the payroll. Attempts by central government to improve the provision of services through autonomous specialized agencies have often produced a mare's nest of overlapping functions and no sense of accountability.

Throughout the region, however, there has emerged a common tendency for decentralization and deconcentration of public-sector activities and for a revival of local democracy. The major features of this new trend are the reform of central-local financial relations, with local government getting a fixed share of the budget (the distribution between municipalities is based on objective criteria); the direct election of municipal leaders; a new rhetoric of participation in local affairs; and the formalization of career structures at the local level.

These changes derive from the increased local consciousness that comes with improved communications. They are also reinforced by the generalized fiscal crisis that so many central governments have suffered from since the onset of the debt crisis in 1982 and by the realization that some burdens and more responsibilities can be shifted.

In spite of the pessimistic traditional view of local democracy, summed up in the proverb "*Pueblo chiquito, infierno grande*" ("A little village is a large hell"), an expansion of the role of local government and the election of local officials offer distinct advantages:

- Local influences have never been effectively controlled by formally centralized systems. Local administrators have enjoyed the advantage of avoiding responsibility and putting the blame on central government. *Caciquismo* (bossism) and *clientelismo* will certainly not disappear with local elections, but who is doing what to whom may become clearer.
- Reserves of talent, civic spirit, and local pride can be tapped. The expansion of higher education in recent years means that there is now no lack of trained personnel for local administration.
- A real outlet is provided for the energies of political minorities, and real guarantees can be given to them against total exclusion from the political system. These advantages can be equally important for conservative parties, for Marxist parties, and for communitarian coalitions.

In 1985 Bolivia revived municipal elections after a 34-year gap. In 1988 Colombia elected mayors for the first time since 1886. In 1989 Venezuela, where formal municipal autonomies have in practice been much reduced by national party domination, passed laws providing for directly elected mayors with a fixed five-year term of office. Similar changes are likely in Mexico.

Brazil has already been something of a leader in local government in Latin America. The election of the PT candidate as mayor of São Paulo in 1988 was the second spectacular gain by the left in a local election in the region (the first was the victory of Izquierda Unida in the Lima elections of 1983). The share of public-sector revenue going to Brazil's municipalities increased from 4 percent in 1979 to 16 percent in 1985 and continues to rise. "Dead at the root" is no longer a just verdict on Brazilian democratic practices in the leading cities of the country.

The most basic premise of democracy is that democratic governments should be responsive. If in the long run democratic forms fail to improve the responsiveness of Latin American governments, then they will have remained mere forms. The picture should not be drawn too dark, however. In certain spheres—for example, in the provision of urban services in expanding cities—one can see the mechanisms working quite well, clientelistic though they may be. Those who want votes see that services eventually get provided—electricity, water, drains, asphalt. But the difference in performance between democratic and authoritarian governments has yet to be clearly demonstrated. There is more to democracy than electricity, water, and drains.

Public Corruption

In theory democratic governments should be less corrupt than authoritarian governments. The varieties and sources of corruption in Latin America also await analysis, but the obvious difficulties of researching the subject are no excuse for ignoring its importance. Governmental corruption is not easily correlated with the age or wealth of a political system, with good times or bad. In certain democracies—in parts of the United States, for example, and in Japan and Italy—practices flourish that are often assumed (not always correctly) to prevail throughout Latin America. Italy, like some Latin American republics, has a large public sector, a private sector heavily dependent on state support and frequently subject to remedial state intervention, and a party system that does not establish clear lines between government and opposition. The result is undoubtedly a high level of corruption in public life. It is a price that this now prosperous country does not much mind paying.

Corruption is not everywhere and at all times such an indifferent matter. In critical times it saps the political confidence of the corrupt: weakness and indecision can derive from a bad conscience. A corrupt politician is one who has chosen to limit his or her own actions on the matter on which he or she is bought but may find that doing so also limits actions and choices across a wider field. For obvious reasons, corruption rarely favors the interests of the poor. A certain amount, necessary grease on the cogs of the machine, can depoliticize some issues and buy off some opponents. Excessive puritanism can have unpleasant consequences for liberty. Nevertheless, corruption beyond a certain degree erodes the legitimacy of governments and of systems. Few would disagree that corruption has increased in the last two decades in Mexico, Panama, Venezuela, Colombia, Ecuador, Peru, Paraguay, Argentina, and Brazil, regardless of the form of government. One of the least corrupt governments has been that of General Pinochet. He inherited a cumbersome but honest system of public administration. The example shows the limitations of simple theory in this question, and perhaps it also helps to explain why Pinochet lasted so long.

Many of these countries are richer than they were. Some increases in corruption were the result of sudden riches—the oil income of the 1970s in the cases of Mexico, Venezuela, and Ecuador—or of sudden illegal riches like drugs as in the cases of Colombia, Bolivia, Peru, and Mexico, with growing ramifications elsewhere. The increases in revenue that occurred in Venezuela after the first OPEC price rise and in Mexico with the vast oil discoveries of the mid-1970s produced unprecedented temptations, which the Mexican system was particularly ill suited to resist.

Democratic systems are vulnerable. But they should not be as vulnerable as authoritarian governments. Vis-à-vis drug money, the government of Colombia has been less corruptible than was the Noriega government in Panama. Drug money is corruption in its most virulent form, as large blandishments are combined with entirely credible threats. Democratic institutions do provide a chance that a government's actions will be subject to some supervision and control, muted by all kinds of calculation though they may be. Authoritarian governments are not commonly honest and are frequently spectacularly corrupt. It is not altogether a coincidence that so much of the region's foreign debt was contracted by such governments. Part of any recovery must be the end of at least some corruption on the grand scale, such as the pharaonic public projects that used to mark each Mexican six-year presidential term.

Corruption can be reduced. The Venezuela of Rómulo Betancourt was certainly less corrupt than that of Marcos Pérez Jiménez. Examples can be set and examples can be made, and the savings may be significant, as well as the political gains. Against a totally defeatist attitude must also be set the cost that a corrupt administration pays in international negotiations. In current circumstances certain types and levels of corruption cannot be sustained. Their political as well as their economic costs will prove too high.

Any government's ability to execute a program depends on the honesty and efficiency of public administration. Efficiency may be increased by some innocuous forms of corruption, but these instances do not counterbalance the distortions, waste, higher costs, and sheer failures to deliver that more frequently result. The control of corruption ultimately depends on the judiciary, the third power, to which too little attention is generally paid.

The Judicial System

Most of the judicial systems of the region share the common defects of the rest of the public administration: complexity, delay, low pay, lack of resources. Too often those best able to defend themselves deplore the results as only a matter of inconvenience to the citizen. The common advice is to steer clear of the judicial system altogether. There is little realization of how fundamental to the proper working of government and the functioning of a democratic system an adequate judiciary is. Without one, there can sometimes be no basic security, as the ability of guerrillas and *narcos* to act without regard to the law in the most violent parts of the region show. The absence of public justice means private justice with all its horrors.

The less spectacular consequences are equally pernicious. Enormous costs, no less burdensome for being frequently indirect, are imposed on those least able to bear them. An inadequate labor code inadequately enforced poisons labor relations. Antique judiciaries have no chance against the advanced sort of international criminal produced by the drug trade. The proper treatment of minorities, a test for all democracies and one on which Latin America's international reputation so often suffers, depends on making law more effective. The efforts to decentralize public administration and to make local government more democratic require reinforcing the local judicial systems. Of all the neglected themes of the last decades, this is perhaps the one that is most important for the survival and consolidation of democracy in this part of the world.

Note

1. J. W. Sloan, *Public Policy in Latin America: A Comparative Survey* (Pittsburgh, 1984), p. 136.

11

Political Prospects

A number of implicit prophecies lurk behind this assessment of the recent development and current state of Latin American politics. This chapter makes them explicit and sometimes more specific.

No intelligent reader should need to be reminded that political prediction is a hazardous business. Earthquakes cannot be predicted, yet they have political effects. Some commentators conclude that the 1973 Managua earthquake was the beginning of the end for Somoza. Nobody predicted the Falklands/Malvinas War of 1982—nobody could have predicted it because it was not meant to occur. Yet it not only ended military rule in Argentina but ended it in a way that had important consequences during the transition to civilian rule.

The same absence of predictability can also be seen in the case of the worst disturbances in Venezuela for several decades: the Caracas riots of February 1989. In the immediate aftermath of the riots, many rushed to connect them with debt, the IMF, and the austerity demanded of debtors. It was also implied by a number of commentators that such unrest was inevitable and, furthermore, that even Venezuela, where one might have expected that belts could have been tightened a few notches without reducing the poor to desperation, could not sustain a genuine democracy.

Yet is such hindsight and pessimism justified? The Caracas riots, the immediate cause of which were sharp price rises—particularly in the domestic price of petrol and in public transport—produced by the implementation of an economic austerity plan by the government of Carlos Andrés Peréz, were spontaneous and unorganized. They were not the result of concerted opposition by political parties. The measures themselves, designed to win IMF support for a substantial rescheduling of current debt maturities and an infusion of new money, were not ill-conceived.

They were, however, poorly implemented. There was too much advance publicity and too little awareness of the effects of delay in certain parts of the program—goods disappeared from shops because shopkeepers had no means of knowing their future wholesale cost. Insufficient control was also exercised over the critical sector of transport—the public unrest was partly sparked by bus drivers increasing their prices by more than was authorized. Another contributory factor was the lack of recent experience among the Caracas police force of disturbances on this sort of scale. The last comparable riots took place some thirty years ago when Vice-President Nixon visited Caracas. This unfamiliarity with large-scale disturbances also partly explains the overconfident manner in which the government handled the introduction of its economic measures. From time to time Caracas and Mérida had experienced student demonstrations that got out of hand, but this was the worst disturbance in decades.

The conclusion to be drawn from Venezuela's experience, and in particular the Caracas riots, are not the oversimplified ones of immediate reaction. Though there have been riots and looting of shops elsewhere—in Argentina, Brazil, and the Dominican Republic—the austerity imposed throughout most of Latin America since 1982 has not been met by violent response. It may have led to more crime, but chaos in the streets has not been a common reaction. Of the major debtors, Venezuela has experienced the least austerity. Explanations of the incidence of disturbance may be sought in relative deprivation and frustration among Venezuelans, but in terms of absolute deprivation Venezuela remains a privileged republic.

The riots produced no political leadership, no demands for political change, no hint of military intervention. The political lesson to be drawn would seem to point to the desirability of more democracy, not less, not in order to embark on some unrealistic populist economic course but to ensure that the government improves its contact with the bases of its own party and with public opinion. Venezuela has since introduced local elections for mayors, who previously were government appointees.

In certain circumstances popular organizations can threaten public order. Civic strikes and general strikes are not always easy to control, but most frequently they are controlled because the organizations behind them feel that they will lose more than they gain by disorder. Subversive groups may have their own plans for such occasions, but they do not create the occasions. They are created by people who ultimately see themselves as talking to governments, which they hope will respond to pressure. They seek to change policy, to redirect resources, not to change governments. Most urban neighborhood organizations appear to be indifferent about what sort of government they deal with or which party is in power. Communitarian organizations, therefore, cannot be regarded as pillars of conventional civilian liberal democratic rule, but at the same time they are interested in pragmatic bargaining, not in widespread disorder.

These observations are preliminaries to an attempt to answer this question: in what circumstances is civilian government likely to break down or to be transformed into something distinctly authoritarian behind a civilian façade?

At various points in the second part of this study, it has been suggested that current and foreseeable circumstances do not favor a return to the excesses of populism. The dangers of such courses are too obvious to the putative populists. In the two republics often considered most prone to populist excess, Argentina and Brazil, neither of the recently elected presidents, Carlos Menem and Fernando Collor, has behaved like a populist. In Chile there is no nostalgia for the *policies* of the Unidad Popular. What Ecuadoreans consider populism, the Guayaquil forces of Assad Bucaram, command only third place in the electorate and are outnumbered by the combined votes of the fragmented socialist and communist left. There is no populist on the Colombian horizon and the designation "populist" never really fit Venezuela's Carlos Andrés Pérez and it won't be heard used of him after the events of February 1989. Neither does the term, loose though it is, have any likely usefulness in Central America or Mexico. The Mexican Corriente Democrática (Democratic Current) certainly differs from the government on economic policy as on the conduct of elections and the future shape of the Mexican system, and its leader (Cuauhtemoc Cardénas) bears a famous and popular name. The movement, however, does not have the characteristics usually associated with the term "populist."

In straitened circumstances most politicians incline toward prudence. The exception of recent years, President Alan García of Peru, was not much of an advertisement for taking too many risks. Bad times and lack of resources make government unenviable, but they alone do not bring governments down. They must be combined with miscalculation and ineptness, or they must deepen into unprecedented crisis. Economic crisis undoubtedly contributes to making cities harder to govern, because services are harder to maintain and expand or subsidize. All governments are aware, for example, of the political sensitivity of urban transport and of energy. The prestige of the Alfonsín government was undoubtedly lowered by the prolonged drought of the summer of 1988–1989, necessitating power cuts and cuts in the Buenos Aires water supply. These inconveniences, however, did not produce widespread protest or disorder: no housewives took to the streets beating empty saucepans; no crucial *gremio* went on strike; no one called for a change of system. All the same, a government that persistently failed to tackle a series of worsening crises of such a sort would undoubtedly risk being overthrown; it would have failed to govern.

An alternative to a breakdown from spontaneous protest or crisis in services is a breakdown that is part of a strategy of terrorism and guerrilla warfare. It does not seem likely that guerrilla activity either in El Salvador or in Colombia will produce a change in the form of government. The Salvadorean army enjoys wide powers and has expanded more in numbers and in the range of its institutional resources under civilian rule than it ever did under previous military presidents. Both from doctrine and from calculation the Colombian army is unlikely to take power unless Colombian civilians fall into far greater discord or act with less than their customary prudence: there would be no obvious gain from doing so, and the risks and losses are plain.

An army is tempted to take power if it feels that its activities are intolerably curtailed; if it feels that it is being subjected to civilian interference in its vital interests; if civilian politics become so conflictive that a substantial part of civilian opinion calls for intervention; if it feels that it can carry out such an intervention without excessive institutional costs. The list is not exhaustive. One can imagine that international disputes might produce coups. One must also consider international opinion and the current inclination—weighty but by no means always decisive—of the United States. Neither national security doctrines, which have been modified rather than abandoned, nor the presence of armed subversion will of themselves produce military seizures of power.

The politically most intractable armed subversion at present is that of Sendero Luminoso in Peru. Colombian and Salvadorean guerrillas are unlikely to fade away rapidly, but the political distance that divides them from the forces that oppose them is by comparison short. Hence the constant, though constantly intermittent, dialogues, ceasefires, and formal and informal truces. In Colombia and El Salvador, both sides know each other rather well, and the rhetoric of "prolonged people's war" leading to socialist revolution needs to be taken with a large grain of salt. Much of the underlying conflict is essentially local in nature, and the inability of the governments concerned to offer physical guarantees is at least as important an obstacle to peace as their incapacity to carry out radical social reforms. In the Guatemalan conflict, as in Peru, there is a strong ethnic element but the balance of forces does not favor the guerrillas. The Guatemalan army is, after the Nicaraguan, the largest in Central America. It is also the most ruthless and most self-confident.

It is in Peru that the strains of resisting insurgency are most likely to produce a coup. At the least, the Peruvian armed forces are likely to demand greater freedom of action, and civil-military relations may become yet more tense. An intensification of conflict in Peru could also produce repercussions in Colombia. Colombia is more likely to be affected than is Bolivia or Ecuador.

Bolivian rural circumstances, history, and political traditions differ from those of the Peruvian *sierra,* and there is no recent guerrilla tradition. The same can be said for Ecuador.

The Brazilian and the Chilean armed forces will preserve their corporate interests during and after the prolonged processes of "transition to democracy" over which they have not lost control. Civil-military relations in Venezuela have been managed without profound disagreements since 1958, and it is unlikely that domestic development will alter this problem or that frontier questions, about which Venezuelan opinion is particularly sensitive, will be so mishandled as to produce a civil-military crisis. The Mexican army is not politically prominent.

Of all the forces of the region, the Argentine military has been the most politicized and the most prone to intervention, and its political divisions have been the most marked. Reading the political entrails of the different branches, factions, and generations involved is a specialized art, conducted through a dense smoke of rumor. The prophets discerned at the beginning of the Menem presidency a division between "liberal-cum-bureaucratic" and "nationalist" currents in the upper ranks of the officer corps, where political initiative have hitherto been made. The nationalists were thought to dream of reproducing Perón's hat trick of a nationalist military in alliance with nationalist trade unions and the masses of the poor. Yet Perón's alliance was unstable and never commanded undivided military support.

President Alfonsín favored "bureaucrat generals" and faced the minor nationalist mutinies of Colonels Aldo Rico and Muhamed Ali Seineldín. Whereas these, though embarrassing the government, failed to effect any significant change, the attack on La Tablada arsenal in Buenos Aires in January 1989 resulted in the creation of a National Defense Council, which in effect restored to the military a role in internal order. It is likely that the intention of reducing conscription from one year to four months will also now be abandoned.

The desire to modernize equipment also pointed the Argentine military toward the United States and to the declared cessation of hostilities in the South Atlantic and resumption of diplomatic relations with Great Britain, a precondition of any major reequipment from that source. By no means all were inclined toward the nonaligned and Latin American orientation identified with Alfonsín's foreign minister Dante Caputo. The new National Defense Council may provide the content with which to bridge the gap between civilians and the military, reducing the isolation of the military from the rest of society, though this bridge building may be more on the military's terms than most civilian politicians are yet inclined to admit. Divisions within the armed forces will persist, and small numbers of civilians will continue to try to exploit them as they have done since 1982. Although there are nationalist elements in the trade unions, the trade unions have yet to show any signs of a new approach to the armed forces. They might do so to oppose the implementation of an orthodox economic plan by a Radical or Radical–Union of the Democratic Center (Unión del Centro Democrático—UCD) government. Though further mutinies and military demonstrations may occur, a seizure of power by the army would still require substantial civilian support, which is nowhere yet apparent.

The most compelling argument for continued democratic civilian rule is that there is no alternative. Arguments from social or economic development, or from the lack of it, are less persuasive: there are no apparent correlations. Nowhere have democracies clearly emerged from changes in social structure, from sudden economic changes, from dawns of enlightenment, or from changes of heart. Most democracies have evolved out of a background of imperfect and limited democratic practice when other methods of government have been seen to fail. Military government is now widely seen as having had little success. It has been repudiated even where most successful, in Chile. There are no convincing revolutionary models. The Soviet Union has no interest in supporting regional conflicts, and Cuba is essentially a moderating influence too. The realistic option for the Latin American left is participation in local government and the agile management of congressional minorities and coalitions, together with the traditional role in trade unions and the more novel opportunities offered by civic, neighborhood and single-issue movements. As has been shown in São Paulo and in Lima, two major cities that in the 1980s elected left-wing mayors, the opportunities or at least the temptations afforded by democratic forms of local government can be substantial. Local administration is unlikely to be transformed in the short term. The left, faced with the overwhelming problems posed by such cities, will probably tackle them in much the same way as its rivals. But the measure of real participation offered to minorities through local elections is important in itself. It can be as important to minority parties of the right as of the left: in Argentina the UCD's most rapid progress has been in Buenos Aires. Such local "apprenticeships" will also have the effect of making it harder for such minorities to be diabolized. It is hard to be diabolical in such a humdrum office as mayor. At least, an elected mayor is unlikely to seem a devil because of his or her party affiliation. Local office can make the role of opposition less of the unqualified disaster that too many Latin American parties consider it to be.

Illusions about democracy's advantages serve only to obscure them. Clientelism—the politics of jobs, favors, and graft—is among the hardiest and most adaptable of political plants. It flourishes just as well in hard times as in good. The power that derives from control over scarce resources can increase with scarcity. Such systems do not depend on ever-increasing bounty. Political honeymoons in Latin America tend to be short, and electoral victories do not seem to bestow much authority. Clientelist machines, alas, deliver votes rather than loyalties, and the votes they deliver are not greatly interested in programs or mandates. Programs and mandates have their limitations in democracies everywhere, but these limitations are particularly apparent in Latin America. Clientelistic practices do not cover the entire map; few parties rely exclusively on them. They do not preclude competition, make elections entirely predictable, or rob governments of all decision and initiative. They are even preferable to some of the alternatives. But they do not contribute to a government's moral authority.

Nevertheless, Latin America's democracies possess advantages that are not illusory and that should be sources of increasing strength. They should perform better in education, particularly in higher education. Though the Brazilian university system was relatively unscathed, the Argentine university system experienced a disastrous decade in the 1970s. First it suffered badly at the hands of civilians, and then it suffered even worse at the hands of the military. Recovery will take a long time. Universities have their own political and sociological significance. Their students demonstrate and aspire to maintain or improve their individual standing—that is generally recognized. Less obvious is the growing need of governments for information and analysis of all kinds. Just as relations between civilians and soldiers in the region must be rethought as a matter of urgency, so must relations between politicians and academics, frequently almost as tenuous as those between soldiers and academics. The strident university of the left is disappearing: the old Marxist certainties no longer attract. Although practical men and women are reluctant to admit it, what is thought in universities does, after some lag, have a practical effect in politics. Some of the surreal activities of the left and many of the activities of those who manage national economies are proof of this. Many politicians are too busy getting votes to have time to think. Many still have an image of their own national universities that is out-of-date. They might do better politically if they exploited their academic resources more: there is less dogmatism, more pragmatism, less theory, more empiricism in the university atmosphere now.

The other advantages of pluralist democracy should be too well known to list. It is more likely—through opposition and alternation, through the function of legislative bodies and uncensored media—to limit government abuses, inhibit grandiose errors, and protect human rights. Virtuous circles can be created. Even the most pessimistic can at least agree that there is some truth for Latin America as well as for Anglo-Saxon America in this observation of H. L. Mencken:

> Turning out gross incompetents, to be sure, does very little practical good, for they are commonly followed by successors who are almost as bad, but it

at least gives the voters a chance to register their disgust, and so it keeps them reasonably contented, and turns their thoughts away from the barricade and the bomb. Democracy, of course, does not work, but it is a capital anaesthetic.[1]

Note

1. Henry Louis Mencken, *A Carnival of Buncombe: Writings on Politics,* edited by Malcolm Moss, with a new foreword by Joseph Epstein. The University of Chicago Press, Chicago and London, 1984, pp. 67–68.

Part

3

ECONOMICS

12

Economic Structure: Resilience and Vulnerability

The economies of Latin America have undergone far-reaching changes in the last twenty-five years. Paradoxically, the changes have increased both resilience and vulnerability to external shocks such as sudden swings in prices and interest rates. The elements of economic management have also changed radically. Who would have thought in 1960, for instance, that the price of cocaine or the U.S. prime rate would today play the roles they do? And, as more and more people have been forced to make work for themselves in the "informal" sector, economic management has become progressively more difficult as more of the economy escapes the reach of conventional management tools.

This chapter sets the scene by summarizing this change in structure and the new elements of resilience and vulnerability. What makes the increase in vulnerability significant is the parallel deterioration in, and greater volatility of, the international economic climate. The first section of the chapter reflects on international trends; the second section turns to trends in the domestic structure of production; the final section considers developments in the 1980s.

Chapter 13 takes up the central issue of macroeconomic policy and its evolution in concept and practice. It looks in detail at the themes of debt, inflation, and commercial policy. Chapter 14 examines welfare issues. Growth prior to the 1980s did not lead to the sharing of benefits by all. Chapter 14 explores this theme in detail and shows that while the structure of poverty became more complex, as parts of the traditional sectors acquired elements of dynamism, the number of those living in absolute poverty increased. Basic-needs indicators showed some improvement, but deficits in health and education remained. Chapter 15 considers prospects.

The International Context

The 1980s confronted Latin America with a world economy that was less stable and less predictable than in earlier decades. Several specific trends originating in the slowdown in the growth of developed countries were particularly damaging to the continent's well-being.

Both the variability and the unpredictability of key variables in the international environment facing Latin America in the 1970s and 1980s increased. Volatility increased for such variables as exchange rates for the major currencies and economic growth rates in the developed market economies. At the same time, there were unpredictable developments like the sharp increase in real oil prices in the 1970s, the subsequent fall of oil prices in the 1980s, the sharp rise in nominal and real U.S. interest rates of the early 1980s, and the drop in commodity prices of the 1980s.

A further problem for the Latin American economies was that in the early 1980s key international economic variables not only became more volatile but evolved in ways that damaged the region's development prospects. As is well known, the rapid growth of the industrial countries, starting in the early 1950s and continuing for the following two decades, started to slow down for structural reasons. In the late 1970s overall macroeconomic policy management in industrial countries became much tighter, particularly after the second large increase in the price of oil. Particularly harmful was the simultaneous shift in the industrial countries toward greater emphasis on monetary policy and reliance on high interest rates. The increase in real interest rates must represent one of the sharpest discontinuities the world economy has experienced. Latin America's growing debt made the region particularly vulnerable to such a change.

Other factors amplified the impact of the resulting recession. The value of commodity exports fell sharply. Decreases in prices were accompanied by proportionately smaller rises, or declines, in volume. Latin America's net barter terms of trade index in 1983 was 26 percent below its 1978 level. Though recovering slightly in 1984, the terms of trade worsened again in 1985 and 1986 and began to improve only in 1989. Another factor that increased the impact of the industrial countries' recession on Latin America was the rise in the exchange rate of the dollar against other major currencies. Since most debt had been contracted in dollars, this rise increased most countries' debt-servicing costs.

As a result of the recession, protectionist tendencies in the United States, Europe, and Japan became stronger, affecting exports of both manufactured and traditional products. Restrictions on traditional exports often took the form of nontariff barriers such as quotas or prohibitions. They were imposed supposedly for other than protectionist reasons, like consumer protection. One example was the "protection" of U.S. consumers from the pesticides said to contaminate Chilean grapes.

This hostile environment impinged on a continent more vulnerable than in earlier years. The changed structure of Latin America's relation with the rest of the international economy represents, if not the worst of all possible worlds, a singularly unfavorable set of circumstances. Reduced trade integration and increased financial integration are a dangerous combination. If countries decide to increase their reliance on foreign finance, they need to ensure that the earnings in foreign exchange will be available in the future to service the borrowing.

Trends in Structure Since 1960

In 1960 the overall picture of the continent still resembled that of a classic developing economy. Primary exports dominated trade, and product concentration was variable but generally high. Industry contributed 22 percent of gross domestic product, ranging from 11 percent in Bolivia to 25 percent in Brazil. Imported consumer goods still accounted for as much as 17 percent on average of total imports and as much as 40 percent in Venezuela and Panama. Agriculture still provided 46 percent of employment, and less than half of the population was urban. In the majority of cases the rural sector still fitted the classic picture of a small export-oriented, plantation-type, modern sector coexisting with a large domestic-market-oriented traditional sector made up of almost feudal *haciendas* and small peasant farms.

The twenty years that followed saw remarkable growth, at least when contrasted with the slow growth of the 1980s. Table 12.1 shows how between 1965 and 1973 the weighted average growth rate of real GDP in Latin America was 7.4 percent, while in South Asia it reached only 4.1 percent. Even East Asia achieved a "mere" 8.3 percent in the same years. Since so much recent writing has castigated Latin America for its failure to match the Asian experience, these figures act as a corrective. Even for the decade 1970–1980, Latin America's growth rate at 5.8 percent was not far below that of East Asia at 8.0 percent and significantly exceeded that of South Asia. The United States, meanwhile, grew less than 2 percent per year during this period.

The most dynamic sector in this pattern of growth was industry. Latin American manufacturing increased rapidly during the 1960s and 1970s. Output at constant prices grew at more than 6 percent per year throughout the

Table 12.1

Comparative economic performance: GDP growth rates in Latin America and elsewhere, 1965–1988

	1965–1973	1970–1980	1980–1983	1984–1988
Latin America				
Argentina	4.3	2.2	–2.8	–1.9
Brazil	9.8	8.4	–1.3	3.7
Chile	3.4	2.4	–3.4	5.5
Colombia	6.4	5.9	1.4	4.3
Mexico	7.9	5.2	0.6	7.3
Peru	3.5	3.0	–2.9	0.6
Venezuela	5.1	5.0	–1.8	2.6
Weighted average	7.4	5.8	–1.1	2.7
East Asia				
Indonesia	8.1	7.6	4.8	3.3
Korea	10.0	9.5	7.3	10.0
Malaysia	6.7	7.8	6.2	5.6
Philippines	5.4	6.3	2.2	1.3
Taiwan	10.4	9.2	5.4	9.3
Thailand	7.8	7.2	5.4	5.4
Weighted average	8.3	8.0	5.3	6.5
South Asia				
Bangladesh	—	3.9	3.6	3.9
India	3.9	3.6	5.4	4.3
Pakistan	5.4	4.1	5.3	7.3
Sri Lanka	4.2	4.1	5.3	3.9
Weighted average	4.1	3.7	5.4	4.5

SOURCE: A. Fishlow, "Some Reflections on Comparative Latin American Economic Performance and Policy," *WIDER Working Papers,* no. 22 (August 1987); IMF database; and ECLAC, *Preliminary Overview of the Economy of Latin America and the Caribbean, 1989* (Santiago, December 1989).

two decades. The rate of growth peaked in the late 1960s and early 1970s. Despite the adverse impact on the region of the first oil shock in 1973, respectable rates of growth were maintained until 1980.

Industrialization

The bedrock of Latin America's increased resilience lies in the development of industry and with it the diversification into new export lines. In the 1960s the fast growth of manufacturing was still sustained principally by import-substituting industrialization. In most countries these years were characterized by falling import coefficients and negligible exports of manufactured products. In 1965, for example, the region's exports of manufactures were worth less than $750 million, compared with total exports of $10.1 billion. In contrast, since the late 1960s the region has seen a rapid expansion of manufactured exports and a parallel growth in imports of manufactured goods.

In real terms, Latin American exports of manufactures grew at an annual rate of 14 percent per year in the 1960s and 1970s. Such exports were boosted by specific trade promotion policies. In some countries, most notably Mexico and some of the Central American and Caribbean countries, export-processing zones were established. In these zones, firms could set up assembly facilities to produce for world markets, free from the import and other restrictions that normally governed domestic production.

Paradoxically, or so it would seem, the various regional integration initiatives that took off during the 1960s and 1970s were not a major reason for the expansion. Economic integration began with the formation of the Latin American Free Trade Area (LAFTA) (originally comprising Argentina, Brazil, Chile, Mexico, Paraguay, Peru, and Uruguay) in 1960 and continued with the formation of the Central American Common Market encompassing El Salvador, Honduras, Guatemala, and Nicaragua in 1961 and the Andean Pact (Bolivia, Colombia, Ecuador, Peru, and Venezuela) in 1969. The hope was that reduced tariffs within the region would stimulate trade and industrial growth and lead to economies of scale that, in turn, would help promote international competitiveness. All of these programs, however, ran out of dynamism as the "easy" concessions came to an end—that is, concessions on products not produced by both partners in the negotiation. Continued development of these regional integration schemes required a greater degree of administrative sophistication and of political will to overcome conflicts of interest and mutual distrust. Neither was present in sufficient quantity.

As a result, intraregional trade did increase, both in absolute and in relative terms, but much of the increase was in primary products. The Central American Common Market and the Andean Pact helped boost manufactured exports in many of the smaller Latin American countries. But in the larger republics the shift of manufacturing production toward the export sector was only marginally affected by regional integration schemes. Thus, for the region as a whole the growth of manufactured exports was determined primarily by sales to the rest of the world.

Despite their rapid growth, however, manufactured exports continued to account for only a small share of industrial output. Even when manufactured exports are broadly defined to include processed raw materials, less than one-fifth of production was exported in most countries. Moreover, Latin America's trade deficit in manufactured goods ($56.5 billion in 1980) continued to widen until the debt crisis hit.

The most significant change in the structure of manufacturing output since 1960 has been the continued decline in the share of nondurable consumer goods. For the region as a whole, the decline was mainly accounted for by the increased share of industries producing inputs for other sectors; the share of capital goods and consumer durables remained virtually unchanged between 1960 and 1979. Even in the most advanced countries of the region (Argentina, Brazil, and Mexico), with the largest capital and consumer durable goods industries, nondurable consumer goods accounted for only a quarter of industrial production, compared to over half in the developed market economies.

This, then, is one indicator of the limited nature of the increased resilience. If the transport equipment industry, a large part of which is made up of car production, is excluded from the figures given above, capital goods account for only 19 percent of manufacturing in Brazil, 14 percent in Mexico, and 12 percent in Argentina. Among the smaller countries in the Andean region the capital-goods sector accounts for less than 10 percent of production and throughout Central America, apart from Costa Rica, less than 5 percent. As a result, capital accumulation in Latin America continues to be highly dependent on imports of capital goods, and industrial growth continues to require substantial foreign-exchange earnings.

Despite the limited growth of the capital-goods sector, an impressive aspect of industrial development has been the growth in technological capacity in the last twenty years. This key element in terms of increased resilience reveals itself in the growth of exports of more technologically sophisticated products from the region, the growth of technology exports through licensing agreements, the sale of "turnkey" plants (plants complete with the required technology), and direct foreign investment by Latin American firms themselves. Though in general the technology gap relative to the developed world continues to grow, some local firms have become internationally competitive on the basis of their technological efforts.

In Argentina, Brazil, Colombia, and Mexico local firms in industries using batch production, such as capital goods and pharmaceuticals, have competed successfully with multinational subsidiaries in domestic and neighboring markets on the basis of indigenous technological capabilities. Although learning has also occurred in continuous process industries, only in Brazil have such firms become internationally competitive. Brazilian firms, with their large and rapidly growing domestic market, have succeeded in approaching the international technology frontier in industries such as steel and machine tools. Elsewhere in the region, however, small-scale production has often prevented internationally competitive levels of production from being achieved.

A feature that has increased both resilience and vulnerability at the same time has been the central role of multinational corporations in industrial growth. Although they contributed to the technological development just described, they also weakened indigenous entrepreneurial and technological capacity, given the easy access they provide to foreign sources of both. In the 1960s multinationals were the most dynamic element in the growth of Latin American industry. The protectionist policies of the import substitution era, together with liberal policies toward direct foreign investment, led to local production by firms which had previously exported—i.e., "tariff-hopping," since they were anxious to preserve their Latin American markets. The multinationals played a major role in dynamic industries such as chemicals, motor vehicles, rubber products, and electrical goods. Their rapid expansion in this period gave rise to a denationalization of local industry. In Argentina, Brazil, and Mexico, for instance, the share of multinationals in manufacturing output increased from under 20 percent in the early 1960s to around 30 percent by the early 1970s.

In the 1970s, the multinational share of industrial production stabilized. It even fell in a number of Latin American countries. In Argentina, for example, the share of multinational production was 30.8 percent in 1973 and 29.4 percent in 1983; in Brazil the multinational share of industrial capital fell from 34.4 percent in 1971 to 22.5 percent in 1979. The decline was partly a result of restrictive policies toward foreign investment introduced in a number of Latin American countries during the 1970s and partly a result of changing strategies by the multinational companies themselves. The result has been the growth of new forms of foreign investment that do not rely on majority shareholdings in local subsidiaries.

Diversity in the Latin American Economies

Within this regional story there have been strong variations. The two largest countries, Brazil and Mexico, have been particularly dynamic. There, industrial output grew at well above the average rate for Latin America as a whole in the 1960s and 1970s. As a result their share of the region's manufacturing increased from less than 50 percent to well over 60 percent. These two countries have also consistently attracted the bulk of direct foreign investment in the region, averaging over 70 percent of the total in this period, as well as having contracted the bulk of commercial loans to the region. There are signs, particularly in Brazil, that a more advanced industrial structure has emerged with the development of a local capital-goods industry. Both Mexico and Brazil have become important exporters of manufactured goods. The sales of the *maquiladora* industries clustered along the U.S.–Mexican border have been particularly buoyant. These factories assemble products from duty-free imported components and re-export the result.

The experience of the Southern Cone countries (Argentina, Chile, and Uruguay) stands in stark contrast. In 1950 these countries had been the most industrialized in Latin America in terms of per capita manufacturing output. Subsequently, however, they experienced low rates of industrial growth. Following the military coups of the 1970s, they adopted policies that encouraged deindustrialization by cheapening imports. This trend was particularly marked in Argentina and Chile. Inspired by the neo-classical critique of import-substituting industrialization (described in the next chapter), these regimes pursued policies of trade liberalization, that together with overvalued exchange rates and high domestic interest rates led to plant closures, falling employment, and declining industrial output.

The Andean Pact countries, aware that their small domestic markets made industrialization difficult, attempted in the 1970s to develop key sectors through a policy of joint industrial programming. With the exception of Ecuador, these countries had grown at rates well below the Latin American average in the 1960s. But despite the ambitious plans the countries made little progress in developing regional sectoral programs in engineering, steel, petrochemicals, and automobiles.

Finally, the Central American Common Market countries, in contrast to those of the Andean Pact, experienced rapid industrial growth in the 1960s. It averaged 8.5 percent per year, compared with 6.7 percent for Latin America as a whole. Rapid growth was stimulated by the expansion of agricultural exports, and the formation of the common market and the increase in intraregional trade. In the 1970s, however, the process lost impetus, and the rate of growth fell below the average for the region as a whole. The decline was largely due to interruptions to integration such as the conflict between Honduras and El Salvador, which upset trade between those two countries for the whole of the 1970s.

Primary Exports

More widespread than the phenomenon of new exports of manufactures has been diversification within the primary export field. Exports of cut flowers from Colombia, shrimp from Ecuador, and fruits and vegetables from Chile, Central America, and the Caribbean are examples of how improved transport and communications, combined with growing technical skills (particularly in marketing), have permitted the region to expand the range of primary commodities in which it enjoys a comparative advantage. Within this picture of increased diversification, however, many countries remain extremely

Table 12.2

Primary exports as a percentage of the merchandise exports of fourteen Latin American countries, 1986

Export	Percentage of Merchandise Exports		
	More Than 90%	75% to 90%	50% to Less Than 75%
Oil	Venezuela Ecuador		Mexico
Minerals	Bolivia (tin) Chile (copper)		
Agricultural raw materials[a]		El Salvador (coffee) Argentina (maize) Colombia (coffee) Paraguay (soybeans) Nicaragua	Brazil (coffee) Uruguay (beef) Costa Rica (coffee)
Balanced exports[b]		Peru	

NOTE: Main primary exports are in parentheses.
[a]Includes fisheries and forestry.
[b]No commodity group accounts for more than 30 percent of primary exports.

SOURCE: World Bank, *World Development Report, 1987* (Washington, D.C., 1987), p. xx; Inter-American Development Bank, *Economic and Social Progress in Latin America, 1987 Report* (Washington, D.C., 1987), pp. 474–476.

dependent on traditional primary product exports and therefore continue to be vulnerable to unfavorable trends in their markets (see Table 12.2).

There has also been a geographical diversification of markets. In 1975, the developed market economies took 65 percent of Latin America's exports of agricultural raw materials, 80 percent of its ores and metals, and 72 percent of its fuels. Ten years later, the corresponding figures were 54, 65, and 71 percent. Among the developed countries, Japan has emerged as a major buyer of Latin American copper, iron ore, and bauxite. The decline in the relative importance of the most developed economies as an export destination for the region's primary exports contrasts with the growing significance of new overseas markets in the Soviet Union, Eastern Europe, and other developing countries, particularly in Asia.

In view of the changes in the commodity composition of Latin America's primary exports since 1960, the most striking feature is the rapid growth of fuel exports, which reflect the emergence of Mexico and, to a lesser extent,

Ecuador as major petroleum producers. The fuel share of Latin American primary exports nearly doubled between 1970 (26 percent) and 1980 (48 percent).

However, treating Latin America as a whole hides important variations in countries' dependence on primary exports and in their mix of commodities. This is illustrated by Table 12.2, which classifies fourteen Latin American countries by these two criteria using data for 1986. Four countries (Venezuela, Ecuador, Bolivia, and Chile), all of them exporters of oil or minerals, still depend on primary exports for over 90 percent of their export revenue.

Vulnerability, Resilience, and Performance in the 1980s

The economic structure of production and exports of Latin America thus changed significantly after 1960. On balance the changes and the growth put the region's economies on a healthier footing. Nevertheless, overall, the continent was more vulnerable to international influences than before, for two major reasons.

First, despite the growth in nontraditional exports, the drop in Latin America's share of world trade during the 1960s and 1970s was greater than that of the rest of the developing world. The fall was in part the product of a deliberate option in favor of import substitution. At the time, the implications of this option for exports were not clearly perceived. Unfortunately, when the policy of import substitution was reversed in the 1970s, the reversal was in the context of world markets that were becoming more difficult to penetrate, especially because the recession of the late 1970s encouraged protection and in the OECD countries productivity was increasing.

Thus today Latin America has a low share of trade in relation to its GDP and continues to depend greatly on primary exports. In this respect there is a clear contrast with South Korea and Taiwan (see Table 12.3). This situation makes for greater vulnerability to fluctuations in primary product prices. At the same time it makes adjusting to a given external shock more difficult because the export base to be used for adjusting is relatively small compared to GDP. Meanwhile, after years of import substitution, Latin America's import structure tends to be inflexible. Imports of consumer goods have fallen to 10 percent of the total, and for some countries food is an important percentage of the intermediate category. By contrast, Taiwan and South

Table 12.3

Indicators of financial and trade structure at the onset of the debt crisis (1980–1981) in selected Latin American and Asian countries

	Structure of External Financial Relations		Trade Structure		
	Percentage of Debt at Floating Rates	Interest Payments as Percentage of Exports	Exports as Percentage of GDP	Exports as Percentage of Tradeables[a]	Basic Commodity Exports[b] as Percentage of Total
Latin America	64.5	28.0	13	27	76
Argentina	58.3	15.1	7	15	79
Brazil	64.3	28.3	9	19	60
Chile	58.2[c]	28.2	20	47	85
Colombia	39.2[c]	16.3	15	26	76
Costa Rica	49.3	12.6	35	71	67
Ecuador	50.5[c]	21.3	23	45	97
Mexico	73.0	19.0	14	30	61
Peru	28.0[c]	19.8	21	40	84
Uruguay	33.5[c]	12.0	12	29	66
Venezuela	81.4[c]	10.4	32	62	98
South Korea	33.3	6.2	38	67	10
Taiwan	—	<5.0	52	—	14

[a]In principle, "tradeables" include all goods that are traded internationally or would be traded in the absence of restrictions. In practice, what is here used is the sum of the agricultural, mining, and manufacturing sectors.
[b]Fuels, minerals, metals, and other agricultural commodities.
[c]1980–1982.

SOURCE: ECLAC, *Preliminary Balance of the Latin American Economy, 1986* (Santiago, December 1986); World Bank, *World Development Report* (Washington, D.C., various years); G. Ranis, "East Asia and Latin America: Contrasts in the Political Economy of Development Policy Change" (May 1986, Mimeographed); and J. Fei, G. Ranis, and S. Kuo, *Growth with Equity: The Taiwan Case* (Baltimore, 1981).

Korea had far higher trade shares with a far lower weight of primary products.

Second, in another and all-important sense, Latin America's degree of integration into the international economy has greatly increased: its integration into world financial markets. Underlying this were institutional and technological changes in the 1970s that permitted and encouraged the greater integration of capital markets worldwide.

The immediate factor behind this increased integration was the boom in lending by private international banks, beginning in 1973–1974. As the banks accumulated deposits from surpluses generated in the OPEC economies as a result of the first oil price rise, and as the banks' usual customers in the developed countries faced the effects of the recession it pre-empted, a wave of loan offers hit developing countries, particularly in Latin America. They rationally took advantage of these offers: real interest rates were negative and public-sector investment projects as always needed finance. By the late 1970s this produced the sort of debt-export ratios shown in Table 12.3. As the table also shows, most of what Latin America borrowed was at floating interest rates and was denominated in dollars. This "new" vulnerability became starkly evident as real interest rates rapidly increased between 1980 and 1981.

Two further elements had a crucial effect. First, capital flight, facilitated by the existence of new channels for capital movement, led to outflows from Latin America that in some countries in certain years were as large as the capital inflows. Second, there was a "contagion" effect. High exposure on capital accounts rendered countries vulnerable to red-lining. International banks viewed the whole area uniformly as uncreditworthy on the basis of sometimes slender indicators.

The trigger was Mexico's statement in August 1982 that the country could no longer meet its debt-service commitments. The abrupt ending of new lending that this statement prompted was an important element in the switch from Latin America's being a net importer of capital to becoming a net exporter.

The cessation of new lending helped produce the unhealthy situation of increased vulnerability that became a hallmark of the 1980s. The attempt to reduce trade dependence was more than usually difficult to implement at a time when world growth was slowing. Also, hindsight shows that it was rash to combine such a program with the accumulation of such heavy external debt. The relatively closed Asian economies survived far better than Latin America because they avoided financial exposure. The highly trade-dependent newly industrialized countries of East Asia did become heavily indebted, but they were better placed in terms of their trade to cope with the problem. They also had a different kind of political economy, a point that is examined in Chapter 13. Because of these advantages, they could continue to call on the financial markets to ease the trade shock. The fact that Latin America had become so indebted during the 1970s meant that it lacked this escape route in the 1980s. It actually became a channel for the shock itself.[1]

As was to be expected, given the diversity of the Latin American economies, the shock took various forms and had different impacts within the region. Argentina was mildly affected on the trade front. Chile was severely affected. The difference reflected the commodity composition of each country's trade. Colombia at that time was the one country not vulnerable on the capital side. In the 1970s against the stream, Colombia had pursued a policy of limiting its borrowing abroad, once again reaffirming the diversity of the Latin American economies. All have become more industrialized and more urbanized, but there is a world of difference between the small Central American economies, with less than 20 percent of their economy in the industrial sector, and the highly sophisticated, if dualistic, Brazilian economy, already exporting capital goods to other developing countries.

Within this diversity, as the examples indicate, size is the main determinant. Resource endowment is not as important, though history, culture, and even chance each play a role in determining the different kinds of policy response that can arise from similar circumstances. But the relative importance of these factors will become clearer in the discussion of macro policy in the next chapter.

As Table 12.1 shows, in the period 1980–1983 the decline in growth rates in Latin America was dramatic, especially when compared with rates in South and East Asia. East Asia's weighted average slowed to a highly respectable 5.3 percent, and that of South Asia actually rose. In contrast, Latin America's rate of growth turned negative.

The contrast is even sharper in relation to industrial growth. Value-added fell in three successive years, and the levels of industrial production of 1980 were not regained till 1986. Not only were the new elements of resilience not strong enough to defend the regional economy, but the effect of the crisis was actually to undermine them. The recession hit investment particularly hard. The region's incipient capital-goods industry was worst hit. Between 1980 and 1985 production fell most sharply for metal products, nonelectrical machinery, electrical machinery, and transport equipment. These industries began to recover only in the second half of the 1980s.

As a result of the economic crisis, some of the technical capability built up during the 1970s was dissipated through the bankruptcy of firms, the breaking up of research teams, and the general downgrading of technological development in the struggle to survive in a contracting market. At the same time, the application of new technologies in the developed market economies widened the technological gap. In the engineering industries, for instance, the use of computer-aided design and the introduction of flexible automation represented a technological leap forward. But, faced with the collapse of their domestic markets, very few Latin American firms were able to respond by investing in these new technologies.

Only agriculture moved in a contrary direction. Given the low income elasticity of demand for food, the recession was bound to affect food demand less severely. Between 1981 and 1987 regional agricultural gross output grew at an annual rate of 1.9 percent, agricultural GDP at 1.6 percent. Although smaller than the historical trend of more than 3 percent, this performance was better than that of the rest of the regional economy.

However, the overall regional growth figure is biased by the weight of Mexico and especially the weight of Brazil, where agriculture performed relatively well. Performance was worse in the Andean region, Central America, and the Caribbean. Between 1980 and 1987, per capita crop and livestock output fell in the fifteen countries of the region for which information is available. Only five countries (Brazil, Chile, Cuba, Paraguay, and Uruguay) experienced noticeable gains in production per capita.

The modest countercyclical role of agriculture is, however, the only favorable trend to be identified in the 1980s. The general picture is one that fully justifies the common description of the 1980s as a "lost decade." To interpret this degree of collapse requires an understanding of policy responses, the subject of Chapter 13.

Note

1. J. A. Fishlow, "Some Reflections on Comparative Latin American Economic Performance and Policy," *WIDER Working Papers*, 22 (1987), p. 8.

13

The Policy Context

The state, as regulator of the economy, has always been important in Latin America. The price signals, to which individual firms and households respond, are affected in a major way by government decisions on tariffs, indirect taxes, and subsidies, as well as by more general instruments such as exchange rates and fiscal and monetary policy. In the period since 1960 the state has also become more involved in economic management as a producer, with large public enterprises now established in basic industries as well as in more traditional activities such as public utilities and transport. In recent years the state has come under pressure—from inside and outside the region—to withdraw from some of its activities. But public policy remains—and will remain—of crucial importance, if only because the price of policy failure remains so high.

Economic policy is guided by ideology. Economic thinking in Latin America, while bearing a family resemblance to ideas in North America and Western Europe, has often had an important autonomous dimension, which in turn has had a strong influence on the evolution of economic policy. The first two sections of this chapter review the evolution of economic thinking over the last three decades, showing how ideas, policies, and events have interacted to produce a complex reality that has varied from country to country. This diversity has become more marked in recent years as policymakers have become increasingly concerned with short-term crisis management.

The importance of economic policy in Latin America, and the diversity to which it has given rise, are most clearly illustrated by inflation. The third section of this chapter examines the problem of inflation, the policies designed to combat it, and the complexity of the issue. In the 1980s the problem of rising prices became ever more acute as inflation was used to reconcile the competing claims placed on scarce resources by the state and private agents alike. The worsening of the situation is directly associated with the debt crisis.

The fourth section is an examination of economic policy in the context of adjustment programs to deal with the debt problem.

The debt crisis has also focused attention on commercial policy in Latin America, the subject of the final section. The need to shift resources toward the external sector to earn the foreign exchange to service the debt has brought to a head the debate on commercial policy that began in the 1960s. The need to promote nontraditional exports is now recognized in all republics, but inconsistencies remain and the international economic environment—over which Latin America has little or no control—remains a powerful determinant of success or failure.

Currents in Economic Thinking

It is difficult to state categorically that economic thinking in Latin America has been truly autonomous. The best examples of autonomous economic thinking in Latin America have been structuralism on the one hand and the dependency school on the other. Structuralist analysis started from the inherited economic and social structures in Latin America and explored structural change through development in order to develop new ideas on inflation, income distribution, and growth. The dependency school took as its starting point the unequal relations of exchange between the "periphery" and the "center" with the distinction applied both to relations between Latin America (the periphery) and the developed countries (the center) and to relations between underdeveloped parts of individual countries (like the northeast of Brazil) and the more advanced regions (like São Paulo).

Even with structuralism and the dependency school, however—both Latin American currents of thought par excellence—there were clear outside influences. Structuralism had close ties to the work of economist John Maynard Keynes, which began to dominate economic thinking in the developed countries in the 1930s. Keynesianism became associated in practice with aggressive state intervention in the economy. In the case of the dependency school, the additional influence of Marxism was also evident. However, these currents of thought, coupled with external influences, produced in Latin America an interpretation of economic and social development that gave them a distinctive regional flavor. These currents also had a strong influence on thinking elsewhere. They became one of the most important foundations for Third World economic thinking in the 1970s but also had a strong influence on academics in the Northern Hemisphere, though this influence was most apparent in the noneconomic social sciences such as sociology.

However, the influence these currents of thinking had in practice on economic policymaking in Latin America is less significant than is often thought. Many of the forms of state intervention advocated by structuralists or by proponents of the dependency school were in fact in wide use well before. These theories, however, gave such intervention intellectual respectability. Furthermore, one of the main defects of these ideas was precisely their inability to provide precise instruments to widen the scope of state intervention and to make it more effective. The most common techniques of planning continued to emerge from other currents of thought, both Keynesian (macroeconomic models) and neo-classical (project evaluation), and even from completely different fields such as input-output models and operations analysis. It is also curious that structuralism contributed relatively little to the analysis of the structure of protection, to which it attached so much importance. A much more crucial contribution to the design of these structures came from neo-classical thought, which has in general provided the main intellectual support for laissez faire during the whole of the past century. Structuralism and the dependency school were much more important in terms of the political and ideological debate over the conceptualization of state action than in the development of new techniques of intervention themselves. Their impact was perhaps most influential on the international bureaucracies serving the Latin American states.

Since the 1970s these currents of thought have lost much of their influence, for many reasons. The most important is the strong swing to the right in political, economic, and social thought in the developed countries—a shift that reflects a crisis both at the technical level (for example, the optimal instruments for state intervention) and in ideology (for example, the goals of socialism). Social democrats continue to argue in favor of interventionism, although with much less force than before as the French and Spanish cases demonstrate, but the latest concepts of laissez faire have won overwhelming acceptance in business circles. In contrast to the 1930s and 1940s, this acceptance reflects renewed faith in the ability of the capitalist system to survive and prosper through the market economy.

The revival of laissez faire in the Northern Hemisphere is not the only influence on economic thinking within Latin America. Economic thinking is being shaped also by rather different influences from within the region itself. In contrast to the enthusiasm of the private sector in developed countries for the unfettered market economy, attitudes among Latin America's business groups tend to be rather more ambiguous. Business depends a great deal on the state, perhaps too much to function efficiently without state support. Although the virtues of privatization are extolled, private debts are sometimes nationalized, as in Chile. Private firms frequently depend crucially on the way in which public-sector contracts are distributed, and the private sector is often the first to resist attempts to reduce levels of protectionism afforded by the state. For this reason, while paying lip service to the neoliberal message, the Latin American private sector also favors a limited form of interventionism—limited to measures on which its own prosperity depends. Only when social conflict begins to threaten the foundations of the system itself—as in Chile in the early 1970s—is the private sector willing to support an openly liberal economic model. Albert Fishlow, a leading authority on the economics of Latin America, is worth quoting on this issue:

> These considerations also illuminate why military regimes seem to find rigorous stabilization packages congenial. The preference does not stem from a firm belief in automatic market adjustment. Military instincts are interventionist. But military leaders can conveniently rationalize political repression in the name of needed price and wage flexibility. The objective is not adaptation to a given economic structure but radical reconstruction of civil society. Falling real income then becomes a symbol of policy success because it shows the determination to stay the course until the underlying economic model is applicable.[1]

Liberalizing trends at the international and regional levels, however, are not the only cause of the decline of structuralist and dependency thinking. Indeed, neither school was ever dominant, still less hegemonic. While both were in fashion, more traditional orthodox ways of thinking in economics survived and in many cases prospered. With the Southern Cone monetarists in the 1970s, for instance, free-market views became well developed in academic circles. This was not the case, however, in Colombia, where a long tradition of economic lawmaking was essentially interventionist in spirit but policymakers tended to be very orthodox in both fiscal and monetary policy. Similarly, the theoreticians of the so-called Brazilian miracle were interventionist, but they were far from being followers of structuralism and dependency. Furthermore, neither structuralism nor the dependency school came up with the policy tools needed to become really influential in economic planning. Then as now, the study of economics was based on macroeconomics and microeconomics, the dominant influences being Keynesian and neoclassical thinking. The exponents of structuralism and dependency tended to be relatively more influential in areas such as economic development, international economics, and economic history; but even in these areas the two theories competed with other traditions of thinking.

The decline of these Latin American schools, however, has given way to an ever greater degree of influence from outside Latin America. The prime academic centers are a number of universities in the United States. The intellectual influence of the World Bank and the International Monetary Fund (IMF) are also of central importance, though perhaps their impact is stronger in circles related to international banking than in the academic sphere. This influence grew rapidly in the 1980s as both the Fund and the Bank widened the scope of their involvement in Latin America in the wake of the debt crisis. Their influence has also been compounded by the wide distribution of particularly influential books. One such book was *Toward a Renewed Economic Growth in Latin America,* by Bela Balassa, Gerardo M. Bueno, Pedro-Pablo Kuczynski, and Mario Henrique Simonsen, which argues the case for growth through liberalization of trade and financial markets.[2] Another is Hernando de Soto's *El otro sendero (The Other Path),* which argues for the removal of restrictive legislation as the most important change needed to liberate the entrepreneurial activities of the poor.[3]

A second effect of the decline of structuralism and dependency has been the loss of influence suffered by important regional intellectual centers in economics. This is especially the case of the United Nation's Economic Commission for Latin America and the Caribbean (ECLAC). Other new regional institutions, such as the Latin America Economic System (Sistema Económico Latinoamericano—SELA), have failed to reproduce ECLAC's previously important influence on the subcontinent. At the same time influential Latin American publishers with a primary focus on social sciences, such as Mexico's Fondo de Cultura and Siglo XXI, have gone into decline. So too has the main academic journal at the regional level, *El trimestre económico.* In neither case have alternatives of any importance been created. All this has to some extent undermined the institutional standing of economists and social scientists in Latin America while the attractions of consulting and the lure of the private sector and of international institutions have all grown in importance.

This does not mean, of course, that there are no important intellectual centers in the region or that the old schools have disappeared entirely. In fact there are a large number of important centers, but their area of influence is usually national. There are centers representing all currents of economic opinion. Some old centers have lost importance, like the Instituto Torcuato di Tella in Argentina or the Colegio de México in Mexico, but others have grown in stature, such as the Economic Research Corporation for Latin America (Corporación de Investigaciones Económicas para América Latina—CIEPLAN) in Chile and the Foundation for Higher Education and Development (La Fundación Para la Educación Superior y el Desarrollo—Fedesarrollo) in Colombia. There are also serious attempts to update and rework some ideas from the old Latin American schools. The most important of these, neo-structuralism, takes on board some recent ideas in economic thinking developed in the United States and favoring a certain degree of state intervention. Neo-structuralism is, however, a widely dispersed current of thought without a clear center. Its best exponent is the Brazilian economist Edmar Bacha, and it has been developed furthest in

Brazil. The various heterodox programs of economic adjustment in recent years show the influence of this school, both in Brazil and in several other countries. Neo-structuralism is currently being revised in the light of the successes and failures of the heterodox adjustment programs.

Some Myths About Policymaking

In the last few years the idea has become widely accepted that the countries of Latin America followed common economic policies until the 1970s, policies responsible for the debt crisis. According to this vision of events, the excessive protection of domestic industry, an artificially low rate of exchange, discrimination against the private sector, the trend toward excessive public expenditure, and an increasing fiscal deficit were all causes of the crisis. This is the basic interpretation of Balassa et al. in *Toward Renewed Economic Growth in Latin America.* It is also an interpretation that has gained currency in international financial and business circles.

The idea of a uniform Latin American economic policy or model is false, even if a long time period is chosen. It is even more false if the ten or fifteen years before the debt crisis began in 1982 are analyzed. In fact, in what may now be regarded as the "classical period" of Latin American economic thought, there were important differences in the form economic intervention took and in the way it was applied in different countries of the region. A rapid review of the main elements in economic policymaking confirms this.

The tendency of structuralists to underrate the orthodox management of public finance and the money supply is well known, if exaggerated. Monetary and fiscal laxity is not, however, a historical constant in the region. High rates of inflation were for a long time the peculiarity of the Southern Cone and Brazil. In the rest of Latin America macroeconomic orthodoxy ruled. Indeed, some countries boast of having had very conservative fiscal and monetary policies for long periods. This was the case, for example, in Mexico (at least before the 1970s), Venezuela, and Colombia.

The same can be said of commercial policy. In the classical period most of the medium-size and large countries developed complex systems of protection for their industries so as to promote the substitution of imports. Yet this was not the universal model. For decades after the Second World War the smaller economies of Central America, and even medium-size countries like Peru and Venezuela, pursued policies that were essentially those of export-led growth combined with some elements of increased protection. These policies were also found in the larger countries during the long period of export-led growth before 1930. What is more important, many of the larger countries that had pursued inward-looking industrial development found that this strategy tended to exhaust itself, and, from the end of the 1960s, they began to develop schemes for promoting manufactured exports. In addition the process of economic integration, beginning at the end of the 1950s, represented a partial external opening. This mixed model, and not the stereotyped inward-looking development model, was defended by Latin American theorists such as Raúl Prebisch in the 1960s.[4]

In terms of the activities of the state, the differences between countries in the region have also been very marked. The social and redistributive policies typical of the welfare state developed fully in only a handful of countries. The tendency of the state to extend its field of interest into productive sectors was also limited to only a few countries. It was a relatively late development, especially compared with Western Europe. Often it was more the result of circumstance, such as the inability of the private sector to invest in key areas, than of ideology.

The uniformity of the development model is debatable even for the classical age of Latin American economic thought. To assert it for the 1970s is absurd. The decade after 1970 is so full of economic and political shocks that it is difficult to talk of a uniform model even for a single country. Chile and Nicaragua are, of course, the extreme cases. Sharp reversals in economic policy in countries such as Argentina and Peru are equally well known. At the comparative level, what common elements can be found between the neoliberal models of the Southern Cone (Argentina, Chile, Uruguay) and the tendency toward further nationalization in such countries as Ecuador, Mexico, and Venezuela, with their oil bonanzas, or in Brazil, managing the adverse shock of the first oil crisis in 1973? In other countries short-term factors began to overwhelm analysis and policy considerations to the point where it was no longer relevant to speak of development strategies of any type at all.

Increasing heterogeneity was thus the chief characteristic of economic policy in Latin America in the 1970s and much of the 1980s. This process had deep political and economic roots and was reflected in the diverse ways the countries of the region accumulated their foreign debts during the 1970s. This is clearly shown in the essay of Carlos Díaz-Alejandro in a volume on economic adjustment in the 1980s edited by Rosemary Thorp and Laurence Whitehead.[5] The debt crisis in the 1980s forced countries to respond in a variety of ways to the problems of internal and external imbalance as first orthodox and then later heterodox adjustment programs failed to achieve the desired targets.

As the 1980s came to an end, however, it was clear that economic policy was once again converging in several areas in the different Latin American republics. Almost without exception, external trade policy began to favor exports in general and nontraditional exports in particular. Countries that, like Venezuela, had not yet joined GATT (General Agreement on Tariffs and Trade) applied for full membership, and the structure of protection began to be overhauled in many countries. Neo-liberal policies were not applied with the same enthusiasm to the domestic economy; but by the start of the 1990s almost all republics had begun to experiment with privatization, and some had opted for financial liberalization in an effort to increase domestic savings and reduce the previous dependence on foreign borrowing. Only in anti-inflation policy was there a marked divergence among countries in the types of programs adopted. This divergence reflected the stubborn nature of inflation in many Latin American republics and the difficulty of breaking inflationary expectations.

Inflation and Stabilization Policy

Repeated foreign-exchange crises, combined with high rates of inflation, have been characteristic of much of Latin America. As Table 13.1 shows, this is not a recent phenomenon. In the 1960s and the 1970s, inflation in the Western Hemisphere was far higher than in Asia and well above the world average. Nonetheless, when Latin America first became known for exceptionally high inflation—in the 1950s and 1960s—only five countries actually had very high rates of inflation. In the majority of Latin American countries inflation rates were not much different from rates in the rest of the world.

One of the five countries with exceptionally high inflation in the early 1950s was Bolivia, which at the time was going through a revolution. The other four were Argentina, Brazil, Chile, and Uruguay. All of these countries belong to the middle-income group and had fairly high degrees of social participation and well-organized pressure groups, such as strong trade unions and entrepreneurial associations. Furthermore, they tended to have governments committed to rapid growth, to ambitious public investment programs, and in some cases to income redistribution and structural change.

One of the most radical of those programs was led by President Salvador Allende in Chile (1970–1973). Allende tried simultaneously to boost production, improve income distribution, and nationalize important parts of the economy. By the third year of the Allende period, Chile had the highest rate of inflation in Latin America at the time and the highest in Chile's history.

Table 13.1

Annual percentage rates of increase in consumer prices by country, 1960–1989

	1960–1970	1970–1980	1980–1984	1984–1985	1986	1987	1988	1989
Argentina	19.6	38.1	290.2	672.1	81.9	174.8	387.7	4,923.8
Bolivia	5.5	18.8	251.7	11,748.0	66.0	10.7	21.5	16.6
Brazil	47.6	35.2	132.5	227.0	58.4	365.9	933.3	1,764.9
Chile	29.1	130.4	19.0	30.7	17.4	21.5	12.7	21.4
Colombia	11.2	21.1	21.9	24.0	21.0	24.0	28.2	26.1
Costa Rica	2.3	10.8	40.2	15.1	15.4	16.4	25.3	10.0
Dominican Republic	1.9	10.4	11.4	37.5	6.5	25.0	57.6	41.2
Ecuador	4.5	12.6	27.4	28.0	27.3	32.5	85.7	54.2
El Salvador	0.7	10.7	12.8	22.3	30.3	19.6	18.2	23.5
Guatemala	0.8	9.6	4.8	18.7	25.7	10.1	11.0	20.2
Haiti	2.8	10.7	8.7	10.6	–11.4	–4.1	8.6	10.9
Honduras	2.4	7.8	7.8	3.4	3.2	2.7	6.7	11.4
Mexico	2.7	16.6	61.4	57.7	105.7	159.2	51.7	19.7
Nicaragua	*n.a.*	*n.a.*	28.7	219.5	747.4	1,347.9	33,602.6	1,690.0
Panama	1.3	7.0	3.8	1.0	0.4	0.9	0.3	–0.2
Paraguay	3.3	13.1	13.5	25.2	24.1	32.0	16.9	28.5
Peru	9.3	30.2	89.1	163.4	62.9	114.5	1,722.6	2,776.6
Uruguay	44.1	64.2	38.7	72.2	76.4	57.3	69.0	89.2
Venezuela	1.0	8.4	11.0	11.4	12.3	40.3	35.5	81.0
Latin America	20.3	38.7	95.9	163.6	64.5	198.5	778.8	1,161.0
IMF world index	4.0	11.0	13.1	13.7	8.5	10.9	13.1	17.0
IMF index for Asia	15.6	9.3	7.0	6.6	9.1	9.8	11.7	10.2

SOURCE: Data for 1960 to 1985 are from J. Sheehan, *Patterns of Development in Latin America* (Princeton, 1987), p. 102. Data for 1986 to 1989 are from ECLAC, *Preliminary Overview of the Economy of Latin America and the Caribbean, 1990* (Santiago, December 1990). The IMF indexes for 1986 to 1989 are from International Monetary Fund, *International Financial Statistics, Yearbook* (Washington, D.C., various issues).

However, the link between radical change and high inflation—though common—is not inevitable, since it can be reduced by prudent economic management and clear political leadership. Thus, more modest economic transformations were carried out in the late 1960s in Chile under the administration of Eduardo Frei and in the late 1960s and early 1970s in Peru under the government of General Juan Velasco without a major upsurge in inflation.

The high levels of inflation in a number of countries in the 1960s and 1970s have a variety of explanations, and most of them emphasize internal factors. A monetarist would argue that the rapid growth of the money supply and large budget deficits caused high inflation in these countries. A structuralist would argue that these economies had problems of inflexibility on the supply side. The inflexibility created bottlenecks that could not be eliminated in the short run through the price mechanism. Inflation was therefore the undenied—but not excessive—cost to be paid for growth and structural transformation. Structuralists in sociology and political science also stressed inflation as a mechanism to dilute and postpone social conflict over income distribution between social groups—for example, between workers and capitalists, between the public and private sectors, or between industry and agriculture. According to this line of thinking, which was particularly influential in Chile, countries with the highest rates of inflation tend to be those with the longest history of political tension and of greater mobilization of different social groups, especially in situations where none of these groups clearly had the upper hand.

In the 1960s and 1970s inflation resulted from the interaction of all these factors. To a significant degree, it was a result of incompatible demands by different social groups and different sectors, especially when accentuated in periods of rapid structural change or economic mismanagement.

Two points in particular need to be stressed. First, high inflation was not always inevitable. In most cases where financial distortions were particularly acute, as in Argentina in the 1970s under Peronism or in Chile under Allende, much of the acceleration in inflation was due to the mistakes made in implementing economic policy. Alternative policies that could have achieved the same social and economic targets at much lower cost, as was the case in Costa Rica in the 1970s, were available. However, they were not perceived or were perceived too late. The fault was not only with economists but also with politicians unable or unwilling to understand the real and financial constraints on their economies and unwilling to explain these restrictions to their electorate—in particular, to their own followers.

Second, although high inflation to an important extent may have been caused by social tensions, it also worsened them and aggravated the political climate. Very high levels of inflation were certainly among the main causes contributing to the overthrow of democratic governments by repressive military regimes in Brazil (1964), Chile (1973), and Argentina (1976). Some inflation, therefore, may oil the wheels of democracy by attenuating social conflict and permitting more rapid growth. Very rapid inflation, however, particularly hyperinflation, can disrupt not only economic mechanisms but also political systems. The line between acceptable and unacceptable inflation is difficult to draw.

In the 1980s, a somewhat different situation emerged, although an important part of the previous analysis remains valid. Inflation became far more widespread within Latin America. The regional average increased dramatically, and countries like Mexico experienced very high levels of inflation for the first time in a very long period (see Table 13.1).

The acceleration of inflation in the 1980s gave rise to the notion of inertial inflation. According to this theory, inflation in the current period is largely determined by inflation in the previous period, because expectations about inflation are so firmly rooted. In such a situation, a reduction in nominal demand—through, for example, a cut in the budget deficit—may have little impact on inflation because agents continue to act as if price rises will continue as before. This was the problem in Brazil in 1985, when the budget deficit was cut quite sharply but inflation continued to accelerate. The idea of inertial inflation was influential in the design of heterodox adjustment programs intended to alter expectations.

Clearly, however, external factors also played a major role in the acceleration of Latin American inflation, as large industrial countries curbed monetary expansion in their own economies in the early 1980s, leading to increased international interest rates and depressed commodity prices. For heavily indebted developing countries—most of Latin America—this contraction implied a loss of creditworthiness and led to a dramatic decline in new private lending. As a result, net external transfers of resources—net payments of profits and interest less net capital inflows—became negative after 1981. For Latin America as a whole, net resource transfers as a proportion of GDP, which were +2.6 percent in the 1973–1981 period, became negative and averaged –3.9 percent of GDP in the 1982–1989 period. The dramatic reversal of net resource transfers, equivalent to nearly 7 percent of GDP, accelerated the inflationary process in at least three ways:

- Because of the inability to finance external interest payments through new borrowing, governments were forced to look internally for the needed resources. The main mechanism to do that—in a context where taxation was difficult to increase and internal capital markets were underdeveloped—was by issuing new currency through what is called the "inflation tax." This tax reduced the purchasing power of the money balances held by the public and increased the resources available to the state.

- The need to generate trade surpluses rapidly so as to be able to make negative net transfers led to major devaluations in an attempt to make exports more competitive and discourage imports. Devaluations inevitably fed through into inflation.
- The trade surpluses required to pay the debt were achieved by a dramatic compression of imports—over 40 percent for the region as a whole between 1981 and 1984. As a result, the supply of imported goods and inputs declined dramatically, thereby further worsening inflationary pressures.

To an important extent, therefore, high inflation in Latin America in the 1980s was the result of the need to "adjust" the economies to a very sharply deteriorated international environment and, in particular, to the massive reversal of net resource transfers. Had Latin America's debt burden been smaller or had it been reduced by way of debt-service limitations when the debt crisis arose, then the "adjustment" effort would have been smaller, the acceleration of inflation less rapid, and—crucially—the sacrifice in growth and development less dramatic.

Particularly vulnerable to the acceleration of inflation in the 1980s were some of the countries undergoing a transition to democracy, such as Bolivia, Brazil, and Uruguay. Argentina had had very high inflation during the last years of military rule. A key problem for Latin American economic policymakers and politicians is the need to design and implement programs for sustainable economic growth and development that allow for a fairer income distribution and make it easier to support democratic political systems without generating large financial disequilibria that lead to unacceptable levels of inflation or to current account deficits. The more unfavorable the external environment, of course, the harder achieving this is.

The acceleration of inflation in Latin America in the first half of the 1980s coincided with the period when IMF influence on economic policy was at its height. The IMF approach, strongly influenced by monetarism, emphasized the budget deficit as the source of inflationary pressures. Orthodox stabilization policy thus focused on measures to reduce government expenditure and raise government revenue. However, by this time in many countries an increasing proportion of government expenditure consisted of interest payments on the internal and external debt. Therefore the orthodox approach required a particularly sharp cut in noninterest public expenditure. The orthodox stabilization policies favored by the IMF to reduce inflation were not notably successful and in some cases, such as that of the Dominican Republic, produced food riots. As a result, a number of Latin American republics started to experiment with heterodox anti-inflation programs.

Heterodox stabilization plans were adopted in Argentina, Brazil, and Peru after 1985 and represented an important attempt to control inflation without paying an excessive cost in growth and development. Through price freezes and monetary reform, these plans attempted to reduce inertial inflation by attacking the mechanisms that propagate inflation, and to link key economic variables such as wages, interest rates, and exchange rates to previous inflation rates. Though initially successful, the heterodox plans generally failed to control inflation in the longer term.

The disappointing long-term results of most of the heterodox plans can be explained in a number of ways. Since each plan relied on price controls after the program was announced, it was essential that the relative prices established at the beginning of the program be equilibrium prices. This goal was not always achieved. Similarly, heterodox programs were often implemented as if fiscal and monetary orthodoxy could be ignored.

This is probably clearest in the case of the Brazilian Cruzado Plan, launched in February 1986. The Brazilian government did not accompany its heterodox measures by control of aggregate demand. On the contrary, real wages increased rapidly, and no serious attempt was made to control the fiscal deficit. As a result of these and other factors, the quantity of money in real terms in the hands of the public increased by as much as 7.1 percent a month during the first year of the plan. The target of zero inflation was clearly unrealistic and led to the refusal to raise some prices to achieve equilibrium prices. Furthermore, the government handled the Cruzado Plan according to short-term political criteria rather than making a longer-term commitment to inflation control. It thus postponed widely perceived necessary changes for electoral purposes. As a result the ruling coalition party won the parliamentary elections in 1986 but lost the battle against inflation. Indeed, the fight against inflation was postponed until President Fernando Collor took office in March 1990.

It has now become evident that heterodox policies on their own cannot control inflation. They need to be accompanied by orthodox measures for controlling aggregate demand (and the money supply) within reasonable limits. Prudence in macroeconomic management is particularly crucial for countries undergoing major structural changes, either in their economy—for instance, a redistribution of wealth—or in their society—the consolidation of democracy. Orthodox policies alone can control inflation, but at a very high cost in terms of a country's output and employment, as the Chilean experience in the early 1980s and the Nicaraguan experience in the late 1980s showed. Heterodox policies alone cannot defeat inflation for more than a short period. A creative synthesis is required—a synthesis that should also stress elements, such as increased taxation, largely neglected by both schools of thought.

In the second half of the 1980s some countries—notably Bolivia and Mexico—adopted stabilization programs that combined orthodox and heterodox policies with considerable success. Bolivia saw the annual inflation rate fall from over 10,000 percent a year in 1984–1985 to 10.7 percent in 1987. This drop was achieved without a dramatic collapse in real GDP and was made possible by an exchange-rate policy that emphasized the fight against inflation at the expense of some overvaluation of the currency. In Mexico, a tripartite agreement between government, business, and labor paved the way for the Pacto de Solidaridad Económica (Pact of Economic Solidarity), launched in December 1987, which helped bring down the annual inflation rate from over 150 percent to under 20 percent in 1989.

These examples are encouraging, yet too much should not be read into them. Both Bolivia and Mexico were able to underpin their stabilization programs with new foreign borrowing—a luxury not open to most Latin American republics—and the labor movement in both countries proved remarkably passive in the face of falling real wages. Both stabilization programs were also laced with a heavy dose of orthodoxy in terms of cutting government expenditure, raising government revenue, and reducing the growth of the nominal money supply. Significantly, neither Bolivia nor Mexico had a long, continuous history of inflation, so inflationary expectations were not deeply entrenched. However, neither country has yet passed the acid test of a revival of growth without renewed inflation. Bolivia's case is particularly dispiriting, though not surprising given the collapse of the tin market. Per capita GDP has fallen in every year from 1985 to 1989, and there is still no sign of any recovery in investment.

Reducing inflation in countries such as Argentina, Brazil, Peru, and Uruguay, where inflation has become endemic, has proved much harder. Orthodox solutions implying a massive drop in real GDP are not a realistic option in the democratic 1990s. Heterodox solutions have been tried and have failed. The creative synthesis outlined above represents the best way forward, but no one should underestimate the complexity of the problem.

Debt-Management Policy

The current debt problems surfaced in 1982 when debt crises became widespread in Latin America and Africa. The main objective of creditors in their dealings with major debtor governments was to safeguard the stability of the international banking system. This stability could have been threatened by the default of one or more of the major Latin American debtors, seriously undermining the growth and volume of world trade.

A formula was thus hammered out, geared toward preserving the stability of the international banks. Amortization payments were postponed, and new "involuntary" lending was squeezed out of the private banks. The issue of any sort of debt relief, either on the principal or on interest payments, was not then part of the agenda for debtor governments and their creditors.

In the formula agreed to at the end of 1982, a crucial role was allocated to the international financial institutions (IFIs), in particular the IMF and the World Bank. The reason was simple. Without the IFIs' seal of approval, no creditors were prepared to lend new money to Latin America; without new money, there was no chance of Latin America adjusting to the debt crisis and enjoying economic growth at the same time.

The IMF since its origins in the 1944 Bretton Woods Conference has been involved in Latin America's balance-of-payments problems as the lender of last resort. However, the funds it is able to lend are strictly limited. The IMF therefore depended on the willingness of commercial banks to extend new loans once a debtor government had agreed to meet the conditions laid down by the Fund.

The World Bank has also been involved in Latin America since the late 1940s, but for most of the period its lending has been confined to projects. In the 1970s, the World Bank began to switch toward program lending designed to help a country meet a variety of targets through a process of structural change. Structural Adjustment Loans (SALs) became more important in the 1980s, as the World Bank used them to underpin strategies for creating the resources needed to service the debt. Thus, in the wake of the debt crisis, several Latin American countries found themselves subject to two sets of conditions imposed by the IMF and the World Bank and to cross-conditionality clauses. Failure to meet the conditions laid down by one IFI would lead the country to be ineligible for further borrowing from the other. By contrast, the Inter-American Development Bank in the 1980s continued to emphasize project lending, on which conditionality has traditionally been milder.

The total lending to Latin America by the IFIs rose sharply after the debt crisis erupted in 1982 but did not disguise the fact that the commercial banks were extremely reluctant to increase their exposure. In a few cases, such as in Mexico, the banks were persuaded to provide a small amount of new lending as a result of pressure not only from the IFIs but also from the U.S. government. Generally, however, the banks took the view that they were overexposed in Latin America and were anxious to scale down their commitments.

As a result, Latin America found that net new capital flows were not nearly large enough to service the debt. The imbalance (some $30 billion a year) had to be financed by building up a trade surplus, which could be achieved only by cutting imports. The sharp fall in imports had serious implications for investment and economic growth and forced most Latin American countries into recession.

By mid-1985 a new phase was under way. There was increased resistance in debtor countries to a strategy of debt-crisis management that was seen to satisfy the objectives of the creditor institutions at the expense of growth in the debtor countries. Many small and medium-size debtors in Latin America began to accumulate arrears. Dissatisfaction was most clearly expressed in the unilateral action taken by the Peruvian government of Alan García, which limited debt-service payments and announced that "Peru's main creditors are its people." Creditor governments and banks feared that debtor radicalism would spread throughout Latin America. The U.S. government retook the initiative with the Baker Initiative, named after U.S. Treasury Secretary James Baker and announced in September 1985. This scheme recognized that the strategy of debt management should also pursue, as a fundamental objective, growth in the debtor economies. It called for more lending by private banks and by the multilateral public institutions. However, net lending from private banks to Latin America actually declined further in 1986, the first year of the Baker Initiative, and became *negative.*

A third phase of debt-crisis management then began in early 1987 with Brazil's unilateral moratorium on interest payments to banks on medium- and long-term debt. Brazil's unilateral action did not have very clear objectives. Furthermore, it was taken at a time when the economy was suffering major disequilibria and the domestic political situation was unsettled. For these and other reasons it did not contribute to higher growth in Brazil. However, Brazil's moratorium changed the framework for debt negotiations. In the short term, other Latin American governments—such as Mexico, Chile, and Argentina—were able to obtain better rescheduling deals than they would otherwise have gotten. More significantly, Brazil's move led major U.S. and British banks to make large loan-loss provisions against developing countries' debt. Other European banks had tended to make such provisions earlier.

This decision by U.S. and other banks had major implications:

- It implied that all the major banks finally accepted explicitly what had been apparent for a long time: the debts of many Third World nations would not and could not be serviced in full.
- The existence of large provisions against losses in all major banks significantly reduced uncertainty about the risks to banks' solvency and stability if debtor governments take (or are forced by circumstance to take) unilateral action.

- Most importantly, it strengthened the feasibility of intermediate solutions that recognized that the real market value of the debt was no longer its face value and that some reductions should—and eventually would—be made either in the level of the debt itself or in its servicing.

The initiative by the major banks did not at first result in any major advantage for debtors, although a small amount of debt was traded in the secondary market and converted into equity (debt-equity swaps) or bonds. The main obstacle was the insistence by creditor governments that the Baker Initiative was still operational. However, the new Bush administration gave priority to a fresh approach to the debt crisis, and early in 1989 the Brady Plan (named after U.S. Secretary of the Treasury Nicholas Brady) was launched.

The Brady Plan, already applied to Mexico, Costa Rica, and Venezuela, and under discussion in other countries, is sufficiently flexible to cope with the different requirements of the Latin American debtors. Essentially, a debtor government must offer a menu from which the creditors can choose. The menu has four basic ingredients:

- An exchange of commercial debt at a big discount for a cash payment by the debtor government.
- An exchange of commercial debt for bonds at a substantial discount but carrying the same rate of interest.
- An exchange of commercial debt for bonds with the same face value but carrying a lower rate of interest.
- Maintenance of the face value and interest rate on previous loans in exchange for new money.

In order to attract banks to this scheme, the Brady Plan stressed the need for involvement of the IMF and the World Bank. In addition, debtors were expected to find sufficient resources to guarantee interest payments for a limited time period on the second or third options. The Brady Plan also envisaged the use of IFI loans to provide resources to enable a debtor to repurchase some of its debt in the secondary market at a substantial discount. Costa Rica, for example, used IFI loans to buy its commercial debt at 16 percent of its face value.

The Brady Plan would probably have succeeded better if it had been adopted earlier. However, as Latin America entered the 1990s, only four republics (Mexico, Colombia, Chile, and Uruguay) were fully servicing their debts. Thus, the attractions of the Brady Plan for debtors had to be set against the option of nonpayment. The latter no longer appeared to carry heavy costs, as more and more banks increased their loan-loss provisions against Latin American lending. Indeed, some banks raised provisions to 100 percent, while only a handful of banks indicated interest in the new money option for Latin America under the Brady Plan.

Latin America's disbursed public external debt at the beginning of 1990 was estimated at $415 billion. Most of this (70 percent) was owed to private creditors, who could expect to see service payments decline, either through the Brady Plan or through nonpayment. The remainder (30 percent) was owed to official multilateral and bilateral creditors. For some countries, particularly the small republics, official debt is the most important. So far, such creditors have been reluctant to agree to any debt-reduction package for Latin America, although they have done so for some African countries. There are some signs, however, that official creditors will adopt a more flexible attitude toward Latin America in the 1990s, and the announcement in 1990 by President Bush concerning the Enterprise for the Americas Initiative contained a reference to the need for official debt-reduction by the United States.

Commercial Policy

Commercial policy in Latin America has undergone a dramatic transformation in the last thirty years. In the late 1960s, trade policy discriminated against exports; exchange rates were frequently overvalued; and a number of countries (including some of the most important) had not joined GATT. The revision of commercial policy began in the late 1960s, but the external shocks of the 1970s and the sharp rise in the price of many primary products exported by Latin America left the process incomplete in many countries. In the 1980s, however, the combination of pressures by international financial agencies and the need to accumulate trade surpluses to service debts produced a major overhaul of commercial policy. Throughout the region, firms were offered new incentives in favor of exports, particularly nontraditional exports, and almost all countries became members of GATT or applied to join.

While Latin America was beginning to shift resources back toward the export sector at the end of the 1960s, the world economy was about to close one of its longest and most successful periods of international trade expansion. Thus, the attempt by Latin America to reverse the sharp decline in its share of world trade was badly timed. Indeed, the new policies have still not succeeded in reversing this decline, which has taken the region's share of both world exports and imports below 4 percent (see Table 13.2).

Table 13.2

Latin America's and other developing countries' share of world trade, 1950–1989

Years	Exports		Imports	
	Latin America	Other Developing Countries	Latin America	Other Developing Countries
1950	11.1	37.5	9.6	33.5
1960	7.7	38.9	7.7	30.7
1970	5.5	22.6	5.7	23.9
1980	5.5	33.1	5.9	27.9
1985	4.5	22.5	6.1	24.1
1987	4.0	20.5	4.7	22.0
1989	3.9	21.4	4.8	22.9

SOURCE: International Monetary Fund, *Direction of Trade Statistics* (Washington, D.C., various years).

Some developing countries outside Latin America, notably in East Asia, have succeeded in increasing their share of world trade. Nevertheless, as Table 13.2 makes clear, Latin America is not alone in facing a decline. International trade is increasingly concentrated among the developed OECD countries, supplemented by the newly industrialized countries of East Asia. The major share of this trade is accounted for by a few hundred of the largest corporations. The challenge facing Latin America is not merely to shift resources toward the export sector but also to develop companies and products that will not be left at the margin of any major expansion of world trade in the future. This means that commercial policy cannot be divorced from policies directed at the creation of an indigenous technological capability and, in several cases, the development of a capital-goods industry.

The change in commercial policy has meant a revision of policies toward multinational companies. Encouraged by generous incentives in the 1960s, the multinational corporations became one of the major instruments for pushing import substitution to extreme limits. The dominant position acquired by the multinationals in many Latin American markets as a result of their superior marketing and managerial skills produced a reaction on the part of policymakers, and enthusiasm for direct foreign investment declined in the 1970s. Now, with export promotion high on the list of policy priorities, policy has shifted back in favor of investment by multinationals, and preference is given to firms exporting the bulk of their output. So far, the economic problems caused by the debt crisis in Latin America have produced only a muted response from multinationals, which have favored East Asia in their investment decisions in recent years. Yet, without an increase in direct foreign investment in the export sector, it will be difficult for Latin America to reverse its declining share of world trade.

Commercial policy in the 1960s discouraged exports to and imports from the rest of the world but was designed to promote intraregional trade under the numerous integration schemes then in force. As a result, the share of imports and exports taken by the region increased (see Tables 13.3 and 13.4). In the case of the region's imports, the main trading partner to lose market share was the United States. In the case of the region's exports, Latin America's increased share was largely at the expense of the European Community. With the onset of the debt crisis and the sharp decline in imports, regional trade was particularly badly hit and the United States regained some of its lost

Table 13.3

Percentage of Latin American exports by destination, 1961–1989

Destination	1961–1963	1977–1979	1980–1987	1987	1989
United States	37.2	35.0	39.2	40.0	36.2
European Community	29.4	21.4	22.4	22.8	23.7
Japan	3.3	4.1	5.1	5.6	6.0
Canada	3.2	3.0	2.3	1.9	2.2
Middle East	0.2	1.4	2.5	1.7	1.5
Latin America	8.4	15.9	15.1	12.8	13.0
Elsewhere	18.3	19.2	13.4	15.2	17.4

SOURCE: International Monetary Fund, *Direction of Trade Statistics* (Washington, D.C., various years).

Table 13.4

Percentage of Latin American imports by country of origin, 1961–1989

Country of Origin	1961–1963	1977–1979	1980–1987	1987	1989
United States	41.8	32.9	35.4	34.0	38.3
European Community	28.1	19.4	20.1	23.0	21.4
Japan	3.7	7.9	6.2	6.4	6.3
Canada	3.0	2.5	2.4	2.2	2.1
Middle East	1.8	9.8	7.2	4.7	4.5
Latin America	10.7	16.9	17.9	13.7	14.0
Elsewhere	10.9	10.6	10.8	16.0	13.4

SOURCE: International Monetary Fund, *Direction of Trade Statistics* (Washington, D.C., various years).

market share—albeit with a much reduced value of exports. The United States also became in the 1980s a much more important export market for Latin America, with market share close to 50 percent. The heavy dependence of the new export promotion strategy on a single market, and one subject to protectionist threats, has been a cause for some concern among policymakers in Latin America.

No aspect of commercial policy in Latin America has changed more since the 1960s than tariff policy. Nominal and effective rates of protection in the region were among the highest in the world. The use of import quotas and licenses (particularly important in Mexico) made the true rate of protection even higher. The process of lowering tariffs began in the 1970s in the Southern Cone, with Chile in particular recording the most dramatic reductions. It continued in the 1980s as policymakers tried to reduce the disincentives against exports caused by high tariffs on imported inputs used by export firms. At the beginning of the 1990s tariffs are still high by international standards, but the trend is downward and firms producing for the home market are learning, in many cases for the first time, how to compete with imports.

One reason that firms have been able to compete has to do with exchange-rate policy. Just as high tariffs in the late 1960s were needed in part to compensate for overvalued exchange rates, so lower tariffs in the 1980s were accompanied by exchange-rate depreciation in both nominal and real terms. The main justification for exchange-rate depreciation, however, has been to protect the balance of payments through stimulating exports and discouraging imports. Because of its impact on inflation, this sort of exchange-rate policy has been unpopular in many circles, but the need to shift resources toward exports and protect the balance of payments has generally taken priority. Exchange-rate policy has been relaxed, causing temporary overvaluation, only when the need for price stability has acquired overwhelming importance. Few countries have yet succeeded, except for brief periods, in combining price stability with competitive exchange rates. This elusive goal may become even more difficult to achieve in the future, as Latin America enters a new round of anti-inflation stabilization policies.

The new tariff and exchange-rate policies have been welcomed by international financial agencies such as the World Bank and the IMF. As a result of the debt crisis, these agencies have acquired an exceptionally high profile in the management of economic policy. Creditor governments welcome the opportunity to promote, through these agencies, the reforms in economic and commercial policy that they regard as essential for sound economic management, and officials of debtor governments have sometimes found the conditions laid down by the agencies a useful discipline in dealing with their own politicians. Yet there are dangers in this approach. Legitimate nationalist aspirations can easily be aroused by an overbearing attitude on the part of international agencies, and policies that do not command widespread domestic support will eventually be reversed.

Commercial and indeed economic policy in Latin America has often been contrasted unfavorably with policy in the newly industrialized countries in East Asia. The poor performance of the Latin American economies in the 1980s, particularly by comparison with East Asia, is a legitimate cause for concern. But too often the wrong lessons have been drawn. What is striking about East Asia is not the limited role of the state but the consistency and conviction with which state policies have been applied in the commercial and other fields. Establishing the consensus that is a necessary condition for the application of consistent policies has been more difficult to achieve in Latin America, in part because of its greater commitment to political pluralism and its higher level of social mobilization. Where consensus has been achieved, as in Costa Rica or, until recently, Mexico, the results have sometimes been impressive.

The complexity of Latin American society continues to justify an important role for the state as regulator, provider, and even in some areas producer. But these functions will be exercised inefficiently if policy is inconsistent. The answer to inefficient policies is not the withdrawal of the state to a minimalist role but greater awareness and increased public debate on the goals and instruments of state policy.

The need for consistency in state policies becomes clearer if the East Asian case is considered in greater detail. The conventional wisdom maintains that the success of South Korea, Taiwan, Singapore, and others is a result of a number of factors: getting prices right, following outward-oriented trade strategies, and limiting state intervention. In contrast, it is often argued, Latin American economies are characterized by substantial price distortions, inward-oriented policies, and excessive state intervention. This view leads to the advocacy of greater emphasis on market forces, trade liberalization, and privatization as ways of creating more dynamic industrial development in Latin America.

Concentrating on South Korea and Taiwan, whose experience is more relevant for Latin America than is the experience of the city-states of Hong Kong and Singapore, one can argue that this picture contains major inaccuracies. In South Korea and Taiwan, key prices, especially interest rates and wage rates, have not been determined by market forces. Moreover, both countries have made extensive use of selective protection to promote industrial production and even industrial exports. Finally, the influence of the state over the economy is pervasive, leading one author to comment that "no state, outside the socialist bloc, ever came anywhere near this [South Korea's] measure of control over the economy's investible resources."[6]

In fact, the differences between the newly industrialized East Asian countries and the Latin American countries are to be found less in the existence or absence of protection or state intervention and more in their basic characteristics. In East Asia protection has been directed toward creating internationally competitive industry and local technological capabilities, whereas in Latin America protection has been described as "frivolous."[7] State intervention in East Asia has been "developmental," seeking to augment market forces in order to accelerate industrialization, whereas in Latin America the emphasis has been more on regulation. Another important difference between the East Asian and Latin American countries has been the role played by foreign capital. That role has been much more limited in Asia than in Latin America. At the same time, foreign capital in South Korea and Taiwan is much more oriented toward export markets than it is in Latin America.

Notes

1. Interamerican Development Bank, *Economic and Social Progress in Latin America, 1985 Report* (Washington, D.C., 1985), p. 147.
2. B. Balassa, G. M. Bueno, P. P. Kuczynski, and M. H. Simonsen, *Toward Renewed Economic Growth in Latin America* (Washington, D.C., 1986).
3. H. de Soto, *El otro sendero (The Other Path),* (London, 1989).
4. Prebisch, the founder of ECLA in 1947, became increasingly aware of the need to move beyond a narrow inward-looking model of development. See, for example, R. Prebisch, *Towards a Dynamic Development Policy for Latin America* (United Nations, 1964).
5. C. Díaz-Alejandro, "Some Aspects of the Development Crisis in Latin America" in *Latin American Debt and the Adjustment Crisis,* ed. R. Thorp and L. Whitehead (New York, 1987).
6. M. K. Datta-Chaudhuri, "Industrialization in Foreign Trade: The Development Experiences of South Korea and the Philippines," in *Export-led Industrialization and Development* (Geneva, 1981).
7. F. Fajnzylber, *La industrialización trunca de América Latina (Latin America's Incomplete Industrialization),* (Buenos Aires, 1983).

14

Issues of Employment, Distribution, Poverty, and Welfare

Income distribution and poverty are affected by variables that modify access to income or to potential income, such as property rights, skills, and capabilities. They are also affected by variables that affect the labor market within given structures and skill endowments. In Latin America, because of the characteristic pattern in demand and supply of labor, the countries that have a higher proportion of the labor force employed tend to be those that enjoy more equal patterns of distribution.

One of the most common characteristics in the Latin American labor market is the excess of population in relation to employment possibilities in the "formal" sector. This excess produces an often large "informal" sector, in which workers generate their own income from forms of production that operate under different rules—basically self-employment in small units of production. In the cities, examples range from making car parts, shoes, or sewing clothes to peddling chewing gum or melons in the streets. In rural areas, the usual form is subsistence peasant production, though artisan production may also develop. Some of this production is economically rational; much of it is profitable only because it is illegal. There are varying degrees of illegality, ranging from nonpayment of taxes or nonobservance of health regulations through to dealing in illegal commodities such as drugs. Some of the illegal activity would simply not be profitable if labor were costed at a market wage. But it provides a form of social insurance: it is preferable to not eating. As a result, in contrast to the situation in developed countries, the average wage and the inadequacy of formal-sector employment is reflected less by open unemployment than by the rate of self-employment.

If wage employment rises in the formal, capitalist sector of the economy, relatively fewer people are left in the self-employed sector and average income within it tends to rise. Meanwhile wage earners in the formal sector can bargain with employers for a better share of the surplus. Thus, for both these reasons an increase in the absorption of labor by the formal sector is crucial for greater equality in distribution.

This is not to say that the informal sector is to be explained only as a residual. Complementarity between formal- and informal-sector firms reveals an element of symbiosis. Formal-sector firms may "put out" work to the informal sector. One example is the sewing of garments. But in either situation the expansion of the formal sector tightens the labor market for those in the informal sector, thereby improving the situation of those in it. Argentina and Venezuela, for example, are countries with relatively high average incomes. They have a high proportion of wage employment—about 74 percent of the economically active population—and relatively low rates of inequality. At the other extreme, Peru and Bolivia have low average incomes, a low proportion of wage employment—around 40 to 45 percent—and extreme inequality.

In the absence of structural changes—such as changes in the structure of property that give new groups greater and more secure access to new sources of income—the growth of employment is the single most important factor in reducing inequalities of income. It reduces the residual fighting for a share of the very low productivity activities outside the formal sector. Conversely, failure to increase employment opportunities in the formal sector means failure to improve distribution. This chapter looks first at the growth in demand and supply of jobs between 1960 and 1980 and during the crisis of the 1980s and then analyzes the evidence on distribution, poverty, and basic needs.

Employment: Demand and Supply

The demand for jobs depends on population growth, migration (mainly between rural and urban areas), and the desire of people to enter the work force (for example, the number of married women who wish to be employed). During recent decades Latin America has seen significant changes in terms of population growth and the geographical and sectoral distribution of population. Indeed, during the period of demographic explosion following the Second World War, population grew steadily at 2.6 percent a year for some twenty years. From 1970, however, population growth started decreasing, and projections for the year 2000 indicate that by then population will grow at a rate of just under 2 percent a year. This rate is still higher than the rate of growth of population today in more developed regions, but it is much lower than in Africa. By the end of the century Latin America will have 540 million inhabitants, or just under 9 percent of the total world population.

The same evolution affects the behavior of the economically active population. Because of the lag that exists between the moment a person is born and the individual's incorporation into the labor market, the decline in the rates of growth of the economically active population started only during the present decade (see Table 14.1). The numerically upward trend will continue to the end of the century at least. Thus, while during the 1970s approximately 31 million jobs had to be created—36 percent of the economically active population of 1970—during the 1990s 41 million jobs will have to be generated in the economy. This volume, though larger in absolute numbers than the number of jobs created during the 1970s, proportionally corresponds to only 27 percent of the economically active population of 1990. Therefore, relatively, the 1970s was the most difficult decade in terms of the number of jobs that had to be created. In future the pressure of labor supply on the labor market may be less.

Table 14.1 shows that the growth of the urban labor force was exceptionally high during the 1970s, mainly because of labor migration from the countryside to the cities. Its rate of growth was almost 50 percent higher than the rate of growth for the total economically active population.

The bases were different in the different countries. Because of the distinct development experiences, there are important variations in the degree of urbanization in different Latin American countries. Argentina, for example, was more urban in 1914 than Bolivia is today. In 1985 the proportion of the population living in urban areas varied from 83 to 85 percent in Argentina, Chile, Uruguay, and Venezuela, to 39 to 45 percent in Bolivia, El Salvador, Guatemala, and Honduras. The importance of this variation is that in the more developed parts of Latin America, there is a limit to future flows of rural migrants to the cities. In Central America the speed of urban growth is likely to be maintained by large-scale migration for some time to come.

Overall, however, the peak of urban growth in Latin America has passed. Although the population share of urban areas in the total population will continue to grow, the rate of growth is slowing, as Table 14.1 shows. This has long been the case in the Southern Cone, where the rural population is now very small in proportional terms. But it is now happening even in late urbanizing areas such as Central America.

Therefore during the 1990s the urban rate of growth will still be higher than the total rate, but both rates will decline and the urban rate will decline more rapidly. This pattern suggests that the pressure on the labor markets in

TABLE 14.1

Latin America: economically active population (EAP) annual rate of growth 1950–2000

	1950–1960	1960–1970	1970–1980	1980–1990	1990–2000
Economically Active Population (EAP)					
Total	2.1	2.5	3.2	2.8*	2.6*
Male	1.9	2.0	2.8	2.6	2.3
Female	2.5	3.6	4.7	3.7	3.1
Urban EAP					
Total	3.6	3.6	4.7	3.7	3.2
Male	n.a.	n.a.	4.3	3.5	3.0
Female	n.a.	n.a.	5.5	4.1	3.6

Note: n.a. = not available.
*Projections (see Celade).

SOURCE: CELADE, *Boletin Demográfico (Demographic Bulletin)*, year 19, no. 35, (Santiago, 1985).

the cities will be less, either because there will be a strong decline in migration or because participation rates (essentially of women) will diminish.

Changes in the participation rates of women have been significant during the last decades. Even though women in Latin America participate less in the labor market than do women in the rest of the world, there has been a continuous increase of women who work. During the 1950s the rates of growth of the participation rates for men and women were very similar. But after 1960 the rapid integration of women into the labor market started, a phenomenon especially evident in urban areas. During the 1980s participation rates started to decline, but by the end of the century the growth of women's rates will still be higher than that of men. Thus, the structure of employment is likely to continue to change in the direction of a more egalitarian distribution by gender, although, because of a relative decline in women's participation, the rate of growth of the total urban labor force will in fact decrease.

These changes in population have not only altered the nature of the supply of labor but have had an impact on the sectoral distribution of employment. The first and most important change took place in agriculture. Migration from rural to urban areas occurs because of expulsion factors found in the rural sector and the attractions cities can offer. One of the most important expulsion factors has been the behavior of agriculture, particularly since modernization has altered technology, land tenure systems, and the pattern of land distribution, in each case reducing the requirement for labor. In 1950, 55 percent of the labor force worked in agriculture. Today, less than one-third does. By the year 2000 only around 20 percent will be engaged in agricultural activities, even though differences among countries in the region will continue to be considerable. For example, some Central American countries still have more than half of their working population engaged in agriculture. Southern Cone countries, in contrast, will have less than 20 percent. By the year 2000 Africa will have 61 percent of its labor force in agriculture, Asia 59 percent, and the Middle East 35 percent. Developed countries with market economies will have only 6 percent.

The massive transfer of people to the cities has also brought changes in the structure of urban unemployment. Indeed, urban employment in the modern sectors has expanded at very fast rates, and the role of industry has been particularly important. During the 1950s labor absorption was low. In the 1960s it improved significantly, so much so that in some countries the rate of growth of industrial employment was higher than the growth rate in all other economic sectors. This was the case in Mexico, Venezuela, Colombia, Chile, Guatemala, and Honduras. The same process took place in Brazil during the 1970s. Today industrial employment typically accounts for one-quarter of the labor force.

Employment in the modern sector consists of activities related to commerce, services, and particularly government. Analysis of employment data since 1950 leads to the conclusion that employment in the service sector is associated with industrialization and therefore is very much linked to modernization in Latin America. It is also related to government activities and to public employment, which has increased at faster rates than nonagricultural employment. Public employment in the early 1980s accounted for 18 percent of total employment, 27 percent of nonagricultural employment, and 40 percent of modern urban employment. In many countries the public sector has been the fastest growing sector in terms of employment creation not only because of the increasing functions performed by governments but also because the public sector plays a buffer role to diminish potential conflicts stemming from the lack of sufficient employment in other areas of the economy. In this sense the public sector has played a political role. In addition, its quantitative importance cannot be overstated because of its strong link with the formation of the middle class in Latin America. As many as 60 percent of all professionals and technicians in Latin America work in one way or another for the government.

Even though job creation in the modern sector has been dynamic, it has been insufficient to absorb the supply of labor in urban areas. Many people have thus had to search for jobs in other areas, generating a particular characteristic of the employment problem in Latin America: the underutilization of labor.

The most visible form of labor underutilization is chronic unemployment. Traditionally chronic unemployment has not been very important in Latin America. Except during the crisis of the early 1980s, it has usually been "only" around 7 percent of the economically active population. Clearly, in the absence of any type of unemployment benefit and insurance, poor people simply cannot afford to be without an income and therefore have to create some sort of employment. Thus, the absence of chronic employment does not mean that in Latin American economies there is adequate utilization of labor.

The Regional Employment Program for Latin America and the Caribbean (Programa Regional de Empleo para América Latina y el Caribe—PREALC) analyzed the underutilization of the labor force during the period 1950–1980 and concluded that chronic unemployment accounts for only one-fifth of total underutilization. The rest is due to underemployment—working people who earn incomes below a certain poverty line. For this reason it has been argued that the employment problem in Latin America is a matter of poverty generated by the insufficient creation of good jobs.

Between 1950 and 1980 one of the most striking features of the functioning of the labor market was that peasant economies and the urban informal sector retained their importance. In effect, the growth of peasant employment during thirty years was more or less equal to the growth of wage employment in agriculture in Latin America, thus representing 60 percent and 40 percent respectively of the active population in agriculture during three decades.

In the cities, urban informal employment—characterized by small enterprises and self-employed workers with scarce capital, low technology, and low productivity—has represented during the same period around one-third of total employment. The permanence of these economic units, despite rapid employment creation in the urban modern sector, shows a structural feature of economic development in Latin America. This is very different from the experience of industrialized countries in which traditional sectors were successfully integrated into the modern sectors. Urban informal activities can be found in almost all nonagricultural economic sectors, but their relative weight is especially important in commerce and services, where they represent between one-half and one-fifth of total employment in each sector respectively.

This conception of the urban informal sector should be distinguished from the concept of an underground economy. There is a tendency to confuse the informal sector with illegal activities, which, it has been argued, are illegal because of barriers imposed by the state, making entry into the formal sector more difficult. A corollary of this view therefore is that if the state eliminated bureaucratic obstacles, informal urban activities would disappear. This view has been put forward with considerable force by Hernando de Soto in *El otro sendero (The Other Path)*. This analysis does not recognize the degree of heterogeneity in the structure of the Latin American economies, or the coexistence of economic units with widely differing levels of productivity and that this is in fact the origin of the informal sector. One of the effects is that many units operate illegally, but this illegal activity is essentially a consequence not a cause.

The trends in unemployment and underemployment just described were accentuated during the 1980s. According to PREALC, because the crisis caused a rapid increase in unemployment, the largest proportion of the cost of the adjustment process was absorbed by groups whose income derives from the labor market. Unemployment rates increased by almost 50 percent as labor was laid off in the modern sector and because the rate of job creation was so low. In addition, the few jobs that were generated were mainly in government and administration. Together with unemployment, the urban informal sector played the role of a sponge, absorbing labor that either had been made redundant in the modern sector or that consisted of new entrants into the labor market who could find employment only in the informal sector.

Inequality, Poverty, and Basic Needs

Given these trends in employment and underemployment, it comes as no surprise that inequality tended to increase in the period under review. Unfortunately there is little by way of systematic and comparable data covering a wide range of countries. The few estimates available are for specific countries. An estimate made by the United Nations' Economic Commission for Latin America and the Caribbean (ECLAC) for a group of countries for 1960 to 1975 showed some increase in concentration. The figures are given in Table 14.2. It indicates that in the seven largest countries of the region, taken together, the share of the poorest 20 percent fell from 2.8 to 2.3 percent. Gains were made by only the richest 30 percent at the top of the distribution. As always, however, such global figures conceal more than they reveal. Within the group of countries included in Table 14.2, in Colombia, where the distribution has been studied with particular care and where the basic situation was one of extreme inequality, there were signs of improvement after 1975. This fact reflects the relatively slight impact of the debt crisis in Colombia. In general,

Table 14.2

Income distribution of Latin American households, 1960–1975

Population Distribution	Share of Total Income 1960	Share of Total Income 1975
10% richest	46.5	47.3
20% middle/high group	26.1	26.9
30% middle group	18.6	18.1
20% second most poor	5.9	5.4
20% poorest	2.8	2.3
Total	100.0	100.0

NOTE: Data are estimates based on a survey of seven countries: Argentina, Brazil, Colombia, Chile, Mexico, Peru, and Venezuela.

SOURCE: ECLAC.

though, the data on distribution are very incomplete. The deteriorating employment situation already described is indicative of a worsening distribution in the 1980s.

Given these trends, even during two decades of strong economic growth, the number of poor increased. Table 14.3 shows that in 1960 the poor represented half of the population and in 1981 they composed around one-third. However, in absolute numbers, because of the increase in population, poverty was greater in 1981. The number of poor people will continue to grow until the end of the century, when it will reach around 170 million people, or 30 percent of the total population. The wide variation among countries is shown in the lower half of the table. The table also shows that, as a result of urbanization, there are about as many poor in urban as in rural areas, even though the *incidence* of poverty is much greater in the rural sector. In 1981 half of the people living in the rural sector were poor, while in the cities poverty engulfed around 20 percent of the population.

The crisis of the 1980s affected the incidence of poverty. An analysis by PREALC suggests that as a result of the recession there was a general increase in poverty in Latin America, particularly in urban areas. The increase was the product not simply of the conditions in the labor market described above, but also of the general increase in levels of inflation experienced in the 1980s (see Chapter 13). The poor generally were much less able to protect their very limited resources against inflation than were the better-off. Typically the poor held a larger proportion of their liquid resources in cash and thus bore the full brunt of the erosive power of inflation. Also typically they suffered

Table 14.3

Estimates of poverty in Latin America, 1960–1981

	1960	1970	1981
Total poor			
Millions	108	112	130
As percentage of total population	50	40	35
Geographic distribution (percent)[a]			
Total	100	100	100
Rural	na	58	51
Urban	na	42	49
Incidence (percent)[b]			
Rural	na	54	51
Urban	na	29	21
Argentina		8	8
Brazil		49	43
Chile		17	16
Colombia		45	43
Costa Rica		24	22
Honduras		65	64
Mexico		34	29
Panama		39	37
Venezuela		25	24

[a]Proportion of urban and rural poor in the total population of poor.
[b]Proportion of poor in total urban and rural population.

SOURCE: ECLAC, *Revista de la CEPAL [Comisión Económica para América Latina] (Review of the Economic Commission for Latin America),* no. 18 (Santiago, 1982); PREALC estimates.

disproportionately from abrupt stabilization measures, which tended to cut real wages and "adjust" prices such as bus fares crucial to the cost of living for the least well-off.

It is estimated that in the 1980s as many as 30 million additional people in the cities fell below the poverty line, representing an increase of 40 percent in poverty levels. The increment was mainly the result of the growth in chronic unemployment. Poor people in the rural areas increased by almost 9 million, representing a growth of 8 percent in the percentage of rural poor.

An alternative perspective on welfare can be gained by examining basic-needs indicators. What are truly valid proxies for the "quality of life"? The consensus today is that infant mortality, life expectancy at birth, and literacy

Table 14.4

Infant and child mortality in 1960 and 1984, with alternative measures of income per capita, by country

Country[a]	Infant Mortality per 1,000		Child Mortality per 1,000		GNP per Capita (Current U.S.$)		Adjusted per capita Income as Percentage of U.S. income in 1974[b]
	1960	1984	1960	1984	1977	1984	
Venezuela	85	38	9	2	$2,625	$3,410	50.6
Argentina	61	34	5	1	1,870	2,230	46.4
Uruguay	51	29	4	1	1,449	1,980	31.1
Brazil	118	68	19	6	1,411	1,720	29.4
Costa Rica	74	19	8	na	1,393	1,190	23.9
Cuba	35	16	2	na	1,317	na	na
Chile	119	22	20	1	1,247	1,700	28.4
Panama	68	25	6	1	1,195	1,980	27.7
Mexico	91	51	10	3	1,164	2,040	26.5
Nicaragua	144	70	30	6	865	860	21.8
Dominican Republic	120	71	20	6	841	970	21.8
Guatemala	92	66	10	5	830	1,160	18.0
Ecuador	140	67	28	5	819	1,150	15.6
Colombia	93	48	11	3	762	1,390	19.2
Paraguay	86	44	9	2	747	1,240	13.9
Peru	163	95	38	11	721	1,000	17.6
El Salvador	136	66	26	5	589	710	14.5
Bolivia	167	118	40	20	476	540	10.2
Honduras	145	77	30	7	424	700	11.6
Haiti	1,182	124	47	22	230	320	na

[a]Countries are listed in descending order of GNP per capita in 1977.
[b]Adjusted income per capita as percentage of U.S. income in 1974 is "Kravis-adjusted" income compared in terms of estimated real purchasing power. See I. Kravis, A. W. Heston, and R. Summers, "Real GDP per Capita for More Than One Hundred Countries," *Economic Journal* 88 (June 1978), pp. 215–42.

SOURCE: J. Sheehan, *Patterns of Development in Latin America* (Princeton, 1987), p. 26. Reprinted by permission of Princeton University Press. Copyright © 1987.

are the most reliable indicators of well-being. However, they cannot be interpreted in isolation, and they are interrelated with other variables. Literacy, for example, is in part a proxy for the skills that enable a person to take advantage of health facilities, which in their turn raise the quality of life.

Infant and child mortality are given in Table 14.4. It is significant that the two countries with the lowest levels of both in 1984, Costa Rica and Cuba, are not the highest in the ranking of GNP per capita. The explanation of their success in reducing child mortality seems to be not simply their greater investment in the social sector but their lower degree of income inequality. For a given degree of inequality, higher income per capita helps the basic-needs situation. But for a given income level, more equal distribution helps just as surely, and possibly more.

However, the moderate improvement in some countries needs to be put into an international perspective. In 1960 the infant mortality rate for the region was 3.6 times higher than in the industrialized countries. By 1984, although the median rate for the region had been brought down by 44 percent, the rate by then was 5 times higher than in the industrialized countries.

An index that incorporates also life expectancy at birth and literacy is the so-called Physical Quality of Life Index, or PQLI. It arbitrarily gives equal weight to each of the three elements. Table 14.5 shows the position of the various Latin American countries in a ranking that includes 125 countries, rich and poor. The position and improvement in Cuba and Costa Rica are remarkable. Uruguay's very high ranking is explained by its past history of investment in its welfare state, though its ranking declined between 1960 and 1980. Chile, on the contrary, improved, basically because of an intensive campaign to reduce child mortality. Argentina is striking for its decline, as are, more understandably, Guatemala and Bolivia.

These comparisons raise the question of the relevance of redistributive strategies. Broadly, redistribution policy can be divided into reformist and structural strategies. Reformist strategies rely on instruments such as taxation and long-term investment in health and education. Structural strategies affect the structure of access to income-generating opportunities, principally by means of land reform or other ownership changes. Examples of the former include Costa Rica, Colombia, Uruguay, and to a lesser extent Brazil. Examples of the latter include Cuba, Nicaragua under the Sandinistas, Chile under Allende and to some extent under Frei (land reform), and Peru under Velasco. Other countries have been notable for paying no more than lip service to either strategy. It is noteworthy that countries from both categories of policy have achieved important gains. Once again Cuba and Costa Rica are the best examples.

The structuralist route can bring great dividends but can also fail totally. Failure occurs partly because of the technical difficulty of restructuring—as evidenced by all land reform programs—but also because of the intervention of political variables. Nicaragua looks like a brave attempt at structural reform that made real gains in its early years but was subsequently eroded by the reduction in government revenue as a result of the collapse of the economy.

What is most noteworthy of all, however, is that, on the basis of the

Table 14.5

Physical Quality of Life Index and GNP per capita by country, 1960 and 1980 (by rankings)

Country[a]	PQLI		GNP per Capita	
	1960	1980	1960	1980
Cuba	29	10	43	68
Costa Rica	36	23	46	49
Uruguay	26	31	29	38
Chile	47	34	32	45
Argentina	31	40	33	41
Venezuela	45	43	27	36
Paraguay	43	46	57	57
Mexico	47	48	39	46
Colombia	51	51	58	59
Brazil	55	57	51	47
Ecuador	57	60	67	58
Dominican Republic	56	61	62	60
El Salvador	60	63	70	75
Nicaragua	62	65	61	71
Peru	64	67	53	65
Honduras	66	68	75	79
Guatemala	61	71	60	62
Bolivia	80	86	84	78
Haiti	96	95	96	104

[a]Countries are listed in descending order of PQLI ranking in 1980.

SOURCE: E. Nissan and R. Caveny, "Relative Welfare Improvement of Low Income Versus High Income Countries," *World Development* (May 1988).

limited evidence available so far, no country that has adopted either strategy has shown greater improvement in basic needs or in distributive indicators, although the initial situation in countries like Argentina may have been much healthier owing to the structure of the labor market. In fact, this group of countries has on the whole performed less well in terms of welfare improvement than the group that has taken a more active approach.

15

Prospects

With the 1980s recognized as the "lost decade" as far as economic growth is concerned, Latin America entered the last decade of the century in a spirit of despondency. The debt crisis has sapped confidence, and long-run development planning has been replaced by short-term crisis management. Given the problems faced by civilian regimes in dealing with apparently intractable economic and social problems, there is genuine fear in several countries of a breakdown of constitutional government and a possible return to authoritarian rule.

The last decade, however, has not been entirely wasted. The majority of the Latin American countries have made some progress in implementing the structural reforms needed to restore the region to economic health in the 1990s. This process, which began before the debt crisis unfolded, has been accelerated both by the demands of international financial agencies and by the exigencies of severe budget and balance-of-payments constraints. Furthermore, structural reform not only has taken place in republics favoring free-market solutions (such as Chile) but has also been introduced by governments (such as the Mexican) that remain committed to a fair degree of state intervention.

More priority is now being given to exports in general and to nontraditional exports in particular. The internal terms of trade have been shifted in favor of traded goods, and new incentives have been created to promote exports. Investors in nontraditional exports have become more aware of the problems of penetrating new markets, and governments are coming to understand that "getting prices right" is only a first step in shifting resources back toward the export sector. The poor performance of traditional, mainly primary, exports in the 1980s has obscured the underlying changes in many countries, but the basis has been laid for a superior export performance in the 1990s.

The second change involves the efficiency of the public sector and the rationality of public expenditure. This process is far from complete, and there are notable exceptions to the rule. The demands of debt servicing have also produced budget deficits that are often far in excess of what can be considered desirable by the orthodox tenets of fiscal and monetary policy. Yet new taxes have been introduced, old taxes have been streamlined and revised, and steps have been taken to overhaul the administration of the fiscal system. The expenditure side of the budget has been more difficult to reform, given the overwhelming importance of public-sector salaries on the one hand and debt-service payments on the other. Nevertheless, many inefficient transfers and subsidies have been weeded out in the search for fiscal economies. Finally, almost all countries have taken steps to enhance accountability in the management of state-owned enterprises, and most governments have also found a welcome source of additional revenue through the sale of some public-sector firms to the private sector.

These changes are to be welcomed and should not go unrecognized, but the region faces the paradox that, after nearly half a century of inward-looking policies, it is more vulnerable than ever to the external economic environment. Thus, its economic performance in the 1990s will depend to a considerable degree on events beyond the region's control. In particular, Latin America's economic prospects depend crucially on steps to resolve the debt crisis, the performance of the world economy, and the response of a number of international actors with responsibilities for and commitments to the region.

The Debt Problem

As is well known, the debt crisis has led to a drain of resources out of Latin America, converting the region from a net borrower to a net lender. This negative net resource transfer—a consequence of debt-service payments exceeding new lending—has also forced Latin America to curtail investment. Future economic growth has been mortgaged to pay the debt.

It is universally agreed that reversing the negative resource transfer is an essential prerequisite for restoring economic health in Latin America. It is also widely recognized that a reduction in the drain of resources from the region will take place in the 1990s, whether or not it is agreed to by the creditors. Yet the manner in which the reduction comes about is important. If it is unilateral, then interest payments on the debt will certainly decline but the region will find it extremely difficult to tap the international capital market.

The absence of new lending will continue to depress investment, and the growth performance will be sluggish at best. If the reduction is multilateral, with the cooperation of creditors, then there is just a chance that the negative net resource transfer of the 1980s could be turned into a positive flow of resources toward the region in the 1990s.

Debt reduction is one of the main stated aims of the Brady proposals unveiled in 1989. However, how to maintain the new lending to meet Latin America's financial needs while undertaking debt reduction is an area of uncertainty in the scheme, one that has been seized on by some commercial banks as a reason for opposing the Brady Plan.

Multilaterally agreed debt reduction may be the preferred solution, but its outcome is not assured. Creditors will have to accept that the debt will not be repaid at par, and the governments of creditor countries will have to accept a fiscal loss as the counterpart of debt relief. These are difficult conditions, but it is already apparent that the solution will eventually take this form. The international banks have already dropped the fiction in their accounts that the market and the par values of the debt are the same, and governments of creditor countries have provided tax relief on the loan-loss provisions set aside by banks.

Debt reduction through multilateral action still requires a leap of imagination by the actors involved. The menu for providing debt relief through multilateral means was far too limited for most of the 1980s and too heavily dependent on debt-equity swaps. The menu has to be broadened with much greater emphasis given to the conversion of existing debt into bonds at prices reflecting market values. This process, known as securitization, allows market forces to play an important role in determining the extent of debt relief and can be coupled with a lowering of interest rates.

Creditor governments have so far shown only a limited interest in securitization. Their reluctance to commit themselves to this form of debt relief was based partly on a belief that the Baker Initiative would make it unnecessary and partly on genuine fears that the international banks could not absorb such losses without serious damage to the international financial system. Neither consideration is now particularly relevant: the Baker Plan is effectively buried, and the balance sheets of the main international banks have been much improved. There are therefore good reasons for believing that securitization will provide the key to debt relief in the 1990s with obvious benefits for Latin America.

The Brady proposals go some of the way toward meeting the needs of Latin American debtors. By recognizing the need for some degree of debt reduction, the proposals pave the way for a more equitable division of the burden of adjustment between creditors and debtors. Clearly, securitization is consistent with the Brady Plan, although the scale of debt relief will depend crucially on the discounts applied to the existing debts. Here there is scope for considerable negotiation, which is likely to be carried out on a country-by-country basis.

In itself, debt relief simply reduces the negative net resource transfer. Its reversal, a much more ambitious task, depends on the supply of new funds, which in turn depends on the response of a number of international actors. Apart from the banks themselves, these actors consist of multinational companies, the governments of Western industrialized countries, and the international financial agencies.

It is not realistic to expect the international banks to play a large part in channeling new funds to Latin America in the 1990s. Nor is it particularly desirable that they do so. Banks lack the expertise to ensure that their funds are used productively when lent to, or even guaranteed by, sovereign countries. And the experience of the 1980s will make them very reluctant to increase their exposure to Latin America voluntarily. Securitization, or other forms of debt relief, is designed not only to reduce the debt burden but also to extricate the banks from an unmanageable situation. Much will depend on how much, and by whom, guarantees are granted on the new bonds. Although some forms of lending will remain attractive for banks, notably short-term trade credits and cofinancing with international agencies, commercial loans in general are not expected to be a dynamic feature of the Latin American financial landscape in the 1990s.

It is therefore particularly important that debt reduction under the Brady Plan, or whatever other plan is finally adopted, be on a sufficiently large scale to compensate Latin American debtors for the risk of a decline in new commercial bank lending. A 10 percent reduction in debt-service payments, for example, would be wholly inadequate to compensate debtors for the expected fall in new bank loans, and banks are going to be very reluctant to commit new resources when old loans are subject to discounts. The reduction in debt-service payments therefore needs to be at least 50 percent, which implies a considerable reduction either in the value of the principal or interest rates or in some combination of the two.

New Sources of Capital

As part of their efforts to promote exports, many Latin American governments have reformed or revised legislation affecting inward investment by multinational companies. Article 24 of the Andean Pact, for example, requiring eventual majority ownership of all foreign investments by nationals, has been phased out and multinational corporations are allowed in many cases to participate in privatization schemes. The new climate favoring investment by multinationals has not been easy to create, and the rewards are still likely to be disappointing. Multinationals are offered even more attractive packages by other developing regions—for example, some of the East Asian countries—and Latin America has lost favor as an area for inward investment. The previous attraction, the large captive domestic market, is no longer so relevant, and the use of Latin America as a base for exports to third markets must be compared with the advantages of other such bases around the world. There will be some areas of remaining interest, notably investment in *maquiladoras* on Mexico's border with the United States, but multinationals will not replace international banks as the primary source of new lending to Latin America in the 1990s.

The official credits provided bilaterally by the governments of advanced industrial countries are already important sources of finance for the smaller Latin American republics, like Costa Rica, and the prospect of a large increase in official bilateral credits to the region in the 1990s has been much discussed. Yet there are many obstacles in the path of such an increase. Some of the relevant governments can expect to run current account deficits in the 1990s and cannot absorb a major transfer of resources to developing countries in general and to Latin America in particular. Japan and West Germany will continue to run current account surpluses, and the possibility of a major transfer of resources by Japan to Latin America has been debated. Yet Latin America promises to remain only on the margin of Japan's foreign-policy priorities in the 1990s, and the transfer of resources to the region is likely to disappoint many expectations. As in the 1980s, only the smaller countries, such as Guatemala, are likely to find that official credits provide a substantial proportion of their foreign financial requirements.

A further problem with the transfer of official credits to Latin America is the competition from Eastern Europe. The Latin American plea in the 1980s that the consolidation of democracy required outside financial support went largely unheeded. Nevertheless, Western official creditors were the first to adopt this argument in the case of Eastern Europe. Thus, the transfer of resources to Eastern Europe in the 1990s will increase sharply. Some of these will be new resources, but there is a widespread fear that part of the transfer will consist of funds that might otherwise have gone to Latin America.

If a multilaterally agreed solution to the debt crisis is adopted, the international financial institutions (IFIs)—particularly the World Bank, the Inter-American Development Bank, and the IMF—will continue to exercise a high profile in the debate over policy and structural reform. Yet their ability to effect a major transfer of resources to the region is likely to be circumscribed. Creditor governments have shown a certain reluctance to increase the agencies' lending capacity. The paramount need to service such loans in full meant that in the late 1980s repayments from many Latin American governments exceeded new lending. The balance can be expected to change in the 1990s so that the agencies at least provide a net flow of funds to the region. The Inter-American Development Bank in particular is set to increase both its gross and its net lending to Latin America substantially as a result of increases in its capital base agreed to at the end of the 1980s.

The major change in the role of the IFIs will be their involvement in debt-reduction packages as guarantors of future interest and principal payments. Although reluctant to become involved in this new venture, the international agencies—particularly the IMF and the World Bank—have little choice because the commercial banks are unlikely to accept debt-reduction proposals without such guarantees. The Inter-American Development Bank should also be able to play a more dynamic role in Latin America in the 1990s, becoming involved for the first time in structural adjustment lending.

The increasing involvement of the international financial institutions in Latin America will bring with it an increase in conditionality. In addition, some other official creditors, like the European Community, are keen to attach conditions to any new lending. Thus, conditionality threatens to become a major issue in the 1990s, as lenders use it to try to force through the changes in economic and social policy that they consider appropriate. With the IFIs subject to growing pressure from influential lobbies to add conditions relating to the environment, human rights, the participation of women, and income redistribution, there is genuine concern that conditionality will come increasingly into conflict with national sovereignty.

Even the most optimistic scenario does not allow for a major increase in external funding for the region. The best that can be hoped for in the 1990s is that the negative net resource transfer will be reversed, leading to a small positive net inflow. Thus, the increase in fixed capital formation that the region desperately needs will have to be financed in the main through domestic resources. Only countries that have successfully overhauled their financial systems to promote domestic savings will be able to raise investment to a rate consistent with the historic rate of growth.

The increase in domestic savings will require greatly improved performance from both the private and the public sectors. In the case of the private sector, new financial instruments will need to be created to reduce the attractions of capital flight. These will include stock-market quotations for new companies as well as an overhaul of the government bond market to make such bonds more attractive to the nonbank private sector. In the case of the public sector, the drive to overhaul the fiscal system, in particular on the revenue side, will have to continue. More governments in the 1990s are likely to experiment with privatization programs as a seemingly painless way of increasing fiscal income.

International Trade and the World Economy

Latin America's economic performance in the 1990s, just as in the 1980s, will be heavily conditioned by developments in the world economy. The experience of the early 1980s, when both the OECD countries and Latin America were in recession, suggested that expansion of the world economy was a necessary condition for growth in the region. The second half of the 1980s, however, witnessed an expansion of world trade and GDP in OECD countries, without an end to stagnation in Latin America. Thus, the growth of the world economy and international trade is a necessary, but not sufficient, condition for the recovery of the Latin American economies.

What was missing in the 1980s were favorable terms of trade for Latin America's traditional exports, which still account for some two-thirds of total exports. Rising prices for a few primary products were swamped by falling prices for many major foreign-exchange earners. Import quota restrictions, applied by consuming countries, were also hardened for many products such as beef and sugar, while agricultural protectionism in the industrialized countries damaged the exports of temperate Latin American countries. As of 1990 international commodity agreements were in disarray, and the Montreal review of the GATT Uruguay Round in December 1988 had failed to make progress on the liberalization of trade in agricultural products.

In recent years, new areas of concern have opened up regarding commodity exports:

- There is heightened awareness of the environmental consequences of primary production. Rapid deforestation in the Amazon Basin has given rise to widespread fears of adverse long-term climatic change, irreversible soil degradation, and the disappearance of many unique species of flora and fauna. Overexploitation of marine resources as a result of free access to a common property resource has required the introduction by national governments of production quotas and closed sport fishing seasons to conserve fish stocks. Air and water pollution from mineral extraction and processing plants has existed for many years in the region but is now being more closely monitored.

- It is argued that the rapid growth in the production of agricultural raw materials for export has occurred at the expense of domestic food output in certain countries. For instance, in Brazil soybeans are displacing black beans. As a result, national food security is felt to be at risk. Though not always well founded, this argument reflects the greater priority that policymakers now give to achieving minimum levels of self-sufficiency in basic food staples.
- The expansion of export-oriented food processing, particularly of fruits and vegetables, has often occurred through foreign investment. This has led to allegations that national food systems have been penetrated by multinational corporations whose objectives may not be compatible with increasing the well-being of the host country. Although this argument merits examination, it is not obvious why foreign investment in the food industry should be treated differently from foreign investment in other industries.

Trade in primary products is notoriously volatile, and there is reason to believe that the performance of primary products in the 1990s will not be quite as dismal as in the 1980s. There are signs that agricultural protectionism in OECD countries will start to be reduced in the 1990s, with or without a successful outcome to the Uruguay Round. The prices of Latin American nonoil minerals have at last shown a welcome tendency to respond positively to the growth of the OECD economies, and the oil price had already started to increase before the Iraqi invasion of Kuwait in August 1990. A modest increase in the volume of Latin American primary product exports can therefore be expected in the 1990s with a somewhat higher (5 percent a year) increase in the value of earnings as a result of firmer prices.

Such an increase is not sufficient to restore Latin America to its historic rate of economic growth. However, nontraditional exports will continue to increase in importance and could represent around half of the region's export earnings by the year 2000. This expansion implies an annual rate of increase in the value of nontraditional exports of 12.5 percent and raises the question of what kinds of goods and services will be exported and to which markets.

Nontraditional exports consist of new primary products, manufactured goods, and services. Various countries have made efforts to diversify agricultural exports. As a result, exports of citrus fruits and tropical and temperate horticultural products—pineapples, melons, vegetables, flowers, fruits, and nuts—have expanded considerably. Substantial growth in demand and world trade for these products can be expected, so there is room for export expansion. There are some limitations, however:

- The size of the world market for these nontraditional exports, many of which are luxury agricultural items rather than basic staples, is likely to remain limited, with exports mostly confined to developed countries.
- Competition will be fierce. Many countries in and outside Latin America are simultaneously trying to diversify exports toward tropical horticultural products, and they may soon crowd what is essentially a not very large market. Competition from domestic producers in developed countries, who will probably continue to enjoy some protection, is likely to affect temperate horticultural products.
- The development of these new export lines requires large investments, sophisticated farm and processing technologies, and fairly complex marketing systems. These needs are likely to exclude from full participation in the potential expansion of nontraditional exports those Latin American countries with comparatively backward agriculture, and also the traditional farming sectors of the more advanced countries.

Manufactured exports vary from technologically simple products such as agro-industrial goods, furniture, and leather products to more sophisticated products such as steel, automobiles, electronics, and petrochemicals. The technological problems are relatively easy to overcome in the first group of products, and many Latin American countries have begun to enjoy rapid rates of growth in such exports. Products in the second group are technologically more demanding, and only the large Latin American republics can expect to increase this type of export substantially. In international trade in manufactures Latin America still has a large deficit, but it should start to fall in the 1990s.

Exports of services are normally associated with the advanced countries. There are, however, good prospects for Latin America in a number of areas such as tourism, which is very sensitive to the real exchange rate. Some of the small republics in the Caribbean Basin should also be able to exploit their proximity to the United States to establish a niche in such areas as data processing and aircraft repair. Latin America as a whole, however, must expect to remain a net importer of services in the 1990s.

The expansion of Latin America's nontraditional exports will depend on access to the markets of the main OECD countries—in particular, the United States and the European Community. Many of the small republics enjoy special access to the U.S. market in nontraditional exports under the Caribbean Basin Initiative (CBI) launched by President Reagan in 1983. But the CBI does not apply to traditional products and some sensitive nontraditional exports such as textiles. In the case of the European Community, the Lomé Convention offers special privileges to sixty-eight small developing countries, but only two—the Dominican Republic and Haiti—are in Latin America. Thus, the special trading schemes in place do not offer much comfort to most of Latin America, and the fear of protectionism in the main export markets is ever present.

Access to the U.S. market is likely to be easier for Mexico, assuming that the current bilateral negotiations between the two countries result in a free trade agreement similar to that signed by Canada and the United States. The negotiations are being followed closely by other Latin American countries, some of whom have responded enthusiastically to the proposal made by President Bush in 1990 (under the Enterprise for the Americas Initiative) for a continent-wide free trade area. Progress is likely to be slow, however, even on the most optimistic assumptions. A free trade agreement between the United States and Mexico is not expected to be in place before 1993, and a broader agreement for all the Americas would take much longer.

In the 1990s the threat of protectionism for Latin American exports depends on a number of factors. The first problem is the U.S. trade deficit. If the deficit fails to respond to the relatively mild measures adopted so far, it will be increasingly difficult for a U.S. president to prevent Congress from adopting overtly protectionist legislation that discriminates most against countries, like Brazil, that run large trade surpluses with the United States.

The second problem is the creation of the European Domestic Market (EDM) within the European Community by 1992. The EDM is designed to eliminate all nontariff barriers on trade within the Community, but it could have the effect of raising nontariff barriers against imports from outside the Community. Although the European Commission has gone out of its way to deny that the EDM implies a "Fortress Europe" policy, critics are quick to point out that in recent years the European Community has increased enormously the number of Voluntary Export Restraint (VER) agreements applied to imports from developing countries.

These are legitimate concerns for Latin America, but they should not be overemphasized. Despite the growth of protectionism in the 1980s, Latin America raised the volume of its exports by 57 percent between 1980 and 1989. Furthermore, this increase was achieved despite the collapse of intraregional trade in the wake of the debt crisis. In the 1990s, intraregional trade seems certain to increase again from its present low level, but one should not expect too much from regional integration. The obstacles that prevented a major expansion of intraregional trade in the past still exist.

There is a shortage of hard currency to settle debts arising from intraregional trade, and many tariff and nontariff barriers still exist. Transport costs remain formidable for many products, and many industrialists are unwilling to accept the full blast of competition. With public policy emphasizing exports outside the region, intraregional exports with a few exceptions will remain fairly undynamic. There is, however, a greater political will in Latin America to experiment with new forms of regional integration and the Rio Group (consisting of Mexico and the South American republics) has put integration high on its agenda.

Economic Policy and Economic Growth

The shift of resources toward the export sector will require the maintenance of competitive exchange rates through periodic devaluations. At the same time, the need to maintain the profitability of private-sector investment will rule out the extended use of price controls. Thus, inflationary pressures will continue in the 1990s despite the slow growth of domestic demand. These pressures will be offset to some extent by tariff reductions and the lowering of budget deficits—if debt-service payments decline. But only exceptional circumstances will permit Latin American countries to enjoy the kind of price stability found in OECD countries. The main policy focus will be on keeping inflation within "acceptable" limits and avoiding its adverse redistributive impact, which caused real wages and salaries to fall so sharply in the 1980s. Experiments with anti-inflation stabilization programs will continue, with policymakers showing greater willingness to mix orthodox and heterodox approaches.

The slow growth of demand in the 1990s and the need to increase efficiency in the private and public sectors will put severe strains on the labor market. Although the growth of the labor force is slowing as a result of the demographic transition, the rate of growth of job creation in the modern sector will be modest. The pressure on firms to lower unit labor costs in order to compete internationally will become more intense, and employers will be anxious to adopt more flexible labor market arrangements through subcontracting, part-time working, and the reform of labor legislation. The public sector, at both central and local government levels, will be under pressure to weed out redundant workers, and sinecures in state-owned enterprises are likely to diminish.

Although educational opportunities will increase and bring with them an increase in educational participation by the young—thus delaying their entrance into the labor force—the process is likely to be slow. Education remains primarily a public-sector responsibility, and the funds will not be available for a major expansion. Female participation rates will also rise, in line with historic trends, so that the gap between supply and demand in the labor market in the 1990s will remain. Real wages will still recover from the trough of the 1980s, but the differential between skilled workers in the full-time modern sector and the rest of the labor force will widen further.

Despite recent rhetoric in favor of the urban informal sector, few governments are likely to base industrial or employment policy on its expansion. Instead, the aim will be to lower the bureaucratic red tape surrounding firms in the formal sector so as to permit them some of the freedom currently enjoyed by the informal sector. Employment and output in the informal sector will still continue to grow, but this growth will reflect that sector's function as employer of last resort rather than any dynamic comparative advantage. The vast majority of traded goods, and exports in particular, will continue to be produced by the formal sector.

The drop in real wages and salaries in the 1980s following the debt crisis led many to suggest that the follies of governments and of the rich, who contracted the debt in the first place, were being paid for by the sacrifices of the poor. There is a great deal of truth in this aphorism, but it is unrealistic to expect a reversal of the situation in the 1990s. Populist policies, such as those followed by the Peruvian government under Alan García, have ended up requiring even greater sacrifices by the poor than those demanded in Pinochet's Chile. There is greater awareness now among politicians of the limits imposed on social policy by economic reality.

The prospects outlined so far suggest that in the 1990s Latin America will not be able to record growth rates comparable to those achieved in the three decades before 1980. Performance, however, should surpass the dismal record of the 1980s, and an annual GDP growth rate for the region as a whole in the range of 3 or 4 percent is feasible. The lack of investment in the 1980s will undermine Latin America's growth potential, though. Also, with population growth still running at nearly 2 percent a year, the chances for a significant increase in real income per capita are slim. Not until the mid-1990s will the 1980 figure for real income per person be surpassed. The gap between living standards in Latin America and many other parts of the world will widen by the end of the century.

Even a growth rate of 3 or 4 percent will require a major effort by the region. On the expenditure side, the growth of private consumption will be restrained by the modest rise in real incomes and the need to increase domestic saving ratios. Public consumption will be affected by the need to reduce budget deficits. Thus, the growth of real GDP will depend heavily on a shift of resources into exports and investment while avoiding a sharp rise in imports. Not all countries can be expected to achieve this. For some, the problem of expanding exports in the face of falling demand for traditional products will prove insuperable. For others, political uncertainty and the lack of entrepreneurial resources will stand in the way of increasing investment.

Nor can the problem of reverse or negative import substitution be ignored. Trade liberalization policies, desirable though they may seem, carry with them a threat to established high-cost industries. Negative import substitution, so important in the Southern Cone in the 1970s, was avoided in the 1980s by the extreme nature of the balance-of-payments constraint. If exports increase in the 1990s and the foreign-exchange constraint eases, some industrial firms may be forced to close. In the most successful countries, the expansion of industrial exports will more than compensate for the closure of inefficient industries, but in less successful countries deindustrialization through negative import substitution will act as a brake on the growth of real GDP.

Regional Differences

The preceding section has surveyed the prospects for the 1990s at the regional level, but regional differences—as always—will be important. Indeed, there is a case for arguing that regional differences will become more important in the 1990s as the international marketplace becomes the yardstick for success.

As the 1980s came to a close, regional differences within Latin America became very marked. As Table 15.1 makes clear, four groups of countries could be identified. Group A consists of three countries that managed to raise real GDP by more than 5 percent a year in 1988–1989—an impressive performance by any standards—and therefore enjoyed an increase in real income per capita. Group B consists of countries where the annual rate of growth of real GDP exceeded 3 percent, but was less than 5 percent. The four countries in this group managed a modest increase in real income per capita.

Group C—by far the largest—consists of all the republics where GDP growth was less than 3 percent per year in the last two years of the 1980s but was at least positive. Many members of this group suffered a fall in living standards because population growth exceeded the growth of real GDP. Group D consists of five countries where real GDP fell and where real income per capita suffered a major decline.

As a guide to performance in the 1990s, real GDP growth in 1988–1989 is

Table 15.1

Annual average rate of growth of real GDP, by country

Group A (more than 5%)		Group B (3% to 5%)	
1988–1989	1990s	1988–1989	1990s
Chile	*Brazil	Colombia	Colombia
Ecuador	Chile	Costa Rica	Guatemala
Paraguay	*Costa Rica	Guatemala	Honduras
		Honduras	*Mexico
			*Nicaragua
			*Panama
			*Paraguay
			*Uruguay
			*Venezuela

Group C (0% to 3%)		Group D (less than 0%)
1988–1989	1990s	1988–1989
Bolivia	*Argentina	Argentina
Brazil	Bolivia	Nicaragua
Cuba	Cuba	Panama
Dominican Republic	Dominican Republic	Peru
El Salvador	*Ecuador	Venezuela
Haiti	*El Salvador	
Mexico	*Haiti	
Uruguay	*Peru	

*Indicates change of group.

SOURCE: Groupings for 1988–1989 are derived from ECLAC, *Preliminary Overview of Latin America and the Caribbean* (Santiago, December 1989), table 2. Used by permission.

of limited value, although it does at least provide a point of reference. However, it does not allow one to determine whether performance was based on temporary factors (such as a sudden change in the external terms of trade) or whether performance was based on a solid foundation made possible by previous policies. Each country's prospects in the 1990s will be affected by both kinds of considerations, but over the long run the second kind are a much more reliable guide to performance.

In the 1980s, the debt crisis and other external shocks forced Latin America to adopt stabilization and adjustment programs. Stabilization is a short-term response to external and internal disequilibria. External disequilibrium is associated with balance-of-payments problems, internal disequilibrium with inflationary pressures. Adjustment programs, by contrast, are designed to create a new framework of price and other incentives to help the economy "adjust" in the desired direction over the medium term. In the context of the 1980s, therefore, adjustment must be thought of as providing the incentives for a shift of resources back to the export sector after many decades of inward-looking development.

Stabilization programs are nearly always associated with recession, since the economy has to accept a strong dose of medicine to cure the twin evils of balance-of-payments problems and inflationary pressures. Adjustment programs are supposed to pave the way for renewed growth, although even with successful adjustment programs it may take some time for the growth rate to accelerate. Thus, a precondition for successful performance in the 1990s is the completion of successful stabilization and adjustment programs.

The completing of stabilization and adjustment programs is only a *necessary* condition for successful performance in the 1990s. It is not a *sufficient* condition. Successful countries must also satisfy a number of other conditions:

- ▼ Promotion of nontraditional exports, without causing the collapse of the traditional export sector.
- ▼ An increase in the rate of fixed capital formation financed in part through an increase of domestic savings and the repatriation of flight capital.
- ▼ An improvement in the efficiency of the import-competing sector without the need for massive deindustrialization.
- ▼ An improvement in the efficiency of state-owned enterprises, with or without privatization.
- ▼ Growth of imports financed in part through expanding exports and in part through reduced debt-service payments.

In the 1990s, three countries (Brazil, Chile, and Costa Rica—Group A in Table 15.1) can expect to record growth rates in excess of 5 percent a year. For Chile, this rate of growth represents a continuation of the trend observed at the end of the 1980s and is due to the successful completion of both stabilization and adjustment programs. The stabilization program, however, was not achieved without a heavy social cost, and Chile—now once again a democracy—can expect to see a modest increase in taxation to pay for increased social expenditures. In addition, Chilean growth in the late 1980s was achieved with scant regard for environmental costs. Thus the new government can be expected to demand that business give more attention to environmental considerations. Both these factors imply a slight reduction in the feasible rate of growth in the 1990s, but the adjustment program has been so successful that Chile should be able to sustain the growth of exports, investment, and imports in a manner consistent with rapid economic growth.

Costa Rica is set to reap the benefits of a successful adjustment program adopted in the mid-1980s and now nearing completion. In addition, the change of government in Nicaragua will benefit Costa Rica. Foreign investors will be less affected by worries over regional instability. Trade within the Central American Common Market should start to increase, and Costa Rican industry is well placed to take advantage of any upturn in that trade. The growth of nontraditional exports, helped by the Caribbean Basin Initiative, will continue at a rapid pace, although a few firms will suffer as export subsidies are phased out over the next few years.

Brazil is the most problematic member of Group A. At the beginning of the 1990s, stabilization was not complete. Yet during the 1980s Brazil succeeded in pushing resources toward the export sector in general and toward manufactured exports in particular in a most spectacular fashion. Thus, Brazil has had lopsided development in which external adjustment has been a success and internal stabilization a failure. If Brazil can sustain a lower rate of inflation coupled with responsible fiscal policies, there is no reason to believe that it cannot achieve rapid growth in the 1990s. Alone among Latin American countries, Brazil has a strong capital-goods industry and is internationally competitive in a range of basic industries including petrochemicals, steel, and automobiles.

The second group of countries (Group B in Table 15.1) consists of those expected to raise real GDP by more than 3 percent a year but less than 5 percent. This group contains nine countries, three of which (Colombia, Guatemala, and Honduras) recorded a similar growth rate in the last two years of the 1980s. It is fair to say that the adjustment process in these three countries is not yet complete, so none is in a position to exploit to the full the opportunities of the 1990s. In addition, Colombia and Guatemala still face a serious problem of public disorder, which will act as a disincentive to productive investment.

The other six members of Group B are one country (Paraguay) that previously enjoyed a higher rate of growth and five countries (Mexico, Nicaragua, Panama, Uruguay, and Venezuela) where growth at the end of the 1980s was lower.

The downgrading of Paraguay is due to the country's failure so far to engage in a serious attempt at either stabilization or adjustment. In addition, the prospect of political upheaval in the transition to greater democracy cannot be ruled out. Paraguay, however, has consistently avoided a massive distortion of relative prices and has only a small foreign debt. Domestic enterprise has achieved a certain efficiency owing to the competition from contraband goods. Growth above 3 percent a year is thus feasible.

In Mexico both stabilization and adjustment programs have taken many years to come to fruition. The process is now nearing completion, and Mexico should be able to achieve a much improved growth rate in the 1990s. Bilateral agreements with the United States, rather than full integration into a North American customs union, will help boost exports from a small number of competitive industries. However, the inefficiency of many branches of industry means that trade liberalization and the proximity of the United States may lead to some industrial closures.

Nicaragua has not yet completed a stabilization program, and an adjustment program has barely begun. Now, however, the main priority is economic reconstruction—rebuilding the economy to levels not seen since before the 1980s. This task requires, above all, foreign aid, and there is good reason to believe that governments in Nicaragua in the 1990s will receive sufficient aid to permit a reasonable rate of economic recovery. Much the same applies to Panama, where real GDP fell by 16.4 percent in 1988 during the intense U.S. campaign to dislodge Noriega.

Uruguay has not yet completed the process of stabilization, and annual inflation rates remain stubbornly high. There has been some success, however, in encouraging exports—particularly nontraditional products—and the adjustment program offers the prospect of further continued growth in the 1990s. Venezuela, by contrast, has barely begun the process of adjustment. But the draconian stabilization program adopted in 1989 has paved the way for a swift introduction of measures designed to guide the economy toward greater diversification and less dependence on oil.

The third group of countries (Group C in Table 15.1) contains the remaining eight republics. Growth is assumed to be very modest and in a few cases will not even exceed the increase in population. None of these countries can be said to have completed an adjustment program, and only one (Bolivia) has had much success with stabilization. The need for tough economic policies in the 1990s to reduce inflation will be the main reason some members of this group (notably Argentina and Peru) will be hard pressed to achieve increases in real income per capita. Elsewhere, as in El Salvador and Haiti, political instability will act as a severe deterrent to productive investment.

Both Ecuador and the Dominican Republic should achieve growth rates close to 3 percent a year. Both countries have had some success in boosting nontraditional exports, but both suffer from accelerating inflation as a result of low fiscal discipline and rapidly depreciating exchange rates. By contrast, Bolivia has been extremely successful in reducing inflation but has so far failed to promote nontraditional exports. In all three cases, a further round of stabilization and adjustment will limit growth prospects in the 1990s, although in all three cases avoiding a fall in real income per capita should be possible.

During some years of the 1980s, Cuba appeared to enjoy the fastest rise in GDP per capita—that is not the same as a rise in living standards—in all the Americas. This feat was due not only to the generous level of support from the Soviet bloc but also to the fact that Cuba was able to avoid recession during the worst years of the debt crisis. In the 1990s, however, Cuba will be doing well if it has any increases at all. A reduction in support from Eastern Europe is certain, and the Soviet Union can no longer be relied on to subsidize the Cuban economy as it has done in the past.

An assessment of prospects in the 1990s by definition cannot anticipate the unexpected. A collapse in the world demand for cocaine, for example, would do severe short-term damage to the economies of Bolivia, Colombia, and Peru, however welcome it might be in the long run. Political upheaval and a return to military rule in some countries could lead to the imposition of trade and other sanctions. The collapse of GATT negotiations could force the world into a series of giant trading blocs from which Latin America might be largely excluded. Nor can the impact of sudden changes in commodity prices—an ever present possibility—be discounted.

All these considerations suggest that prospects for individual countries should be treated with caution. Taken as a whole, however, the picture is not as gloomy as many commentators seem to think it is. Furthermore, for those republics that use the next decade to restructure their economies in line with new opportunities, the first decade of the next century could be more promising. By the end of the twentieth century, some republics—such as Brazil and Mexico—may have joined the small club of developing countries with an indigenous technological capability, an important capital-goods industry, and the ability to create markets in new high-technology industries. Other countries, though still heavily dependent on foreign technology and imported capital goods, will have earned their place in the international division of labor.

Food sufficiency by this time should have increased across the continent, and some agro-industrial enterprises may have grown to the point where they are multinational companies with production and distribution facilities in many countries. Some of the giant state-owned enterprises in Latin America, in oil, banking, and basic industries, will prove that they can expand their activities overseas. That expansion will give them a stake in the expansion of the advanced industrial countries and improved knowledge of the international marketplace.

If Latin America returns to economic growth, foreign confidence will slowly be restored. Multinational companies, banks, and even bondholders may then take a fresh look at a region that tends now to hold little attraction. There is the risk that the excessive pessimism of the 1980s will be replaced by excessive optimism that subsequent performance cannot sustain. One of the lessons of the 1980s debt crisis was foreign bankers' chronic misjudment of the region's absorptive capacity. Latin America cannot isolate itself from the world economy and the international capital market, but it cannot risk another debt crisis. Policymakers will have to learn how to identify their country's needs independently of foreign "expert" advice. This will be true not only of their dealings with the private sector (multinational corporations and banks) but also with the public sector (the World Bank and the IMF). This lesson will be difficult for both sides to learn.

Part

4

INTERNATIONAL RELATIONS

16

Latin America and the United States

Trends in the 1980s

In the decade following the 1979 Sandinista revolution in Nicaragua, the United States was preoccupied with shoring up its traditional security position in the Central American isthmus. President Ronald Reagan came to office in 1981 committed to the view that his predecessor's weakness in defending U.S. interests had opened the way to Soviet-Cuban adventurism in Central America and that this trend could be reversed only by forceful policies. At times it seemed that U.S. congressional and media liberals and Latin American social democrats were as much the target of Reagan administration hostility as the isthmian *comandantes* (commanders).

This Latin American policy—first stiffening the Salvadorean government's resistance to a strong insurgent challenge, then escalating pressure against the Sandinista regime in Managua, and finally attempting to remove the drug-dominated military regime in Panama—dwarfed most other hemispheric concerns. It meant that Washington concentrated most of its energies and resources on a handful of the smallest and weakest Latin American republics, neglecting previously far more important relationships—for example, with Brazil. Indeed, for a short while, to an extraordinary degree, Washington seemed to base its relationship with major Latin American republics on how much they could be counted on as allies in the anti-Sandinista campaign. U.S. relations with President Leopoldo Galtieri's Argentina provide a vivid example of this: the United States would play down human-rights issues in return for military assistance in Central America. Covert action and counterinsurgency programs and the unilateral use of force took priority over more conventional and respectful forms of interstate relationship.

U.S. policy toward Latin America also highlighted unsavory aspects of inter-American history, reawakening memories of the "big stick" diplomacy employed by the United States in the Caribbean before President Franklin D. Roosevelt launched the "Good Neighbor Policy" in 1933. As a result, unease grew among many friends of the United States in the region and among some of Washington's allies in Europe. A long series of regional peace initiatives were launched, from the Contadora process in 1983, amid fears that the United States might invade Nicaragua through Honduras, to the Esquipulas peace proposal of 1987, which laid the basis for the peaceful resolution of the conflict between the Sandinistas and the U.S.-backed Contras. All aimed at reducing the polarization in Central America and at coaxing Washington toward a more low-key, cooperative, and diplomatic modus operandi in the isthmus.

Not just in Central America had opinion been polarized, and not just in Latin America had Washington alienated natural allies. Within the U.S. body politic, divisions were also pronounced. A substantial body of press and public opinion was closer to the Latin American view of the issue than to the official position of the U.S. government. This internal division on Latin American priorities was in marked contrast to the relatively more united stance of U.S. opinion in the 1950s and early 1960s. It was probably the deepest split since the late 1890s and the early 1900s, when anti-imperialists assailed U.S. military actions in the Caribbean.

Although Latin America is frequently classified as a low priority in statements about Washington's hierarchy of foreign-policy concerns, it is not a region that can safely be neglected for too long. Regional problems that are allowed to fester soon assume threatening proportions, in part because of the direct impact of Latin America on many U.S. concerns (for example, drugs), in part because of the negative symbolism of a world power failing to manage its local relationships effectively, and in part because the domestic consensus that Washington needs to conduct foreign policy can easily be shattered by the mismanagement of hemispheric relations.

A remarkable amount of congressional time and presidential energy was therefore devoted to internal conflicts over the purposes and methods of Washington's Central American policies. The Boland amendment suspending military aid to the *contras*, the Kissinger Commission which was established in 1983 to provide recommendations on the overall policy in Central America that would command broad domestic political support, and the Iran-*contra* scandal all testify to how deeply this controversy penetrated U.S. domestic politics. The Republican administration under President Reagan never succeeded in winning a clear majority of U.S. public opinion over to its hard-line views. And the Democratic majority in the House of Representatives (and also, after 1986, in the Senate) never shook the conviction of the administration that its priorities were right.

After a decade of inter-American relations in this mold, the results have been relatively disheartening for almost all parties, and Washington has begun to shift gently toward a different stance, though without explicitly renouncing any past mistakes. The alleged "national security threat" from Nicaragua has been effectively stifled, although at a disproportionate cost. Between 1982 and 1988 the Salvadorean insurgency was contained, although not eliminated, again at a high cost. Only after a long and messy confrontation was the unsavory regime of Manuel Noriega finally ousted from Panama in December 1989, through an act of intervention that won acclaim within the United States but left many lingering problems to be tackled in Panama.

In the meantime non–Central American issues that had been neglected for so long were demanding attention. Eight years after the debt crisis broke, all the sovereign debtors of Latin America still found themselves virtually cut off from voluntary commercial-bank lending. The cumulative net transfer of resources out of the region between 1982 and 1989 totaled $203 billion. At the close of the 1980s most of Latin America remained cut off from new sources of commercial credit, and a majority of countries in the region had found no option but to accumulate arrears of unpaid interest to their creditors. Five were even significantly behind in their payments to the World Bank and IMF (International Monetary Fund).

Debt-reduction initiatives taken in 1989 may eventually diminish the net outflows of capital from the region, but without necessarily restoring regional creditworthiness or beginning to reverse the economic damage done by the decapitalization of the 1980s. The burden of the outflows of that decade on the developing economies of Latin America were much heavier and more lasting than the reparations burden borne by Weimar Germany before the advent of Hitler. Washington policymakers, who had for years downplayed the debt problem, claiming that it would fade with world economic recovery, were faced with increasingly inescapable evidence to the contrary.

The two most celebrated recent U.S. initiatives on the debt problem, the Baker Initiative launched by Treasury Secretary James Baker III in September 1985 at a meeting of the IMF/World Bank, and the Brady Plan unveiled by Treasury Secretary Nicholas Brady in March 1989, have both been viewed as evidence that at the highest levels U.S. policymakers were prepared to make sharp changes of direction in the face of evidence that the problem required new remedies. Yet these two episodes—the details of which are discussed in a later chapter—can be interpreted differently to indicate that Washington's response is always likely to be too little, too late. This lag may be in part the result of commitment to a particular economic ideology. Increasingly, however, in contrast to the situation in the aftermath of World War II when the United States launched the Marshall Plan to aid the reconstruction of Europe and in the early 1960s which saw the establishment of the Alliance for Progress, the United States lacks either the resources or political will to act effectively. With Communism in a state of collapse (or retreat) across the globe, there is no longer the Communist threat to spur the U.S. taxpayer into action. It is also probably the case that some believe that U.S. interests are best served by leaving the Latin Americans to face the consequences of their own misguided economic policies.

Despite the strenuous efforts at economic adjustment made by many Latin American governments, the deterioration of most of their economies seemed to be accelerating. Average annual inflation throughout the region had risen from under 100 percent before the debt crisis to a new record of almost 1,000 percent in 1989. The value in current dollars of Latin America's exports in 1988 was barely higher than in 1984 or in 1981, and not until 1989 did the nominal value of imports rise above the 1982 level. In real terms (adjusted for dollar inflation) or, worse still, as a share of world trade, Latin America's trade performance in the 1980s was lamentable.

The region's poor trade performance during the 1980s represented a grave problem for the Latin American governments, many of which were presiding over investment levels too low to maintain the capital stock, let alone provide additional employment for a growing and potentially more productive labor force. The problem also was an increasingly urgent foreign economic policy issue for the United States, since a chronic deficiency in Latin America's capacity to import was reflected in a chronic weakness of U.S. exports to this hitherto major and buoyant external market. Moreover, the problem affected U.S. security by stimulating drug trafficking and other forms of illegal economic activity.

The U.S. trade deficit was seriously aggravated by the Latin American debt crisis. The U.S. banking system was weakened, especially in comparison to the rival Japanese. Parts of the U.S. labor market may face strain in the event of an upsurge in Hispanic immigration. Clearly in the 1990s the United States will be obliged to pay more attention to inter-American economic issues and to scale back its obsession with Central American security issues.

Another increasingly prominent issue in U.S.–Latin American relations is the illegal trade in narcotics. In the early 1980s some Washington policymakers tended to subsume this issue under the heading of anticommunism by the device of linking subversion, drug trafficking, and terrorism. Such oversimplification contained just enough truth to keep the argument going for several years.

At least some of the guerrilla movements in Peru and Colombia established tactical understandings with the drug barons, even though the ultimate objectives of the guerrillas and the *narcotraficantes* provided far less ground for cooperation. The conditions that favored political gunrunning and kidnapping in Central America also attracted profit-oriented crime. The often shakily established legal order was the main target of both gunrunners and kidnappers.

It seems clear that on ideological principle Washington would have ruled out any form of contact or cooperation with the Cubans or the Nicaraguans, for example, to hamper the growth of the drug trade. However, the reality was that those persons most interested in drug trafficking were the least committed to socialist revolution. Their aim was private enrichment without regard to the law or the long-term sociopolitical consequences. During the 1980s they were often left free to pursue this aim, at least partly because Washington's attention was so narrowly focused on combating Marxism that the other, equally grave threats to American interests in the hemisphere were neglected. The evidence uncovered by the Iran-*contra* hearings leaves little doubt that for a while some powerful agencies in the U.S. bureaucracy chose to work in collaboration with drug-trafficking interests in order to assist in overthrowing the Sandinista government in Nicaragua. Since the Sandinistas proved resilient, some agencies of the U.S. government became involved in a protracted relationship with key intermediaries in the narcotics trade, including interests sheltered by Noriega and the Panamanian National Guard.

This policy was not only questionable from the standpoint of the U.S. national interest; it was also inherently unstable. With the passage of time and the failure to dislodge the Sandinistas, Washington's tactical allies became more self-confident and more visible, until in 1988 the underlying conflict burst into the open in the form of an overt U.S. campaign to oust General Noriega from power in Panama. But by that time the economic and institutional power of the narcotics interest had become so entrenched that, to the U.S. public's surprise and alarm, establishing a "clean," pro-American regime, even in Panama, proved unexpectedly difficult.

Policy Prospects

During the 1990s Washington is likely to try to compensate for its past laxity toward certain South American drug interests by conducting highly visible and possibly rather indiscriminate campaigns against the drug trade, no longer subordinating the U.S. antidrug program to more directly political foreign-policy goals. There is also likely to be a stronger campaign against drug trafficking *within* the United States, which may make a hard line on international narcotics dealing more palatable. Without such a campaign, many Latin Americans will conclude that their countries are being made a scapegoat for U.S. reluctance to tackle the demand for drugs within U.S. borders, and a major additional source of friction between the United States and many Latin American governments can be expected.

Although U.S. leaders remain somewhat divided about the wisdom and balance of their country's Latin American policies in the 1980s, there is fairly general agreement about the lessons to be learned and the shifts of emphasis to be undertaken in the 1990s. Future policymaking is likely to be more consensual, placing greater emphasis on consultation between Congress and the president. The 1988 elections not only ratified Republican control over the presidency but also reinforced the Democratic party's majority in both houses of the legislature. Apart from continued friction with an increasingly isolated Cuba, ideological confrontation will be reduced, in part because the "dominoes" are unlikely to fall in Central America. This reduction is partly due to the general easing of international tensions with the Soviet Union, but it also reflects widespread weariness with the sterile, inconclusive, and now irrelevant debate over aid to the *contras*. However, the $3 billion spent on shoring up the regime of President José Napoleon Duarte in El Salvador only bought time without resolving any of the underlying problems there, so that tension could still flare up, especially if congressional parsimony over aid to the new right-wing government is followed by another guerrilla offensive. Nor is El Salvador the only potential insurgency problem. The Peruvian guerrillas made headway during the Reagan years, and political-cum-narcotics violence has risen to new levels in Colombia.

Notwithstanding those difficulties, Washington's attention is likely to shift toward the major republics of the hemisphere—especially toward Mexico (no longer viewed as Moscow's final domino but recognized instead as a severely troubled polity in its own right) and toward the new, probably more congenial administration of President Fernando Collor in Brazil. In both cases, attempts to establish a more productive and respectful relationship will be fraught with difficulties.

Mexico urgently needs debt relief and trade concessions. But its nationalist reflexes remain strong, and there is still guarded enthusiasm among Mexicans even in government for the open and free-market types of economic remedy that seem so rational to U.S. policymakers. Nor will a North American "common market" or bilateral trade agreement that would expose the Mexican market to the full force of U.S. competition meet with Mexican support. Mexican sensitivities will be further aroused by the probable increase in critical U.S. comment on domestic Mexican political matters, such as the legitimacy of the electoral system, the integrity of the police force, and the competence of the judiciary.

At first glance, relations with Brazil might seem easier to mend than with Mexico, but again United States and Brazilian nationalist sentiments may easily come into conflict.

In the 1990s the United States may look at the activities of some international agencies (the United Nations, the Organization of American States, and possibly even the Inter-American Development Bank) in a more sympathetic light, but the effect will probably be no more than a more flexible and subtle approach to the pursuit of the same underlying objectives. Thus, other forms of multilateral cooperation that are seen as inconsistent with Washington's priorities, such as the Caracas-based Economic System of Latin America (Sistema Económico Latinoamericano—SELA) which was set up in 1975 to provide a means of establishing common economic positions and promoting regional economic cooperation, or the Cartagena Group of major Latin American debtors, which met periodically in the 1980s to formulate common positions on debt issues, may fare less well. The advice of U.S. allies, such as Japan (especially important in view of America's continuing budgetary difficulties) and Western Europe (useful on some political matters), will be considered rather than brushed aside. Even so, the Panama invasion confirmed that more old-fashioned reflexes remain strong across a wide range of U.S. political opinion.

Alone, a shift toward a consensual and multilateral approach to policy formation would augur well for the improvement of U.S.–Latin American relations in the 1990s. But other prospective developments point in the opposite direction.

The shift from ideological to economic issues may not ensure any relaxation of tension, since so many of these issues have become highly charged. Whereas Mexican authorities might welcome a shift in U.S. attention from Central America toward their own economic difficulties, they may feel less enthusiasm if Washington's interest seems focused primarily on such touchy problems as drug trafficking.

On some political issues, Latin Americans would welcome an increased input from the Democratic majority in Congress. However, on economic and social questions such as trade protection and labor migration, they may well feel that the U.S. executive branch is more open to reason than the legislature is. Even on matters of pressing concern to the Latin Americans, such as debt (where influential voices in Congress have been in favor of proposals more favorable to the region), a more open and consensual process of policymaking may not prove a net advantage, since the result could be that every new proposal will be delayed, diluted, and distorted by the many diverse interests that will have to be accommodated. In the domestic and international climate likely to prevail in the early 1990s, many members of Congress with diverse persuasions will find it safer to cut expenditure on Latin America than to raise it. Even the reconstruction fund for postinvasion Panama has suffered from this effect.

Not just in Congress do Latin American policies tend to become bogged down. Within the executive branch, formulating a coordinated long-term policy toward any one Latin American republic, let alone toward the region as a whole, has often proved remarkably difficult. Each agency tends to have its own modus operandi. The Iran-*contra* affair illustrated the lengths to which an administration might be driven in the face of not only congressional but also interagency resistance to its policies. Moreover, various states (California, Florida, and Texas) have their own distinctive Latin American priorities, as do individual cities like Los Angeles and New York.

But, if U.S.–Latin American relations remain unsatisfactory during the 1990s, the basic reason will be that the United States's room to maneuver has shrunk in precisely the areas where Latin America's need for a new deal is most acute. An effective strategy to ease many of the outstanding issues troubling inter-American relations would require increases in U.S. government expenditure that seem most improbable given underlying fiscal difficulties. For example, the principal obstacle to a more farsighted U.S. policy on Latin American debt is the acute difficulty any administration would face in persuading Congress to approve substantial direct budgetary expenditures to provide more economic aid, to fund some Marshall Plan type of initiative, or even to subscribe capital to underwrite some enhanced multilateral financial facility. Any such expenditure would have to displace spending targeted on some domestic political constituency like the farm-credit system or the construction industry. In such circumstances, no matter how strong the general foreign-policy interest may be in easing the debt problem, many members of Congress will always be tempted to vote down any specific plan of expenditure. Of course, failure to find a realistic debt-relief initiative could lead to economic consequences that eventually involve a heavier drain on the U.S. budget, but this is a hypothetical outcome, the timing of which is uncertain. In any case members of Congress have to worry more about recorded votes on expenditures than on the indirect spending consequences of their failure to approve such an initiative.

Washington's room to maneuver will be cramped in the 1990s in areas other than fiscal. On trade issues the United States will have little choice but to adopt aggressive export-promotion policies and to make repeated use of the retaliatory provisions of the 1988 Trade Act, if there is to be timely progress on eliminating the massive trade deficit. The alternatives for Washington are a major recession, which would cut U.S. imports and even more sharply curtail Latin American exports, a large further devaluation of the dollar with potentially inflationary consequences, or further rapid and dangerous accumulation of foreign debt.

None of these alternatives offers much attraction to Latin America. Even the prospect of dollar inflation, which would boost primary export prices and erode the real value of outstanding debt, would be viewed with apprehension because the probable result would be another period of very high interest rates as in 1981–1982.

U.S. policymakers can therefore be expected to make continuing efforts to open the Latin American economies for U.S. exports and to compete strongly with Latin America for sales in markets outside the hemisphere, especially in farm products. If these efforts are insufficiently successful, then U.S. markets may become more closed to Latin American exports. The range of Latin American exports subject to restrictions in the United States is already considerable—beef, sugar, textiles, shoes, avocados, and steel.

In its defense, Washington can rightly argue that most Latin American markets are far more protected against U.S. exports and indeed that the United States is still clearly the most open market for new Latin American exports. It can also point to such measures as the Caribbean Basin Initiative enacted by the U.S. Congress in 1983 (which aimed, by a combination of financial incentives, to promote closer integration of the area's countries into the U.S. market) that (albeit in a discriminatory manner) have improved access for some Latin American exporters.

But the dominant pattern, which is likely to persist into the 1990s, remains: while Latin America, running a substantial trade surplus, liberalizes its imports, the United States, with an apparently structural trade deficit, tightens foreign access to its internal market. And if this approach fails to show sufficient signs of being effective quickly enough to reassure the United States' foreign creditors, then U.S. interest rates will have to be pushed to premium levels in order to continue attracting the necessary foreign funds.

Two rather ominous conclusions follow for the Latin American economies in the 1990s. First, the United States is unlikely to provide a much more buoyant market for their exports in the next decade than it did in the last. Second, Washington's borrowing needs may well continue to crowd out other sovereign debtors from the available pool of international dollar lending. Moreover, the profound changes occurring in Eastern Europe will add a major new set of claimants to available Western investible funds, with both a political and quite possibly an economic priority claim over debt-weary Latin America. If so, even the most creditworthy Third World borrowers would be blocked from a return to voluntary lending, and the interest-rate pressure on those crippled by an excessive burden of external debt would intensify. Continuing pressure would also be exerted on Latin American economies in favor of the continuing flow out of the region of flight capital and against its return from abroad.

Until the United States resolves its budget and trade deficits, these adverse side effects will continue to work powerfully against the restoration of economic confidence in Latin America. Of course, this is a purely bilateral and narrowly economic view of the relationship. At a more global and strategic level, the analysis of U.S.–Latin American relations should be derived from a broader assessment of the United States and its changing place in the world power structure.

In the late 1980s, the theme of "imperial decline" became fashionable among U.S. opinion makers, reflecting unease at the scale of Japanese economic success and the possibly growing autonomy of a more united Western Europe. The downgrading of superpower rivalry as the difficulties facing the Soviet system became more apparent had the paradoxical effect of disorienting the apparent victor of the Cold War. How was U.S. leadership over the United States' industrial allies to be maintained if the common enemy proceeded to withdraw hurt from the contest and the central power in the dominant international coalition seemed to be slipping from its former position as an economic superpower? Whether the post-Reagan phase of self-doubt anticipates a downturn in the United States' international authority remains to be seen. A good countercase can perhaps be made that, despite some slippage in certain areas, the overall centrality of the United States in the advanced Western capitalist system remains intact. However, not only does the overall centrality of the United States have implications for its relations with its hemispheric neighbors, but also sectoral and geographical shifts of emphasis within its alliance system have implications as well.

The economic rise of Japan (and the related rise of California within the U.S. polity, not to mention Florida and Texas) provides one example of such shifts that can be expected to continue in the 1990s. Japanese economic policy receives substantial attention in Chapter 19. From a broader strategic viewpoint, as Europe turns east, Latin Americans need to reflect on the growing importance of the Pacific as a source of leadership and innovation and on the shift in significance and content of the old Atlantic networks.

Another international trend that is already apparent and that could easily become more pronounced in the next decade is the tendency of the various industrialized centers to strengthen their ties with adjoining parts of the Third World to the detriment of more distant areas. Japan's role in East and part of Southeast Asia provides one example of this pattern, and West European ties with adjacent peoples to the east but also in the Mediterranean provides another. The implication for Latin America would be that the "Americas" would form a logical bloc within such an emerging system of regional groupings. But although this notion is fashionable, it needs to be placed in a historical perspective.

For much of the twentieth century the availability of Latin America as a strategic reserve and zone of security was an important source of strength to the United States. Most other major powers, by contrast, had to contend with potentially hostile neighbors and vulnerable supply routes. Latin Americans may have chafed at the asymmetrical pattern of their relations with the "Colossus of the North," but Latin Americans too were relatively favored, certainly as compared with the weaker neighbors of the European great powers or the less developed countries adjoining Japan.

During the 1960s and especially the 1970s decolonization and economic diversification widened interrelationships in all parts of the Third World. Forty years of sometimes uneasy peace between the major powers reduced the salience of such notions as strategic reserves and security zones. However, peace between the major powers was accompanied by a series of regional conflicts that periodically reawakened the old reflexes. The Cuban Revolution of 1959 and the Nicaraguan Revolution of 1979 had this effect in the Western Hemisphere.

During the 1990s, however, inter-American relations are not likely to be restructured in accordance with some overarching regional security project. In Washington it has recently become fashionable to propose "political democracy and economic liberalism" as an alternative basis for inter-American solidarity, and perhaps the various republics of the Americas will indeed be drawn together by their common espousal of liberal democratic forms of government. But it seems equally likely that they will find themselves coming together in a hemispheric bloc defined by negative characteristics: *not* part of the European Community, *not* recent former colonies of Europe, *not* ultra-dynamic Asian economies. In view of U.S. ideas of political democracy, the United States may from time to time find Latin American electoral choices disconcerting. Even if this source of discord can be sidestepped, tension runs deep between the policies of market liberalism that Washington associates with democracy and the possible prospective demands of Latin American electorates.

Latin America is no longer a regional source of strength that boosts U.S. capabilities as a world power. On the contrary, its problems have become a symptom of the United States' growing difficulties in asserting world leadership. Equally well, Latin Americans are no longer so clearly favored by their proximity to the United States, as compared with Third World countries adjoining Japan or even with the European Community. No doubt there will be some limited new opportunities for the reinvigoration of Pan-American cooperation, but the hopes and illusions of the Alliance for Progress period are unlikely to be rekindled. Mexico might be seeking some closer and more structured association with the English-speaking nations of North America, but it may be at the cost of further weakening Mexico's solidarity with the rest of Latin America.

In general, Latin Americans are likely to resist tendencies toward compartmentalization of the world. They will seek ties with Japan and Western Europe quite as eagerly as ties with the United States. Whatever their economic difficulties, Latin Americans will still want to cultivate connections outside the Western Hemisphere for political reasons, to act as a counterweight to undue dependence on the United States and Canada. Such political reasons may not find much favor in the United States, but Washington will be eager to spread the burden of contending with Latin America's economic difficulties. The entry of Canada into the Organization of American States (OAS) brings both a moderating voice and an additional source of finance. Latin Americans will be eager to extend such links beyond the hemisphere.

Cuba

U.S. relations with Cuba require a brief separate treatment. For thirty years, Cuba's defection from the Americas into the Soviet bloc has signified a profound breach in the U.S. system of regional security and political ascendancy. The ideological challenge posed by the Cuban example may have faded, but Fidel Castro's regime remains entrenched and largely resistant to U.S. threats and sanctions. Moscow has invested so much in the Cuban alliance that until recently it seemed to be an immutable fixture of the international order. But clearly the Soviet retrenchment of the late 1980s implies a recasting, and indeed a downgrading, of Cuba's position within the Soviet-led alliance system. The downgrading can be attributed to a confluence of factors, including some that are long-term and irreversible and others that reflect divergences of doctrine.

Cuba, located so close to the United States that it circumvents many of Washington's defense lines, has served as a valuable military and intelligence base for the Soviet Union. However, because of improved satellite communications and other shifts in military technology, this advantage to Moscow seems clearly to be declining. The hard-currency cost of bolstering the Cuban economy has proved more burdensome than the Soviets can have expected, and in conditions of economic stress at home Comecon governments have become increasingly restive at the scale of the subsidies required in distant Latin America. (Comecon, the Council for Mutual Economic Assistance, has coordinated the economic activities of the Soviet-bloc countries.)

It is already evident that the Cuban economy will be severely affected by a switch to arms-length trading with the Soviets at market prices, all the more because oil prices have risen as a result of the Gulf crisis and because Cuba's other main trading partners (East Germany, Poland, Czechoslovakia) have virtually discontinued new transactions. The island's structure of trade has long been extremely ossified. According to official figures, three-quarters of all Cuban exports were sugar, three-quarters of which went to the Soviet Union. The prospects for early diversifications are bleak, regardless of how the politics evolve.

Until the advent of Soviet leader Mikhail Gorbachev, Cuba was enormously useful to the Soviet Union's campaign for influence within the Third World. Following the current withdrawal of Cuban troops from Angola (leaving in place a radical, but precarious, government that in Havana's eyes has been successfully defended against South African aggression), Moscow is likely to consider Castro's Cuba an encumbrance rather than an asset in relation to Gorbachev's new international priorities. The proposal for *Aeroflot* to route its South American flights through Miami rather than Havana is symptomatic in this regard. Apart from Angola, other Soviet-Cuban projects—or perhaps they should be called Cuban-Soviet projects, given the prominence and autonomy of the Cuban input into the joint policymaking—have been less successful. In the Western Hemisphere the 1983 overthrow of a Cuban-backed Marxist regime in Grenada by U.S. Marines was the most notable setback, but Moscow and Havana have also developed growing differences of opinion over Central America with Gorbachev seeking to disengage from regional conflicts.

For some time to come, Washington could be faced by a still entrenched Marxist regime in Cuba—but one that is under heavy pressure from Moscow to be restrained in foreign policy and to undertake domestic economic reform. At the time of this writing, however, the likelihood in the medium-term of Castro's regime either remaining in power or undertaking significant reforms seems small. Communist parties have relinquished their monopolies of power so abruptly and in so many countries that Castro's proclaimed determination to soldier on entirely defiant of world trends seems quite as foolhardy as his original assault on the Moncada barracks in 1953. Many Washington policymakers seem to hope that if the pressure is maintained, Castroism will simply self-destruct, whereas most Latin American governments would probably prefer a negotiated transition to a more liberal order. The Cuban leadership seems determined to rely on its not inconsiderable reserves of internal strength in order to disappoint all such hopes or expectations.

This highly unpredictable situation could present major new headaches for inter-American relations, although potentially it also offers the possibility for the ending of a major unresolved source of international tension. If, as seems currently all too possible, the issue is approached in a spirit of triumphalism (on the U.S. side) pitted against a Masada complex (on the

Cuban side), it is by no means certain that the outcome will be so clear and uncontested as in either Eastern Europe or in Panama. Castro made the Cuban Revolution before enlisting Soviet support, and he based it not only on "military socialism" but also on anti-Yankee nationalism.

With the exception of Cuba then, the ideological concerns that dominated U.S.–Latin American relations in the 1980s are likely to be replaced in the 1990s by pragmatic bargaining, mainly about economic issues. It also seems clear that the deterioration of U.S.–Latin American ties has hurt not only the southern republics but also the economic interests and international leadership capacities of the United States. But until Cuba's future becomes clearer, an analysis of Latin America's international role solely with reference to one of what were until recently called the superpowers will not be possible.

Since 1917, and especially since 1945, the Soviet model of economic political organization has rivaled the U.S. model and has been an alternative source of ideological inspiration. This view made the Soviet Union an inspiration to the critics of the existing social order, a threatening agency of subversion and instability in the eyes of established elites, and a prime source of assistance and guidance in pursuing liberation to the radical counterelites. The Cuban Revolution gave this imagery a new lease on life in the 1960s, when the appeal of bureaucratic socialism might otherwise have faded; and to a much lesser extent the Nicaraguan Revolution did the same while it lasted. But in the late 1980s, the hopes and fears inspired by the Soviet experience were dissipated throughout Latin America. The abrupt transformation of international perceptions of the Soviet Union is likely to reshape the entire world order, not only directly but also through many indirect routes still to be defined. The implications of this change for Latin America are considered in the next chapter.

17

Latin America and the Soviet Union

Commercial Interests

From the Soviet standpoint the 1960 Cuban reversal of alliances can be regarded essentially as a lucky accident. However that may be, the consequences were momentous. Thenceforth Cuba became a vital strategic asset, a crucial source of information and guidance, and a potential platform for further Soviet gains in the Western Hemisphere. In addition, Cuba was also for the first decade or more a wayward dependency and, over the long haul, a very costly and potentially embarrassing economic one.

The Cuban Revolution could not without great discredit to the Soviet Union be allowed to falter, nor could the Cuban economy be seen to fail. Thus Moscow has found it far from easy to limit the costs of its Western Hemisphere exposure or to consolidate the gains that initially seemed in the offing.

Even in the freak year 1981, following the U.S. grain embargo, which greatly boosted Argentina's trade with the Soviet Union, Soviet trade with Cuba exceeded trade with all the rest of Latin America. In more normal years about four-fifths of all Soviet economic transactions were focused on this one physically isolated Caribbean island. Indeed Cuba is thought to have accounted for up to 5 percent of all Soviet external trade. According to some estimates, Soviet aid may be equivalent to as much as 25 percent of Cuban GNP, comparable in scale to the U.S. transfer of resources to the Puerto Rican economy.

In contrast, Soviet trade with the rest of Latin America normally accounts for less than 1.0 percent of Soviet imports and absorbs less than 0.25 percent of Soviet exports. The imbalance means that Moscow has to pay in hard currency for most of its Latin American purchases. Less than 2.5 percent of Soviet military deliveries to the Third World go to Latin America.

There is an almost total lack of complementarity between the Soviet economy and non-Communist Latin America, across virtually the entire range of industrial products and financial services. Soviet consumer goods compare unfavorably with Latin American industrial output; and although Soviet industry may be stronger in some capital goods, the sectors are those in which the Latin Americans normally purchase from the most developed First World suppliers. Soviet exports cannot normally compete either in quality or in the provision of credit, and Soviet products are not compatible with most of Latin America's established industrial plant. Apart from weapons, then, the main economic inducements Moscow has to offer are oil (the basis of its export relationship with Cuba and Sandinista Nicaragua) and gold.

In spite of these strict economic constraints, which are worsening, some of the changes taking place in the Soviet Union and the possible impact of changing Soviet foreign policy on Latin America are nevertheless worth exploring.

Glasnost and *Perestroika*

The changes initiated by *perestroika* and *glasnost* in the Soviet Union soon opened up more effective channels of communication for sectors traditionally outside the Communist party. These changes also created between state and party a separation that has led seemingly inexorably to the eventual loss of the party's legal monopoly on state power. Already the emergence of much clearer separate spheres of activity carries important political implications.

In a society where scarcity is the norm and where questions of productivity are so much in the forefront, a separation between state and party tends to place limits on the unlimited access to public resources formerly enjoyed by the party organization. Although the party had a huge defined allowance within the budget of the Soviet state, the budget has been both flexible and without effective controls because the party leadership decided how it should be spent and that leadership coincided exactly with the leadership of the government. Furthermore, all this went on in a quasi-hermetic situation in which the leaders "interpreted" the needs and demands of the masses in spite of the fact that it was not possible for the people to make their own views known or to press for their implementation.

There is now likely to be more debate about the allocation of funds for international solidarity, though such money will continue to be used to advance the global interests of the Soviet Union. Complaints about poor management of the Cuban economy or turmoil in the Nicaraguan economy will carry more weight than in the past. There will be less scope for adventurism and less favorable conditions for the Soviet Union's undertaking risky commitments in Third World countries, especially in Latin America.

In general, in the coming years the Soviet Union will be seeking to develop its trading relationships mainly with the western industrialized countries in order to facilitate domestic economic reform. The Soviet Union will not totally ignore developing countries, but its own economic problems compel it to avoid potentially burdensome overseas commitments. As a result, the increasingly pressing imperatives of domestic reform will substantially constrain the Soviet Union's ability to allocate resources to assist Third World development.

Even in the era of Leonid Brezhnev (1964–1982), the internationalist inclinations of countries like East Germany, Czechoslovakia, Poland, and Hungary (Bulgaria was something of an exception) tended to be much more limited than those of the Soviet Union itself. Except for certain types of technical aid, like engineering, military assistance, and some naval projects, cooperation was very restricted unless the particular projects represented advantages not only for the recipient but also for the donor. The removal of Communist parties from supreme power in all these countries in 1989 accentuated the lack of interest in solidarity policies, leaving the Soviet Union to shoulder the financial burden almost alone. Politically inspired commitments by non-Soviet Comecon members to Latin America have already disappeared.

The position of Latin America in the global strategy of the Soviet Union is also changing. Those who saw revolutionary potential in the Third World's pitting itself against imperialism have suffered an irreparable defeat with the new policy orientations of *perestroika.* In the new Soviet thinking, the role of national liberation struggles is different. First, conflicts in the Third World tend to be seen as regional conflicts that have the potential to spark off major world confrontations and even nuclear conflict. Second, the cost of establishing and maintaining "socialist" regimes is increasingly being questioned, particularly as the Soviet Union has little capacity to take full advantage of the raw materials or human resources thereby made available. These considerations reduce the attractions of such ventures just when the Soviet people themselves are beginning to voice their discontent at the way in which the Soviet system has worked in the past. Moreover, with one-party regimes being dismantled in the heartland of the Eastern bloc, it becomes almost impossible to argue for the promotion of such regimes elsewhere. Instead, "democracy" has become the approved formula (possibly, but not necessarily, with a social democratic flavor).

As recently as 1982 the Communist party conference in Havana declared that the center of gravity of Latin American revolution had shifted to Central America and the Caribbean. This view seemed confirmed by the Nicaraguan

Revolution and the role of armed struggle in achieving it. At that time this perspective was still in line with Soviet global strategies. But it overestimated the Soviet Union's real economic capacity to sustain support for socialist governments in that part of the world.

When Gorbachev was appointed general secretary of the Soviet Communist party and *perestroika* was initiated, a realistic reappraisal of the Soviet Union's international stance was required. From the Soviet viewpoint it was argued that in many Latin American countries the right conditions for the functioning of what Moscow used to call "bourgeois" democracy existed and that in practical political terms any attempt to change this state of affairs would require lengthy preparation. Moscow concluded that the hour of the revolution had passed, at least for the foreseeable future. The new thinking was reflected in *Pravda,* which on December 14, 1986, had this to say:

> Violence on that continent [Latin America] can easily become transformed from the midwife to the gravedigger of history. The birth of socialism may end in the death of socialism. In the present situation any local conflict may escalate into regional and even world conflict . . . the nuclear age demands of revolutionary forces the most serious consideration of decisions over armed struggle and the definitive rejection of actions characteristic of leftist extremism.[1]

Perestroika is a response to the deep and complex needs of Soviet society itself, and the problems it seeks to address will not be solved in the short or medium term. Its reappraisal of the role of social and political change in the periphery may in effect represent a long-term strategic withdrawal, all the more so as Soviet power visibly crumbles near Moscow.

Wherever possible the Soviet Union will seek to maintain a presence while reducing the costs such a presence entails. Where this tradeoff is not possible, the Soviet Union will try to withdraw while exacting a significant political price. This strategy can preserve its influence or guarantee it certain other advantages.

The Soviet Union and Communist Parties in Latin America

The Cuban leadership cannot be expected to share Soviet concerns. It tends, for instance, to view adverse developments in Central America as a direct threat to the security of Cuba's own revolution. In contrast, the Soviet Union tended to regard Sandinista Nicaragua as a distant bargaining counter, expendable in the last resort. Ideologically, the Cuba of Fidel Castro is far more committed to revolutionary activism in the region than is the Soviet Union of Mikhail Gorbachev.

However, Cuba has responded to the new Soviet external policy. Although domestically Cuba rejects *perestroika,* in its foreign policy it has been more responsive. During the late 1980s Cuba sought to develop closer political and economic ties with the other countries of Latin America and end its diplomatic isolation. Cuba wants to present itself as a "normal" state, adhering to the principles of international coexistence.

The unrelenting pressure of the U.S. trade embargo (in effect since 1962) and growing uncertainty about the strength of support available from Moscow appear to have tempted the Castro regime into some technological smuggling with the help of deposed General Manuel Noriega in Panama and the U.S. financier Robert Vesco. This activity seems to have had limited success, and it created severe problems inside the Cuban armed forces, which culminated in the show trial and execution of General Arnaldo Ochoa—a key figure in the Angolan War—and some associates in July 1989. The U.S. invasion of Panama in December 1989 cut off this outlet for Cuban enterprise seeking to circumvent the U.S. blockade. The channeling of imports to Cuba through Nicaragua has also failed. The Sandinistas suffered their own embargo since 1985 and in 1990 lost power.

Turning to the rest of the Latin American left, Soviet leaders have said they understand the difficulties faced by the Latin American Communist parties in applying "the new political thinking." However, all the indications are that those difficulties are even greater than anticipated. On the left there are significant groups that often exceed in number, activity, and political vigilance the traditional Communist parties and are controlled neither by Cuba nor by the Soviet Union. Indeed, the Communist parties themselves, influenced by previous Soviet rhetoric and radicalism, have generated a revisionist spirit that is difficult to reverse. This spirit is illustrated by the strong showing of Luís Inácio da Silva (popularly known as "Lula") in the Brazilian 1989 presidential elections.

One can foresee, on the one hand, further splits in the Latin American left and, on the other hand, political ambivalence—more in private than in public—in the direction of the Cuban Communist party, which will be trying not to lose contact with any one group. Politically, one can also foresee Moscow seeking a strengthening of political ties and a greater openness between Communist parties and international social democracy.

The new Soviet direction is likely to be demonstrated in the development of trade and economic relations with the major countries in Latin America. Ultimately, such development may have a much greater significance for the Soviet Union than political relations would have had. Countries like Brazil and Argentina are potentially important trading partners, and they also hold out the possibility for obtaining raw materials and providing more of an outlet for Soviet exports than at present. This is especially true of Brazil. Argentina is valued as a source of temperate agricultural products when Soviet harvests fail or if supplies from North America are interrupted for political reasons.

The preoccupation with forging trading links with Latin America, which led the Soviet Union to overvalue the real importance of bodies like SELA, may become more pronounced as it tries to find areas that can supply goods, services, and technology to ease production and consumer problems in the Soviet Union itself.

In Central America, the Soviet Union maintains its commercial presence even in Guatemala and Honduras. In El Salvador, however, the Cubans are likely to maintain the especially high regard they hold for the FMLN guerrillas. The Soviet Union still has a fairly strong influence over the Salvadorean Communist party and is likely to push it in a social democratic rather than in a radical direction. It is not clear how far the Castro regime can go in reinforcing the more militant tendency against the explicit opposition of Moscow.

In Chile, the Communist party for a long time has relied on preferential treatment from the Soviet Union. A daily slot of almost two hours on Radio Moscow has been allotted to the party and to no other. In addition, the party's illegal Radio Magallanes also transmits with the clear, direct endorsement of Moscow. Until 1989, the political line adopted by the Chilean Communist party was still oriented toward armed struggle, but it was dropped in time for the December 1989 presidential election.

Moscow has been slow to apply the new thinking to Chile, in part because the Chilean Communist party is one of the largest, oldest, and most pro-Moscow parties in Latin America. Moreover, there have been and still are large numbers of Chilean exiles in Moscow.

Soviet Interest in the Pacific

The related changes within the Soviet Union and in the broad direction of its foreign affairs have encouraged the Soviet Union to focus on new areas of strategic interest, from both an economic and a military point of view. Soviet interest in the Pacific zone and, by extension, in the Latin American countries bordering it has been steadily increasing. One aspect of this interest that has received relatively little attention concerns the Soviet presence in Nicaragua in particular and with Soviet policy toward the Latin American states with a Pacific coastline in general.

The interests of Japan, the United States, the new industrial and trading powers of Southeast Asia, and the People's Republic of China are converging on the Pacific coastal region of Latin America. For their part, the Soviets have completed the construction of the Baikal-Amur railway, which terminates on the Pacific coast at the port of Vostochni, near Najodka. It has given the Soviet Union a strategic line of communication ensuring the linkup of its European territory with Siberia and the Far East as well as with Asia and the Pacific region. Not surprisingly, then, the Soviet port of Najodka has been the regular venue since 1974 for International Seminars on Cooperation in the Pacific, at which there has been a high level of Latin American participation.

In the Pacific, considerations of military strategy have historically preceded the trend toward economic rapprochement and have even been its stimulus. There are signs of a maturing politico-military rapprochement. Japan and the United States are trying to interest Latin America in the formation of a new Pacific regional organization, promoting a Trade and Development Organization for the Countries of the Pacific as a prototype for a Pacific community. According to the Japanese Center for Economic Studies, the organization would be set up as an intergovernmental consultative body.

The Soviet Union believes that integration in the Pacific would be a significant event in world history and fears that the Soviet Union could be excluded. This belief was confirmed by the visit of the former Japanese prime minister Yasuhiro Nakasone to the Soviet Union. According to the news agency TASS, in his welcoming speech Gorbachev revealed development plans for the Soviet Far East and also for Siberia. Such plans, Gorbachev is reported as saying, provide for a more rapid development for those regions than for the rest of the country. There is also a Soviet proposal to make the port of Vladivostock, situated on the Pacific coast of the Soviet Union opposite Japan, an open port for foreigners in the near future. Whether the leadership in Moscow will still possess the motivation and authority to take such initiatives in the early 1990s remains questionable, but the Soviet navy is still a significant factor in Moscow's policymaking.

Military aspects also seem to be playing a role in the growing importance being conceded to the Pacific region. Recent information tends to indicate increasingly fierce competition for control of remote areas of the Pacific Ocean, with an eye to the use of outer space for ground surveillance that could have military ends. This increased competition helps explain why, since 1986, the Soviet Union has been negotiating fishing agreements in the South Pacific with some small islands and has extended its diplomatic presence in the area, offering favorable trade agreements to several countries. U.S. officials view such moves as part of a strategy to undermine the Western presence and influence in the region. In recent years the Soviets have also increased their deployment of high-technology ships for monitoring and gathering military intelligence in the South Pacific. U.S. and Australian military observers, in a joint communiqué at the end of June 1988, confirmed that the Soviet Union was increasing its military capability for use in the Pacific. The importance of the South Pacific for the control of space is one of the reasons that the Soviet Union has sought in recent years to penetrate the region and the United States has decided to maintain and strengthen its own presence.

Prior to the electoral defeat of the Sandinistas in Nicaragua in 1990, Moscow may still have had some residual interest in Puerto Corinto on the Pacific coast of Nicaragua. It is reported that the port had been equipped to harbor the most advanced Soviet submarines. But although such traditional strategic thinking cannot yet be entirely discarded as a possible lens for interpretation of Soviet activities in Latin America, to magnify these possibilities out of all proportion, as became a common Western practice in the 1980s, would be to entirely misjudge the dominant trends in world politics. Insofar as the Soviet navy has a Pacific strategy, the Soviet Union seems to be more intent on finding port facilities for its naval, military, and commercial activities than on seeking new military bases.

Note

1. *Pravda,* December 14, 1986. Cited in Rodolpho Cerdas Cruz, "New Directions in Soviet Policy towards Latin America," *Journal of Latin American Studies,* 21 (1989), p. 11.

18

Latin America and Western Europe

Historical Ties

The subcontinent is known as "Latin" America for a good reason: cultural ties with the old imperial mother countries, Spain and Portugal, and with Italy and France, remain extremely strong. Similarly, in the political realm the Latin American countries are all in a rather direct sense "children of the French Revolution," having corresponding conceptions of popular sovereignty, individual rights, the left-right ideological spectrum, the nation state, and nationalism. In this, the contrast between Latin America and other areas of the Third World is marked. The retreat of Western influence in the Middle East, Africa, and Asia has given rise to the expression of a wide range of political, cultural, and religious traditions that are at least partly a repudiation of European models. Only in Latin America have recent trends in resistance to great-power hegemonies actually involved reaching out to the new Europe being constructed after two world wars.

Over the past generation, Latin America has achieved a degree of cultural emancipation and originality that has greatly raised its prestige in the outside world. Latin cultural influence has grown within the United States and has also made an impression in Europe. Although in the 1990s Japan may well emerge as a major source of *economic* influence in Latin America, rivaling the United States and overshadowing Europe, in *cultural* terms Latin America's affinity with Europe will remain unsurpassed.

In the economic realm, Latin America developed with an overwhelmingly outward orientation (coastal and indeed centrifugal) that lasted from the conquest until about 1930. During that period of more than four centuries the economic orientation was not so much outward as "Europe-ward"—first to the Iberian Peninsula, then to Britain and to a lesser extent France, Germany, and Italy. It was partly because the Europeans destroyed their own presence and international position through internecine warfare that Latin America fell so completely under the influence of the United States. As this unrivaled U.S. supremacy gradually declined—both globally and regionally—from the late 1950s onward, Latin America's historical orientation toward Europe began to revive.

The Growth of Relations

In addition to powerful cultural and historical affinities, the rapid economic growth of Western Europe in the postwar period and the expanding needs of Latin America meant that by the early 1980s Europe had acquired substantial economic interests in the region. Europe had become a major trading partner. In 1980 the European Community (EC) accounted for 24 percent of Latin America's exports and 20 percent of its imports. Foreign investment expanded so that, by the mid-1980s, Europe accounted for about 35 percent of direct foreign investment in the region (double its share in 1971). Moreover, the pattern of European investment differed markedly from that of the United States and was far more heavily concentrated in manufacturing. Finally, by the 1980s the countries of the EC had become the largest source of official aid. Between 1979 and 1983 they gave $2.6 billion of official aid jointly or individually, against $1.9 billion from the United States and $850 million from Japan.

On top of this steady expansion of the economic relationship, the 1980s saw four developments that led to an increase in European interest and activity in the region. First, Western European banks and financial institutions were directly threatened by the debt crisis that broke in the autumn of 1982. By 1986, for example, 34.4 percent of total Latin American external bank debt was owed to Western Europe (around $82 billion), only slightly below the 37.7 percent ($90.5 billion) owed to the United States.

Second, the severity of the Central American crisis focused European attention both on the general problem of insecurity in the Third World and on the implications of this particular crisis for U.S.–European relations. A substantial groundswell of popular and political opinion in Europe was strongly critical of U.S. policy in Latin America. This viewpoint created a common perspective with much of Latin America and introduced an increasingly political dimension to Europe's Latin American policy. For the first time,

Europe appeared willing to challenge U.S. policy in what it had previously accepted to be a U.S. sphere of influence. Strong French criticism of U.S. policy (as in the Franco-Mexican Declaration of 1982 which recognized the Salvadorean guerrillas as a legitimate political force), the creation of regular foreign ministerial consultations (the San José Dialogue, under which foreign ministers of the European Community meet annually with all their Central American counterparts, (including the Nicaraguans) and the inclusion (against direct U.S. pressure) of Nicaragua within the EC's expanding economic aid programs to the region were important illustrations of this trend.

Third, the widespread shift away from military rule in Latin America both increased European interest in Latin America and drew Latin American attention toward Europe. Not only did European governments offer strong verbal support for democracy but many subnational European groups—the Catholic Church, the party internationals, the European trade unions—played an active role in the process of democratic transition. Many Latin Americans believed that Europe's postwar experience might offer some lessons of special relevance to the region's re-emerging democracies and that at least some of the political and social currents in Europe would understand and sympathize with Latin American dilemmas.

Fourth, two European countries, Italy and Spain, became more forceful advocates of the need for Europe to intensify its relations with Latin America. Italy has close cultural and human ties with the region. Between 1857 and 1930, for example, nearly half of the 3.5 million immigrants who went to Argentina came from Italy. More importantly, the strength of the Italian economy has both increased Italy's ability to provide investment and aid and led to a more activist foreign policy in the Third World generally. Between 1981 and 1986 there was a 264 percent increase in the overall amount of Italian official aid—against, for example, an 18 percent fall in British aid in the same period—and in 1986 over 16 percent of Italian aid commitments were to Latin America. The clearest sign of increased Italian interest was the signing in December 1987 of a major bilateral cooperation treaty with Argentina aimed at channeling $4.5 billion of new investment and loans to that country over a five-year period.

In Spain the expansion of European–Latin American relations became a central focus of the foreign policy of the socialist government. Spain laid great weight on its historical, cultural, and ethnic ties with the region. The Spanish Socialist Party (Partido Socialista Obrero Español—PSOE) had long maintained close relations with many center-left democratic movements in Latin America. Trade with Latin America was more important for Spain than for any other European country. Between 1975 and 1982 Latin America's share of Spanish foreign investment rose from 13 percent to 37 percent, and the region's share of Spanish loans and credits rose from 14 percent to 48 percent.

Spanish leaders repeatedly pointed to the country's dual role as a European country but one with a Latin American projection and vocation. As Spain entered the European Community in 1986, it saw its role as that of a bridge between the two regions. For many Latin American countries too, Spain's return to democracy offered an instructive precedent.

If these factors help explain the increased attention paid to Latin America, it is important to note a further distinctive feature of the relationship—namely, that European–Latin American links were not confined to a bilateral level. The 1980s saw an expansion of multilateral ties by the EC. In 1982, for example, the European Coal and Steel Community made a $600 million loan to Brazil for the development of the Carajás iron-ore project. In 1983, the EC signed a cooperation agreement with the Andean Pact. 1984 saw the start of a series of ministerial-level conferences between the EC and the countries of Central America. There were also regular conferences between the European Parliament and Latin American politicians and between the EC and SELA.

There was also increased activity at other levels. Close contacts and flows of money developed between European (especially West German) church groups and Latin America. The European party internationals—the Christian Democrats, the Social Democrats, the Liberals, and the Conservatives—expanded their work in the region. In this effort they were aided by the fact that 95 percent of the members of the four party internationals came from Europe and Latin America and by the close links that existed between the party internationals and the West German political foundations, which had been steadily acquiring a presence and expertise in the region since the 1960s. In the area of political and religious relations, the depth of the cultural and historic relationship became most visible, with institutions like the Catholic Church and the Christian Democrat and Socialist internationals providing a channel for the transmission of ideas, support, and resources.

Constraints and Limitations

Despite the activity, the expectations, and the rhetoric that accompanied European–Latin American relations in the 1980s, serious problems remain and the prospects for the immediate future are mixed. Trade between the EC countries and Latin America has been badly hit by the depth and severity of the economic crisis that has plagued Latin America since 1982. Because of recession and the need to cut back imports and build up trade surpluses, EC exports to Latin America fell by 25 percent between 1981 and 1983 and in 1987 remained 18 percent below the 1981 level. While EC imports from the region continued to rise between 1982 and 1985, European countries could claim that they were helping Latin America build up trade surpluses and thereby service the debt. But EC imports from the region fell by 35 percent between 1985 and 1987, and the trade surplus dropped from 15.252 million European Currency Units (ECU) to 5.861 million ECU. The largest falls were in oil imports (Mexico's exports to the EC fell by 43 percent, Venezuela's by 69 percent), but there was also a 31 percent drop in the level of Brazilian exports.

Of greater concern is the continuing marginalization of Latin America in overall EC trade. Latin America's share in imports from outside the European Community declined from 8.7 percent in 1965 to 7.5 percent in 1985 to 5.7 percent in 1987. Latin America's share of EC exports to countries outside the Community shrank from 6.4 percent in 1965 to 4.1 percent in 1985 and to 3.9 percent in 1987. Within Latin America, EC trade is heavily concentrated in Brazil, Argentina, Mexico, Venezuela, and Chile. In recent years the dominance of Brazil has become more marked: in 1987 Brazil's share of total EC imports was 38 percent (up from 35 percent in 1985), and Brazil's share of total EC exports was 25 percent (up from 18 percent in 1985). Brazil also produces around half of all Latin American manufactured exports sold to the European Community.

In addition to this marginalization, Latin America has long complained of growing protectionism within the EC and of the adverse impact of the Common Agricultural Policy. Latin America is at the bottom of the "pyramid of privilege" and does not enjoy the trade benefits extended to certain African, Caribbean, and Pacific countries associated with the EC through the Lomé Conventions and to the Mediterranean states through bilateral and multilateral agreements. Although there is disagreement over the extent of damage, the Common Agricultural Policy has not only severely limited Latin American access to the European market but has led to increased instability in world markets and to the emergence of Europe as a major exporter of (often heavily subsidized) agricultural products in competition with Latin America. Argentina and Uruguay are the most severely affected. This situation led to conflict between Latin America and the European Community during the current Uruguay Round of GATT (General Agreement on Tariffs and Trade) multilateral trade negotiations. Latin America has made common cause with the United States and with members of the Cairns Group of agricultural exporters against the EC's agricultural policy. In addition, Latin America finds itself pitted against both the EC and the United States over the question of trade in services.

Apart from agriculture it is unclear exactly how much Latin America has suffered at the hands of European protectionism. Certainly, Latin America has fallen afoul of the wide range of nontariff barriers used by European countries to limit sensitive manufactured imports. Latin America has been adversely affected by the progressive tightening of the Multi-Fiber Agreement controlling textile exports, and Brazil has been pushed to "negotiate" Voluntary Export Restraint (VER) agreements covering steel and footwear. Yet despite these barriers, Latin American manufactured exports to the European Community have grown and have increased their share of total exports to the EC from 4.9 percent in 1970 to 24 percent in 1987. The percentage of manufactured exports in total Brazilian exports to the EC rose from 8 percent to 32 percent over the same period.

There is also concern over growing marginalization of Latin America in terms of investment. In the short term, investment has been hit by the economic crisis in Latin America and by political uncertainties in many countries, particularly Brazil. Yet there have also been important shifts in the overall pattern of European outward investment. Increasing emphasis on high-technology production techniques is undercutting the advantages that drew investment to Latin America in the 1970s: cheap labor and access to raw materials and energy. European investment has been directed increasingly away from the developing world and toward other industrialized countries—above all, the United States. Moreover, Latin America may be declining as a preferred target for investment, even within the developing world. Support for this view can be drawn from one analysis of the OEM (Original Equipment Manufacturing) Arrangement whereby transnational enterprises increasingly obtain some of their products through long-term contractual relationships with independent but less well established competitors. In a list of twenty-eight illustrative cases of such arrangements involving the Third World, not a single case involved a Latin American producer.

Finally, the 1980s saw clear limits on the Western European policy on the management of the debt crisis. Latin American hopes of support in its efforts to reduce the burden of adjustment went unheeded in Europe. For most of the period from 1982 to 1987, despite some rhetorical support from France, European governments, central banks, and private banks followed U.S. preferences on the debt. Indeed, West Germany and Britain at times went further than the United States in their warnings against the dangers of the more extensive schemes of debt relief. It is also important to note that the European Commission has been at the center of moves to intensify relations with Latin America but that the debt crisis falls outside its competence—as well as outside the competence of most European foreign ministries.

For many in Latin America, the political limits to European relations with Latin America were underlined by developments in the 1980s:

- The degree of European support for Britain and the imposition of an economic boycott against Argentina over the Falklands/Malvinas War in 1982 shocked many Latin Americans and underscored the limits of the relationship. The Falklands/Malvinas issue itself, however, has gradually faded from the scene as Britain and Argentina have moved to improve relations, a process that culminated in the restoration of diplomatic relations in early 1990.
- European rhetoric of supporting democratization may well have been sincere, but the discrepancy between the abundance of rhetoric and the absence of solid economic measures (above all on the debt) has led to a degree of skepticism and disillusion in many parts of Latin America.
- The decline in the willingness of Europe to criticize the excesses of U.S. policy in Central America, followed by a more general falloff in interest, prompted many Latin Americans to question the strength of the political relationship. In some cases the change reflected a change in governments, as in the transition from a Social Democrat to a Christian Democrat government in West Germany in 1982. In other cases, such as in France and Spain, political attention was attracted elsewhere and the costs of criticism appeared to outweigh the benefits. In still other cases, such as among the parties of the Socialist International, in the late 1980s there was a marked falloff of enthusiasm over the pattern of events inside Nicaragua. Against these developments it is fair to say that policy at the EC level has been more consistent, offering firm support for a regional peace settlement and repeatedly pledging to increase economic aid to assist regional reconstruction. The extent to which the pledges are fulfilled will be an important indicator of Europe's political concern for the region.

1992

The moves of the European Community toward further economic integration in the form of the completion of a single market and further progress on monetary union have aroused substantial misgivings in Latin America. However, evaluating their economic impact with any precision is extremely difficult because no one knows how many of the proposed measures will be enacted (and implemented) and because much depends on the future performance of the world economy.

Optimists argue that Latin America will in general stand to benefit from this process. In the first place, movement toward 1992 will lead to a reduction in the overall level of protectionism because the ability of individual states to impose nontariff barriers will be reduced. In addition, the need for increased structural adjustment assistance for weaker members of the European Community will increase EC budgetary constraints and thereby force a radical change in the Common Agricultural Policy. It is also argued that Europe will resist the temptation to retreat into "Fortress Europe" because of the possible retaliation which such a withdrawal would provoke and because so many European companies are firmly tied into the world market.

More importantly, optimists argue that the move toward 1992 will improve the overall growth performance of the European Community and that an economically dynamic and prosperous Europe will have a number of positive benefits for Latin America. Europe will have significant trade-creating industries that are less likely to press for protectionist measures against Third World products. These stronger industries will be well placed to seek investment opportunities in Latin America. Economic success will strengthen Europe's ability to stabilize the international monetary system and offset the negative impact of recent U.S. monetary policy. And finally, an economically strong and successful Europe is a precondition for a more politically active Europe. Only on this basis will Europe be able to become a more genuinely autonomous and independent partner for Latin America.

There are, however, substantial problems with this optimistic scenario. The potential dangers for Latin America center on the very real risk of increased protectionism. The danger is not so much the creation of high tariff walls, which would clearly lead to reprisals; rather the threat is more one of increased use of Voluntary Export Restraints and a further shift toward managed trade. The basis of this managed trade would be determined by the political and economic weight of Europe, the United States, and Japan; other states would be left very much on the margins.

More specifically, there are five potential problems for Latin America:

- Completion of the internal market will involve heavy adjustment costs. To help absorb these costs, several states and many firms may exert strong pressure (already visible) for temporarily increased protection against third parties. Once in place, "temporary" protection is rarely removed.

- The adjustment costs will reduce the ability of the EC to raise overall levels of foreign aid and assistance.

- Many large European companies are so heavily geared toward the European market that they would be prepared to accept the threat of increased international protectionism as the cost of strengthening their position within the EC.

- The move toward majority voting within the EC will increase the political weight of the southern European states, which are most protectionist and have the greatest range of nontariff barriers.
- If the EC changes in 1992 are a success, investment opportunities *within* the European Community will increase, and multinational investment in the developing world will decline further.

In trade terms, 1992 is likely to have a negative impact on Latin American trade, although not dramatically so. The trends toward trade marginalization will continue, although Latin American countries able to produce internationally competitive manufactured goods will be able to find a market. If there is an improvement in the current economic and political situation in Brazil, it is possible that the dominance of Brazil in EC–Latin American trade will increase and the Brazil–German link will remain at the heart of the relationship.

European corporations are unlikely to significantly increase their interest in Latin America. Large companies already established in the region will expand as and when the situation improves, but the trend toward world production—for instance, in the automobile industry—is unlikely to involve Latin America to the extent that it did in the 1970s. Italian investment may well prove to be the most notable exception to this pattern. In general, continued budgetary constraints and other demands both inside and outside the European Community will prevent any dramatic increase in aid levels.

Europe After the Cold War

The debate over 1992 has been overshadowed by the dramatic recasting of the political map of Europe that has followed Gorbachev, the collapse of communism in Eastern Europe, as well as the rapidity of German reunification. These developments have enormous implications for Europe's international role in general and its policy toward Latin America in particular. In the short and medium term (the next seven years) these changes are likely to reinforce Europe's introspection. A bewildering number of issues have been opened (or reopened) that will dominate the foreign-policy agenda of all the major European states and of the EC for the foreseeable future: the German problem, the reintegration of Eastern Europe into the European mainstream, the need for a new European security system, concern over the consequences of the disintegration of the Soviet empire, and the adaptation of the European Community to these developments. Not only will these issues remain the dominant concern of politicians and public opinion, but they will also have important economic implications. First, the massive aid programs that have already been announced for Eastern Europe will reduce the scope of European initiatives in foreign aid and foreign-debt relief. Second, the decline in European foreign investment in Latin America will be worsened as companies, particularly German companies, expand their activities in Eastern Europe.

The decline in the political salience of Third World issues that was so visible in 1989 and 1990 will therefore continue. Moreover, this decline will be further strengthened by the shift toward more U.S.–Soviet cooperation on a number of major regional conflicts in the Third World. Africa and the Middle East are likely to remain the two most important areas: Africa because of the institutionalization of the Lomé system and because of the extent of European interests in the continuing crisis in southern Africa; the Middle East because of the likely renewed tightening of the oil market, continued regional instability (graphically illustrated by the Iraqi invasion of Kuwait), and geographic proximity.

Two factors will influence the attention given to Latin America. First, however much politicians may wish to concentrate on other issues, they may well be forced to look to Latin America. Whether or not a "Fortress Europe" is created, Western Europe will remain vulnerable to events in Latin America in at least two areas: debt and the global environment. There are already many signs of a shift in European attitudes toward the debt and an increased recognition that the present system of debt management is unsustainable economically and because of the social strains that it imposes on Latin America. The French, for example, strongly support a more generalized system of debt reduction, and West Germany has reacted positively to at least some aspects of the Brady Plan. Britain remains, and will probably remain for some time, the major opponent of change. Given the strength of the environmental lobby and the perceived seriousness of the threat, European governments may well be prepared to provide substantial assistance to Latin America in this area (see Chapter 23).

Second, the degree of attention paid to Latin America will depend a great deal on how the internal balance of power within the European Community evolves. The existence of a Latin American "constituency" in West Germany is well established, and the country will continue to have the largest direct economic stake in the region. However, events in Eastern Europe and the reunification of the two Germanys are bound to absorb the greater part of

German foreign-policy energies, and it is difficult to see Latin America playing the kind of role in German foreign policy that it did in the mid-1970s. Britain is likely to prove the most generally unresponsive to Latin American concerns, although Britain's enthusiasm for an open and outwardly oriented post-1992 Europe and for environmental issues could work to the region's advantage.

Italy and Spain will remain the most forceful advocates of a more active policy toward the region. Of these, Italian support is likely to prove the most firmly rooted both because of the momentum that Latin America has acquired in the country's foreign policy and because of Italy's growing economic position. However, even in Italy there has been a significant shift of political and economic attention away from Latin America and toward Eastern Europe.

There are also some important limitations on Spain's role, particularly if economic or financial assistance is involved. Latin American expectations that Madrid would be able to modify EC policy are likely to remain unfulfilled. The bases of EC policies were firmly established before Spain entered in 1986, and most of Spain's energies at least for some years will be absorbed with the challenge of internal adaptation to EC membership. Moreover, Spanish public opinion may not be so strongly committed to the Latin American cause (or in such agreement about how to promote it) as official rhetoric tries to suggest. In addition both Spain and Italy are among the most protectionist of the European states and the least likely to support significant tariff concessions to Latin America.

French policy is the hardest to predict. In general, France's attitude toward the region in the 1980s was apparent in rhetoric rather than in action. Yet there are indications that the French may become more actively involved in, for example, efforts to resolve the debt crisis. France has always played a major role in the overall direction of European policy toward the Third World and occupies a pivotal position that could tip the balance in favor of a more assertive European policy toward Latin America.

The balance of forces in Europe, however, is almost certainly insufficient to guarantee an across-the-board activist and responsive European policy toward Latin America in the short and perhaps medium term. During this period, the major aim of Latin American countries will be to try to exploit the Latin American "constituency" in Europe in order to prevent further marginalization, especially in economic terms. The major tactic will be to try to link the areas in which there is genuine interdependence (debt, the environment, drugs) in order to secure concessions in other fields. In the longer term—in seven to ten years—the prospect of Europe as a major center of political and military power with the internal unity and cohesion necessary to develop a broader and more active international role cannot be discounted. One can certainly argue that Latin America would benefit from a genuinely more multipolar international system of this kind. Yet the formation of such a system will be a gradual process, and the extent to which Europe will be able to devote significant attention to developments in Latin America is unlikely to increase very rapidly in the 1990s.

19

Latin America and Japan

Historical Ties

Historically Japan's relations with Latin America have been limited and certainly of lesser importance than those with either the United States or Western Europe. Yet the 1970s saw an expansion of economic ties that were far more soundly based than were ties with any of Latin America's other nontraditional partners. Moreover, the continued growth of Japan's economic and particularly financial power, the increasing salience of Latin America for policymakers in Tokyo, the recent signs of a more assertive Japanese policy toward the region, and the clear potential for further commercial expansion will make the Japanese connection a more central feature of Latin American foreign relations in the 1990s.

The first significant historic link between Japan and Latin America developed as a result of Japanese emigration to the region. Large-scale Japanese emigration was prompted by several factors, but perhaps most important were domestic concerns over population growth and rural poverty. Initially, most Japanese emigrants headed for the west coast of the United States and Hawaii. But as anti-Japanese sentiments continued to increase in the United States and Canada, ultimately leading to restrictive immigration laws (especially the 1924 Oriental Exclusion Act), the destination of these immigrants increasingly shifted to Latin America.

Between 1908 and 1942 around 200,000 Japanese emigrated to Latin America, around 70 percent in the peak years from 1926 to 1935. Emigration was encouraged by both Latin American and Japanese governments. Thus Japan established a special company to streamline the emigration procedures, and from 1921 this Overseas Development Company received direct government financial assistance. In contrast to the United States, in Brazil there was no mass internment of the Japanese community during World War II.

A second, smaller wave of Japanese emigration occurred after the war, with 60,000 people moving in the period between 1953 and 1968. Today there are an estimated 1 million people of Japanese descent living mainly in São Paulo but also in Paraguay, Peru, and Mexico. This is the largest population of ethnic Japanese outside mainland Japan.

The significance of Japanese migration is hard to assess. By far the largest number of ethnic Japanese live in Brazil, virtually all in and around the city of São Paulo. Their presence was a major factor in the early phases of Japanese investment in that country. Perhaps more importantly, the presence of a large Japanese community continues to play a significant role in Japanese perceptions of the region. Japanese immigration is mentioned in nearly every Japanese government discussion of Latin America. The immigrants are viewed as a natural bridge between Japanese and Latin American firms. Tokyo has encouraged educational opportunities for the immigrants in Japan and continues to promote Japanese–Latin American cultural exchange.

Yet the ethnic factor should not be exaggerated. Japanese businesses in Brazil have become less dependent on Brazilian Japanese, relying instead on managers from Japan. In addition, and this largely accounts for the recruitment patterns of the Japanese firms, the Japanese community in Brazil has established a well-integrated position in society. Although cultural and social affinity with Japan often remains strong, the feeling of being Brazilian and belonging in Brazil has grown stronger with each generation. Japanese-language schools, for instance, are declining. The Japanese community is disproportionately represented in higher education, and many ethnic Japanese have risen to high positions in Brazilian business and government, including a former head of Petrobrás, the state oil company.

Japanese economic interests in Latin America have expanded significantly since the late 1960s. Japan has become the second most important trading partner for most Latin American countries. Excluding Panama, with which trade consists largely of "paper" transactions relating to ship registering, Mexico and Brazil are Japan's most important trading partners. Over 70 percent of trade is conducted with just four countries: Brazil, Mexico, Peru, and Venezuela. Latin America's mineral resources have always been a major attraction for resource-poor Japan. Japan is Mexico's second largest oil customer, and Brazil is a major exporter of iron ore, which alone represents 40 percent of Brazilian exports to Japan. Although the pattern of trade is predominantly one of Japan importing raw materials and exporting manufactured goods, Brazil has achieved some success in increasing the percentage of manufactured exports from 12 percent in 1976 to 30 percent in 1984.

Direct foreign investment has also expanded significantly. Latin America accounted for 19 percent of Japan's accumulated foreign investment between 1951 and 1985, behind the United States (32 percent) and Asia (23 percent).

Again, Brazil and Mexico were the two major targets for Japanese investment, with Japan the third largest foreign investor in both countries behind the United States and West Germany. Mexico was particularly attractive because of its proximity to the United States, and recently Japan has increasingly invested in the *maquiladora* industries. In addition to its direct investment Japan is also the most important source of products that enter the United States under the *maquiladora* tariff codes. In the case of Brazil, Japanese investment was primarily attracted by the size and potential of the domestic market, but investment in large-scale mineral production, processing, and transportation has also been a significant feature.

Pressures for Greater Involvement

By the mid-1980s, Japan had acquired substantial economic interests in Latin American trade, investment, and mineral imports. More recently the salience of Latin America for Japanese policymakers has grown as the result of these factors: the debt crisis; U.S.–Japanese relations; account surpluses in Japan; and Japan's desire to enhance its prestige abroad.

The Debt Crisis

Japanese interests in the region have been profoundly affected by the debt crisis, which now represents the single most important link between Japan and Latin America. Japan's stake in managing the Latin American debt crisis is both direct and indirect. The direct stake is based on the estimated $30 billion owed by Latin America to Japanese private banks. According to the most widely cited estimates by the Mitsui Bank, the exposure of Japanese banks in Brazil was $8.9 billion, in Mexico $10.8 billion, in Argentina $5.0 billion, in Venezuela $2.3 billion, and in Chile $1.6 billion.

Japan's indirect stake in the current economic crisis in Latin America is based on its overall dependence on an open and growing international economy—dependence on imported raw materials and on export markets. Indeed, Japan is dependent on the global environment to a much greater degree than a cursory review of Japanese export figures might suggest. Although in 1985 the ratio of Japan's exports to GNP was 10.2 percent—considerably lower than ratios in several European countries, especially West Germany—this is not an all-inclusive explanation. The areas in which Japan is most dependent are also the areas most critical to the nation's overall productive capacity. Thus, for example, 55.1 percent of automobile production, 46.1 percent of electronics and electrical machinery, and 32.7 percent of crude steel products were exported in 1985. The impact of this dependence is magnified by Japan's self-perception of being an isolated and insecure nation, dependent on others both for continued economic success and for security. Outsiders see an economic colossus when they look at Japan, but the Japanese constantly remind themselves of their overseas dependence.

U.S.–Japanese Relations

Other pressures on Japan are the result of the dynamics of U.S.–Japanese relations. Japan's interest in Latin America is not motivated exclusively by its involvement in the debt issue or even based solely on its economic interests in the region. Tokyo forms its Latin American policies with one eye fixed firmly on the United States and with the clear intention of moderating the growing economic friction between the two countries. Thus when U.S. trade complaints become unusually vocal, Tokyo responds by demonstrating its commitment to international economic stability by means of increased aid to the Third World. During 1988 and 1989, when Congress was working on what Tokyo believed was an extremely protectionist trade bill, Japan unveiled a string of debt and development initiatives.

This linkage has been encouraged by Washington. Congress has consistently stressed the relationship between the need for "burden sharing" by Japan and Europe and the United States' ability to compete. Furthermore, both the president and Congress have urged Japan to demonstrate its commitment to international economic stability by doing more than buying raw materials from Latin America. Rather, they believe Japan should help stimulate Latin American economies by increasing investment, sending more economic assistance, and buying more manufactured goods.

In short, it is difficult to overestimate the impact of the United States on Japan's Latin American policies. Tokyo believes that Third World issues are one area where Japan can successfully combat U.S. economic friction and cement the critical U.S.–Japanese relationship.

Current Account Surpluses

Japan has been prompted to increase its involvement in Latin America because of the sheer size of its current account surplus, now running at about $80 billion a year. The "recycling" of this surplus has been aimed primarily at the United States, Western Europe, and Asia. But in all these areas there are political limits to the extent of Japanese economic expansion. Given the depth of the economic crisis facing Africa, Latin America emerges as the one other area where a substantial increase in the Japanese presence is possible. In addition, for Latin Americans Japan has been seen as an attractive partner. It has no political ambitions in the area. Its economic involvement does not carry the same political implications as U.S. economic involvement. And the extent of Japan's economic success adds to the attraction of its technology and managerial know-how.

International Prestige

An increased presence in Latin America and activism on the debt crisis are seen as means of enhancing Japan's international prestige and of highlighting its status as a responsible economic superpower. Japanese officials believe that the country is uniquely qualified to assist economic development by "recycling" its financial resources to the developing countries. Unlike the United States, Japan has the resources to adopt a long-term view of Third World economic development. The gradual move toward a more assertive role on development issues, therefore, forms part of a general desire to play a larger role on the world stage.

These pressures—to protect Japanese economic interests, to appease U.S. trade complaints, and to enhance Japan's prestige—have had important implications for Japanese policy in the region, most crucially on the debt issue. In the early phases of the debt crisis Japan adopted a very low-key and cautious approach; it supported the idea that the U.S. government should take the regional lead in managing the Latin American debt crisis, and it publicly backed both the Baker Initiative and IMF orthodoxy. More recently, the pressures outlined above have led to a broader and more assertive approach.

In 1987 Tokyo permitted twenty-eight Japanese lenders to establish a "paper" company in the Cayman Islands. The company buys a portion of Japanese banks' nonperforming loans to Mexico and Brazil at a discount. The banks are able to write off their losses for tax purposes and improve their net worth. In the case of default, the factoring firm rather than the banks would take the losses. Although the scheme does nothing to ameliorate the situation of the debtor countries, it has helped to placate Japanese creditors.

Also in 1987, Japan launched a three-year, $30 billion program to assist the major debtor countries. The plan consisted of $10 billion in subscription to multilateral institutions and $20 billion to be recycled directly to the debtor countries, primarily through untied loans. The initial announcement appeared to be directed at Latin America—both because of the gravity of the debt crisis in the region and because Japan was under pressure to expand the geographic scope of its economic assistance. However, when the Association of Southeast Asian Countries expressed concern about being overlooked, Tokyo announced that Asia would receive a healthy portion of the recycling funds. Central America and South America are now expected to receive around one-fifth of the $20 billion.

Japan has consistently advocated that multilateral agencies play a more active role in coordinating a solution to the debt crisis. One proposal would have the multilateral agencies act as a marketplace or information center for debt-equity swaps; another would establish a special account with the IMF. Debtor nations would contribute currency reserves to the account, which the IMF would manage and use as security against possible defaults. In return, banks would negotiate with debtors to convert debt into securities and to reschedule other portions of the debt. More recently, Japanese spokesmen have responded positively to the Brady Plan, although the death of Emperor Hirohito and the seriousness of the 1989 Recruit bribery scandal have temporarily blunted Japanese activity in this area.

The central feature of the recent Japanese initiatives is the stress that they place on continued and expanded private-sector participation. Where they differ sharply from U.S. policies is Tokyo's belief in the necessity for a more active role for governments in order to generate private-sector interest.

Between 1982 and 1988 the total equity of Japanese lending banks rose fourfold in dollar value, whereas that of British and American banks barely doubled. As a result of this very profitable expansion, the Japanese banks found themselves in a much stronger position than their Anglo-Saxon rivals to take large write-downs on their Latin American loans. Largely for domestic tax reasons there was a long time-lag before these losses were recognized, but in February 1990 twenty-nine Japanese banks took 70 percent write-downs against $5.3 billion of Mexican debt, which they swapped for bonds under the Brady debt-reduction scheme. The ministry of finance paved the way for this transaction by raising the provision level on total Third World debt eligible for tax relief to 15 percent in 1989–1990 and to 25 percent in 1990–1991. Even the most exposed Bank of Tokyo will suffer only about a 7 percent drop in reported profit, since it can realize portfolio gains elsewhere to offset these losses.

But despite the relative ease with which Japanese commercial banks have been able to absorb their Latin American losses, their willingness to undertake future lending to the region has evidently been severely impaired. There were no Japanese takers for the "new lending" option to Mexico, and Tokyo bankers express the intention of directing their loanable funds to more trustworthy clients nearer home.

Japanese official aid to the Third World has grown significantly, and in 1988 Japan had the world's largest aid budget. Although Latin America receives only around 10 percent of Japanese official aid, the absolute volume for Latin America had grown to $317 million U.S. dollars in 1986. It is remarkable to note how important a donor Japan has become to many Latin American recipients. In 1985 Japan was the largest donor to Brazil, Paraguay, and Guyana and the second largest donor to Honduras, Jamaica, Panama, Argentina, Bolivia, Colombia, and Uruguay. Latin American countries have also been encouraged by the announcement in June 1988 of a plan to disburse $50 billion in official development assistance between 1988 and 1992.

Constraints on Japanese Actions

Although Japan's stake in Latin America and the pressures on Tokyo have grown substantially, certain constraints limit Japan's willingness and ability to expand its role in the region:

- The relative place of Latin America in Japan's overall foreign policy is unlikely to change. Foreign investment and the expansion of Japan's overseas banking activities will continue to be targeted primarily at the United States, Asia, and Western Europe. The majority of official aid will go to Africa and Asia. Yet over the next decade the same relative share of a rapidly growing pie will still lead to a substantial increase in the Japanese presence in Latin America.
- Much of the talk in the 1970s of a natural complementarity between Japan and Latin America exaggerated the role of Japan's mineral dependence. Changes in Japan's industrial structure, the move away from heavy industry and into the high-technology and service sectors, and a less pessimistic view of the extent of worldwide mineral scarcity have all led to a downward revision of estimates for the country's mineral needs in the 1990s.
- Important institutional barriers complicate any increase in Japanese aid to Latin America. On the Japanese side, Tokyo is unable to rely on a corps of trained development specialists such as the U.S. Agency for International Development (USAID). For this reason Japan's aid program stresses private-sector participation in utilizing the large sums that are being pumped into Latin America. Already the pipeline of undisbursed funds is quite long, reaching three to four times the amount

of Japan's annual aid budget. On the Latin American side, there is the problem of finding and managing sufficient projects to absorb the increased aid.

- A contradiction exists between the emphasis that Japanese debt initiatives place on the importance of direct foreign investment and the visible reluctance of Japanese firms to expand their activities in the region. According to a 1986 survey of the 100 largest Japanese investors in Brazil, the vast majority said they were satisfied with the present level of investment and 68 percent said that they had already invested more than necessary. This reluctance results from two factors. First, it reflects the difficulty of finding suitable investment opportunities given the financial instability still prevalent in Latin America. Second, as in Europe, it reflects broad shifts in the pattern of outward investment toward high-technology processes and toward other developed countries.

- In its relations with the United States, Japan has generally been supportive of the concept of geographic spheres of influence and has certainly tended to view Latin America as lying within Washington's sphere. Thus it has consistently avoided any political initiatives or criticism of U.S. policies. U.S. political concerns are clearly the main reason Japan has had no aid program in Cuba or Nicaragua, and it is difficult to conceive of a Japanese aid program in Jamaica, El Salvador, Honduras, or Costa Rica without U.S. urging and encouragement. In addition, Tokyo clearly hopes that its more forthcoming policies on the debt will help appease U.S. trade complaints and cement the U.S.–Japanese relationship.

The dilemma of balancing an increased economic role in Latin America against respect for Washington's political interests remains real. There have already been reports of U.S. displeasure at the lack of prior consultation on Japan's debt proposals and of U.S. pressure for most Japanese money to be channeled through multilateral agencies. Together with Britain and West Germany, Washington has made no secret of its opposition to Japan's debt initiatives at the Toronto and Berlin economic summits. Thus, although the United States has been in the forefront of those calling for an expanded Japanese role in the region, many in Washington are wary of an expanding Japanese presence in Latin America. The Japanese are well aware of this and are sometimes at a loss as to how to receive the credit for greater regional burden sharing without creating negative repercussions in the United States.

It can be argued from the Brady Plan and the increased recognition in Washington that a new approach to debt management is unavoidable and will lead to a greater convergence of U.S. and Japanese policies toward the region. However vague the Brady Initiative, it has served to broaden the agenda of debt management and may provide a platform around which a future increased Japanese role could be constructed. Against this likelihood, there remains a considerable distance between the voluntary and case-by-case approach that seems to characterize U.S. thinking in the Brady Plan and the more extensive and the generalized Japanese approach. More important, the political terms on which Japanese money will be forthcoming remain to be decided.

The Future

Japan's economic role in Latin America will continue to expand. Between 1985 and 1990 Japan became the largest source of external finance to Latin America, providing 50 percent more funds than the United States. Moreover, even if Latin America maintains the same relative ranking for Japan, Tokyo's prominent position will continue to develop as aid, credits, and investment funds from Europe and the United States remain constant or decline. By the mid-1990s Japan may have established the largest economic presence across a whole range of indicators. The partial falloff in Japanese activism on the debt as a result of the Recruit scandal will only be temporary, and the pressures pushing Japan to implement new mechanisms for tackling the debt crisis are likely to remain. Moreover, not only are the current policies of debt management clearly insufficient, but the United States will become both less willing and less able to adopt any more constructive, long-term solutions to the problem. For Washington an increased Japanese role will become more necessary.

Although Japanese investment is unlikely to increase in the short term, the prospects for the longer term are encouraging. On the one hand, Latin American governments are being forced, out of economic necessity, to reconsider restrictive policies against foreign investment. On the other, the pressure from Japan will continue. The Japanese government will continue to insist that private investment remain a central part of any solution to debt and development problems and will press Latin American governments to provide conditions conducive to foreign investment. The one area on which there has been little movement so far concerns the opening of the Japanese market to Latin American manufactured goods.

Although an expansion of the Japanese presence represents one of the few signs of movement on the international horizon, it is not a panacea for Latin America's problems nor will it occur without friction. The Japanese are likely to adopt a hardheaded approach to the region. Indeed the other side of increased Japanese assertiveness is a tendency toward bargaining more toughly and toward tying aid and investment to strict conditions. Crucial questions for the relationship will include these: What kind of conditionality will be demanded? How will Japan seek to implement these conditions? How acceptable will they prove to be to Latin America? The economic relationship—and especially the ability to manage conflict and divergence—between Latin America and the United States has evolved over a long period. The learning process in Japanese–Latin American relations will not be smooth and will certainly create friction and misunderstandings.

Japan will not assume a new leadership role in Latin America. Its involvement will remain heavily focused on economic issues. Tokyo is uncertain over how Japan should respond to the changing relationship with the United States. No clear overall strategy has been worked out, let alone a strategy involving Latin America. Indeed, both at the company and at governmental level, past success is often attributed to "flexible rigidity" and to Japan's ability to respond quickly and efficiently to opportunities as they emerge. Thus, although its presence in Latin America will expand significantly, Japan is not likely to seek a prominent leadership role in the region actively, and its involvement will probably remain heavily focused on economic issues in which it has a direct stake.

Although friction with the United States will continue (both in general and over the details of policy toward Latin America), Tokyo will seek to avoid excessive conflict with Washington and will remain less likely than Western Europe to challenge U.S. political interests in the region. There will thus be only limited opportunities for Latin America to "play the Japanese card." Continuing preoccupation with the critical U.S.–Japanese relationship will reinforce Tokyo's low-key approach to Latin America, and a major deterioration of U.S.–Japanese relations would have to occur for this situation to change. Because such a deterioration is not likely and because of the nature of Japanese economic policies, the Japanese connection, though important, will fall short of Latin American hopes.

20

Latin America and Other Regions

China

The cumulative effect of the rise of Japan, the emergence of a unified Europe, and the relative decline of the United States are likely to create considerable flux in the primary international relationships of all Latin American countries in the coming decade. It is in the light of these fluctuations that some of the subcontinent's most marginal international relationships can most profitably be analyzed. Of these marginal relationships, the links that a number of Latin American countries have established with the People's Republic of China are of some significance.

The initial interaction between China and the countries of Latin America was far from propitious. Despite the triumph in 1949 of revolution led by the Chinese Communist party on the Chinese mainland, the countries of Latin America continued to recognize the Kuomintang government of Jiang Jieshi (Chiang Kai-shek) on the island of Taiwan as the legitimate government of China. These countries provided the bulk of the votes that were used by the United States to deny Beijing a seat in the United Nations and were consequently seen by the Chinese Communist leadership as little more than tools of U.S. imperialism.

The success of the Cuban Revolution in 1959 focused international attention on Cuba, abruptly pushing Latin American issues into the consciousness of the elites of Asia and Africa. To the leadership in Beijing, the Cuban Revolution signified that Latin America could not be written off as a region permanently under the hegemony and control of U.S. imperialism. China therefore began to include Latin America in the Chinese strategy of an Afro-Asian "United Front Against Imperialism." For the Chinese, the impetus was clearly ideological: even after the establishment of diplomatic links with Cuba in 1960, China's Latin American policy remained the responsibility of the party rather than the government, the possibility of future armed revolutions in the region being the focus of interest. Sino-Cuban relations therefore worsened inexorably as the Sino-Soviet schism became a concrete reality.

Nearly all the Communist parties in Latin America were greatly influenced by the Sino-Soviet split and were themselves soon divided into pro-Soviet and pro-Chinese factions. At the Tricontinental Conference in Havana in 1966, Castro's denunciation of the "Chinese line" was direct and harsh. With China's public proclamation in 1969 that the Soviet Union was China's "principal enemy," Sino-Cuban relations, already highly strained, became totally frigid. During the Cultural Revolution, all Chinese governmental and diplomatic activity in Latin America was stopped. Only the links that existed between the Chinese Communist party and some Latin American revolutionary parties and movements continued to be maintained.

China's Latin American diplomacy was reactivated in 1970 in response to the election of Salvador Allende as president of Chile. However, Sino-Chilean diplomatic relations were never intimate; in the ideological climate of the Cultural Revolution, the "Chilean Way" of socialism through the ballot could not be reconciled with Maoism.

The combined effect of two events—Sino-Soviet military clashes over the Ussuri River in 1969 and General Augusto Pinochet's coup in Chile in 1973—finally induced China to look at Latin America in a nonideological way. Soviet hostility forced China to come to terms with the fact that China could no longer, to use Mao's phrase, "stand alone in the world." The Pinochet coup clearly demonstrated the relative strengths of reactionary Latin American governments and juntas on the one hand and revolutionary parties and movements in the region on the other. It was perfectly logical for the leadership in Beijing to decide that China needed the support of the former far more than it needed the latter.

Thus, for the first time, China began to see its relations with Latin America in diplomatic and state-centered terms rather than ideological terms. This new view led to a break with revolutionary movements and guerrilla bands that had till then been China's only constituency in the region. China alone among the socialist countries did not make a formal break with Santiago after the coup, even though one of the junta's first foreign-policy decisions was to downgrade Chile's diplomatic representation in Beijing.

In the aftermath of the Sino–U.S. détente there was a deluge of recognitions of China by Latin American countries. By 1974 Brazil, Mexico, Peru, and Argentina had established diplomatic relations with China. China's diplomatic presence in Latin America was reinforced in the post-Mao period, thereby further isolating Taiwan diplomatically in the international community. Also, because of its desire to receive universal recognition, China views Latin America as important to this end because 11 of the 21 countries that still recognize Taiwan are situated there and in the Caribbean. China now maintains diplomatic relations with seventeen Latin American countries, which represent about 90 percent of the subcontinent's territory and population. This is clearly China's most important diplomatic stake in the Western Hemisphere.

China's attitude toward Cuba remains a matter of some interest. Statements from the top Chinese leadership have indicated that a gradual improvement in Sino-Cuban relations is to be expected. But China is also laying a great deal of emphasis on economic relations with the countries of Latin America. By asserting that China, like the countries of the region, is a developing country, Beijing is laying claim to greater economic interaction with Latin America, since economic relations between developing countries are, in the Chinese view, mutually supportive rather than exploitive. Also, in pursuit of an economic strategy to conserve its foreign-exchange reserves, China has long been advocating some kind of barter trade with prospective trade partners in Latin America. China regards its economic ties with the major countries of Latin America as an important aspect of its relations with the region as a whole.

China and Argentina have signed economic cooperation agreements in vegetable and fruit growing and processing, construction of granaries, processing of grain and oil-bearing seeds, management of grazing grounds, marine and freshwater fisheries, forest plantations, multipurpose use of timber, and the exploration, development, and smelting of nonferrous metals. China and Venezuela have signed a government trade agreement, with China supplying farm produce and Venezuela rolled steel, aluminum ingots, and petrochemical products. The two countries have also signed a protocol of cooperation in oil exploration and development, a matter of some importance to both signatories. China and Colombia have signed two agreements and have had three exchanges of notes on economic and technical cooperation and trade. These agreements relate to Chinese financial support for the construction of power stations in Colombia as well as for the purchase of coffee, cocoa, and sugar.

However, Sino-Brazilian relations appear to be the central focus of China's economic strategy in Latin America. In recent years the Chinese and Brazilian governments have signed five documents on developing their bilateral relations. Of particular importance are the protocols on cooperation between the two governments in the iron and steel industry and geological science. The documents mention commercial questions, such as Brazil's interest in augmenting its sales of iron ore, metallurgical products, cellulose, timber, aluminum, and automobiles, and China's interest in increasing its sales of oil, cola, corn, and cotton.

A strategic dimension has entered Sino-Brazilian relations with the Chinese showing an interest in purchasing and exchanging technology particularly in aerospace, solid fuels, and armored vehicles. China has also expressed the desire to collaborate with Brazil in electricity generation, particularly with regard to the proposed Three Gorges Dam on the Yangtze. Unlike Brazil, China does not have the technology for enterprises as large as the Itaipú Dam, the massive hydroelectric project on the Paraná River between Brazil and Paraguay.

Sino-Latin American trade has increased almost thirteen-fold in the last two decades, from $130 million in 1969 to $1.65 billion in 1984. Areas of economic cooperation now include timber, fisheries, mining, oil exploration, construction, and textiles. However, Sino–Latin American trade accounts for only 3 percent of China's total and 1 percent of Latin America's.

In the post-Mao years, China has substantially upgraded its diplomatic presence in Latin America. In August 1984 China's foreign minister Wu Xueqian visited four major Latin American countries—Mexico, Venezuela, Argentina, and Brazil—and briefly stopped over in two others—Panama and Peru. Wu's trip was followed a little over a year later by official visits to Colombia, Brazil, Argentina, and Venezuela by Zhao Ziyang, then the Chinese premier. Since then, a number of Latin American heads of state have paid state visits to China.

In conclusion, the following generalizations can be made about China's foreign policy toward the countries of Latin America:

- There is no longer an ideological element in China's Latin American policy. China has relinquished any interest in, or intention of, supporting any guerrilla movement or insurrection in the region. The Chinese leadership at the highest level has declared that China has no links with the Peruvian Sendero Luminoso (Shining Path) guerrilla group, which is generally regarded as being Maoist.

- Latin America is of marginal interest to China as far as international politics and the global division of power are concerned. China regards the region as lying in the sphere of influence of the United States. China might express disapproval of specific U.S. policies and actions in the region but has no intention of challenging U.S. domination of the subcontinent. Also, China's relations with the Soviet Union—China's cardinal international relationship—play virtually no role in Chinese diplomacy in Latin America because the Soviet Union wields so little influence in the region outside Cuba.

- Maintaining a large and visible diplomatic presence in Latin America is in China's national interest, since a number of governments in the region continue to retain diplomatic links with Taiwan. By placing an emphasis on establishing links with all the countries in Latin America, China is attempting to hammer the final nails in the coffin of the political concept of "two Chinas."
- Chinese foreign policy today has an economic orientation: it is geared to the promotion of China's "four modernizations." When Premier Zhao Ziyang visited four Latin American countries in 1985, the most important members of his entourage were Chen Muhua, president of the People's Bank of China, and Wei Yuming, vice minister of foreign economic relations and trade—a clear indication of the importance that China gave to economic relations during the visit. The fact that China's Latin American policy, while not neglecting the smaller countries, is nonetheless focused on the large reveals that China's interest in the region is primarily economic. Since economic relations between China and Latin America are likely to remain minimal in the coming decade, it is safe to conclude that Sino–Latin American ties will remain slender.

The Middle East

The turbulent and volatile politics of the Middle East has an effect on all parts of the world, even on a region as geographically removed and culturally distinct as Latin America. All Latin American countries with the exception of Cuba voted in favor of the scheme to partition Palestine into a Jewish state and an Arab state; 40 percent of the 33 states that supported the U.N. resolution that led to the creation of Israel in 1948 were from Latin America. Today, however, nearly all Latin American countries have adopted a much more nuanced position and there is a good deal of variation in support for Israel. Cuba, Guyana, and Nicaragua have virtually no ties, but Israel's U.S.-backed involvement in Central America has resulted in the establishment of warm relations with El Salvador and Honduras.

In general, the economic importance that the Arab world has enjoyed since 1973 has had little effect on the way the Arab-Israeli equation is perceived in Latin America. The Arab world buys little from Latin America, and Latin American oil importers have largely relied on regional or non-Arab extraregional suppliers. Thus trade between the Arab world and Latin America, with the exception of Argentina, Brazil, Cuba, and Uruguay, has been minimal. This factor, coupled with the lack of economic assistance in the form of concessionary loans from Arab oil-supported development funds, has resulted in little Arab leverage in the region on the Palestine issue. The Latin American shift away from Israel is a reaction to Israeli actions since 1967: the occupation of Arab lands in 1967, the annexation of the Golan Heights in 1981, the annexation of eastern Jerusalem, the Israeli invasion of Lebanon, and Israel's refusal to contemplate any sort of settlement of the Palestinian question. It is significant that Latin American support for U.N. resolutions that recognize the Palestine Liberation Organization (PLO) as the sole legitimate representative of the Palestine people has been on the increase since 1974.

Recognizing its increasing respectability in the region, the PLO has refrained from any terrorist activities in Latin America since its attack on the Israeli embassy in Asunción, Paraguay, in 1970. The *intifada,* the ongoing Palestinian uprising against the 21-year-old Israeli occupation of the West Bank and Gaza, has further tarnished Israel's image, although Israel's undoubted loss of ground is less acute in this region than in other parts of the developing world. Most Latin American states continue to maintain cordial relations with Israel and continue to limit their support for the PLO to the multilateral level only, while avoiding bilateral recognition and the opening of PLO offices in their countries. The six Latin American states that have permitted the opening of PLO representation are Bolivia (1982), Brazil (1975), Cuba (1974), Mexico (1976), Nicaragua (1980), and Peru (1979). Brazil's dependence on Arab oil has influenced its policy in this regard.

If the recent PLO recognition of Israel were to lead to the proclamation of a U.N.–sponsored Palestinian state, Latin American states could be expected to support it. The Latin Americans, however, would be extremely reluctant to get directly involved in any pro-PLO move that was not carried out under the auspices of the United Nations, particularly if the move went against U.S. policy in the region.

Apart from the Palestinian issue, Latin America and the Middle East impinge on each other in the areas of arms and energy exports. Israel's security concerns and desire to achieve a measure of self-sufficiency in military hardware have resulted in a large arms industry that has to export to survive. If the value of Israel's arms sales to Latin America is included in Israeli trade statistics, its $56 million deficit in trade with Latin America turns into a surplus. The exception is Mexico, which in the early 1980s supplied 24 percent of Israel's oil needs of 160,000 barrels a day and ran a $400 million trade surplus with Israel. Unlike Brazil, which has successfully traded its goods and services in exchange for Arab oil, Israel has not been able to sell anything of value to Mexico in exchange for its energy purchases. Mexico's proximity to the U.S.–based parent companies and the small scale of its arms-procurement needs have prevented that.

When the oil glut forced Mexico to slash its prices in June 1981, Israel attempted to put pressure on Mexico to supply oil on a countertrade basis by threatening to move to suppliers willing to do so. Mexican unwillingness to increase significantly its intake of Israeli products and commodities led to a fall in Israel's oil purchases from Mexico in 1986 to the present level of 39,000 barrels per day. Israel is willing to cut but unwilling to terminate oil imports from Mexico.

Ecuador, in contrast, has bartered or countertraded oil for military aircraft from Israel on two occasions and supplies oil to Israel through U.S. middlemen because of the sensitivities of its Arab partners in OPEC (Organization of Petroleum Exporting Countries). On the energy-for-arms front, Israel's countertrade with Colombia is a recent development that has some implications for the future. Israel's coal needs have increased with its shift from oil to coal-fired electricity-generating plants. South Africa once supplied two thirds of Israel's coal imports, but this share has dropped to 50 percent as Israel attempts to distance itself from the apartheid regime. Initially, Colombia was unwilling to accept anything but cash for its coal, but in April 1988 it signed a four-year agreement with Israel worth $60 million covering the supply of 2 million tons of coal. Colombia appears to have accepted the notion of countertrade, because it is buying $200 million worth of military hardware, including fourteen Kfir combat aircraft, from Israel.

Israeli arms sales to Latin America have been greatly assisted by U.S. restrictions on arms flows, such as the Carter administration's linkage of arms sales to human-rights criteria, the Reagan administration's post–Falkland/Malvinas arms embargo on Argentina, and congressional restrictions on U.S. arms sales to Central American states. Latin American purchasers have been attracted by Israel's no-strings-attached outlook. Nevertheless, a number of factors work against a long-term Israeli presence in the Latin American arms market: the rapidly developing regional arms industry, particularly in Brazil; and the U.S. desire to prevent a further erosion of its share of the Latin American arms market. An important growth area for Israel could be the supply of Israeli know-how or components to the Latin American weapon producers—the Elta radar for the Brazilian-Italian AMX aircraft is a good example—but the fact that the Arab countries continue to remain Brazil's best customers of military hardware will militate against a close collaboration in military technology.

The most important single relationship between the two regions concerns Brazil. Brazilian interest in the Middle East was largely the result of Brazil's heavy dependence on Middle Eastern oil imports. In 1974 Brazil imported 79 percent of its oil requirements, of which 77 percent came from the Middle East. Successive price rises drove up Brazilian Middle East oil imports from $1.9 billion in 1974 to $7.6 billion in 1980. In order to counter this situation, Brazil launched a determined drive to increase its exports to the region. These grew from $357 million in 1978 to $1.5 billion in 1983 and consisted of food, manufactured goods, service exports (the construction of large-scale civil engineering projects), and weapons. Indeed, the Middle East quickly became the major market for Brazil's rapidly expanding production of light armored vehicles, artillery systems, and trainer aircraft. In addition, these economic realities led to an important shift in Brazil's position on the Arab-Israeli issue and to a vocal pro-Arab alignment symbolized by the support in 1975 for the U.N. resolution denouncing Zionism as a form of racism.

The relationship will become less important through the 1990s. As the Iraqi invasion of Kuwait demonstrated, Brazil will remain vulnerable to the disruption and increased cost of oil supplies, but to a lesser extent than in the past. Due to the alcohol-fuel program (producing automobile fuel from sugar cane) and increased domestic oil production, Brazilian imports from the Middle East fell from $7.6 billion U.S. dollars in 1980 to $1.9 billion U.S. dollars in 1986. Brazil will also continue to seek to expand its export markets in the region, especially of food and manufactured goods. But here again the overall importance will decline. The Gulf War killed off any Brazilian ideas of developing a special relationship with Iraq and led to the cancellation of many export orders and construction projects. Hopes of large-scale Arab investment in Brazil have long since evaporated.

Even as regards arms exports, the 1990s is likely to see a decline in the role of the Middle East and Brazil's position as a major developing country arms exporter is likely to come under strain. In the short term, arms sanctions against Iraq and unpaid Iraqi debts for earlier arms purchases have put severe financial strain on several of Brazil's major arms companies. More importantly, increased competition from producers in the industrialized world (due to the falloff in the arms market because of the end of the Cold War) and stricter controls on the export of advanced weapons technology to developing countries will make it far harder for Brazil to compete in the world arms market of the 1990s. These difficulties, together with the more general desire of the government of President Collor to improve relations with the United States, will lead on the political front to a low-key approach to the Middle East and a further modification of Brazil's earlier pro-Arab policies.

Africa

Apart from Cuba's role in Angola, the growth of relations between Latin America and Africa in the 1970s was largely focused on Brazil. In the period after 1974 Brazil's Africa policy was the center point of its drive to expand relations in the Third World. By the early 1980s, Brazil was selling arms to seven African countries. It was constructing dams and houses in Algeria, roads in Mauritania, a telecommunications network in Nigeria, and a supermarket chain in Angola; it was involved in large-scale agricultural projects in Nigeria and the organization of rural cooperatives in Mozambique. Total exports had risen from $24 million in 1969 to $1.7 billion in 1981, 89 percent of which consisted of manufactured goods. The cornerstones of the relationship were Nigeria and Portuguese-speaking Africa.

As was the case with the Middle East, the 1980s have seen a falloff in Latin American relations with Africa due largely to the severity and uniformity of the economic crisis on that continent. In 1987, exports were 44 percent and imports 74 percent below their 1981 levels. Unless there is a dramatic improvement in Africa's economic fortunes, it is very unlikely that Africa will again play the kind of role in Brazilian diplomacy that it did in the 1970s. The partial exception will be Portuguese-speaking Africa, especially Angola. Although the rhetoric of Portuguese-language solidarity is often overblown, Brazil's relations with Angola have been deeper and more intensive than with the rest of the continent. In addition, exports to Angola have continued to grow despite Angola's chronic economic problems. In 1987, exports were double their 1980 level. Finally, Cuba's declining role and the shifts in Moscow's attitudes to its erstwhile Third World allies have left Brazil as one of Angola's major allies. Nevertheless, Brazil's own economic difficulties will limit the extent to which good relations are reflected in concrete economic cooperation.

The Third World Movement

Until the mid-1960s, the extent of U.S. dominance over Latin America, buttressed by the pro-Western and anti-Communist sentiments of Latin American elites, meant that there were strong grounds for viewing the region as a Western sphere of influence or at least as an area distinctly separate from the Third World. Latin America remained distant from both the Afro-Asian and nonalignment movements. Within the region, in the decade after the 1955 Bandung Conference there was little identification with the driving forces behind the Third World movement: decolonization, nonalignment in the Cold War, and the struggle for racial equality. It is therefore not surprising that in the 1950s and early 1960s relations between Latin America and the newly emerging nations of Asia and Africa were tenuous.

A significant change took place in the mid-1960s. The change could be seen in many areas:

- The central role played by the twenty Latin American states in the creation and consolidation of the Group of 77.
- The expansion of Latin American involvement in the Non-Aligned Movement (NAM) from the presence of just Cuba and three former Commonwealth Caribbean observers at Belgrade in 1961 to the participation of fifteen Latin American and Caribbean states and eight observers at New Delhi in 1983.
- The leading role of Mexico, Peru, and Venezuela in the formulation and promotion of the New International Economic Order in 1974.
- The activities of Venezuela and Ecuador within OPEC.
- Latin American involvement in commodity groups in cocoa, copper, sugar, and coffee.
- The central role played by Latin American governments in the negotiations for a new Law of the Sea.

Latin American theories of dependency contributed to the demands of the Third World for the reform of the international system. The rise of *tercermundismo* (third-worldism) was the result of various factors. The increasing preoccupation of the Non-Aligned Movement after 1970 with economic issues and its de facto merger with the Group of 77 opened up a broader area of common interest between Latin America and the countries of Africa and Asia than had existed hitherto. The success of OPEC and the belief that a unified Third World coalition could force significant concessions from the industrialized countries helped increase support from many conservative Latin American leaders who felt little instinctive attraction to the notion of the Third World. Increased involvement with the Third World formed part of a broader trend in Latin America toward increased international assertiveness and the diversification of its international relations.

Yet, even at the height of *tercermundismo,* in the mid-1970s, Latin America's identification with the Third World remained qualified. Interest and support continued to be based on economic issues. The region's relatively high income levels and resource abundance often complicated the formation of a unified negotiating position and made Latin America wary of all proposals that singled out the poorest developing states for special treatment. The degree of alignment varied greatly from country to country and from regime to regime. Most important, rather than reflecting any deep-rooted identification with Africa and Asia, *tercermundismo* was seen by many Latin American governments as a pragmatic and useful additional source of leverage in what remained the major area of concern: relations with the United States. *Tercermundismo* was thus often viewed as a means of improving a country's position within the West and only rarely reflected a challenge to Western values and interests.

The 1980s witnessed a decline in Latin American interest in the Third World movement. As the Third World coalition lost its coherence and momentum with the decline of OPEC's power and the hardening of attitudes by the industrialized countries, its attractiveness and value to Latin America declined. Moreover, many of the economic pressures that pushed Latin America toward the Third World in the 1970s weakened as economic divergences between the region and the rest of the Third World became more apparent. Thus the decline in the ability of Third World markets to absorb Brazilian exports and the turnaround in Brazil's energy position reduced, though did not remove, the economic importance of the Third World. More important, the Third World movement has been useless for all except rhetorical purposes in dealing with the single most pressing international problem facing Latin America: the external debt crisis.

However, this decline in interest does not mean that the countries of Latin America are going to break all links with the Third World movement in the coming decade. In institutional terms there has been little reduction in Latin American attendance at Third World gatherings. Although the focus has clearly shifted away from grandiose plans for global economic reform and redistribution, building coalitions on specific issues and coordinating economic positions will remain important. The group of developing countries led by Brazil and India in the debates within the GATT over trade in services provides a good example of this.

The Uruguay Round, however, can be seen as an example of the erosion of the rigid North-South alignments of the 1970s and may well provide a pointer to the increased complexity of multilateral diplomacy in the 1990s. Thus, concerning trade in services, Latin America finds common cause with the developing world against the United States, Japan, and the EC. As regards trade in agriculture, Latin America finds itself allied with such countries as Canada and Australia in the Cairns Group and partially supports U.S. attacks on European agricultural protectionism. Meanwhile, on the question of the reform of GATT procedures (the rules which bind signatories to the GATT), Brazil has allied itself with the EC against the United States. Moreover, if Moscow's rhetoric about global interdependence and Washington's rediscovery of the virtues of international organizations prove durable, there may well be a revival in the importance of multilateral diplomacy. In such a situation, this more complex pattern of coalition building will need to be an important part of Latin America's diplomatic arsenal.

21

International Financial Institutions and Latin America

The IMF and the World Bank

The International Monetary Fund (IMF) and the International Bank for Reconstruction and Development (IBRD, known as the World Bank) were established at the Bretton Woods Conference in 1944. The IMF was to stabilize international payments and the IBRD was to provide growth capital for economic reconstruction and development—especially in wartorn Europe. It was argued at the time that creating two separate agencies to perform these tasks would prevent an overconcentration of power and the cost of errors of judgment. When the Bretton Woods system of fixed but alterable exchange rate broke down in 1972, the main raison d'être of the IMF disappeared. Although the Fund was no longer expected to defend a rigid exchange-rate regime, it still had to contend with the short-term balance-of-payments difficulties of member countries. During the 1970s the Fund sought a new operational role, but it did not regain its former pre-eminence until 1982, when Mexico declared that it was unable to meet its external debt obligations.

Initially the Latin American debt crisis was viewed as a short-term liquidity problem best managed by some slightly modified variant of the IMF formula for adjustment. But as the crisis dragged on, and the IMF's harsh prescriptions seemed incapable of restoring client governments to international creditworthiness, demands grew for a more long-term growth-oriented strategy of adjustment.

Under the Baker Initiative of 1985 the World Bank was brought in on the debt crisis strategy. It has been suggested that the Bank was brought in to signal to the debtors that some of their calls for less austerity and more growth had been heard. The Bank's reputation was less sullied than the IMF's since traditionally the Bank's task lay in providing capital for specific development projects. In 1990 both institutions are involved in the latest phase of debt management—schemes for market-based, voluntary reduction of debt and debt service obligations.

In fact, the two institutions' roles have been converging since the 1970s. The IMF's traditional role was in short-term balance of payments disequilibria (exchange rate policies and the provision of short-term funds). As of the 1974 creation of the Extended Fund Facility, however, the IMF started moving into more medium-term lending—providing support for structural adjustment. In 1979 the World Bank also became increasingly involved in lending for structural adjustment. Hence, both agencies came to provide funds to support programs of economic reform supposedly designed to increase the efficiency and flexibility of the economies of member countries. Additionally, in the 1980s, both agencies became involved in collaborating with the private sector in the supply of funds: the IMF through "concerted lending" and the World Bank through "co-financing." There has also been some switching of traditional roles: while the World Bank became involved in Latin America (previously IMF turf), the IMF, through the Structural Adjustment Facility (1986) and the Enhanced Structural Adjustment Facility (1988), became more involved in Africa.

Some suggest that the convergence of tasks has brought the agencies into conflict with each other. Some friction between the institutions must be inevitable. Personalities, bureaucratic rivalry, and differences in approach offer some explanation. The breaching of traditional roles and norms could also contribute to friction, such as the World Bank's loan to Argentina before Argentina had received IMF approval of its adjustment program. The convergence of the IMF and World Bank roles has also produced anxiety among developing countries who fear that increasing links between the two sources of funds will further tighten conditionality and leave them with less room for maneuver.

Evolution of the IMF in the 1980s

The IMF has come in for much criticism, both among the debtor countries and within the academic community, for its handling of the adjustment process. Jeffrey Sachs comes to the conclusion that

> for most countries, IMF programs have not proven to be highly successful. On a narrow level, most IMF program targets are not achieved, and a large proportion of programs break down. On a broader level, most debtor countries that have borrowed from the IMF in recent years under Stand-by arrangements have failed to recover. (Stand-by arrangements provide a country with an assurance of a right to draw monies over some future period, should the need arise.) These failures have brought the IMF into serious disrepute in the creditor countries as well as the debtor countries.[1]

The aim of this section is to review some key policy changes made by the IMF in the 1980s and to examine their relevance for the Latin American region. The policy changes to be reviewed bear on the magnitude of resources provided by the IMF—that is, SDR allocation, quota increases, and enlarged access to IMF resources—and the Baker Initiative for dealing with the debt problem.

SDR Allocation

SDR (Special Drawing Rights) is an international reserve asset created by the IMF in 1970 as a supplement to gold and U.S. dollars used for international payments by member governments. Six allocations have been made to member countries for a cumulative amount of SDR 21.4 billion. The most recent allocation was made in 1981. The opposition of the United States, West Germany, and the United Kingdom has prevented further issues of unconditional liquidity via the SDR, despite broad support from other members. Latin America has been denied this resource, which would have been available on an unconditional basis.

Quota Increases

These are the sums subscribed by members to the Fund which are used to tide them over balance of payments difficulties. The seventh general review of quotas raised the IMF's resources from SDR 39.8 billion to SDR 60 billion in 1980. The eighth review raised the total to SDR 89.2 billion in 1984. Notwithstanding these nominal increases, the IMF has experienced a sharp fall in quota resources in relation to world trade, and correspondingly the drawing rights of members have been constrained. A major struggle took place in the U.S. Congress over the eighth quota review. After the ninth quota review, the IMF's Board of Governors agreed on June 28, 1990 to increase members' quotas so as to expand the size of the IMF by fifty percent (to approximately SDR 135.2). This increase was the result of considerable negotiation and compromise—the United States originally having been opposed to the increase and the IMF itself advocating it.

Enlarged Access

The Hamburg meeting of the Interim Committee in April 1980 decided that the IMF should play a growing role in the recycling process and that it should borrow to supplement quota resources. The cumulative, combined limit of IMF drawings was put at 600 percent of quota over three years, compared with 305 percent earlier. This policy became operational in May 1981. Since then, the limit was reduced to 450 percent. The managing director helped arrange financial packages for several Latin American debtors, undertaking adjustment by obtaining contributions from commercial banks. The IMF made its own assistance conditional on these contributions from other creditors. The management of the IMF interpreted very conservatively the access rules decided on by the Interim Committee.

The Baker Initiative

The International Monetary Fund and the World Bank expressed strong support for U.S. Treasury Secretary James Baker's view, outlined in October 1985 in Seoul, that adjustment had to be "growth-oriented." By implication Baker recognized that previous adjustment-policy packages had been recessionary and that such reforms could not be sustained. Baker's Initiative was an attempt to reverse the flow of resources out of Latin America and ensure that adjustment did not jeopardize the debtor's growth prospects and long-term debt servicing capacity. The Initiative faded when it became apparent that despite the efforts of the IMF and World Bank, the commercial banks were not prepared to "play their part" in providing new funds to the region.

Although the Baker Initiative remains the official doctrine, most observers acknowledge that the commercial banks have not played their part. In July 1988, Michel Camdessus, the IMF managing director, said:

> Net lending (from commercial banks) has remained negligible. . . . What is of concern is that assembling financing packages for countries that are making a genuine effort has remained difficult and has been often subject to extended delay. This carries the risk of sending quite the wrong signal to countries contemplating bolder adjustment policies. Such a signal is doubly unfortunate at a time when, in a growing number of countries, there is much less debate on what needs to be done, but many difficulties, politically, in

> putting urgently needed policy reforms into practice. . . . Unless the banks do more to support the adjustment efforts of middle-income countries, the notion that our debt strategy is a collaborative one oriented to growth will be put into question.[2]

The gross drawings of Latin American countries from the IMF (excluding those in the reserve tranche) rose from SDR 292 million in 1981, the year before the debt crisis occurred, to a peak of SDR 4,273 million in 1984. Since then, gross drawings have fallen sharply in each year and reached SDR 1,283 million in 1987.[3] Figures on a net basis for Latin America are not easily available, but they would be much lower. For all IMF members, net drawings turned negative in 1986, and the figure for 1987 was minus SDR 2,994 million.

In May 1989 the Fund adopted a new set of guidelines to provide funds for operations that aimed to reduce debt or debt service. These guidelines were immediately applied. Costa Rica secured a Stand-by arrangement for SDR 661 million as did Mexico for SDR 2,979 million (in addition to a drawing of SDR 454 million under the compensatory and contingency financing mechanism). In June 1989 the Fund approved a three-year extended arrangement for Venezuela in the amount of SDR 3,703 million.

The Baker Initiative's premise that the debt problem can be solved without reducing existing debt has provoked considerable skepticism and was finally discarded in early 1989, when the incoming Bush administration moved Baker to the State Department and placed Nicholas Brady at the Treasury. Brady quickly launched the so-called Brady Plan, which accepted that voluntary debt reduction (funded by IMF and World Bank loans) would have to be a part of any viable debt strategy.

Issues Under Consideration by the IMF

The aim of this section is to capture the flavor of the ongoing debate on a number of key issues. Some decisions have been taken, but these subjects remain active.

IMF Conditionality

The IMF board conducted a comprehensive review of conditionality in 1979 leading to the formulation of lending guidelines, including one that emphasized the need to conduct periodic reviews of the guidelines. The most recent review of conditionality was completed in April 1988 and concluded that there was no need to make any changes. This was a remarkable conclusion given the growing criticism of IMF conditionality from the less developed countries (via the Group of 24 [G-24]), the Nordic Council, and prominent academics. IMF board decisions, however, are made on the basis of weighted voting and reflect the relatively large votes of the United States (19.11 percent), United Kingdom (6.62 percent), West Germany (5.78 percent), France (4.80 percent), and Japan (4.52 percent). IMF guidelines on conditionality mirror the views of treasuries and central banks of these major shareholders. The IMF says it has no political philosophy, but critics see in recent behavior the clear impact of Reaganomics and Thatcherism.

The G-24 produced a major critique of the IMF approach to adjustment and conditionality in 1987. Their criticisms focused on such things as the excessive speed of adjustment required by Fund programs; the rigidity of specific targets (as opposed to ranges) for assessing performance; the dominance of IMF staff in determining the content of adjustment programs; and the need for contingency mechanisms in adjustment programs.

The Group's May 21, 1990 Communiqué (IMF survey) reveals quite a shift in the Group's view of the IMF. The heat previously directed towards the IMF is turned in the direction of commercial banks, government creditors, and the external policy environment. While note is made of "excessive conditionality," the Group commends the recently modified policy of the Fund on financing assurances, and calls on the IMF and World Bank to "enhance further their support for debt and debt-service reduction." Contingency mechanisms (having now been included in some Fund agreements—Mexico was the first) are suggested as appropriate for inclusion in agreements with all creditors.

The following criticisms of the IMF have been made by prominent academics:

- The IMF has overreached its technical competence (and that of the economic profession generally) in the way that it "markets" the Stand-by programs. IMF programs purport to be based on a macroeconomic framework that can reliably relate policy instruments to policy targets in the short run. Such a powerful framework does not exist. Many policies championed by the Fund, such as interest-rate liberalization or dramatic trade liberalization, have little basis in historical experience.

- Most IMF agreements are negotiated between a technocratic team in the debtor government and the IMF staff, under conditions of secrecy. The letter of intent itself is generally not made public by the debtor government. At worst, the IMF actually writes the program for the country. The result is that the agreement with the Fund has little internal political support and calls for actions by parts of the government (for example, the legislature) or the private sector (for example, the union organizations) that were not privy to the decision. The IMF ends up with a beleaguered ally within the government that has little political force in the country. The rest of the political actors in the country feel little inhibition in breaking "agreements" that they had no part in formulating.

- The enforceability of IMF conditionality is relatively weak. The IMF often lends repeatedly to countries, and even to specific governments, that fail to honor IMF agreements. Moreover, since the creditor governments often have political interests in providing financial support to a particular regime, even when the regime has failed to live up to previous commitments, the sanction of failing to honor IMF agreements is weak.
- Unsuccessful implementation of IMF recipes has been the norm in Latin America, not the exception. A high proportion of Stand-by programs has failed to push key indicators of government finance and domestic credit even in the right direction. The power of the IMF remains a useful myth for governments seeking a scapegoat to explain difficult economic disequilibria, but the ability of the IMF to impose programs from the outside is distinctly limited.

Former IMF managing director Jacques de Larosière responded to critics who alleged that IMF programs frequently led to a deterioration in the economic condition of vulnerable groups in member countries. He pointed out that IMF conditionality applied to macroeconomic variables and that governments had to choose specific, microeconomic measures that determined how the domestic burden would be allocated among various socioeconomic groups. The IMF would be prepared, however, if requested by governments, to advise on alternative sets of measures that had different implications for poverty groups. Whether or not the statement by de Larosière had any operational implication is not easy to determine. Perhaps very few, if any, Latin American governments have requested advice in this area.

IMF Surveillance

Latin American observers have long emphasized the one-sidedness of IMF conditionality, which tends to make the burden of adjustment disproportionately large for developing countries. It was argued, for example, that the debt problem acquired the severity it did because industrial countries responded to the second oil-price increase in 1979 by precipitating a sharp rise in interest rates, a fall in commodity prices, and a sharp slowing down in world trade. According to the IMF charter, the IMF was supposed to exercise firm surveillance over the economic policies of the Group of Seven (G-7), but it failed to do so.

Surveillance of G-7 apparently meant little more than periodic discussions of IMF reports as required by Article IV. Those discussions were supplemented in recent years by multilateral discussions of the annual IMF exercise called *World Economic Outlook.* In 1986 the Interim Committee put some force behind the need to coordinate the economic policies of the G-7. The board of the IMF decided to broaden the coverage of policies subject to IMF surveillance. Board members decided to develop a set of indicators aimed at highlighting international interactions of domestic policies within a medium-term framework. In February 1987 the G-7 met in Paris (with the IMF managing director participating) to hammer out the Louvre Accord and to review progress on exchange rates since James Baker had masterminded the 1985 Plaza Accord in New York. The Venice Summit in 1987 confirmed the earlier decision to pursue coordination with the IMF's assistance. In their Spring 1990 statement, the Group of Seven reaffirmed their commitment to economic policy coordination, including cooperation on exchange markets.

The central issue is power. The IMF has considerable leverage vis-à-vis Latin American members because they are financially distressed and the IMF is the gatekeeper that might assist them by releasing its own and other external funds. By contrast, the IMF depends on the G-7 for resources and is in no position to get the G-7 to adopt good global economic management. The IMF can provide analytical support, however, if the initiative is taken by the big players.

The Debt Overhang

Debt overhang simply means an economy crippled by an excessive burden of debt. In 1983 and 1984 the IMF echoed the U.S. Treasury in expecting world economic recovery and Latin American austerity to overcome the debt crisis in a year or two. The Latin Americans obliged by reducing imports, suffering increasing unemployment, and paying interest on the debt. IMF conditionality demanded avoidance of arrears on interest payable to commercial banks. The IMF has since modified its policy, tolerating arrears in specific and defined circumstances where the achievement of adjustment program objectives might be jeopardized. The Baker Initiative promised growth-oriented adjustment, but the commercial banks were determined not to play the game. Many commodity prices fell in 1985, adding to the already severe strains.

Brazil declared a moratorium on debt-service payments in February 1987 and proposed a plan for swapping new securities for outstanding debt based on values in the secondary market. These values had declined progressively in recent years. In 1989 both the IMF and the World Bank have become actively involved in market-based schemes of debt reduction.

The major commercial banks have greatly improved their financial position, and some have signaled their willingness to participate in an organized debt-reduction scheme in the collective interest of creditors. Debt reduction was finally taken up by the United States in the Brady Plan (on a case-by-case voluntary basis), and the IMF and World Bank each undertook to provide $12 billion toward the $30 billion facility envisaged as backing for new bond issues to replace existing debt.

Mexico was the first and largest beneficiary of this debt-reduction process, though even in its case the debt relief obtained was modest in relation to the underlying imbalances. In March 1990, various options for reducing Venezuela's commercial-bank debt were presented to creditors under the aegis of the Brady Plan. Costa Rica is also set to benefit, and negotiations in process may result in some debt relief for other debtors. But all this will take time and may yield only very limited benefits. Probably the most important effect of the Brady Plan was to disengage the IMF from the creditor banks, enabling the Fund for the first time to extend Stand-by agreements even to debtors not in compliance with their commercial obligations. On the negative side, the Fund began to find its own very strong credit rating under challenge as various debtors built up arrears. Peru was even threatened with expulsion from the Fund, but a compromise was reached.

World Bank Response to Latin America in the 1980s

In 1980 a major change in World Bank policy occurred when the Bank decided to provide financial support for a program of reforms, rather than to fund particular investments. The reform agreements are negotiated by the Bank with member governments. Some of these measures must be put into practice before the Bank provides loans; others are to be implemented according to an agreed schedule. The staff monitors the situation, and tranches of the loan are released when agreed measures are adopted by governments. Structural Adjustment Loans (SALs) aim at raising efficiency on an economy-wide basis.

Sectoral Adjustment Loans (Secals) support reforms that are relatively narrowly based. SALs and Secals are intended to disburse much more rapidly than project loans, and they finance general imports, except for some specified items. They are attractive to governments because of these two features.

In Latin America, the World Bank financed mainly development projects until the early 1980s. The bulk of lending went to agriculture and rural development, transport, development finance companies, and water supply/sewerage. The only exceptions before the debt crisis of 1982 were Jamaica, Guyana, and Bolivia, which obtained policy-based SALs or Secals. Between the beginning of the crisis and the Baker Initiative, the list of countries securing policy loans was extended to Panama, Costa Rica, Brazil, Mexico, and Uruguay, but such loans remained a small share of the total number of policy loans disbursed. Only after the start of the Baker Initiative did the role of the World Bank change significantly, and the list of countries receiving SALs or Secals was further extended to include Argentina, Colombia, Ecuador, and Chile. Such loans constituted 20 percent of total World Bank loans to Latin America in fiscal year 1987. By 1988 the World Bank was the single largest source of new financing for the heavily indebted countries. The Bank's involvement has included both guaranteeing new loans and, as mentioned above, its role in supporting debt reduction schemes.

A large amount of support in the form of policy loans has been provided in particular to Bolivia (69 percent of total World Bank lending to Bolivia), Chile (61 percent), Colombia (39 percent), Uruguay (65 percent), Costa Rica (97 percent), Jamaica (61 percent), and Guyana (70 percent). In Mexico, World Bank policy-based operations became the basis for obtaining financial support from commercial banks. Other countries did not obtain much Bank support because they were not able to develop a coherent and credible medium-term adjustment strategy. Their programs had a pronounced "stop-go" character.

A large number of policy operations focused on trade reforms, including replacement of quantitative restrictions on imports by tariffs. Some loans have helped change agricultural policies and rationalize public enterprises, but progress in this area and in the area of public expenditures remains insufficient.

During the early years of the new policy of supporting reforms, the main emphasis was on improving resource allocation, raising resources, and making institutions more effective. As time passed, it became clear that Latin America's economic problems were not going to be solved quickly and that meanwhile severe human costs were being incurred, particularly by the poor. The World Bank responded recently by making an effort to improve the design of agreed reforms so that poverty groups would be protected from at least some of the burden of adjustment. A good example is the 1987 Bolivian program, which included emergency relief through food distribution and vaccination as well as employment generation through small-scale irrigation. Another example is the Mexican Agricultural Sector Loan, which supported expansion of food coupon and milk distribution programs.

A recurrent theme of public debate in the 1980s was the appeal by Latin American governments for international agencies in general and the World Bank in particular to take into account the need to assist fragile democratic regimes to preserve their political freedoms. Many countries in the region have been unwilling and tried to put off submitting to the strenuous and harsh policy reforms required. Policies of austerity and adjustment needed to be designed with this political goal in mind, it was said. World Bank officials were generally cool to this appeal, pointing to the terms of the charter, which preclude politically motivated lending. Less will probably be heard of this objection in the 1990s, since the main shareholders of the Bank are anxious to shore up the fragile new democracies beginning to emerge in Eastern Europe. But even though the principle of pro-democratic conditionality may now have been conceded, the funds available for Latin America under this rubric are likely to remain negligible.

Issues Under Consideration in the World Bank

Division of Labor with the IMF

As discussed above, the distinction between the IMF and the World Bank was quite clear during much of the 1970s and in earlier decades. The IMF focused on short-term balance of payment difficulties at the macro level. The World Bank specialized in the design and financing of long-term investments. Recent policy moves of the two, however, have enlarged the area of overlap. The IMF began to take increasing interest in structural adjustment of supply-side issues in a medium-term context, and the World Bank got more heavily involved in macroeconomic management in a short-term context.

These trends have resulted in turf-raiding behavior or bureaucratic competition between the two organizations, in the view of many critics. This behavior can be rationalized as the inevitable result of two organizations trying to respond innovatively to important changes taking place in their global environments.

The second oil-price increase and the manner in which G-7 members responded to the ensuing turbulence created a situation in which the earlier compartmentalization of short-run macroeconomic policy and long-term investment policy did not make sense. The interface between project, sector, and macro issues on the one hand and between short-run, medium-term, and long-run questions on the other acquired critical importance.

In January 1989 IMF Managing Director Michel Camdessus wrote a letter to the World Bank proposing that the IMF should be the final arbiter of disagreements over the economic conditions to be attached to loans. With the IMF in that position, the line demarcating the role of the two institutions would have been redefined. The World Bank, however, opposed the idea because it might have granted the IMF a veto over the World Bank's area of activity. The 1966 memorandum governing the relationship between World Bank and the International Monetary Fund has just been renegotiated, but in practice the new division of labor will have to be worked out from experience as test cases arise. During 1989 the two organizations produced a set of principles to guide their collaboration of the debt issue.

Observers in Latin America have reacted to these developments by expressing concern about cross-conditionality—that is, the increased inflexibility encountered by Latin American policymakers, who have to adhere to both Bank and Fund conditions in the same subject area. The Bank will not disburse if the Fund is dissatisfied, and vice versa. Officials of developed countries and IMF/World Bank executives deny that there is cross-conditionality in the technical legal sense, but they worry about the rising burden of coordination that has to be shouldered by the two organizations.

Measures have been taken to encourage staffs of the two institutions to exchange information, to consult regularly, and to thrash out differences in policy perspectives. Such coordination has improved considerably. Differences in institutional orientation, in the relative weight attached to policy objectives (for example, financial balance, economic growth, protecting the poor), and in the time-horizon for policy formulation persist, however. Superimposed on these problems are bureaucratic rivalries.

Latin American countries that have a strong, local policymaking machinery and are not financially desperate can usually sort out coordination problems between the IMF and the Bank. In other instances, Latin American governments have to cope with inevitable frictions. In the perception of the Bank staff, the IMF has dominated the policy arena except in specific cases, such as Colombia, where the IMF's role has been confined to one of surveillance. The IMF continues to insist on staff adherence to a formally defined division of labor (periodically revised by the two managements). The Bank emphasizes the need to work out joint approaches given linkages between subject areas and policy instruments.

Net Resource Transfer

During the 1980s the World Bank raised its commitments, disbursements, and net transfers to Latin America very sharply. For example, net transfers (disbursements minus debt-service payments) rose by 137 percent during 1980–1986, but the increase could not be sustained subsequently. The setback was partly the result of wavering policy commitments of regional governments, which made those governments ineligible for SALs and Secals, and partly it was a symptom of the near exhaustion of the Bank's capacity to lend. According to the Articles of Agreement, the value of disbursed and outstanding World Bank loans cannot exceed the Bank's subscribed capital plus reserves. The available "headroom" has diminished considerably, thereby making a general capital increase an urgent necessity. In April 1988 the board of directors of the Bank approved an increase in the authorized capital from $97 billion to $171 billion (3 percent of this amount will have to be paid in; the rest is callable). This infusion should allow an increase in the Bank's sustainable level of lending by about 10 percent per year during the next five years. Over 1988–1989, the Bank increased its lending program to the region by 11 percent, bringing its total lending commitment to $5.8 billion. More than half of this commitment was in the form of adjustment lending to support economic policy reforms.

Some liberal members of Congress in the United States tried to make ratification of the capital increase conditional on a change in the debt strategy of the U.S. administration. They wanted the Bank to play a much bigger role and to manage a debt-reduction scheme for "adjusting" debtor countries. This plan was strongly resisted by Baker. The capital increase was always expected to pass despite these frictions because the United States could not afford to lose its veto power in the Bank's board. Currently the U.S. vote is 19 percent of the total. An 85 percent vote is required for important changes, such as alteration of the Bank's articles. In the extreme case, if the United States did not participate in the capital increase and Japan secured 40 percent of the U.S. allocation, the United States would be displaced by Japan as the Bank's largest shareholder. In practice, a more gradual shift can be anticipated, with the United States eager to defend its single-country veto.

The Brady Plan accepts the principle of voluntary debt reduction on a case-by-case basis, but it seeks to maintain (and possibly even enhance) the strong conditionality that had characterized official adjustment lending during the 1980s. To that effect, the Plan stipulates that in order to qualify for assistance in debt reduction, debtor governments must first adopt economic programs sanctioned by the IMF and World Bank. For this plan to work, the two agencies will have to reach greater agreement on the conditions they must promote to achieve a return to economic growth, not just stabilization.

The Inter-American Development Bank

Set up in 1960 with strong Latin American representation, the Inter-American Development Bank (IADB) was long viewed as the most attractive source of multilateral financing for many Latin American projects, especially in the public sector. Although Canada, the Western European countries, and Japan subscribed capital in the 1970s, the United States retained a 34.5 percent shareholding and therefore exercised a decisive voice in the bank's affairs (the United States vetoed lending to Chile and Nicaragua when those countries had governments that Washington viewed as hostile). After the debt crisis broke, the IADB found itself under heavy pressure from both sides, and its lending capacity was restrained by a U.S. refusal to authorize any capital replenishment until it adopted the more stringent conditionality that characterized lending by the World Bank and the International Monetary Fund. This obstacle was removed in March 1989 when a $26 billion capital increase was authorized for the years of 1990–1993. However, the IADB had to agree that at least for the first two years its sectoral development loans would be cofinanced with the World Bank and would therefore be subject to World Bank policy conditions. Ironically, then, at the same time that the World Bank was refusing to accept IMF conditionality, it was successfully imposing its policy conditions on the regional bank.

Prospects for the 1990s

Looking beyond the various immediate interagency disputes and rivalries, in the longer run the really important question will be which (if any) of these institutions—the World Bank, the IMF, the IADB—has discovered a satisfactory lending formula that will enable the Latin American debtors to work their way out of the current external financing impasse to restore investment and growth and to regain the capacity for effective national economic policymaking. This task may be larger than any of the multilateral agencies (or even all of them taken together) will be in a position to handle. The experience of the 1980s indicates that all three of these Washington-based organizations made significant misjudgments about the nature of various regimes' economic problems and the speed with which they could be corrected. Although these agencies all contain many high-caliber people and have formidable financial resources at their disposal, they are certainly not in any position to substitute for effective national economic management in debtor countries, especially in view of the number of problem areas that they have to deal with simultaneously. In fact, despite their efforts to project themselves as authoritative judges of the course of international economic development, the first priority of the agencies is much more modest and practical: to administer the funds with which they have been entrusted in a manner that preserves the credibility and high credit rating of their own institutions.

Large though these banks may seem, their funds are in fact modest in relation to the fiscal and foreign-exchange flows of debtor governments. Their impact in the 1990s will depend on how well they engage with much larger forces and how strongly they are backed by the leaders of the developed countries. If their policy reforms restore the confidence of private banks and foreign investors, then they will succeed. If their programs of conditionality induce a transformation in the financial practices of debtor governments, the same will apply. But if they are not very successful in these two respects, costly transfusions from the governments of the developed countries may be needed to shore up the authority of the IADB and these aging Bretton Woods institutions.

Notes

1. J. Sachs, "The Role of the IMF in the International Debt Crisis" (Paper presented at the NBER Conference on Developing Country Debts. Reprinted by permission.
2. *IMF Survey,* July 25, 1988, p. 254.
3. *IMF Annual Report* (Washington, D.C., 1987), p. 50.

22

Cooperation and Conflict in the Region

Patterns of Regional Cooperation

Despite the generally disappointing record of schemes for economic cooperation and integration in the postwar period, the 1980s have seen an upsurge of interest in regional cooperation and concrete progress in several areas. Various factors lie behind this advance:

- Emphasis on regional cooperation resulted from the severity and uniformity of the economic crisis and from the extent to which the countries of the region found themselves confronting a similar range of problems, above all in relation to the foreign debt.
- Feelings of common interest were strengthened by the widespread shift away from military rule and by the extent to which democracy provided a common ideological basis for cooperation and a further range of shared problems and concerns.
- The crisis in Central America provoked a widely shared concern about the dangers of the region becoming a focus for East-West rivalry and a general, though not completely uniform, reaction against the policies of the Reagan administration.
- The Falklands/Malvinas War of 1982 provided an indirect but significant impulse to cooperation. This cooperative impulse was partly the result of the widespread, though far from complete and unconditional, support for Argentina over its claim to the islands—particularly in the period since the end of the war. It also followed from the general belief that U.S. support for Britain in the war represented the final nail in the coffin in the Inter-American Military System.

- The relative absence of alternative foreign-policy options and the disillusion with the results of the attempts at diversification that had characterized the 1970s, together with the decline of the Third World movement as a viable focus for international negotiations, strengthened the trend toward regional introspection and the emphasis on a limited kind of "group power."

Two additional features of this process should be noted. The first, and more recent, is the gradual improvement of relations between Cuba and the rest of Latin America. The second is the "Latin-Americanization" of Brazilian foreign policy.

For much of the 1970s, relations between Brazil and its neighbors were either cool (as in the case of Venezuela and Peru) or overtly hostile (as in the case of Argentina). Brazil's military government saw itself as distinct from the region and placed much greater emphasis on expanding relations with Europe, Japan, and other parts of the Third World, not including Latin America. The shift began in the mid-1970s with the improvement and expansion of relations with its Andean neighbors, as, for example, in the conclusion of the Amazon Pact in 1978. The shift gathered pace with the beginnings of rapprochement with Argentina in 1979. By the time Brazil moved to civilian rule in March 1985, Latin America had become the central focus of its foreign policy. Given Brazil's size and importance, this change represents a major shift in the pattern of international relations in the region and is an important factor influencing the prospects for future cooperation.

One important feature of regional cooperation in the 1980s is the extent to which the focus has shifted away from schemes aiming at formal economic integration, often modeled on the European Community, and toward less institutionalized forms of cooperation. On one level this change can be seen in the dramatic increase in bilateral visits and meetings between presidents and ministers of the various countries. On another level, it can be seen in such multilateral forums as the Contadora Support Group, the Cartagena Consensus, and, most importantly, the Group of Eight. The Group of Eight was founded in December 1986 to provide a flexible, nonbureaucratic forum for consultation and for the negotiation of joint positions on such questions as debt, Central America, and Cuba. The forum has led to two presidential summits and five foreign ministers' meetings.

How significant is this process, and what are the prospects for the future? There have certainly been many more words than deeds, and there has been little concrete success on the crucial question of the foreign debt. Latin America has not managed to translate potential "debt power" into an effective negotiating strategy. The obstacles to the creation of a viable debtors cartel have proved insuperable:

- The unwillingness of the major debtors to run the risks and face the uncertainties that might follow from a radical confrontation.
- The difficulty of agreeing on a formula for the distribution of the costs that might follow from such a confrontation.
- The lack of synchronization between the negotiating cycles of the major debtors.
- The ability (at least until Brady) of the creditors to maintain effective unity—at the level of governments, private banks, and multilateral institutions.
- The capacity of the creditors to provide concessions to individual debtors.

Nevertheless, this increased pattern of informal and semi-institutionalized cooperation has represented a realistic and useful additional foreign-policy instrument. It has provided external legitimacy for the difficult process of democratic consolidation. Such cooperation has provided the framework for efforts at a regional settlement in Central America and for the improvement in relations between Cuba and Latin America; it can even claim some success in helping convince the outside world about the unsustainability of the present framework of debt management. If expectations are kept modest, this kind of cooperation will continue to prove useful and could well become more important in the future. If, for example, a new framework for debt management with a greater multilateral emphasis does emerge, or if there are multilateral negotiations on the global environment, then the benefits to be gained from constructing joint positions will be heightened.

This pattern of cooperation is also likely to prove durable. It is unlikely, for example, that any of the major states will pursue a foreign policy entirely divorced from, or in opposition to, the policies of its neighbors, as was the case, for example, with Brazil in the early 1970s. Increasingly close ties between Mexico and the United States may represent a possible exception here and would undoubtedly weaken the overall cohesion of the region. Serious problems would also be caused by the failure of democratization in a major state. That would force the others to decide whether democracy is a prerequisite for cooperation. Panama has already been suspended from the Group of Eight for this reason.

Finally, however limited the gains may be, no realistic alternative exists. In particular, far-reaching schemes for economic integration will probably prove as problematic in the future as they have in the past. The kind of economic interdependence that underpins European integration is unlikely to expand rapidly in Latin America, and other contacts will continue to lag even further behind. The economic crisis of the 1980s hit interregional trade especially hard, and the barriers to integration will remain strong:

- The great disparities between the countries of the region in size and level of economic development.
- The still marginal character of interregional exports, especially manufactured exports.
- The physical barriers to integration and the high costs of interregional transport.
- Continued political unwillingness to bring national economic and industrial policies into line.

Efforts at increased economic cooperation are not doomed to fail. But future cooperation agreements will need to be more flexible and more limited both in geographical and in sectoral terms. Such flexibility can already be seen in the introduction within the Latin American Integration Association (Asociación Latinoamericana de Integración—ALADI) of Bilateral Commercial Agreements as a central mechanism of regional integration. The need for flexibility and limits also emerges as one of the major lessons of the Brazilian-Argentine cooperation (see below).

Patterns of Regional Conflict

Alongside a degree of regional cooperation, however, must be set an equally long history of border and territorial disputes and of deep-rooted suspicions and resentments between the states of the region. Few wars have been fought in Latin America in the past century, and only one of these, the Chaco war between Paraguay and Bolivia between 1932 and 1935, can be compared in intensity and duration to a European war. All the same, the number of potential disputes and rivalries is by no means negligible. Among the most important have been the historic rivalries between Brazil and Argentina and between Argentina and Chile and the territorial disputes between Venezuela and Guyana, Venezuela and Colombia, Bolivia and Chile, Peru and Ecuador, Nicaragua and Colombia, Guatemala and Belize, and El Salvador and Honduras.

The origins of these conflicts can often be traced back to the lack of any clear and complete demarcation of frontiers in the early postindependence period and to the problems that arose as the newly established states sought to consolidate their power and expand their influence. To outsiders the disagreements themselves often seem to be trivial matters. Yet, over time, many of these disputes have become encrusted with a powerful nationalist mythology and have led to a widely held feeling among a country's citizens that the nation has lost a territory or a role to which it was historically "entitled." This feeling has been strengthened by the strong geopolitical tradition, in both military and civilian elites, that sees international life as an unavoidable struggle for survival and that places great weight on the importance of utilizing the territorial resources of a country.

Moreover, in the early 1980s, a number of commentators argued that the significance and seriousness of these conflicts was increasing. Several factors were adduced to support this view:

- The struggle for natural resources had drastically increased the stakes: hydroelectric resources on the Paraná River between Brazil and Argentina; access to offshore oil, fishing, and seabed minerals in the case of Chile and Argentina (and, allegedly, between Britain and Argentina); access to oil again in the disputes between Peru and Ecuador, Venezuela and Guyana, and Venezuela and Colombia.

- The intensification of superpower rivalry in the Third World had increased the chances that a regional conflict in Latin America would become an issue in East-West relations.

- The overall decline of U.S. hegemony and the erosion of the Inter-American Military System had reduced the ability of Washington to maintain "discipline" within its own sphere of influence.

- The Central American conflict, the border clash between Peru and Ecuador in 1981, and the Falklands/Malvinas War of 1982 had all demonstrated the increasing reality of armed conflict in the region.

- The pace of militarization had increased with a significant trend toward both increased arms imports and the development of domestic arms industries.

However, although these factors need to be noted, there is little clear evidence that the region is in general becoming more conflict-prone.

Various important points of friction have been resolved, particularly the Beagle Channel dispute between Chile and Argentina, and relations between Brazil and Argentina have improved dramatically. Levels of military spending fell in the second half of the 1980s, and the trend toward democracy reduced, although it certainly did not eliminate, the influence of the military and the kinds of extreme geopolitical thinking with which some military figures are associated. As noted above, the debt crisis and the common struggle for democratic consolidation have provided the focus for a renewed emphasis on regional cooperation. In addition, the Soviet reassessment of regional conflicts and the improved climate of superpower relations have reduced the chances of Latin America becoming a focus of East-West rivalry. In Central America, there are clear signs that the Soviet Union is actively pressing for a regional settlement. Finally, the evolution of Cuban foreign policy toward the region has reduced the ideological element in regional conflicts.

The general trend therefore appears favorable, and levels of interstate conflict are likely to remain low. Yet the possibility of conflict cannot be totally discounted. Many border disputes remain unresolved, and the prevalent hyperconsciousness about borders and national territory is not going to disappear completely in the near future. In addition, the ability of governments to control events on distant borders—such as Brazilian informal "colonization" of Paraguay or Brazilian miners working illegally in the Venezuelan Amazon—will remain limited. Border issues can therefore heat up without the involvement of governments. Moreover, the weakness of military command and control systems (and, in some cases, of diplomatic channels of communication) can make it difficult to prevent an isolated incident from becoming a small-scale border skirmish. Although minor border skirmishes are not likely to become the focus for war, they would represent a considerable setback to the cause of regional cooperation and add one more complication to the nationalist myths in which they are embedded.

Domestic shifts may represent the most critical factor influencing the future level of interstate conflict. Governments (civilian and military) may be tempted to use nationalism to bolster popularity and legitimacy—as happened in Argentina over the Malvinas/Falklands in 1982. And there is always a chance that a major breakdown of domestic social structures will spill over into the international realm. After all, around 85 percent of all armed conflicts in the postwar world have been *intrastate* rather than traditional *interstate* conflicts. Although the decline of Central America as an East-West issue and the growth of regional cooperation are undoubtedly positive steps, the underlying fragility of domestic social, political, and economic structures remains unresolved. Elsewhere, a radical breakdown in the process of democratic consolidation, continuing economic stagnation, increased political polarization, and the expansion of organized violence whether from *narcotraficantes* or guerrilla groups could become a focus for regional instability, particularly in Peru but perhaps also in Colombia and Bolivia. Although this remains a low probability, it cannot be totally discounted.

Brazil and Argentina

Although the relationship has been one of both conflict and cooperation, the historic rivalry between Brazil and Argentina has been a central characteristic of Latin American international relations. The 1970s witnessed a period of particularly tense relations between the two countries, with conflicts over the construction of hydroelectric plants, a struggle for influence in the border states of Paraguay and Bolivia, competition in the South Atlantic, and barely concealed nuclear rivalry. However, in the period since 1979 the picture has changed dramatically. In particular the presidencies of José Sarney and Raúl Alfonsín saw the signature of a complex network of agreements covering economic, scientific, technological, and nuclear cooperation. This new climate of confidence was symbolized by the visits of the two presidents in 1988 to each other's previously secret nuclear research facilities, and by the July 1990 presidential summit at which plans were announced for the creation of a full common market by 1994.

The solidity of this rapprochement and the success of these cooperation agreements are both important in themselves and will an indicator for the more general balance between conflict and cooperation in the region. What are the prospects?

The overall prospects for continued stable relations are relatively good, although the gap between rhetoric and reality is likely to remain considerable. The rapprochement is based on deep-rooted and parallel shifts in the foreign policies of the two countries—shifts that show little sign of changing in the immediate future. On the Brazilian side, the shift of policy toward Argentina grew out of an awareness that both the dreams of *grandeza* (greatness) of the early 1970s and the hopes pinned on the policy of diversification were exaggerated. Brazil not only came to see that it needed Latin America but also realized that hostility toward Argentina was counterproductive, merely fueling anti-Brazilian sentiment in the region. In addition, the erosion of the U.S.–Brazilian relationship undercut the traditional Argentine perception of Brazil as Washington's stalking horse in Latin America. Finally, the shift of Brazilian strategic priorities away from the South Atlantic and Antarctica removed a source of potential friction with Argentina. These changes were paralleled in Argentina by the shared perception of a hostile external environment, the shared difficulties of relations with Washington, and an underlying awareness that the disparity of power between Argentina and Brazil had grown so great that competition and hostility were futile.

A reasonable degree of stability has been achieved in the nuclear relationship. The failures of the Brazilian nuclear program both increased the need for cooperation and reduced Argentine fears of rapid Brazilian progress. Brazil and Argentina now share a belief in the importance of acquiring nuclear technology and of resisting external attempts to prevent the spread of such technology. In addition to these common economic and technological incentives (which exist also in the armaments industry), a belief has emerged—at least among the civilian elites—that the security aspects of the nuclear relationship can best be safeguarded by a bilateral system of inspection and by confidence-building measures.

Finally, the two countries appear to have learned many of the lessons from earlier efforts at economic cooperation. Agreements between them have been flexible and based on specific sectors, and they have yielded some concrete results, above all in trade in capital goods. Moreover, the recent decision to press ahead with further bilateral integration is underpinned by the parallel shifts in the domestic economic policies of the Collor and Menem governments toward increased economic liberalization and greater openness to the international economy.

Yet the case should not be overstated. The process of economic cooperation has not been completely smooth; old suspicions have not been entirely overcome (particularly between the two military establishments), and several important potential problems persist. The overall expansion of trade has been modest; there has been a persistent imbalance of trade in Brazil's favor; and on a large number of agreements very little real progress has been made. Also the danger that the benefits and viable scope for economic cooperation have been oversold lurks amid all the presidential rhetoric and talk of integration and common currencies. Furthermore, external events—such as a protracted crisis in Paraguay or Bolivia—could well be difficult to manage on a cooperative basis and could reawaken old suspicions. Finally, much of the impetus for improved relations came from the personal initiatives of Alfonsín and Sarney and was backed by their personal relationship. Equally, a return to military rule in either country could pose a potentially greater threat, although it should be remembered that the process of rapprochement was initiated by two military governments.

Central America

Despite their ideological disagreements and conflicting international allegiances, the five Central American republics—Costa Rica, El Salvador, Honduras, Nicaragua, and Guatemala—have consistently maintained a certain level of cooperation and commitment to shared progress. Even in the period of greatest tension the five central bank presidents kept up regular communications and presented something of a common front to external aid-givers. All the foreign ministers met regularly with the foreign ministers of the European Community, and starting in 1987 the presidents began to hold periodic summits that have given rise to concrete agreements. It was planned that this collaboration would be further institutionalized through the creation of a Central American parliament, consisting of twenty directly elected delegates from each of the five republics, but at least for the time being this initiative is in abeyance due to Costa Rican resistance. The parliament will be an advisory body, although its influence over the process of regional integration will be fairly direct. To avoid a conflict of jurisdictions with the various national assemblies, the "executive" counterpart to the parliament will be composed of the five regional vice presidents.

This institutional heritage of regional cooperation is an asset that will be badly needed in the coming decade if Central America is to make any progress toward overcoming the past decade's legacy of political polarization and economic decline. The obstacles to be overcome are formidable, even after the Nicaraguan election of February 1990. Although that democratic contest resulted in the exit from government of the defeated Sandinistas, they remain the best organized and most cohesive political force in Nicaragua, with considerable support and the potential for shaping their country's politics for many years to come. Even the U.S. and Salvadorean military are increasingly resigned to the view that it is not possible to completely eliminate the revolutionary left from El Salvador, and Guatemalan politics remains as bunker-like as ever. So Central America will continue to be riven by disputes between political forces of fundamentally divergent persuasions, even if these disagreements can be contained within a framework of nonbelligerence. Despite the cosmetic democratization of various regimes, principled commitment to political pluralism is still hardly a dominant feature of regional affairs. In fact the enmities created by a decade of brutal civil war in three of the five republics will live on as a source of danger for years to come. Moreover, the disequilibrium between the five republics has grown worse during the 1980s—in terms of both military power and economic well-being. Nicaragua and El Salvador have relapsed a quarter-century in economic terms. This decline will take at least a generation to reverse. In contrast, Costa Rica is emerging relatively unhurt, and Honduras has also been strengthened in relative terms. Institutions like the Central American Common Market and the Bank for Economic Integration have also suffered devastating setbacks.

On the positive side, compared to the rest of Latin America the isthmian republics have received substantial external support, not all of it destructive. The counterpart to this, however, is the danger that if the five regional governments do begin to reduce tension and settle some of their most severe outstanding differences, their various external backers may react by cutting back on external aid. There is already some sign of this by both the United States and the Soviet Union. Without generous, long-term multilateral assistance for reconstruction, the outlook for any progress for the Central American region will be persistently bleak. In the past decade, educational systems have been shattered, infrastructure destroyed, markets lost, and entrepreneurs alienated. This generalization applies to Panama about as much as to Nicaragua or El Salvador. Guatemala, Costa Rica, and Honduras are somewhat more fortunate. What will be the material basis for renewed growth in Central America in the 1990s? Even with optimistic assumptions about pacification and democratization, the economic panorama is discouraging. Traditional agricultural exports are unlikely to achieve a new dynamism. The regional market has been crippled, and nontraditional exports will require systematic promotion over a long period before they can offer an alternative route to progress. So the leaders of Central America will have to show great persistence and ingenuity to build the fragile system of tacit coexistence into an effective regional formula for reconstruction.

23

Latin America and International Management of the Environment

Over the past five years international concern for the environment has grown substantially and will become an important factor influencing the attitudes and policies of the industrialized countries toward Latin America. Although the range of environmental problems facing the region is wide, the focus of international concern has been tropical deforestation, primarily in the Amazon Basin but also in Central America.

International concern for the environment dates at least from the 1972 U.N. conference on the environment in Stockholm. Yet the salience of the issue has grown appreciably for two reasons. In the first place, the world has become far more aware of the seriousness of the threat posed by environmental degradation. The links between the destruction of the rain forests and gradual climatic deterioration resulting from the greenhouse effect are by now well established. Although there is serious disagreement over the extent of both climatic change and deforestation, there is no doubt that the loss of forests is proceeding at a historically unprecedented rate. There is also great concern over the way in which deforestation is leading to the forced extinction of large numbers of both plant and animal species and the consequent reduction in the amount of genetic material available for new medicines and other purposes.

Second, environmental concern has become heavily politicized. On one level, politicization has resulted from the growth of a worldwide network of pressure groups and nongovernmental organizations (NGOs), many of which combine mass membership with extremely effective lobbying. On another level, "green" politics has become part of the established political agenda in many developed countries. The growth of the Green party in West

Germany in the 1970s led the way. The party often captured as much as 10 percent of the popular vote in the local election and, more importantly, forced other parties to include environmental issues on their party platforms.

Environmental problems are also taken very seriously in Scandinavia and the Netherlands and recently have begun to figure more prominently on the political scene in France, Italy, and Britain. The year 1989 saw the emergence of a small but growing "green" lobby in the U.S. Congress. In the Soviet Union, environmental threats have formed an important part of Gorbachev's talk about "interdependence" and the "global community." Japan appeared to be the major exception to this trend and remains the focus of much protest by environmental NGOs. However, by 1990 there were signs of change as, for instance, in the rapid growth of Japanese loans for environmental projects.

Although it is important not to exaggerate the extent or influence of the green lobby, pressure groups have already been successful in changing the lending policies of the World Bank, the European Community, and some private commercial banks. There is every likelihood that this trend will grow. Similarly, in many developed countries a genuine shift in popular attitudes toward the environment is almost certainly going to persist and may well strengthen in the coming years.

Effective management of the global environment is an issue in which Latin America and its international partners have common interests. At the most fundamental level, environmental degradation represents a threat to the future of all life on Earth. All will lose by depletion of the ozone layer or a reduction in the genetic stock. Indeed it is apparent that Latin America is already more severely affected by environmental degradation than are many other parts of the world. Thus incentives for unilateral action are strong, and the outside world, with justification, expects the countries of the region to do more on their own to protect the environment.

Certainly, Latin American attitudes and policies toward the environment are changing, although the extent and pace of change are uneven. Brazil, for instance, has seen the emergence of an incipient green lobby. There have also been significant shifts in Brazilian government policy: the ending of many fiscal subsidies that encouraged deforestation (and totaled over $1 billion between 1975 and 1986); the declaration of the "Our Nature" policy in April 1980; and the naming of the prominent environmentalist, José Lutzenberger, as environmental secretary by the newly inaugurated Collor government in March 1990.

Yet the ability of Latin American countries to cope with environmental damages on their own will remain limited. In the first place, these nations need technology from the industrialized world, whether in the form of satellite data or environmentally more efficient production processes. Second, many of the most serious threats can be tackled only on a multilateral basis.

This limitation applies most clearly to global climatic deterioration but also to transborder air pollution and sea pollution. Third, and most crucially, Latin America will need assistance with the costs of adopting environmentally more rational policies. The cost of "saving" the Amazon forest or of decontaminating Mexico City's atmosphere will be extremely high.

On one level the costs are specific. Extensive research on, for example, sustainable agriculture in the Amazon Basin is expensive. Similarly the short-term costs of adopting alternatives to chlorofluorocarbon (CFC) gases in refrigerators may well be out of reach for many developing countries. On another level, the question of costs is related to the extent to which underdevelopment and poverty themselves are the most fundamental causes of environmental degradation in the developing world.

Who is likely to bear such costs in the coming decade? Clearly, even the governments of Brazil and Mexico—let alone the smaller republics—will be unable to afford more than token gestures out of their own resources. This prediction would probably have been true in the absence of the debt crisis, and is certainly valid after the "lost decade" of development and investment.

Latin America, then, has a strong incentive and an excellent case for seeking assistance with environmental protection and for trying to engage the developed world in bilateral and multilateral negotiations. Moreover, the environment represents an issue where there is genuine interdependence between North and South. Unlike trade and investment, where, according to some analysts, interdependence has been diminishing and is in any case asymmetrical, the developed world is directly threatened by the long-term impact of environmental degradation, and thus has a strong incentive to take Latin America seriously.

An effective regime for the global environment can be constructed only with the active and cooperative participation of Latin America. Such a situation opens the possibility (but does not guarantee the success) of genuine bargaining in which Latin America can press for an equitable distribution of the costs and in which it can argue its case for the linking of the environment to the deeper problems of underdevelopment.

Yet, in spite of the fact that there is a clear common interest worldwide in safeguarding the Earth's environment, and interdependence of this kind creates a strong incentive for cooperation and collective management, it would be a mistake to assume that this incentive will easily translate into effective action. Environmental degradation has already acquired strong momentum, as statistics on the rate of deforestation or the build-up of urban pollution and congestion clearly testify. Simply to slow these negative trends before they result in irreparable ecological damage will require an extraordinary combination of will, foresight, international collaboration, and the well-targeted application of massive resources. In addition, simple links between the debt crisis and tropical deforestation, for example, underplay the extent to which environmental degradation is often deeply rooted in the broad pattern of a country's political and economic development—a pattern that goes back over many decades.

Moreover, even if governments are committed to protecting the environment and even if external assistance is forthcoming, control and enforcement will remain a serious problem. The fragility of political structures, the weight of domestic lobbies, and the often very limited capacity of central government to control events in distant and remote areas are all factors that work against any dramatic and immediate change in the situation.

There is also the problem of priorities. For Latin Americans, it is far from clear that the most pressing environmental dangers are those stressed in the industrialized world. It may well be both politically and environmentally sensible to devote the greatest attention to the enormous environmental threat posed by air and water pollution in the big cities. On the other side, the United States clearly has environmental issues at home that will demand both political attention and scarce resources. Just as the cost of safeguarding the U.S. savings and loan industry (up to $300 billion U.S. dollars) has weakened Washington's room for maneuvering on the debt crisis, so the massive costs connected with the environmental problems of the U.S. nuclear industry will weaken Washington's policy on the international environment.

Another major difficulty in achieving effective environmental management is that agreed criteria for the distribution of costs (between different groups and different countries and over time) will inevitably be a problem to determine. Those who benefit from environmental management are real but are generalized and dispersed. Those bearing its immediate costs tend to be concentrated and politically vocal. In addition, the Western cultural tradition is by no means entirely an advantage here because, throughout the Americas, European colonists became accustomed to the idea that land and natural resources were virtually limitless and so need not be cherished. Similarly, the Western emphasis on the autonomy and rights of uncoordinated economic agents can make organizing an adequate collective response to such dangers very difficult, even when the costs to individuals of noncooperation are crystal clear. Finally, the question of costs is magnified by the continuing paucity of scientifically accredited information about even the scale of environmental damage, not to mention the most effective means of correcting it.

What is the likelihood that the developed countries will commit substantial resources to the preservation of the environment in Latin America? The weight of environmental concern may force governments to move in this direction, yet such moves will be limited. In the United States the economic and fiscal constraints on the administration are clear. In Japan, the country with the greatest financial resources, emphasis on environmental questions is still limited, although increasing slowly. In Western Europe the pressure to protect the environment will be greatest and at least some increase in resources can be expected. As in the case of debt relief, however, Europe's response is likely to fall below Latin American expectations.

A final problem concerns Latin American sensitivity about external interference. This sensitivity is most marked in Brazil, where it was a prominent feature of Brazilian diplomacy in the early 1970s. It was forcefully restated in 1989 by the Brazilian president, José Sarney, who repeatedly denounced what he saw as "green imperialism" aiming to "restrict Latin America's autonomy and progress." Indeed, the kind of intense campaigning necessary to persuade electorates in the industrialized countries to bear the costs of effective environmental management runs the risk of provoking an equally emotional resistance in Latin America. The rhetoric of green lobbies in the developed world is all too likely to be interpreted as yet another excuse for infringing on the sovereignty of Latin American states and yet another manifestation of the arrogance of the developed countries and their unwillingness to accept Third World governments as copartners in a common endeavor.

In light of well-publicized examples of continued environmental damage and of such nationalist response, there may well be a strong temptation to try to force the countries of the region to "improve their behavior." Although external lobbying has certainly been important in fostering awareness of environmental issues and, to a certain extent, in changing government policy, making debt relief or trade concessions conditional on environmental improvements runs the risk of strengthening nationalist resistance. However negligent Latin American countries may have been or may be toward their environment, external pressure alone is unlikely to improve the situation, particularly since First World governments also have such a poor record on this question.

Nationalist feeling in Latin America may also be encouraged by the growing mood among many in the industrialized world that effective environmental management means going beyond the national state and reducing the rigidity of state sovereignty. Such approaches are unlikely to find favor in Latin America, where the nation state will remain the bulwark of national autonomy in the unequal struggle to reduce the pressure of increased levels of external economic dependence.

Environmental issues will therefore be of rising importance in North-South relations in the coming decade. They have the potential to bring governments and opinion leaders of different parts of the world together in a shared, scientifically based endeavor to protect the environment for future generations. And if there is any region of the world where such issues are potentially manageable and where a common framework of understanding exists, it is the Americas. There the man-land ratio is most favorable; the population and wealth of the North are greatest in proportion to the need for assistance in the South; and the South's capacity for remedial action is best developed. Also the Americas contain an established network of institutional links between government, scientific, and environmental communities, rooted in a shared Western liberal cultural tradition. If a constructive outcome to global environmental problems is to come about, Latin America is the most promising region to pioneer such a project.

The obstacles to effective practical action and the possibility that the environment will become a source of mutual suspicion and even conflict are also very real. To overcome the problems, the industrialized governments would have to take a far more serious and long-term view of global environmental issues than has been evident so far. The scientific basis of international policymaking would have to be enormously reinforced, and a multilateral approach would have to be adopted in which the developed countries showed themselves willing to accept limitations on their own sovereign rights to pollute and despoil before they can convincingly demand similar restraint by Latin America.

All these changes would have to be matched by a very large and sustained (and responsibly managed) collaborative effort, which might well cost taxpayers in the developed countries considerably more than would have been required in the 1980s to overcome the debt crisis. The short-term uncoordinated, cost-cutting, and opportunistic approach to ecology that has so far predominated at the government level in both North and South would have to be transformed. That is clearly a tall order, but the magnitude of environmental dangers that are now emerging could soon bring with them the need for such a far-reaching response.

24

Conclusions and Prospects

The international setting for the 1990s will not prove easy for Latin America. Yet not all the major trends in the contemporary international system are entirely unfavorable to the region. The much-discussed decline of U.S. hegemony could prove a positive development. It should create more space for regional actors to develop independent and autonomous foreign policies. Less U.S. dominance should also help in promoting regional cooperation and conflict resolution, above all in Central America; it should also open the way to a more plural and multipolar international system, which should increase the number of foreign-policy options open to the region.

Against this, the United States will remain the dominant external power for some time, and the Monroe Doctrine reflex is far from dead. Indeed the fear of growing regionalism in both Europe and the Far East has already led Washington to revive ideas of greater hemispheric unity under U.S. leadership. This can be seen, for instance, in the U.S.–Canadian free trade agreement and the negotiations for its extension to include Mexico, and in President Bush's proposal for an Initiative for the Americas. However, there remains a large gap in official perceptions which has opened up a number of major bilateral questions—the scale and terms of debt relief, the pace of market liberalization, *narcotráfico,* and environmental issues. The leaders of major Latin American states are not about to fall into line with Washington's interpretation of the nature of their problems, and U.S. public opinion may react uncomprehendingly to international differences of view. Crisis points like Panama can easily reawaken Latin American suspicions of U.S. motives and methods. Moreover, Latin American expectations about the concrete economic benefits of greater hemispheric unity are unlikely to be fully satisfied.

Of equal concern to Latin Americans is the fact that efforts to diversify the range of their foreign relations will not prove easy. Western Europe will remain in many ways their most natural target because of the density of historic, cultural, political, and economic ties. Yet the economic relationship with Europe will provide Latin American countries with little scope for significant growth. The probable result in 1992 will be a negative impact on Latin America's trade prospects, though not a dramatic one. The trend toward trade marginalization is likely to continue, although industries able to produce competitively will still be able to penetrate the European market. Any significant upturn in European direct investment is also unlikely despite the change in the investment climate in many Latin American countries. Similarly, continued budgetary constraints and other demands both inside and outside the European Community will mean that no dramatic increase in aid levels can be expected. However, even though Europe will be forced to act out of self-interest—on the debt and perhaps also on the environment—Latin America will find a greater degree of responsiveness.

On the political side, the short-term outlook is also not encouraging. It is true that a significant Latin American "constituency" has become established in Western Europe at the level of public opinion, in national governments, and at the European Commission. This constituency is most deeply rooted in Spain, Italy, and West Germany and, on aid and human-rights issues, in the Netherlands and Scandinavia. This degree of interest will probably ensure that the formal political dialogue between Europe and Latin America will continue. Yet the political and economic implications of events in Eastern Europe and the Soviet Union, together with continued instability in the Middle East, will dominate the attention of public and political opinion and push Latin America down on the agendas of all the major European states.

The most substantial new opportunities will center on Japan. Through the 1990s Japan's economic role in Latin America will continue to expand, and it is not inconceivable that Japan will establish the largest economic presence across a whole range of indicators. Even if Latin America maintains the same relative ranking for Japan, levels of foreign aid, trade, and direct foreign investment are all likely to increase substantially. Moreover, the trend toward a greater role for Japan in the management of the debt crisis—a trend already evident—will gather speed in the next few years.

An expansion of the Japanese presence represents one of the few signs of movement on the international horizon, but it is not a panacea for Latin America's problems, nor will it come about without friction. There is no clearly worked out plan in Tokyo to assume a leadership role in the region, and Latin America will continue to rank well below the United States, Asia, and Europe on Japan's foreign-policy agenda. It will remain heavily conditioned by relations with Washington, and Tokyo will be less likely than Western Europe to challenge U.S. political interests in the region. Moreover, the amounts of Japanese economic assistance and the conditions attached will fall well below Latin American expectations. Indeed, the other side of increased Japanese assertiveness is the tendency toward harder bargaining and toward tying aid and investment to strict conditions.

A second major trend concerns the dramatic improvement in superpower relations that has occurred over the past two years. If it continues, this advantageous development should reduce the chances of having regional instability, whether in Central America or elsewhere, become the focus of the East-West struggle with all the dangers of militarization and the polarization that entails. If Washington's policy of seeking to reassert its hegemony over the region was driven by Cold War imperatives, then a new détente should open the way to a more relaxed and responsive policy. On the Soviet side, Gorbachev's "new thinking" has laid much greater emphasis on expanding economic relations with major Third World states, including those of Latin America.

There is, however, another side to the picture. The reduced salience of the Third World in East-West relations can all too easily become a reason for according lower priority to Latin America, whether in Western Europe or in the United States. There is already a tendency to assume that, because there is a greater degree of superpower understanding over regional conflicts, such conflicts can be safely ignored. Similarly, Latin American expectations of what can be gained economically from relations with Moscow are likely to exceed reality. *Perestroika* will have to produce far-reaching improvements in Soviet economic efficiency and will have to overcome very deep-seated internal difficulties within the Soviet bloc before there can be any substantial and durable payoff for Latin America. If this happens at all, a decade or more will be needed to work it through.

Both these trends—the decline in overall U.S. power and the improvement in superpower relations—will force the countries of Latin America to rethink their security arrangements. The prospects for international stability within the region are reasonably good. Latin America does not seem to be becoming more conflict-prone. Several points of tension have been significantly reduced, particularly between Brazil and Argentina and between Argentina and Chile. Levels of military spending have fallen back, and the debt crisis and the common struggle for democratic consolidation have created a new impulse toward regional cooperation. Stabilizing this situation and preventing the many other historic border disputes from reemerging will call for increased cooperation and a greater emphasis on specific confidence building. Given the nearly total demise of the Inter-American Military System, discussion of an exclusively regional security system may well become more relevant in the years ahead.

The major threat to regional stability will remain the breakdown of the social and political order within states—in Central America and, conceivably, also in Peru. In the case of Central America some progress has been made toward a regional settlement, and this progress will need to be built on in the coming years. The great challenge remains the need to find an effective formula for regional reconstruction together with a significant degree of external assistance. Doing so will be no easy task.

No magic key, no new sets of relationships, will either represent a solid base for a more autonomous international role or provide substantial economic assistance for the region's economic development. In general, Latin America will remain a low priority of the foreign-policy agendas of most states. This ranking will place a high premium on efforts to increase cooperation within the region, both to increase Latin America's bargaining power and to yield specific economic gains. The economic barriers to formal integration, however, will remain strong. The kind of economic interdependence that underpins European integration is unlikely to expand rapidly in Latin America, and the degree of societal contracts will continue to lag even farther behind.

In the past, there was a tendency to think of Latin American foreign policies in terms of broad models of "options." In the 1970s, for instance, a widespread debate occurred in several countries of the region as to whether they formed part of the First World or the Third World. Yet neither "option" will provide a solid basis for foreign policy in the 1990s. On the one hand, Latin America will be unable to count on special treatment from any major developed country. On the other, the Third World movement has been gravely weakened by internal cleavages and other problems and by the shift in attitudes by the industrialized world. Cooperation with other developing countries on a wide range of issues (trade, technology, the environment) will remain important; Third World markets will provide some, albeit uneven, opportunities; and particular relationships may flourish over the longer term (for example, between Brazil and China). Yet the overall scope here, though greater than in the 1980s, will be well below the pattern of the 1970s.

Recently, an alternative "model" has been suggested, that of the "Asian tigers." Yet not all countries (not even all Latin American countries) can be exporting "tigers" at the same time. Latin America currently has almost five times the population, three times the GNP, and over a hundred times the territorial extension of the four East Asian territories—all these differences limit the extent to which Latin America can imitate their extreme trade orientation. Both the demands of internal development and the internal constraints of "super-exporting" would act to limit Latin America's outward orientation long before the region could reach current East Asian levels of trade dependence. None of these observations argue against greater Latin efforts at export promotion, but they do cast doubt on whether the Asian NICs offer an appropriate model.

Latin America will need to get away from thinking in terms of such models or simple foreign-policy principles. It will also need to avoid building excessive hopes on any single relationship—Japan appears the most obvious current example, but Western Europe and the Soviet Union have also been viewed in this way. In the past, such thinking led inevitably to frustration and disillusion and a lack of follow-through to maximize the concrete gains that can be achieved. Latin American relationships with Europe provide a good example of this pattern.

The need for pragmatism, realism, and persistence points to the importance of the domestic aspects of foreign policy. Diplomatic and negotiating skills, technical expertise, and the flexibility to seek tradeoffs across a wide range of issues and areas will all be important. So too will access to knowledge about Latin America's international partners. Although the level of knowledge of the United States is high, only in recent years have Latin American states made a concerted effort to exploit the bargaining advantages that result from the decentralized nature of the U.S. political system. The pattern of decision making within the countries of the European Community and the complex process of coalition building on which it is based represent another important area where opportunities exist and can be developed. In the case of Japan the cultural gap makes the task of developing a productive and manageable dialogue both more difficult and more urgent. Expanding knowledge nearer home is also necessary: Latin American countries remain all too ignorant about each other.

Bibliography

This bibliography makes no pretense to be exhaustive. It seeks to provide readers with easily available titles, most of them in English, should the reader wish to follow up on individual topics or countries mentioned in the text. There are, in addition to the references below, useful articles on contemporary Latin America and its historical background to be found in the *Journal of Latin American Studies,* the *Latin American Research Review,* the *Hispanic American Historical Review,* the *Journal of Interamerican Studies and World Affairs,* and *Interamerican Economic Affairs,* to name but a few of the most important English-language journals. Also, a comprehensive survey along with a detailed bibliography is to be found in the volumes of the *Cambridge History of Latin America,* which deal with the twentieth century. For further bibliographical references, see the *Handbook of Latin American Studies,* published annually by the University of Texas Press.

1. Society

Demography

Sánchez Albornoz, N., *The Population of Latin America,* University of California Press, Berkeley, 1974.

Saunders, J., (ed.), *Population Growth in Latin America and U.S. National Security,* Allen and Unwin, Boston, 1986.

Teitelbaum, M., *Latin American Migration North,* Council on Foreign Relations, New York, 1986.

Urban Migration/Urbanization

Butterworth, D., and Chance, J., *Latin America Urbanization,* Cambridge University Press, Cambridge, 1981.

Gilbert, A., and Ward, P., *Housing, the State and the Poor: Policy and Practice in Latin American Cities,* Cambridge University Press, Cambridge, 1985.

Hunter, J., Thomas, R., and Whiteford, S., *Population Growth and Urbanization in Latin America,* Schenkman, Cambridge, Mass., 1983.

Agrarian Change

De Janvry, A., Sadoulet, B., and Wilcox, L., *Rural Labour in Latin America,* World Employment Programme Working Paper 79, ILO, Geneva, 1986.

Grindle, M., *State and Countryside: Development Policy and Agrarian Politics in Latin America,* Johns Hopkins University Press, Baltimore, 1986.
Redclift, M., *Sustainable Development: Exploring the Contradictions,* Methuen, London, 1987.
Reinhardt, N., *Our Daily Bread. The Peasant Question and Family Farming in the Colombian Andes,* University of California Press, Berkeley, 1988.

Race/Ethnicity

Degler, C., *Neither Black nor White,* University of Wisconsin, Madison, 1986.
Fernandes, F., *The Negro in Brazilian Society,* Columbia University Press, New York, 1969.
Fontaine, P-M., *Race, Class and Power in Brazil,* Center for Afro-American Studies, University of California, Los Angeles, 1985.
Solaún, M., and Kronus, S., *Discrimination without Violence: Miscegenation and Racial Conflict in Latin America,* John Wiley, New York, 1973.

Class/Social Mobility

Palomino, H., *Cambios Ocupacionales y Sociales en Argentina 1947–85,* CISEA, Buenos Aires, 1987.
Portes, A., "Latin American Class Structures: Their Composition and Change during the Last Decade," *Latin American Research Review,* vol. 20, no. 3, 1985.
Touraine, A., *La Parole et le Sang: Politique et Societé en Amérique Latine,* Odile Jacob, Paris, 1988.

Women

Jaquette, J., *The Women's Movement in Central America: Feminism and the Transition to Democracy,* Unwin Hyman, Boston, 1989.
Jelin, E., *Women and Social Change in Latin America,* Zed, London, 1990.

Culture

Franco, J., *Modern Culture of Latin America,* Penguin Books, Harmondsworth, 1970.
Hines, H., and Tatum, C., (eds.), *Handbook of Latin American Popular Culture,* Greenwood Press, Westport, 1985.
King, J., *Magical Reels,* Cinema in Latin America, Verso, London, 1990.
Martin, G., *Journeys through the Labrynth. Latin American Fiction in the Twentieth Century,* Verso, London, 1989.

2. Politics

Democracy/Democratization

Boeker, P., *Lost Illusions: Latin America's Struggle for Democracy as Recounted by Its Leaders,* Markus Weiner, New York, 1989.

Diamond, L., Linz, J., and Lipset, S., *Democracy in Developing Countries,* (Volume 3), Rienner, Boulder, 1988.

Drake, P., and Silva, E., *Elections and Democratization in Latin America 1980–85,* University of California Press, San Diego, 1986.

O'Donnell, G., Schmitter, P., and Whitehead, L., *Transitions from Authoritarian Rule: Latin America,* Johns Hopkins University Press, Baltimore, 1986.

Stallings, B., and Kaufman, R., *Debt and Democracy in Latin America,* Westview Press, Boulder, 1989.

Political Parties

Alexander, R., *Political Parties in Latin America,* Praeger, New York, 1973.

McDonald, R., *Party Systems and Elections in Latin America,* Westview Press, Boulder, 1989.

Labor/Social Movements

Davis, S., and Goodman, L., *Workers and Managers in Latin America,* D. C. Heath, Lexington, 1972.

Eckstein, S., (ed.), *Power and Political Protest: Latin American Social Movements,* University of California Press, Berkeley, 1989.

Epstein, E., *Labour Autonomy and the State in Latin America,* Unwin Hyman, Boston and London, 1989.

Greenfield, G., and Maram, S., (eds.), *Latin American Labor Organizations,* Greenwood Press, Westport, 1987.

Spalding, H., *Organized Labor in Latin America,* New York University Press, New York, 1977.

Zapata, F., "Towards a Sociology of Labour", *Journal of Latin American Studies,* vol. 22, part 2, May 1990.

The Church

Keogh, D., (ed.), *Church and Politics in Latin America,* Macmillan, London, 1990.

Levine, D., (ed.), *Churches and Politics in Latin America,* Sage, Beverly Hills, 1980.

Wilde, A., and Mainwaring, S., (eds.), *The Progressive Church in Latin America,* University of Notre Dame Press, Notre Dame, 1989.

Armed Forces

Cammack, P., and O'Brien, P., (eds.), *Generals in Retreat,* Manchester University Press, Manchester, 1985.

Rouquié, A., *The Military and the State in Latin America,* University of California, Berkeley, 1987.

Stepan, A., *Rethinking Military Politics: Brazil and the Southern Cone,* Princeton University Press, Princeton, 1988.

Guerrillas

Deas, M., "Colombian Peacemaking," *Third World Quarterly*, vol. 8, no. 2, April 1986.
Dunkerley, J., *Power in the Isthmus: A Political History of Modern Central America*, Verso, London, 1988.
McClintock, C., "Why Peasants Rebel: The Case of Peru's Sendero Luminoso," *World Politics*, vol. 37, no. 1, 1984.

Local Government/Administration

Centro Latinoamericano de Administración para el Desarrollo (CLAD), "Administración y Reforma Tributaria Municipal en América Latina. Estratégias para su Implantación y Desarrollo," CLAD, Caracas, 1987. *Planning and Administration*, vol. 12, no. 2, Autumn 1985. Special on Latin America. IULA-IFHP. The Hague, Netherlands.
Sloan, J., *Public Policy in Latin America*, University of Pittsburgh Press, Pittsburgh, 1984.

Drugs

Arrieta, C., et al., *Narcotráfico en Colombia: Dimensiones Políticas, Económicas e Internacionales*, Ediciones Uniandes/Tercer Mundo, Bogota, 1990.
Journal of Interamerican Studies and World Affairs, vol. 30, no. 1, Spring 1988 issue devoted to the drug problem.
Pacini, D., and Franquemont, C., (eds.), *Coca and Cocaine: Effects on People and Policy in Latin America*, Cultural Survival/Cornell Latin America Studies Programme, Cambridge, 1986.

3. Economics

General

Hartlyn, J., and Morley, S., (eds.), *Latin American Political Economy: Financial Crisis and Political Change*, Westview Press, Boulder, 1986.
Sheahan, J., *Patterns of Development in Latin America: Poverty, Repression and Economic Strategy*, Princeton University Press, Princeton, 1987.

Economic Performance

Anglade, C., and Fortin, C., "The State in Latin America's Strategic Options," *CEPAL Review*, 1988.
Belassa, B., et al., *Toward Renewed Economic Growth in Latin America*, Institute for International Economics, Washington, D.C., 1986.
Dietz, J., and Street, J., (eds.), *Latin America's Economic Development: Institutionalist and Structuralist Perspectives*, Rienner, Boulder, 1987.
Williamson, J., *Latin American Adjustment: How Much Has Happened?* Institute of International Economics, Washington, D.C., 1990.

Industrialization

Blomstrom, M., *Transnational Corporations and Manufacturing Exports from Developing Countries*, United Nations, New York, 1990.

Gwynne, R., *Industrialization and Urbanization in Latin America*, Croom Helm, London, 1985.

Jenkins, R., *Transnational Corporations and Industrial Transformation in Latin America*, Macmillan, London, 1984.

Katz, J., (ed.), *Technology Generation in Latin American Manufacturing Industries*, Macmillan, London, 1987.

Tokman, V., "Global Monetarism and the Destruction of Industry," *CEPAL Review*, 1984.

Commodities and Trade Policy

Ffrench-Davis, R., and Tironi, E., (eds.), *Latin America in the New International Economic Order*, Macmillan, London, 1982.

Wirth, J., (ed.), *Latin American Oil Companies and the Politics of Energy*, University of Nebraska Press, Lincoln, 1985.

Economic Thinking and Policy

Foxley, A., *Latin American Experiments in Neo-Conservative Economics*, University of California, Berkeley, 1982.

Kay, C., *Latin American Theories of Development and Underdevelopment*, Routledge and Kegan Paul, London, 1989.

Ocampo, J., "New Economic Thinking in Latin America," *Journal of Latin American Studies*, vol. 22, no. 1, February 1990.

Inflation

Bruno, M., et al., *Inflation Stabilization: The Experience of Israel, Argentina, Brazil, Bolivia, and Mexico*, MIT Press, Boston, 1988.

Cole, J., *Latin American Inflation: Theoretical Interpretations and Empirical Results*, Praeger, New York, 1987.

Debt/Debt Management/Stabilization

Feinberg, R., and Ffrench-Davis, R., (eds.), *Development and External Debt in Latin America: Bases for a New Consensus*, University of Notre Dame Press, Notre Dame, 1988.

Griffith-Jones, S., (ed.), *Managing World Debt*, Harvester Press, London and St. Martins Press, New York, 1988.

Kuczynski, P-P., *Latin American Debt*, Johns Hopkins University Press, Baltimore, 1988.

Sachs, J., (ed.), *Developing Country Debt and Economic Performance. Volume 2, Country Studies—Argentina, Bolivia, Brazil, Mexico*, National Bureau of Economic Research, University of Chicago Press, Chicago and London, 1990.

Thorp, R., and Whitehead, L., (eds.), *Latin American Debt and the Adjustment Crisis*, Macmillan, London, 1987.

Employment

De Soto, H., *The Other Path,* Taurus, London, 1989.
Handelman, H., and Baer, W., (eds.), *Paying the Costs of Austerity in Latin America,* Westview Press, Boulder, 1989.
Portes, A., Castells, M., and Benton, L., (eds.), *The Informal Economy: Studies in Advanced and Less Developed Countries,* Johns Hopkins University Press, Baltimore, 1989.
Wells, J., *Empleo en América Latina: Una Búsqueda de Opciones,* PREALC, Santiago, 1987.

Income, Distribution, Poverty and Welfare

Carrière, J., Haworth, N., and Roddick, J., (eds.), *The State, Industrial Relations and the Labour Movement in Latin America,* Macmillan, London, 1989.
U.N. Economic Commission for Latin America and the Caribbean (ECLAC), *Changing Production Patterns and Social Equity: The Prime Task of Latin American and Caribbean Development,* ECLAC, Santiago, 1990.
Morley, S., *Labour Markets and Equitable Growth. The Case of Authoritarian Capitalism in Brazil,* Cambridge University Press, Cambridge, 1982.

4. International Relations

General

Pope Atkins, G., *Latin America in the International Political System,* Westview Press, Boulder, 1989.

The United States and Latin America

Lowenthal, A., *Partners in Conflict: The United States and Latin America,* Johns Hopkins University Press, Baltimore, 1987.
Middlebrook, B., and Rico, C., (eds.), *The United States and Latin America in the 1980s,* Pittsburgh University Press, Pittsburgh, 1986.
Schoultz, L., *National Security and United States Policy Toward Latin America,* Princeton University Press, Princeton, 1987.

Latin America and the Soviet Union

Blasier, C., *The Giant's Rival. The USSR and Latin America,* University of Pittsburgh Press, Pittsburgh, 1988.
Miller, N., *Soviet Relations with Latin America 1959–1987,* Cambridge University Press, Cambridge, 1989.

Latin America and Western Europe

Bulmer-Thomas, V., (ed.), *Britain and Latin America: A Changing Relationship,* Cambridge University Press, Cambridge, 1989.

Durán, E., *European Interests in Latin America*, RIIA/Routledge and Kegan Paul, London, 1985.

Grabendorff, W., "Relations with Central and Southern America: A Question of Over-reach," in Edwards, G., and Regelsberger, E., (eds.), *Europe's Global Link*, Frances Pinter, London, 1990.

Latin America and Japan

Doherty, E., *Japan's Response to the Latin American Debt Crisis*, Japan Economic Institute Report 29A, Washington, D.C., July 1987.

Hollerman, L., *Japan's Economic Strategy in Brazil*, Lexington Books, Lexington, 1988.

Stallings, B., "The Reluctant Giant: Japan and the Latin American Debt Crisis." *Journal of Latin American Studies*, vol. 22, part 1, February 1990.

Latin American Regional Conflict and Integration

Gauhar, A., (ed.), *Regional Integration. The Latin American Experience*, Westview Press, Boulder, 1985.

Martz, M., "SELA, The Latin American Economic System: Ploughing the Seas." *Inter-American Economic Affairs*, vol. 32, (Spring) 1979.

Nuñez del Arco, J., Margain, E., Rachells, C., (eds.), *The Economic Integration Process of Latin America in the 1980s*, Inter-American Development Bank, Washington, D.C., 1984.

Latin America and the Environment

Goodman, D., and Hall, A., (eds.), *The Future of Amazonia*, Macmillan, London, 1990.

Hall, A., *Developing Amazonia: Deforestation and Social Conflict in Brazil's Carajás Programme*, Manchester University Press, Manchester, 1989.

World Resources Institute, *World Resources 1990–91*, Oxford University Press, Oxford, 1990. Chapter 3: Latin America: Resource and Environment Overview.

5. Individual Countries

Argentina

Crassweller, R., *Peron and the Enigmas of Argentina*, W. W. Norton, London and New York, 1987.

Di Tella, G., and Dornbusch, R., (eds.), *The Political Economy of Argentina 1946–1983*, Macmillan, London, 1989.

James, D., *Resistance and Integration: Peronism and the Argentine Working Class*, Cambridge University Press, Cambridge, 1988.

Bolivia

Dunkerley, J., *Rebellion in the Veins: Political Struggle in Bolivia 1952–82*, Verso, London, 1984.

Ladman, J., (ed.), *Modern-Day Bolivia: Legacy of the Revolution and Prospects for the Future,* University of Arizona Press, Tucson, 1983.

Malloy, J., and Gamarra, E., *Revolution and Reaction 1964–88,* Transaction Books, New Brunswick, 1988.

Brazil

Bacha, E., and Klein, H., (eds.), *Social Change in Brazil 1945–85: The Incomplete Transition,* University of New Mexico Press, Albuquerque, 1989.

Skidmore, T., *The Politics of Military Rule in Brazil 1964–85,* Oxford University Press, New York, 1988.

Stepan, A., *Democratizing Brazil,* Oxford University Press, New York, 1989.

Wirth, J, et al., (eds.), *State and Society in Brazil: Continuity and Change,* Westview Press, Boulder, 1987.

Caribbean

Clark, C., (ed.), *Society and Politics in the Caribbean,* Macmillan, London, 1991.

Lowenthal, D., *West Indian Societies,* Oxford University Press, Oxford, 1972.

Sutton, P., *Europe and the Caribbean,* Macmillan, London, 1991.

Central America

Bulmer-Thomas, V., *The Political Economy of Central America Since 1920,* Cambridge University Press, Cambridge, 1987.

Carmack, R., (ed.) *Harvest of Violence: The Maya Indians and the Guatemalan Crisis,* University of Oklahoma Press, Norman and London, 1988.

Christian, S., *Nicaragua: Revolution in the Family,* Random House, New York, 1985.

Dunkerley, J., *Power in the Isthmus: A Political History of Modern Central America,* Verso, London, 1988.

Williams, R., *Export Agriculture and the Crisis in Central America,* University of North Carolina Press, Chapel Hill, 1986.

Chile

Arriagada Herrera, G., *Pinochet: The Politics of Power,* Unwin Hyman, Boston, 1988.

Garretón, M., *The Chilean Political Process,* Unwin Hyman, London, 1989.

Valenzuela, J., and Valenzuela, A., *Military Rule in Chile: Dictatorship and Opposition,* Johns Hopkins University Press, Baltimore, 1986.

Colombia

Hartlyn, J., *The Politics of Coalition Rule in Colombia,* Cambridge University Press, Cambridge, 1988.

Urrutia, M., (ed.), *40 Años de Desarrollo: Su Impacto Social,* Banco Popular/Fedesarrollo, Bogota, 1990.

Peeler, J., *Latin American Democracies: Colombia, Costa Rica, Venezuela,* University of North Carolina Press, Chapel Hill, 1985.
Herman, D., (ed.), *Democracy in Latin America: Colombia and Venezuela,* Praeger, New York, 1988.

Cuba

Horowitz, I., (ed.), *Cuban Communism,* 7th ed., Transaction Books, New Brunswick, 1989.
Smith, W., *The Closest of Enemies. A Personal and Diplomatic Account of U.S.-Cuban Relations Since 1957,* W. W. Norton, New York, 1987.
Szulc, T., *Fidel: A Critical Portrait,* Coronet, Sevenoaks, 1986.

Dominican Republic

Wiarda, H., *The Dominican Republic: Nation in Transition,* Praeger, New York, 1988.

Ecuador

Hurtado, O., *Political Power in Ecuador,* Westview Press, Boulder, 1985.
Martz, J., *Politics and Petroleum in Ecuador,* Transaction Books, New Brunswick, 1987.
Schodt, D., *Ecuador: An Andean Enigma,* Westview Press, Boulder, 1987.

Haiti

Nichols, D., *Haiti in Caribbean Context: Ethnicity, Economy, and Revolt,* Macmillan, London, 1985.

Mexico

Aguilar Camín, H., *Después del Milagro,* Cal y Arena, Mexico, 1989.
Cornelius, W., Gentleman, J., and Smith, P., *Mexico's Alternative Political System,* University of California, San Diego, 1989.
Riding, A., *Distant Neighbors: A Portrait of the Mexicans,* Knopf, New York, 1985.

Peru

Crabtree, J., *Peru under Alan Garcia,* Macmillan, London, 1991.
McClintock, C., and Lowenthal, A., (eds.), *The Peruvian Experiment Reconsidered,* Princeton University Press, Princeton, 1983.
Thorp, R., *Economic Management and Economic Development in Peru and Colombia,* Macmillan, London, and University of Pittsburgh Press, Pittsburgh, 1991.

Paraguay

Nickson, R., "Tyranny and Longevity: Stroessner's Paraguay," *Third World Quarterly,* vol. 10, 1988.

Valdéz, L., *Stroessner's Paraguay: Tradition vs. Modern Authoritarianism*, Universidad Interamericana, Puerto Rico, 1986.

Uruguay

Finch, H., *A Political Economy of Uruguay Since 1870*, Macmillan, London, 1981.
Weinstein, M., *Uruguay: Democracy at the Crossroads*, Westview Press, Boulder, 1988.

Venezuela

Levine, D., *Conflict and Political Change in Venezuela*, Princeton University Press, Princeton, 1973.
Martz, J., and Myers, D., *Venezuela: The Democratic Experience*, Praeger, New York, 1986.
Naim, M., and Piñango, R., *El Caso Venezuela: Una Ilusión de Armonía*, Ediciones EASA, Caracas, 1985.

Index

AD (Democratic Action party), 84, 92, 100
Adjustment programs, 241–242
Administrative system, 160–164
African–Latin American relations, 300–301
Age, of population, 12–13
Agriculture, 19–24, 34, 43, 45, 275
  cash-crop, 19–20
  dualism in, 19, 20
  peasant, 20–24
  slash-and-burn, 35
AIDS, 10
Air pollution, 331, 332
ALADI (Latin American Integration Association), 322
Alcohol consumption, 12
Alemán, Miguel, 72
Alfaro Vive guerrillas, 152
Alfonsín, Raúl, 25, 69, 87, 120, 122, 137, 142, 170, 172, 325
Allende, Isabel, 68
Allende, Salvador, 89, 101, 110, 128, 200, 202
Alliance for Progress, 42, 66, 81, 252, 259
Amazon Basin, 329, 331
Amazonia, 33, 35, 143
Amazon Pact, 320
American Popular Revolutionary Alliance (APRA), 84, 94, 102, 103
Amerindians, 31, 32–36, 148, 149
Andean Pact, 183, 186, 231–232, 274
ANDI (National Industrialists' Association), 114
APRA (American Popular Revolutionary Alliance), 84, 94, 102, 103
Aramburu, Cardinal, 131
ARENA (National Republican Alliance), 105, 156
Arenas, Reynaldo, 69
Argentina
  Church in, 131
  cities in, 25
  corruption in, 165
  culture in, 70–71, 72, 75–76
  debt management in, 208, 285
  democracy in, 69, 81, 82, 83, 84, 85, 86, 87, 88–89, 91, 94, 96, 97, 134, 170
  economic growth in, 182, 184, 185, 186, 241, 244
  economic policy of, 199
  economic problems of, 190
  education in, 56, 58, 59, 60, 61, 64, 65
  Falklands/Malvinas War, 131, 135, 136, 141, 142, 168, 277, 319, 323, 324
  income in, 217, 224, 225
  inflation in, 200, 201, 202, 203, 204, 205, 206
  labor unions in, 117, 118–119, 121–122, 123, 125
  military in, 135, 136, 137, 138, 140, 142, 143, 168, 172
  minorities in, 36
  political actors in, 127, 135, 136, 137
  political parties in, 101, 103, 105, 107, 108–109, 110–111
  political violence in, 157, 169
  population of, 5, 6, 7, 8, 9, 12, 13, 14, 15, 16, 17, 18, 218
  relations with Brazil, 325–326, 337
  relations with China, 295
  relations with other Latin American countries, 322, 323, 337
  relations with United States, 249–250
  relations with Western Europe, 273
  social structure in, 42–43, 48
  trade by, 187, 189, 268, 275, 295
  World Bank loans to, 305
Argentine Anticommunist Alliance, 157
Arias, Oscar, 154
Armed forces. *See* Military
Arms sales, 298, 298, 301
Aymara Indians, 33
Azcarraga, Emilio, 72
Aztecs, 33

Bacha, Edmar, 197
Baggio, Sebastino, 132
Baker initiative, 208, 209, 230, 251, 287, 304, 306, 307–308, 311, 316
Balassa, Bela, 197, 198
Bananas, 45
Barco, Virgilio, 108, 146, 154
Belaúnde, Fernando, 25, 108, 120
Belize, 37, 322
Belmont, Ricardo, 109
Bemberg, María Luisa, 70, 72
Benedetti, Mario, 69
Betancourt, Rómulo, 166
Betancur, Belisario, 108, 153–154
Bicycling, 76–77
Bilateral Commercial Agreements, 322
Birth control, 6–7, 133
Black Caribs, 37, 38
Black Panthers, 38
Black Rio movement, 38
Blacks, 31, 36–39
Black Salvador movement, 38
Blades, Rubén, 78
Bloque sur, 146
Bogotá, 29, 30, 38, 65
Boías frías, 23
Boland amendment, 250
Boleteo, 158
Bolivia
  agriculture in, 23, 34, 45
  cities in, 27
  corruption in, 165
  culture in, 71, 72
  debt management by, 313–314
  democracy in, 81, 87, 91, 96
  economic growth of, 244, 245
  education in, 56, 60, 61
  exports of, 187, 188
  income in, 217, 225
  inflation in, 200, 201, 204, 206
  labor unions in, 123
  military in, 135, 138, 139
  minorities in, 32, 33, 34
  political actors in, 127, 135
  political parties in, 101, 102, 103
  political violence in, 150, 152, 172
  population of, 5, 6, 8, 9, 12, 13, 14, 15, 17, 18, 22, 218
  public administration in, 164
  relations with other Latin American countries, 322, 324
  social structure of, 46–47, 48, 52
Bolivian Workers Central (COB), 123, 150
Borges, Jorge Luis, 68
Borja, Rodrigo, 106
Boxing, 77
Brady plan, 209–210, 230, 231, 251, 280, 288, 290, 291, 308, 312, 316, 321
Brasília, 24, 50
Brazil
  agriculture in, 21, 22, 24, 35, 192
  Church in, 130–131, 133
  cities in, 24, 30
  corruption in, 165
  culture in, 71, 72, 73, 75, 76
  debt management in, 208, 285, 312
  democracy in, 81, 82, 85, 86, 87, 88, 89, 91, 96, 97, 100, 170
  economic growth in, 182, 184, 185, 192, 196, 241, 242, 243, 245
  economic problems of, 191
  education in, 56, 57, 60, 61, 64
  environmental concerns in, 329, 331, 333
  income in, 224, 225
  inflation in, 200, 201, 203, 204, 205, 206
  Japanese emigration to, 283–284
  labor unions in, 117, 118, 119, 120, 125
  military in, 135, 136, 137, 138, 140, 143, 172
  minorities in, 31, 33, 36, 37, 38
  political actors in, 126, 128, 129, 135, 136, 137
  political parties in, 102, 103, 106, 107, 108
  political violence in, 157, 169
  population of, 4, 5, 6, 7, 10, 12, 13, 14, 17, 18
  public administration in, 161, 164, 165
  relations with Africa, 300–301
  relations with Argentina, 325–326, 337
  relations with China, 295–296, 338
  relations with Middle East, 299–300
  relations with other Latin American countries, 320, 321, 322, 323, 324, 337
  relations with United States, 255
  social structure of, 48, 50, 52, 53
  trade by, 187, 189, 267–268, 275, 284, 295–296, 299–300, 303
Brazilian Democratic Movement Party (PMDB), 121
Bretton Woods Conference (1944), 304
Brezhnev, Leonid, 265
Britain
  Falklands/Malvinas War and, 131, 135, 136, 141, 142, 168, 277, 319, 323, 324
  relations with Latin America, 276, 277, 281
Brizola, Leonel, 108
Bucarám, Assad, 102, 170
Bueno, Gerardo M., 197
Buenos Aires, 24, 25, 64, 137, 170, 173
Bureaucracies, 161–164
  local, 163–164
  national, 162–163
Bureaucratic authoritarianism, 88
Bush, George, 209, 210, 237, 335

Cabrera Infante, Guillermo, 69
Caciquismo, 97, 164
Cairns Group, 275
Camdessus, Michel, 307–308, 315

Camila, 70
Capital, new sources of, 233–236
Caputo, Dante, 172
Caracas, 25, 28, 30, 65, 87, 168–169
Carajás (Brazil), 35
Carajás iron-ore project, 274
Caribbean Basin Initiative (CBI), 237, 243
Car ownership, 30–31
Carpentier, Alejo, 68
Cartagena Consensus, 255, 320
Carter, Jimmy, 299
Castro, Fidel, 69, 74, 81, 86, 87, 145, 260, 261, 262, 267, 268, 294
Catholic Church, 35–36, 57, 104
  European–Latin American relations and, 273, 274
  in politics, 129–134
Caudillo, 97
Ceduc, Paul, 71
Center, political parties of, 105–107
Central America, relations among countries in, 326–328
  See also Costa Rica; El Salvador; Guatemala; Honduras; Nicaragua
Central American Common Market, 183, 186, 243
CGT (General Confederation of Labor), 120, 121
CGTP (General Confederation of Peruvian Workers), 122
Chagas disease, 12
"Chicha" music, 34
Chile
  Church in, 130, 131, 133, 134
  culture in, 74, 75
  debt management in, 208, 209, 285
  democracy in, 81, 82, 85, 86, 87, 88, 89, 90, 95, 96, 98, 99, 100, 170
  economic growth in, 182, 186, 192, 202, 241, 242–243
  economic policy of, 199
  economic problems of, 190, 195, 239
  education in, 55, 56, 60, 61, 64
  income in, 224, 225
  inflation in, 200, 201, 202, 203, 205
  labor unions in, 117, 118, 122, 125
  military in, 135, 136, 137, 138, 140, 141, 143, 172
  political actors in, 114, 127, 128, 135, 136, 137
  political parties in, 101, 102, 105, 108, 110
  population of, 5, 6, 8, 9, 12, 13, 14, 15, 16, 17, 18, 218
  relations with other Latin American countries, 322, 323, 337
  social structure in, 42–43, 46, 48
  relations with Soviet Union, 268
  trade by, 186, 187, 188, 189, 213, 275
Chinese–Latin American relations, 293–297, 338
Chocó, 39
Christian Brothers, 57
Christian Democrat Parties, 92, 101, 105, 106
Christie, Julie, 72
Churches, 129–134
  See also Catholic Church
Cien años de Soledad (García Marquez), 67, 68
CIEPLAN (Economic Research Corporation for Latin America), 197
Cimarrón, 38
Cinema, 70–72
Cities. *See* Urban areas; *names of specific cities*
Ciudad Guyana (Venezuela), 24
Classes, 40–42
  middle, 47–50
  upper, 50–51
  urban working, 46–47
CLAT (Latin American Central of Workers), 119
Clientelism, 82–83, 95, 97–98, 99, 162, 164, 173–174
COB (Bolivian Workers Central), 123, 150
Coca farming, 34, 43, 45
Cocaine, 34, 45
Colegio de Médicos (Chile), 114, 197
Colleges, 59–66
Collor, Fernando, 87, 109, 170, 205, 254, 300, 326, 330
Colombia
  agriculture in, 21, 45
  Church in, 133
  cities in, 24
  corruption in, 165, 166
  culture in, 71, 72, 76–77
  debt management in, 209
  democracy in, 82, 84, 86, 87, 88, 91, 92, 94, 95, 96, 98, 100, 170
  economic growth in, 182, 184, 196, 241, 243, 245
  economic policy of, 198
  economic problems of, 191
  education in, 55, 56, 57, 58, 60, 61
  illiteracy in, 56
  income in, 222, 224, 225
  inflation in, 201
  labor unions in, 117, 118, 119, 120, 122, 123
  military in, 138, 141, 143, 153, 171
  minorities in, 33, 34, 35, 36–37, 38
  political actors in, 114, 126, 128, 129
  political parties in, 101, 103, 104, 106, 107, 108, 110, 111
  political violence in, 145, 146, 148, 149, 150, 151, 152, 153–154, 155, 156, 157–158, 171, 252
  population of, 5, 6–7, 12, 14, 15, 16, 22
  relations with China, 295
  relations with other Latin American countries, 322, 323, 324

social structure in, 41, 42, 46, 47, 48, 53
trade by, 186, 187, 189, 295, 299
Colombian National Federation of Coffee Growers, 114
Colombian Revolutionary Armed Forces (FARC), 96, 146, 148, 150, 154, 156, 158
Comecon (Council for Mutual Economic Assistance), 260, 265
Comic books, 75
Commercial policy, 198–199, 210–215
Common Agricultural Policy, 275, 278
Communism and Communist parties, 88, 95, 101, 102–104, 122, 132, 137, 148, 156, 158, 194, 252, 253, 261, 266–268
See also Soviet Union
CONACYT (National Council for Science and Technology), 63
CONADEP (National Commission on the Disappeared), 69
Concertación, 114, 124
Condorito, 75
Confederation of Colombian Workers (CTC), 122
Confederation of Mexican Workers (CTM), 120, 121
Confederation of Workers (Brazil) (CUT), 121
Conflict, regional, 322–324
Congreso del Trabajo (Mexico), 120
Conservative political parties, 104–105
Contadora Group, 88, 320
Contadora process, 250
Contraceptive use, 6–7, 133
Contras, 147–148, 149, 250, 253, 254
Cooperation, regional, 319–322
COPEI (Christian Democrat party), 92
Cordero, León Febres, 104, 106
Córdoba University reform of 1918, 64
Coronel, 97
Corruption
government, 165–166
labor union, 119–120
political, 82–83, 97–98
Cortázar, Julio, 68, 69
Costa-Gavras, Constantin, 70
Costa Rica
debt management in, 209, 312
democracy in, 82, 91, 92, 95, 96
economic growth of, 241, 242, 243
economic policy in, 202
education in, 56, 59, 60, 61
income in, 224, 225
inflation in, 201
labor unions in, 119
military in, 138, 139, 141
political parties in, 101, 106
population of, 5, 6, 8, 9, 14
social structure of, 48
trade by, 187, 188, 214
CROC (Revolutionary Confederation of Workers and Peasants), 120
CROM (Regional Confederation of Mexican Workers), 120
Cruzado Plan, 121, 205
Cuba
culture in, 69, 70, 72, 74, 76
democracy in, 69–70, 81, 84, 86, 87, 88
economic growth of, 192, 241, 245
education in, 55, 58, 65
income in, 225
military in, 138, 140
minorities in, 31, 37
political parties in, 103
political violence and, 151
population of, 5, 6, 8, 9, 12, 14
relations with China, 293–294, 295
relations with other Latin American countries, 320, 324
relations with Soviet Union, 261, 263–268
relations with United States, 254, 260–262
trade by, 260–261, 263–264
Cuban Revolution, 259, 262, 263, 293
Culture, 67–78
cinema, 70–72
mass culture, 72–78
novels, 67–70
television, 72–75
writers, 67–70
Cuna de Lobos, 73

Death squads, 152, 154, 157
Debt crisis, 136, 168, 189–191, 199, 229–231, 276, 280, 285–286, 287–289, 290–291, 311–312
Debt-management policy, 206–210, 290–291
Debt overhang, 311–312
Deforestation, 35, 329, 330, 331, 332
Democratic Action Party (AD), 84, 92, 110
Democratic Convergence, 151
Democratic Current, 94, 106, 170
Democratic tradition, 81–90
Demonstration elections, 92–93, 99–100
Dengue, 12
Derecho de Nacer, 73
Desaparecidos, 69, 128
de la Madrid, Miguel, 25
de Soto, Hernando, 47, 105, 115, 197, 222
Díaz-Alejandro, Carlos, 199
Disease, 9–10, 12
Di Stefano, Alfredo, 76
Dominican Republic
blacks in, 37
democracy in, 87, 89
economic growth of, 241, 244
education in, 60, 61
income in, 225
inflation in, 201, 205
military in, 138
political parties in, 101, 107
political violence in, 169
population of, 5, 6, 8, 9, 12, 14, 15

social structure of, 48
trade by, 237
Dorfman, Ariel, 75
Drugs, 12, 34, 43, 143, 150–151, 158, 166, 245, 252–254, 255
Duarte, José Napoleon, 254

Echeverría, Luis, 71, 126
Economic Commission for Latin America and the Caribbean (ECLAC), 19, 197, 222
Economic diversity, 185–186
Economic growth, 182, 184, 185, 186, 192, 196, 202, 238–246
Economic issues, 216–227
debt crisis, 136, 168, 189–191, 199, 206–210, 229–231, 276, 280, 285–286, 287–289, 290–291, 311–312
employment, 217–222
inequality, 222–227
inflation, 200–206, 252
poverty, 222–227
trade. *See* Trade
Economic performance, 188–192
Economic policy, 193–215
commercial, 210–215
debt management, 206–210
economic prospects and, 238–240
economic thinking and, 194–198
inflation and stabilization, 200–206
myths about, 198–200
Economic prospects, 228–246
debt problem, 229–231
economic policy, 238–240
growth, 238–240
new sources of capital, 231–234
regional differences in, 240–246
trade and world economy, 234–238
Economic Research Corporation for Latin America (CIEPLAN), 197
Economic structure, 179–192
economic diversity and, 185–186
industrialization and, 182–185
international context of, 180–181
primary exports and, 186–188
Economic System of Latin America (SELA), 255, 268, 274
Economic thinking, 194–198
Ecuador
corruption in, 165
democracy in, 81, 85, 91, 96
economic growth of, 241, 244
economic policy of, 199
education in, 55, 56, 59, 60, 61
income in, 225
inflation in, 201
labor unions in, 119
military in, 135, 136, 137, 138, 140, 143
minorities in, 33, 35, 36–37
political actors in, 126, 135, 136, 137
political parties in, 102, 104, 106, 108, 111
political violence in, 152
population of, 5, 8, 12, 14, 15
relations with Israel, 299
relations with other Latin American countries, 322, 323
social structure of, 48
trade by, 186, 187, 188, 189, 297
Education, 55–66, 174
expenditures by country, 56
higher education, 59–66
primary and secondary, 55–59, 60, 61
Elections, 90–100
demonstration, 92–93, 99–100
exclusions and, 94–95
media and, 98–99
vetoes and, 94–95
violence and intimidation in, 95–97
voter participation in, 90–94
ELN (National Liberation Army), 146, 148, 150
El Salvador
Church in, 133
culture in, 72
democracy in, 81, 89, 90, 91, 93, 95, 96, 99
economic growth of, 241, 244
education in, 56, 60, 61
exports of, 187
income in, 225
inflation in, 201
military in, 135, 136, 138, 139, 141, 153
political actors in, 126, 135, 136
political parties in, 105, 106
political violence in, 145–146, 149, 151, 152–153, 154, 155, 156, 157, 158, 171
population of, 5, 8, 13, 14, 16, 218
relations with other Latin American countries, 322, 326–328
relations with Soviet Union, 268
relations with United States, 254
social structure in, 41, 46, 48
El otro sendero, 105, 115, 197, 222
Embrafilme, 71
Employers' associations, 113–115
Employment, 25–27, 46–53
as economic issue, 217–222
in public administration, 161–162
Enhanced Structural Adjustment Facility of IMF, 305
Enterprise for the Americas Initiative, 237
Environmental concerns, 329–334
EPL (Popular Liberation Army), 146
Esquipulas peace proposal of 1987, 250
ERP (People's Revolutionary Army), 157
Ethnic minorities, 31–39
Amerindians, 31, 32–36, 148, 149
blacks, 31, 36–39
European–Latin American relations, 271–282, 335–336
after Cold War, 279–282
constraints and limitations on, 274–277

growth of, 272–274
history of, 271–272
in 1992, 277–279
trade and, 273, 274–276, 278–279, 336
Exports, 181, 182–183, 186–188
See also Trade
Extended Fund Facility of IMF, 305

Falklands/Malvinas War, 131, 135, 136, 141, 142, 168, 277, 319, 323, 324
Family planning, 6–7
Farabundo Martí National Liberation Front (FMLN), 96, 145–146, 148, 151, 155, 268
FARC (Colombian Revolutionary Armed Forces), 96, 146, 148, 150, 154, 156, 158
Farmers, 19–24
Favelas, 37
FDR (Revolutionary Democratic Front), 96, 151
Fedesarrollo (Foundation for Higher Education and Development), 197
Ferreira, Wilson, 94
Fertility rates, 3, 6–7
Films, 70–72
Fishlow, Albert, 196
FMLN (Farabundo Martí National Liberation Front), 96, 145–146, 148, 151, 155, 268
Foquista guerrilla movement, 145, 147, 148, 150
Forests, 329, 330, 331, 332
Fotonovelas, 75
Foundation for Higher Education and Development (Fedesarrollo), 197
France, relations with Latin America, 273, 277, 280, 281
Franco-Mexican Declaration of 1982, 273
Franqui, Carlos, 69
Franz Fanon Study and Research Center, 38
Frei, Eduardo, 202
Frente Nacional, 94
Fresno, Cardinal, 130
Frondizi, Arturo, 134
Fuentes, Carlos, 68–69, 77
FUNAI (National Indian Foundation), 36

Galtieri, Leopoldo, 131, 249
García, Alan, 103, 108, 120, 155, 170, 208, 239
García Márquez, Gabriel, 67, 68, 69, 70, 73, 77
Garimpeiros, 35
Gaviria, César, 108, 170
General Agreement on Tariffs and Trade (GATT), 200, 210, 234, 245, 275, 303
General Confederation of Labor (CGT), 120, 121
General Confederation of Peruvian Workers (CGTP), 122
Germany, relations with Latin America, 274, 276, 277, 279, 280–281
Glasnost, 264–266
Gómez, Juan Vicente, 85
"Good Neighbor Policy," 250
Gorbachev, Mikhail, 261, 266, 267, 269, 279, 337
Goulart, João, 121, 130
Government
adminstrative system of, 160–164
corruption in, 165–166
judicial system of, 160, 166–167
Green party, 329–330
Gremios, 114, 115, 170
Gross domestic product (GDP), 181, 182, 188, 203, 206, 234, 239–240, 241, 243, 244, 245
Gross national product (GNP) per capita, 226, 227
Group of 77, 302
Group of Eight, 320
Guadalajara, 26
Guardapolvo, 58
Guatemala
Church in, 133
democracy in, 81, 89, 90, 91, 93, 95, 96
economic growth of, 241, 243
education in, 55, 56, 60, 61
income in, 225
inflation in, 201
military in, 136, 138, 139, 141, 171
minorities in, 32, 33, 34
political actors in, 136
political parties in, 106
political violence in, 145, 147, 149, 152, 154, 157, 158
population of, 5, 8, 9, 12, 13, 14, 16, 218
relations with other Latin American countries, 322, 326–328
social structure of, 48
Guatemala City, 38, 147
Guerrillas, 34, 95–96, 131, 137, 141, 142, 143, 145–158, 171, 252–254, 268, 324
factors favoring, 149–152
future of, 155–156
government response to, 152–155
ideology of, 148
threat posed by, 145–148
Guevara, Che, 150
Guyana, 31, 38, 322, 323

Hacendados, 23–24
Haciendas, 45, 149
Haiti
blacks in, 37, 38
economic growth of, 241, 244
education in, 60, 61
income in, 225
inflation in, 201
military in, 138
population of, 5, 6, 8, 9, 10, 12, 13, 14
trade by, 237

Health care, 9, 12
Hermosillo, Jaime, 71
Historia official, 70, 71
Hobbes, Thomas, 158
Hogar Dulce Hogar, 73
Honduras
  democracy in, 81, 91
  economic growth of, 241, 243
  education in, 55, 56, 60, 61
  income in, 224, 225
  inflation in, 201
  military in, 138, 139, 141
  population of, 5, 6, 8, 13, 14, 218
  relations with other Latin American countries, 322, 326–328
  social structure of, 48
Hora de los hornos, 70
Housing, 27–29
How to Read Donald Duck: Imperialist Ideology in the Disney Comic (Dorfman and Mattelart), 75
Humanae Vitae, 133

Imports, 188–189
  See also Trade
Income, unequal distribution of, 217, 222–227
Indians. *See* Amerindians
Indígenismo, 31–32, 34
Industrialization, 182–185
Industries, 26–27, 35, 182–185
Infant mortality, 8, 9
Inflation, 200–206, 252
Infrastructure, 30
Initiative for the Americas, 335
Institutional Revolutionary Party (PRI), 69, 84–85, 93, 94, 99, 105–106, 120, 121
Instituto Torcuato di Tella (Argentina), 197
Inter-American Development Bank (IADB), 62, 207, 232, 233, 255, 317
Inter-American Military System, 319, 323, 337
International Bank for Reconstruction and Development. *See* World Bank
International Confederation of Free Trade Unions (ICFTU), 119
International financial institutions (IFIs), 304–318
  Inter-American Development Bank, 62, 207, 232, 233, 255, 317
  International Monetary Fund, 196–197, 204, 207, 209, 213, 232, 233, 246, 251, 287, 288, 304–312, 317
  World Bank, 163, 196–197, 207, 209, 213, 232, 246, 251, 304–305, 312–316, 317
International Monetary Fund (IMF), 196–197, 204, 207, 209, 213, 232, 233, 246, 251, 287, 288, 304–312, 317
  conditionality, 308–310
  criticisms of, 309–310
  division of labor with World Bank, 314–315
  evolution in 1980s, 305–308
  issues under consideration by, 308–312
  surveillance, 310–311
Intimidation, 95–97
Iran-*contra* scandal, 250, 253
Isaura the Slavegirl, 73
Israeli–Latin American relations, 297–298, 299
Italian–Latin American relations, 273, 281
Izquierda Unida, 102–103, 106, 148, 155

Japanese–Latin American relations, 283–292, 336–337
  account surpluses and, 286–287
  constraints on, 289–291
  debt crisis and, 285–286, 287–289, 290–291
  future of, 291–292
  history of, 283–285
  prestige and, 287–289
  trade and, 284–285, 286
  U.S.–Japanese relations and, 286
Jaramillo, Bernardo, 154
John Paul II, Pope, 132–133
Joint ventures, 51
Juantorena, Alberto, 76
Judicial system, 160, 166–167

Kelly, Sir David, 75–76
Keynes, John Maynard, 194
Keynesian economics, 194, 195, 196
Kissinger Commission, 248
Krauze, Enrique, 69
Kuczynski, Pedro-Pablo, 197

Labor market, 115–118
Labor unions, 115–125
  corruption in, 119–120
  government and, 120–122
  membership and organization of, 118–119
  militancy of, 118
  political role of, 123–125
LAFTA (Latin American Free Trade Area), 183
Laissez faire, 195
Landholding, inequities in, 19
Landowners, in social structure, 41, 42
Land reforms, 20–21
Language, 33
Larosière, Jacques de, 310
Las Truchas (Mexico), 24
Latifundios, 19, 23, 42
Latin American Central of Workers (CLAT), 119
Latin American Film Foundation, 70
Latin American Free Trade Area (LAFTA), 183

Latin American Integration Association (ALADI), 322
Law of the Sea, 302
Left-wing political parties, 101–104
Lever, Janet, 76
Lezama Lima, José, 70
Life expectancy, 8, 9–10
Lima, 24, 34, 147, 150, 173
Lispector, Clarice, 68
Lomé Convention, 237, 280
López Trujillo, Alfonso, 132
Lutzenberger, José, 330

Malnutrition, 9
Maradona, Diego, 76
Marijuana, 43, 45
Marilu, 73
Marinho, Roberto, 72
Mariscal de Ayacucho, 62–63
Marxism, 102, 103, 132, 148, 156, 194, 253, 261
Mass culture, 72–78
Mattelart, Armand, 75
Maya Indians, 33
Medellín, 38, 132
Media
  culture and, 67–78
  politics and, 98–99
Mencken, H. L., 174–175
Menem, Carlos Saúl, 105, 109, 111, 170, 326
Mexico
  agriculture in, 21, 45
  Church in, 130, 133
  cities in, 24, 25, 26, 30
  corruption in, 165, 166
  culture in, 71, 72, 73, 75, 77
  debt management in, 207, 208, 209, 285, 287, 312, 313, 314
  democracy in, 69, 81, 82, 84, 86, 87, 88, 90, 91, 93, 94, 96, 97, 99, 100, 170
  economic growth in, 182, 184, 185, 192, 241, 243, 244, 245
  economic policy of, 198, 199
  economic problems of, 190
  education in, 56, 57, 59, 60, 63, 64, 65
  environmental concerns in, 329
  income in, 224, 225
  inflation in, 201, 203, 206
  labor unions in, 117, 119, 120–121
  map of, 116
  migration to United States, 16
  military in, 138, 140, 172
  minorities in, 31–32, 33, 34
  political actors in, 115, 126
  political parties in, 105, 106
  political violence in, 149
  population of, 5, 6, 7, 8, 10, 12, 14
  public administration in, 161, 164, 165
  relations with Israel, 299
  relations with other Latin American countries, 321
  relations with United States, 254–255
  social structure in, 46, 48, 50
  trade by, 189, 214, 237, 275, 284, 299
Mexico City, 24, 25, 29, 30, 50
Middle classes, 47–50
Middle East–Latin American relations, 297–300
Migration
  international, 13–16, 283–284
  rural-urban, 17–18, 45, 47
Military
  guerrillas and, 152–153, 171–173
  Israeli arms sales to, 298, 299
  in politics, 134–143
Minifundios, 19
Mining, 35, 45, 124
Minorities. *See* Ethnic minorities
MIR (Movement of the Revolutionary Left), 103
Miskito Indians, 148, 149
Missionaries, 35
Miss Mary, 72
M-19, 146, 148, 150, 154
Mobility, social, 51–52
Monterrey, 26
Montoneros, 131, 157
Mortality rates, 7–12
Mothers of the Plaza de Mayo, 128
Movement of the Revolutionary Left (MIR), 103
Movement to Socialism (MAS), 92, 102
Movies, 70–72
MRTA (Revolutionary Tupac Amaru Movement), 147, 148, 150
Mulattos, 36, 37
Multi-Fiber Agreement, 276

Narcotraficantes, 151, 158, 253, 324, 335
  See also Drugs
National Action Party (PAN), 94, 105–106
National Commission on the Disappeared (CONADEP), 69
National Council for Science and Technology (CONACYT), 63
National Defense Council, 172
National Front, 94
National Indian Foundation (FUNAI) (Brazil), 36
National Industrialists' Association (ANDI), 114
National Liberation Army (ELN), 146, 148, 150
National Peasant Confederation, 150
National Renewal, 105
National Republican Alliance (ARENA), 105, 156
Neo-structuralism, 197–198
Net resource transfers, 314
New International Economic Order, 302

Nicaragua
  culture in, 72
  democracy in, 70, 90, 91, 93, 99, 100
  economic growth of, 241, 243, 244
  economic policy of, 199
  education in, 55, 56, 60, 61
  exports of, 187
  income in, 225
  inflation in, 201, 205
  military in, 138, 139
  political actors in, 126
  political parties in, 102, 106
  political violence in, 145, 147–148, 149, 156, 158
  population of, 5, 6, 8, 12, 13, 14
  relations with other Latin American countries, 322, 326–328
  relations with Soviet Union, 268, 270
  relations with United States, 249, 250, 251, 253
  relations with Western Europe, 273, 277
  social structure of, 48
Nicaraguan Revolution, 87–88, 259, 262, 265
Nixon, Richard, 169
Non-Aligned Movement, 302
Noriega, Manuel, 166, 244, 251, 253, 267
Novels, 67–70

Ochoa, Arnaldo, 267
O'Donnell, Guillermo, 88
Odría, Manuel, 28
OEM (Original Equipment Manufacturing) Arrangement, 276
Official Version, 70, 71
Oligarchy, 41, 50
Olmos, Edward James, 78
One Hundred Years of Solitude (Garcia Marquez), 67, 68
OPEC, 165, 190, 299, 302, 303
Organization for Economic Cooperation and Development (OECD), 119, 188, 211, 234, 235, 236, 238
Organization of American States (OAS), 255, 260
ORIT (Regional Inter-American Organization of Labor), 119
Ornetti, Juan Carlos, 68

Pacific zone, Soviet interest in, 268–270
Pact of Economic Solidarity, 206
Padilla, Heberto, 69
Palenque, Carlos, 109
Palestine Liberation Organization (PLO), 298
Pambelé, "Kid," 77
Panama
  corruption in, 165, 166
  culture in, 77
  democracy in, 84, 88, 93, 99
  economic growth of, 241, 243, 244
  education in, 56, 59, 60, 61
  income in, 224, 225
  inflation in, 201
  labor unions in, 119
  military in, 138
  minorities in, 37
  population of, 5, 6, 8, 14
  relations with other Latin American countries, 321
  relations with United States, 251, 253, 255, 256, 267
  social structure of, 48
Panamanian National Guard, 253
PAN (National Action Party), 94, 105–106
Pantanal, 73
Paraguay
  corruption in, 165
  culture in, 72
  democracy in, 86, 134
  economic growth of, 192, 241, 243
  education in, 56, 60, 61
  exports of, 187
  income in, 225
  inflation in, 201
  military in, 138
  political parties in, 107
  population of, 5, 8, 12, 14, 15
  relations with other Latin American countries, 322, 324
  social structure of, 48
Paramilitares, 158
Pardo Leal, Jaime, 154
Pardos, 36, 37
Pastoral Land Commission of the National Council of Brazilian Bishops, 127
Patriotic Union (UP), 96, 151, 154
Patronage, 82–83, 95, 97–98, 99
Paul VI, Pope, 133
Paz, Octavio, 68, 69, 71
Paz Estenssoro, Víctor, 103
Paz Zamora, Jaime, 103
Peace Committee, 130
Peasant organizations, 125–127
Peasants, 20–24, 45
Pentecostalism, 133–134
People's Revolutionary Army (ERP), 157
Perestroika, 264–266, 267, 337
Pérez, Carlos Andrés, 108, 168, 170
Pérez Jiménez, Marcos, 111, 166
Permanent Congress of Trade Union Unity of Latin American Workers (CPUSTAL), 119
Perón, Juan, 76, 94, 99, 108, 123, 172
Peronism, 108–109, 110–111, 121–122, 123, 131, 202
Personalismo, 161
Peru
  agriculture in, 21, 23, 45, 126
  cities in, 25, 27
  corruption in, 165
  culture in, 71, 73
  debt management in, 208

democracy in, 69, 81, 82, 84, 85, 87, 89, 91, 94, 95, 96, 170, 337
economic growth in, 182, 202, 241, 244, 245
economic policy of, 198, 199
education in, 56, 58, 59, 60, 61
income in, 217, 225
inflation in, 201, 205, 206
labor unions in, 118, 119, 122, 123, 125
military in, 135, 136, 138, 139, 140, 141, 143, 153
minorities in, 31, 33, 34, 35, 36
political actors in, 126, 127, 135, 136
political parties in, 101, 102–103, 104, 106–107, 111
political violence in, 145, 146–147, 148, 149, 150, 152, 154, 155, 156, 157, 171, 252
population of, 5, 8, 9, 12, 13, 14, 15, 22
relations with other Latin American countries, 322, 323, 324
social structure in, 42, 46, 47, 48, 52
trade by, 187, 188, 284
Physical Quality of Life Index (PQLI), 228
Piñera, Virgilio, 70
Pinochet, Augusto, 74, 85, 88, 89, 95, 96, 102, 108, 114, 122, 130, 134, 135, 136, 137, 165, 239, 294
Pizarro, Carlos, 154
PMDB (Brazilian Democratic Movement Party), 121
Political actors, 113–144
armed forces, 134–143
churches, 129–134
employers' associations, 113–115
labor unions, 115–125
organizations of peasants and rural workers, 125–127
other social movements, 127–129
professional organizations, 113–115
Political parties, 84–85, 101–112
center, 105–107
left, 101–104
populists, 107–112
right, 104–105, 156–159
See also names of specific parties
Political prospects, 168–175
Political violence, 95–97, 145–159, 168–170
by guerrillas, 34, 95–96, 131, 137, 141, 142, 143, 145–158, 171, 252–254, 268, 324
from right, 156–159
Politics, 69–70, 81–100
clientelism, 82–83, 95, 97–98, 99, 162, 164, 173–174
corruption in, 82–83, 97–98
democratic tradition, 81–90
elections, 90–100
exclusions, 94–95
media and, 98–99
vetoes, 94–95
voter participation in, 90–94
Pollution, 331, 332
Polonoroeste scheme (Brazil), 35
Poniatowski, Elena, 68
Popular Liberation Army (EPL), 146
Population, 3–16
age structure, 12–13, 14
basic size of, 3–6
ethnic minorities, 31–39
fertility rates, 3, 6–7
growth of, 5, 217–219
life expectancy, 8
migration patterns, 13–16
mortality rates, 7–12
of urban areas, 17–18
Populists, 107–112, 239
Postgraduate courses, 63
Poverty, 222–227
PREALC (Regional Employment Program for Latin America and the Caribbean), 221, 222, 223
Prebisch, Raúl, 199
PRI (Institutional Revolutionary Party), 69, 84–85, 93, 94, 95, 105–106, 120, 121
Professional organizations, 113–115
Protestantism, 133–134
PSOE (Spanish Socialist Party), 273
PT (Workers' Party), 102, 121, 128
Public administration, 161–164
Public services, 29–30
Puig, Manuel, 68
Puenzo, Luis, 70
Punto Fijo, Pact of 1959, 111

Quadros, Jânio, 108
Quechua-speaking Indians, 33, 34
Quito, 65
Quotas, 304–305

Radio Magallancs, 266
Rain forests, 329, 330, 331, 332
Ranchos, 28
Reagan, Ronald, 237, 247, 250, 299, 309
Regional Confederation of Mexican Workers (CROM), 120
Regional Employment Program for Latin America and the Caribbean (PREALC), 221, 222, 223
Regional Inter-American Organization of Labor (ORIT), 119
Religion. *See* Catholic Church; Churches
Renovadores, 109
Research, 63
Revolutionary Confederation of Workers and Peasants (CROC), 120
Revolutionary Democratic Front (FDR), 96, 151
Revolutionary Tupac Amaru Movement (MRTA), 147, 148, 150

Rico, Aldo, 172
Right to Be Born, 73
Right-wing political parties, 104–105, 156–159
Rio de Janeiro, 27, 38
Rio Group, 238
Ripstein, Arturo, 71
Roa Bastos, Augusto, 68, 69
Roads, 30
Rojas Pinilla, Gustavo, 114
Rondônia (Brazil), 35
Roosevelt, Franklin D., 250
Rosas, Juan Manuel de, 70
Rouquié, Alain, 49, 134–135
Rural areas
  agriculture in, 19–24, 43, 45
  education in, 57
  migration to urban areas, 17–18, 45, 47
  social structure in, 43–45
Rural workers, organizations of, 125–127

Sábato, Ernesto, 69
Sachs, Jeffrey, 305–306
Salinas, Carlos, 121
Sandinistas, 88, 145, 147–148, 149, 156, 249, 250, 253, 327
Sanguinetti, Julio Mario, 88
San José Dialogue, 273
San Salvador, 146
Santiago, 24, 29, 128, 130, 294
São Paulo, 25, 30, 38, 50, 121, 173, 194, 284
Sarney, José, 87, 88, 120, 121, 325, 333
Second General Conference of Latin American Bishops, 132
Second Vatican Council, 132
Sectoral Adjustment Loans (Secals), 313, 316
Seineldin, Muhamed Ali, 172
SELA (Economic System of Latin America), 255, 268, 274
Sendero Luminoso guerrilla organization, 34, 96, 103, 146–147, 148, 149, 150, 151, 152, 153, 155, 156, 171, 296
Señora de Nadie, 70
Silva, Luís Inácio da ("Lula"), 102, 121, 267
Silva, Raúl, 130
Simonsen, Mario Henrique, 197
Simplemente Maria, 73
Soccer, 75–76
Soccer Madness (Lever), 76
Social Conservative party (Colombia), 104
Socialist party (Ecuador), 102
Social structure, 40–54
  classes, 40–42
  of middle classes, 47–50
  mobility and, 51–52
  of rural society, 43–45
  of Southern Cone, 42–43
  of upper classes, 50–51
  of urban working classes, 46–47
  women and, 52–54
Somoza, Anastasio, 145, 156, 168
Sotomayor, Javier, 76
Southern Cone, 42–43, 46, 47, 186, 218, 220
  See also Argentina; Chile; Uruguay
Soviet Union
  interest in Pacific, 268–270
  relations with Cuba, 261, 263–268
  relations with Latin America, 263–270, 337
Spain, relations with Latin America, 271, 273–274, 277, 281
Spanish Socialist Party (PSOE), 273
Special Drawing Rights (SDR), 306, 308
Spoils systems, 82–83, 95, 97–98, 99
Sports, 75–77
Stabilization, economic, 200–206, 241–242
State of Siege, 70
Stroessner, Alfredo, 86, 107, 134
Structural Adjustment Facility of IMF, 305
Structural Adjustment Loans (SALs), 207, 312–313, 316
Sucre, Antonio José de, 63
Surinam, 38

Tablada arsenal, 143, 172
Tariffs, 185, 213, 237–238
  See also Trade
Taxation, 30
Telenovelas, 72, 73, 74
Televisa (Mexico), 72, 73, 74
Television, 72–75, 98–99
Television (Williams), 74
Tercermundismo, 70, 302–303
Terrorism, 137, 152
  See also Political violence
Thatcher, Margaret, 281, 309
Third General Conference of Latin American Bishops, 132
Third World movement, 301–303, 338
Third World Priests movement, 131
Tlachtli, 75
Tobacco consumption, 12
Torres, Camilo, 133
Touraine, Alain, 46, 50
Toward Renewed Economic Growth in Latin America (Balassa et al.), 197, 198
Trade
  with Africa, 300–301
  with China, 295–296
  economic growth and, 182–183, 185, 188–189
  economic policy on, 210–215
  with Europe, 273, 274–276, 278–279, 336
  international, 234–238
  with Japan, 284–285, 286
  with Middle East, 297–300
  with Soviet Union, 260–261, 263–264, 267–268
  with Third World, 303
  with United States, 252, 256–257
Trade Act of 1988, 256

Trade and Development Organization for the Countries of the Pacific, 269
Transportation, 30–31
Tricontinental Conference (Havana, 1966), 294
Trimestre económico, 197
Trujillo, Rafael, 86, 107
Tupamaros, 135, 148
TV-Globo (Brazil), 72, 73, 74

UCD (Union of the Democratic Center), 105, 173
Unidad Popular, 89, 99, 102, 114, 128, 170
Union of Colombian Workers (UTC), 122
Union of the Democratic Center (UCD), 105, 173
United Left, 102–103, 106, 148, 155
United Nations, 255
  Economic Commission for Latin America and the Caribbean (ECLAC), 19, 197, 222
  Educational, Scientific, and Cultural Organization (UNESCO), 65
United States
  Hispanic population in, 15–16
  relationship with Latin America, 249–262, 335
  trade with, 252, 256–257
UP (Patriotic Union), 96, 151, 154
U.S. Agency for International Development (USAID), 289
UTC (Union of Colombian Workers), 122
Universities, 59–66
University of Buenos Aires, 59
University of Mexico (UNAM), 59
Upper classes, 50–51
Urban areas, 24–31
  employment in, 25–27
  geographical concentration in, 24–25
  growth of, 17–18
  housing in, 27–29
  infrastructure in, 30
  services in, 29–30
  social structure in, 43–51
  transportation in, 30–31
  See also names of specific cities
Urrutia, Miguel, 114
Uruguay
  culture in, 72
  debt management in, 209
  democracy in, 81, 84, 85, 88, 90, 94, 96, 100
  economic growth of, 192, 241, 243, 244
  economic policy of, 199
  education in, 55, 56, 58, 59, 60, 61, 64
  income in, 225
  inflation in, 200, 201, 204, 206
  labor unions in, 117, 125
  military in, 135, 137, 138
  minorities in, 32
  political actors in, 127, 135, 137
  political parties in, 101, 108
  population of, 5, 6, 7, 8, 12, 13, 14, 17, 18, 218
  social structure in, 42–43, 47, 48
  trade by, 187, 188
Uruguay Round of GATT, 234, 275, 303
Utilities, 30

Vargas Llosa, Mario, 68, 69, 77, 104
Velasco, Juan, 202
Velázquez, Fidel, 121
Venezuela
  Caracas riots, 87, 168–169
  cities in, 24, 26, 28
  corruption in, 165, 166
  culture in, 71, 72, 77
  debt management in, 209, 285
  democracy in, 82, 83, 84, 85, 86, 87, 88, 91, 92, 96, 98, 168–169, 170
  economic growth in, 182, 241, 243, 244
  economic policy of, 198, 199, 200
  education in, 56, 59, 60, 61
  income in, 217, 224, 225
  inflation in, 201
  labor unions in, 118
  military in, 138, 139, 140, 143, 172
  minorities in, 33, 37
  political actors in, 127, 129
  political parties in, 101, 106, 107, 110, 111
  population of, 5, 6, 8, 12, 14, 15, 218
  public administration in, 161, 164, 165
  relations with China, 295
  relations with other Latin American countries, 322, 323, 324
  social structure of, 48, 53
  trade by, 187, 188, 189, 275, 284, 295
Verónico Cruz, 71
Vesco, Robert, 267
Videla, Jorge, 76
Video technology, 73–74
Viedma (Argentina), 25
Violence. *See* Political violence
Voluntary Export Restraint (VER) agreements, 237, 276, 278
Voter participation, 90–94
Vuelta, 69

Water pollution, 332
Western Europe. *See* European–Latin American relations
Williams, Raymond, 74
Women, in social structure, 52–54
Workers' organizations
  labor unions, 115–125
  peasants and rural workers, 125–127
Workers' Party (PT), 102, 121, 128
Working classes, 46–47

World Bank, 163, 196–197, 207, 209, 213, 232, 233, 246, 251, 304–305, 312–316, 317
division of labor with IMF, 314–315
issues under consideration in, 314–316
net resource transfer, 316
response to Latin America in 1980s, 312–314
World Cup (soccer), 76, 77
World Economic Outlook (IMF), 311
Writers, 67–70

Zamora, Rubén, 154
Zapata, Emiliano, 149